DALIT FEMINIST THEORY

Dalit Feminist Theory: A Reader radically redefines feminism by introducing the category of *Dalit* into the core of feminist thought. It supplements feminism by adding caste to its study and praxis; it also re-examines and rethinks Indian feminism by replacing it with a new paradigm, namely, that caste-based feminist inquiry offers the only theoretical vantage point for comprehensively addressing gender-based injustices.

Drawing on a variety of disciplines, the chapters in the volume discuss key themes such as Indian feminism versus Dalit feminism; the emerging concept of Dalit patriarchy; the predecessors of Dalit feminism, such as Phule and Ambedkar; the meaning and value of lived experience; the concept of *Difference*; the analogical relationship between Black feminism and Dalit feminism; the intersectionality debate; and the theory-versus-experience debate. They also provide a conceptual, historical, empirical and philosophical understanding of feminism in India today.

Accessible, essential and ingenious in its approach, this book is for students, teachers and specialist scholars, as well as activists and the interested general reader. It will be indispensable for those engaged in gender studies, women's studies, sociology of caste, political science and political theory, philosophy and feminism, Ambedkar studies, and for anyone working in the areas of caste, class or gender-based discrimination, exclusion and inequality.

Sunaina Arya is a Senior Research Fellow at the Centre for Philosophy, Jawaharlal Nehru University, New Delhi, India. She is completing a dissertation on feminist philosophy from a Dalit perspective. Her areas of research include Ambedkarite social and political philosophy, philosophy and psychology, and the philosophy of social sciences.

Aakash Singh Rathore is Visiting Professor at O.P. Jindal Global University, Sonepat, and Fellow of the Indian Institute of Advanced Study, Shimla, India. He is author of A Philosophy of Autobiography: Body & Text (2019), Plato's Labyrinth: Sophistries, Lies, and Conspiracies in Socratic Dialogues (2018), Indian Political Theory: Laying the Groundwork for Svaraj (2017), and co-author of Rethinking Indian Jurisprudence: An Introduction to the Philosophy of Law (2018). His 18 authored/edited books range from political philosophy, law, and religion to literature, sports, and wine. He is also the Series Editor of 'Ethics, Human Rights and Global Political Thought'. As professor of politics, philosophy, and law, Rathore has taught at Jawaharlal Nehru University and the Universities of Delhi, Rutgers, Pennsylvania, Toronto, Humboldt-Berlin, and LUISS-Rome. He is a regular contributor to The Indian Express and Outlook magazine with bylines in The Times of India, Firstpost, Huffington Post, and Scroll.in. Rathore serves as advisor to policymakers, thinktanks, educational and political bodies, and has featured on Asia News Network, News18 and NDTV 24X7. He is also India's number 3 Ironman triathlete, and has finished six Ironman Triathlons. Among his forthcoming works are Vision for a Nation (with Ashis Nandy), Ambedkar's Preamble: A History in Six Concepts, and B. R. Ambedkar: A Definitive Biography.

DALIT FEMINIST THEORY

A Reader

*Edited by Sunaina Arya and
Aakash Singh Rathore*

Routledge
Taylor & Francis Group

LONDON AND NEW YORK

First published 2020
by Routledge
2 Park Square, Milton Park, Abingdon, Oxon OX14 4RN

and by Routledge
52 Vanderbilt Avenue, New York, NY 10017

Routledge is an imprint of the Taylor & Francis Group, an informa business

© 2020 selection and editorial matter, Sunaina Arya and Aakash Singh Rathore; individual chapters, the contributors

The right of Sunaina Arya and Aakash Singh Rathore to be identified as the authors of the editorial material, and of the authors for their individual chapters, has been asserted in accordance with sections 77 and 78 of the Copyright, Designs and Patents Act 1988.

All rights reserved. No part of this book may be reprinted or reproduced or utilised in any form or by any electronic, mechanical, or other means, now known or hereafter invented, including photocopying and recording, or in any information storage or retrieval system, without permission in writing from the publishers.

Trademark notice: Product or corporate names may be trademarks or registered trademarks, and are used only for identification and explanation without intent to infringe.

British Library Cataloguing-in-Publication Data
A catalogue record for this book is available from the British Library

Library of Congress Cataloging-in-Publication Data
Names: Arya, Sunaina, editor. | Rathore, Aakash Singh, editor.
Title: Dalit feminist theory : a reader / edited by Sunaina Arya and Aakash Singh Rathore.
Description: Abingdon, Oxon ; New York, NY : Routledge, 2020. | Includes bibliographical references and index.
Identifiers: LCCN 2019020446 (print) | LCCN 2019981185 (ebook) | ISBN 9780367276812 (hardback) | ISBN 9780367278250 (paperback) | ISBN 9780429298110 (ebook)
Subjects: LCSH: Feminist theory—India. | Feminism—India. | Dalit women—India—Social conditions. | Caste—India.
Classification: LCC HQ1191.I4 D35 2020 (print) | LCC HQ1191.I4 (ebook) | DDC 305.420954—dc23
LC record available at https://lccn.loc.gov/2019020446
LC ebook record available at https://lccn.loc.gov/2019981185

ISBN: 978-0-367-27681-2 (hbk)
ISBN: 978-0-367-27825-0 (pbk)
ISBN: 978-0-429-29811-0 (ebk)

Typeset in Bembo
by Apex CoVantage, LLC.

Sunaina Arya dedicates this work to all Dalit women:
To everyday contributors, like my mother Kunti Devi and sister Anjana Devi;
To inspiring achievers, like Devyani Khobragade;
To those risking their lives fighting for justice, like Bhanwari Devi;
To those who have lost their lives in this struggle, like Delta Meghwal, Jisha and Payal Tadvi.

CONTENTS

List of figures	x
Notes on contributors	xi
Acknowledgements	xv

Introduction: theorising Dalit feminism *Sunaina Arya and Aakash Singh Rathore*	1

PART I
Indian feminism vs Dalit feminism 23

1 A critical view on intersectionality *Nivedita Menon*	25
2 Problems for a contemporary theory of gender *Susie Tharu and Tejaswini Niranjana*	40
3 Indian feminism and 'Dalit patriarchy' *Gopal Guru; Uma Chakravarti; V. Geetha*	60

PART II
Predecessors of Dalit feminism 63

4 Dalit women's agency and Phule-Ambedkarite feminism *Shailaja Paik*	65

5	Ambedkarite women *Wandana Sonalkar*	88
6	Ramabai and Ambedkar *Sharmila Rege*	94

PART III
Lived experience as 'difference' — 101

7	Brahmanical nature of violence against women *Sharmila Rege*	103
8	Vilifying Dalit women: epics and aesthetics *Vizia Bharati; Y. S. Alone*	117
9	Dalit women's autobiographies *Sharmila Rege*	131

PART IV
What difference does 'difference' make? — 137

10	'Difference' through intersectionality *Kimberlé Crenshaw*	139
11	Dalit women talk differently *Gopal Guru*	150
12	Debating Dalit difference *Sharmila Rege*	154

PART V
Intersectionality in India — 171

13	Why intersectionality is necessary *S. J. Aloysius, J. P. Mangubhai and J. G. Lee*	173
14	The Dalit woman question *Susie Tharu*	182
15	Responses to Indian feminists' objections *Mary E. John; Meena Gopal*	188

PART VI
Toward a Dalit feminist theory   199

16 Feminist fictions: a critique of Indian feminism   201
    Julie Stephens

17 Revitalising Dalit feminism   211
    Smita M. Patil

18 Dalit women's experience: toward a Dalit feminist theory   223
    Kanchana Mahadevan

Index   *237*

FIGURES

8.1	Savi Sawarkar, *Untouchable and Devdasi*, mixed media, 29 × 23 cm	123
8.2	Savi Sawarkar, *Two Untouchable Women and Yellow Cloud*, mixed media, 321 × 45 cm	124
8.3	Savi Sawarkar, *Devdasi with Crow*, etching, 40 × 28 cm	125
8.4	Savi Sawarkar, *Untitled*	126
8.5	Sudharak Owle, photograph from the Kamathipura series	127
8.6	Nandakumar, *Blind Faith*	129

CONTRIBUTORS

Y. S. Alone is Professor in Visual Studies, School of Arts and Aesthetics, Jawaharlal Nehru University, New Delhi, India, and has written on Ancient Indian Art, critique of Walter Spink, Buddhist caves, modern Indian art, neo-Buddhist visual culture, Dr Ambedkar's critical interpretative framework, and the concept of 'protected ignorance'. He is the author of *Early Western Indian Buddhist Caves: Forms and Patronage* (2016).

S. J. Aloysius is Program Director of the Research, Advocacy, and Human Rights Education Department at the Institute of Development Education, Action and Studies in Tamil Nadu, India.

Vizia Bharati is Deputy Director, Telugu Akademi, Hyderabad, Andhra Pradesh, India.

Uma Chakravarti is a feminist historian who taught at Miranda House, University of Delhi, India, from where she took early retirement in 1998. She has been associated with the women's movement and the movement for democratic rights since the late 1970s. She writes on Buddhism, early Indian history, the nineteenth century and contemporary women's issues.

Kimberlé Crenshaw is an American civil rights advocate and a leading scholar of critical race theory. She is a full-time professor at the UCLA School of Law and Columbia Law School, USA, where she specialises in race and gender issues. Crenshaw is also the founder of Columbia Law School's Center for Intersectionality and Social Policy Studies (CISPS) and the African American Policy Forum (AAPF), as well as the president of the Berlin-based Center for Intersectional Justice (CIJ).

V. Geetha is an independent scholar who writes in Tamil and English. She has authored, co-authored, and co-edited works including *Gender* and *Towards a Non-Brahmin Millennium: From Iyothee Thass to Periyar* (1998), *Essays on Science, Women and Society, Gender in Economic Theory and Practice*, and *Women and the Household: Structural and Cultural Dimensions*. She is editorial director, Tara Publishing, Chennai.

Meena Gopal is Professor at the Advanced Centre for Women's Studies, School of Development Studies, Tata Institute of Social Sciences, Mumbai, India. She has published and worked on projects related to child marriage, wage labour, caste and sexuality, gender and labour, political economy of health, welfare and development, and social movements.

Gopal Guru is currently editor of *Economic and Political Weekly*, and Professor Emeritus, Centre for Political Studies, Jawaharlal Nehru University, New Delhi, India. He has published several books and articles on gender, caste and political theory, including *The Cracked Mirror: An Indian Debate on Experience and Theory* (2017) and *Humiliation: Claims and Context* (ed., 2011).

Mary E. John is Senior Fellow and previously Director at the Centre for Women's Development Studies, New Delhi, India. She has written widely on feminism and women's studies. Her publications include *Discrepant Dislocations: Feminism, Theory and Postcolonial Histories* (1996), *French Feminism: An Indian Anthology* (co-ed., 2002), and *Contested Transformations: Changing Economies and Identities in Contemporary India* (co-ed., 2006).

J. G. Lee is Assistant Professor at Williams College, USA, and a former researcher at the Indian Institute of Dalit Studies. He completed his PhD from Columbia University, New York. He teaches and conducts research on religion, language, caste and the state in South Asia. In particular, his work concerns the ways in which Dalits combat structural deprivation, navigate the politics of religious majoritarianism and contend with the sensory and environmental entailments of sanitation labour in colonial and postcolonial India.

Kanchana Mahadevan is Professor at the Department of Philosophy, University of Mumbai, India. She works on the areas of gender studies, critical theory, political thought and film theory. She is the author of *Between Femininity and Feminism: Colonial and Postcolonial Perspectives on Care* (2018). She was formerly Visiting Professor at the Department of Political Science & Centre for Ethics and Global Politics, LUISS University, Rome.

J. P. Mangubhai is Research Programme Director at the Centre for Social Equity and Inclusion, New Delhi, India. She has worked as a consultant in the human rights and development field in India for the past 13 years, with a focus on the rights of Dalits and Adivasis, especially women from these communities. She received her PhD from the Netherlands Institute of Human Rights, University of Utrecht, the Netherlands.

Nivedita Menon is Professor, Centre for Comparative Politics and Political Theory, Jawaharlal Nehru University, New Delhi, India. She is the author of *Seeing Like a Feminist* (2012) and editor (with Aditya Nigam and Sanjay Palshikar) of *Critical Studies in Politics: Exploring Sites, Selves, Power* (2013). An active commentator on contemporary issues in newspapers and on the blog kafila.org, she has translated fiction and nonfiction from Hindi and Malayalam into English.

Tejaswini Niranjana is a professor, cultural theorist, translator and author. She specialises in culture studies, gender studies, translation and ethnomusicology, particularly relating to different forms of Indian music. She has an MA in English and Aesthetics from the University of Bombay, an MPhil in Linguistics from the University of Pune, and a PhD from the University of California, Los Angeles.

Shailaja Paik is Assistant Professor of History and Women's, Gender, and Sexuality Studies, Affiliate Faculty at the University of Cincinnati, USA. She works on Ambedkar, Phule, education, gender and caste and is the author of *Dalit Women's Education in Modern India* (2014).

Smita M. Patil is Assistant Professor in the School of Gender and Development Studies at Indira Gandhi National Open University (IGNOU), India. Her doctoral research was on the intersections of caste and gender from the Centre for Political Studies, Jawaharlal Nehru University. She was also a doctoral fellow at the Centre for the Study of Developing Societies (CSDS), Delhi. She was a recipient of The Australia-India Council Junior Fellowship for the research on 'Politics of Race, Caste and Gender: Exploring the Social Spaces of Indigenous Women in Australia and Dalit Women from India' at National Centre for Australian Studies of Monash University, 2011–2012.

Sharmila Rege was an Indian sociologist, feminist scholar and author of *Writing Caste, Writing Gender* (2006). She led the Krantijyoti Savitribai Phule Women's Studies Centre at University of Pune, a position she has occupied since 1991. She received the Malcolm Adiseshiah award for distinguished contribution to development studies from the Madras Institute of Development Studies (MIDS) in 2006. She contributed greatly to Ambedkar's feminist scholarship with her work such as *Against the Madness of Manu: B R Ambedkar's Writings on Brahmanical Patriarchy* (2013).

Wandana Sonalkar is Professor Emeritus, Advanced Centre for Women's Studies, School of Development Studies at the Tata Institute of Social Sciences, Mumbai, and Director of Tarabai Shinde Women's Studies Centre, India. She was a graduate in Mathematics, Economics at the University of Cambridge and received a

PhD from the Department of Economics at Dr Babasaheb Ambedkar Marathwada University.

Julie Stephens is an Honorary Professor, teaching and researching on sociology and politics at College of Arts & Education, Victoria University, Melbourne, Australia. She has published on social movement theory, feminist oral history and memory studies including *Confronting Postmaternal Thinking: Feminism, Memory and Care* (2012) and *Anti-Disciplinary Protest: Sixties Radicalism and Postmodernism* (1998).

Susie Tharu is Professor in the Department of Cultural Studies, EFL-U, and a founding member of Anveshi, Research Centre for Women's Studies, Hyderabad, India. Co-editor of the two-volume anthology, *Women Writing in India*, and author of several influential papers, she has been active in the Indian women's movement and is a member of the Subaltern Studies Collective. She is co-editor of dossier I, *No Alphabet in Sight* (2011).

ACKNOWLEDGEMENTS

The editors gratefully acknowledge the following contributors and/or their publishers for granting permission to reproduce material for use in this Reader.

Nivedita Menon, 'Is Feminism about "Women"? A Critical View on Intersectionality from India', in *Economic and Political Weekly*, Vol. L No. 17, April 25, 2015, pp. 37–44.

Susie Tharu and Tejaswini Niranjana, 'Problems for a Contemporary Theory of Gender', in Shahid Amin and Dipesh Chakrabarty (eds.), *Subaltern Studies IX: Writings on South Asian History and Society*, New Delhi: Oxford University Press, 1996, pp. 232–60.

Uma Chakravarti, *Gendering Caste: Through a Feminist Lens*, Kolkata: Stree, 2013, pp. 83–88.

V. Geetha, *Patriarchy*, Kolkata: Stree, 2009, pp. 108–9.

Shailaja Paik, 'Modern Dalit Women as Agents', Chapter 4, in *Dalit Women's Education in Modern India: Double Discrimination*, New York: Routledge, 2014, pp. 146–86.

Wandana Sonalkar, 'Translator's Introduction' of Urmila Pawar and Meenakshi Moon (eds.), *We Also Made History: Women in the Ambedkarite Movement*, translated and introduced by Wandana Sonalkar, New Delhi: Zubaan Academic, 2014, pp. 9–20, 26–33.

Sharmila Rege, 'Introduction' of Ambedkar, B. R. *Against the Madness of Manu*, Selected and Introduced by Sharmila Rege, New Delhi: Navayana, 2013, pp. 21–27, 36–40.

Sharmila Rege, 'Caste and Gender: The Violence against Women in India', Chapter 3, in P. G. Jogdand (ed.), *Dalit Women in India: Issues and Perspectives*, New Delhi:

Gyan Publishing House in collaboration with University of Poona, Pune, 2013, pp. 18–36.

Vizia Bharati, 'Hindu Epics: Portrayal of Dalit Women', Chapter 6, in P. G. Jogdand (ed.), *Dalit Women in India: Issues and Perspectives*, New Delhi: Gyan Publishing House in collaboration with University of Poona, Pune, 2013, pp. 93–104.

Sharmila Rege, 'Debating the Consumption of Dalit "Autobiographies": The Significance of Dalit *'Testimonios"* of Sharmila Rege (ed.), *Writing Caste/Writing Gender*, Zubaan, July 1, 2013, pp. 10–19, 84–103.

Kimberlé Crenshaw, 'Demarginalizing the Intersection of Race and Sex: A Black Feminist Critique of Antidiscrimination Doctrine, Feminist Theory and Antiracist Politics', in *University of Chicago Legal Forum*, Vol. 1989. Reprinted with permission from the *University of Chicago Legal Forum* and the University of Chicago Law School.

Gopal Guru, 'Dalit Women Talk Differently', in *Economic and Political Weekly*, Vol. 30 No. 41/42, October 14–21, 1995, pp. 2548–50.

Sharmila Rege, 'Dalit Women Talk Differently: A Critique of "Difference" and Towards a Dalit Feminist Standpoint Position', in *Economic and Political Weekly*, Vol. 33 No. 4, October 31–November 6, 1998, pp. WS39–WS46.

S. J. Aloysius, J. P. Mangubhai, and J. G. Lee, 'Conceptual Framework', Chapter 1, of S. J. Aloysius, Jayashree P. Mangubhai, and Joel G. Lee (eds.), *Dalit Women Speak Out: Violence against Dalit Women in India*, New Delhi: Zubaan, 2006, pp. 47–57.

Susie Tharu, 'The Dalit Woman Question', *Indialogs*, Vol. 1, 2014, pp. 152–59.

Mary E. John, 'Intersectionality: Rejection or Critical Dialogue', *Economic and Political Weekly*, Vol. L No. 33, August 15, 2015, pp. 72–76.

Meena Gopal, 'Struggles around Gender: Some Clarifications', in *Economic and Political Weekly*, Vol. L No. 33, August 15, 2015, pp. 76–78.

Julie Stephens, 'Feminist Fictions: A Critique of the Category "Non-Western Woman" in Feminist Writings on India', in Ranajit Guha (ed.), *Subaltern Studies VI: Writings on South Asian History and Society*, New Delhi: Oxford University Press, February 1, 1994, pp. 92–125.

Smita M. Patil, 'Revitalising Dalit Feminism: Towards Reflexive Anti-Caste Agency of Mang and Mahar Women in Maharashtra', Review of Women's Studies, *Economic and Political Weekly*, Vol. XLVIII No. 18, May 4, 2013, pp. 37–43.

Kanchana Mahadevan, 'Experience and Representation: Beyond Hierarchy', *Labrys, etudes feminists/estudos feministas* No. 27, January–June 2015, pp. 1–20. Retrieved from http: www.labrys.net.br.

INTRODUCTION
Theorising Dalit feminism

Sunaina Arya and Aakash Singh Rathore

Why *Dalit Feminist Theory*? We seek to begin to canonise this discipline in order to not just supplement but to alter Indian feminism; to reorient Indian feminism so that it is more able to function adequately for gender justice. Obviously, there are severe challenges in the methods and approaches of doing feminism in the Third World, and within this context we require theoretical engagement with Indian feminism.

Feminism as an academic discourse recognises that our sociopolitical lives are fundamentally based on inequality between men and women (and other gender minorities). Feminist thinkers hold various standpoints concerning the origin and causes of gender inequality and put forward significant measures that may correct this hierarchical social order based on gender. Consistent with these efforts, this Reader broadly looks into some major developments in feminist thought and presents a new orientation from the Indian context, with an aim of achieving a more authentic feminist theory.

Broadly, there are two primary challenges for the development of that sort of Indian feminist thought that we champion. First, caste-privileged feminists have been at the forefront of the debate and consequently claim to represent *all* women's issues in India. This is deeply problematic. Second, there have been sophisticated theoretical claims that a contemporary theory of gender seems to be impossible since women cannot be homogenised, especially in the Indian context (Tharu, Niranjana, 1996). The latter challenge emerges from the Dalit feminist camp itself, in an effort to problematise the scope and direction (and hegemony) of Indian feminism. Thus, we are forced to re-examine Indian feminist discourse from a theoretical perspective and seek to find ways that the discipline may help us to fulfil the goal of gender justice in India. This Reader attempts to engage with, analyse and evaluate various perspectives and methodologies on gender presented by foremost feminists of India. We seek to resolve the lacuna found in the works of Indian feminist writers, by theorising an alternative perspective (i.e., a Dalit feminist perspective). Thus, *Dalit Feminist Theory* attempts to provide a more complete picture of gender-based inquiry and attempts to fill this unfortunate gap in so-called Third World feminism.

Indian feminists have a widespread inclination towards taking the feminist thesis as their premise and abandoning women's relation to caste. The neglect of *Dalit* in the Indian discourse on gender is deeply problematic because Dalit women occupy subordinate positions in most organised production of feminist knowledge. In the beginning of the twenty-first century, feminists have increasingly begun to recognise this oversight, and several books have emerged highlighting Dalit women's contribution to Indian feminism. But mainstream Indian feminists have by-passed this rectifying body of knowledge, despite its importance and relevance. Indian feminist discourse, which ought to bring gender-justice to *all* Indian women, at least in theory, has suppressed the caste question to such an extent that 'feminism' itself has been seen as a modality of subjugating women from Dalit communities.[1] Thus there are not just theoretical flaws within mainstream Indian feminism but ideological flaws as well.

Theorising feminism within the Indian context therefore entails the need to interrogate and redefine mainstream Indian feminism from a *Dalit* point of view. This necessitates rethinking notions of patriarchy, feminism and 'difference' in a caste-sensitive manner. Only then can we begin to (re)build an adequate theory of Indian feminism. This book offers such a redefinition by exploring the implications of gender politics, of the influence of feminist scholars' social 'location', and 'Indian' feminism from the Dalit feminist perspective. *Dalit Feminist Theory* investigates the relation between gender and caste considering the perspectival limits of the feminist thesis. As mainstream feminists for the most part have neglected the question of caste, the inclusion of Dalit feminist thought substantively furthers the feminist ideals of freedom, equality and solidarity, where they can acquire a more collective tone.

Caste-based exploitation of women: need for a Dalit feminist approach

The recent 'name and shame' movement (which emerged under the spotlight of #MeToo[2]), and the controversy surrounding the feminist collective behind the *Kafila* blog[3] issuing a statement criticising the 'name and shame' uprising and ironically urging for bourgeois 'due process' instead, serves as a point of reference for the deep underlying tension between Dalit feminist lifeworlds and Indian feminist ideology.

However, the difference in approaches between Dalit feminists and Indian feminists is a long-standing one, going back in clear public awareness at least to the anti-Mandal agitation by 'upper'[4] caste women with placards reading '*We don't want unemployed husbands*'.[5] We can also look back at divergent responses to the ban on bar dancing by the Maharashtra government in 2005. Bar dancing was banned, in the words of the Maharashtra Home Minister, because it 'perverts the morals of our young men'.[6] Although many Dalit feminist groups supported the ban, Marxist feminists were opposed to it. Heated debates ensued nationwide between Marxist feminists and Dalit-Bahujan feminists. Mainstream feminist groups opposed the ban as a resistance to 'moral policing' by the state and argued for women's 'choice' to earn the way that they want to. Dalit feminists, on the contrary, welcomed the ban because the 'semi-respectable' occupation of bar dancing inevitably led women – predominantly from marginalised castes – into prostitution. Instead of focusing fundamentally on the moral issue, Dalit-Bahujan feminists demanded rehabilitation of those women who would lose their jobs as a result of the ban.[7]

Articulating the Marxist-feminist position, Nivedita Menon argues that professions like sex-work should be seen with respect as they are chosen. She writes:

> There is no more or less agency exercised in 'choosing' to work as a domestic servant in multiple households for a pittance and with minimum dignity, or to be exploited by the contractors in arduous construction work, than there is in 'choosing' to do sex work – whether as the sole occupation or alongside other work.[8]

Menon argues that an equal degree of agency is exercised by women choosing sex-work as by those choosing domestic or construction-labour work. She also mentions the findings of the first pan-India survey of sex-workers, that is, that about 71% of female sex-workers *choose* sex-work over other occupations.[9] The reasons for their choice are found in the inadequate and insufficient pay and the lack of regular work.[10] These women predominantly focused on the economic issues over the concerns about dignity, as they were unable to run a household with the incomes they were offered. Menon, however, plays down the economic focus of the sex-workers themselves. In order to strengthen her argument to dignify sex-work, she gives the example of the institution of marriage. Just as women's conditions within marriage are unfavourable, the course we opt is not to abolish marriage but rather to create laws to improve women's conditions within the institution. Analogously, Menon says that we must find ways to improve the status of women in sex-work instead of abolishing the profession.[11]

Menon's position on sex-work is problematic from the perspective of Dalit feminism. In cases of sex-work, we cannot ignore that the choice made by women has certain limitations. Choice is a particular capacity of rational beings to prefer a course of action from among various alternatives. In this case, the choice is not between preferring a profession of dignity to one void of dignity but to choose between two options both without dignity, one of which provides a higher wage. A woman choosing sex-work may technically be an agent, but her agency has no meaning if she does not have sufficient opportunity to exercise broader freedom of choice. Obviously, if women were availed of dignity through another occupation while earning a similar wage, they would prefer the other profession over sex-work.[12]

The category of being a 'sex-worker' also alienates these women from non–sex-worker women, who regard them as 'other'.[13] Thus Menon's analogy between the institution of marriage and the occupation of sex-work is false. The point of *othering* also illustrates a difference in the approaches of the sex-workers themselves and the feminist defenders of sex-work. The former operates primarily from within an economic perspective (broader choices being historically inaccessible to them), whereas the latter deploy liberal agendas of 'my body, my rights'. This *difference* has been characterised as 'subaltern versus elite', which provides a hint about the differing social locations that horizon the perspectives of the feminists who enjoy caste-class privileges over the workers whose rights they claim to defend. Neither discrimination in the form of *othering* nor factual *difference* should be ignored in our endeavour to establish a gender-just society. The aims behind feminist discourse will never be met unless each and every woman is in a systemic position to avail of equal treatment and dignified status in society.

The reports of the National Federation of Dalit Women (NFDW) and National Campaign on Dalit Human Rights (NCDHR), which establish the structural violence inherent in caste-ordained linkages between sexuality and labour, also pose challenges to the Marxist feminist standpoint on sex-work.[14] Menon ignores the factual aspect of the issue which calls our attention to the foundations of the dehumanisation of these women. On the contrary, the feminist philosophy of B.R. Ambedkar provides a direct and clear position on this. Ambedkar advocates that women should give up the disgraceful life of prostitution, which has long been a profession populated predominantly by Dalit women.[15] Some critics accuse Ambedkar of disdaining these women by calling them a 'shame to the community',[16] and arguing that his view attempts to curb women's freedom to deploy their sexuality in the manner they desire. But those critics have ignored the underlying issue, that prostitution is a systemic option primarily limited to the disadvantaged, and is thus part of a larger system of social exploitation within which individual choice or sexual freedom functions as hardly more than a bourgeois abstraction. Hence Ambedkar's advice in the same impugned speech, that women should 'not live under conditions *which inevitably drag [them] into prostitution*',[17] has been brushed aside. Ambedkar thus brings into focus the caste-ordained linkages between labour and sexuality.[18]

Building on Ambedkar's analyses of the issue and the previously mentioned survey reports, Dalit feminist theorist Sharmila Rege suggests that subordinate caste women's 'entry into a life of sex work is dictated by their birth into specific untouchable communities that are expected to provide sexual favours to caste Hindu men, and not by choice'.[19] Rege's position thus runs contrary to that of mainstream feminism. The revealed linkages between caste and gender show that sex workers' lives are largely predetermined in a caste-stratified society. Therefore, Rege concludes that 'caste determines the division of labour, sexual division of labour and division of sexual labour'.[20]

Within this historical context, sex-work cannot be abstracted from its broader systemic framework and regarded simply as a 'profession' per se. The notion of a profession entails an agent's voluntary exercise, which in this case is empty, as the freedom to choose has always been denied to Dalit-Bahujan women.[21] It is thus not only their economic status but their social status that has constrained the field of choice for these women. What this implies is that in addition to the gender axis alone, Indian feminist thought needs to take seriously the junctures of gender and caste, as well as caste as such. Seeing the issues of feminism from the intersections of caste, class and gender is referred to as intersectionality, to which we now turn.

On intersectionality and gender justice[22]

Amongst the many disputes between mainstream Indian feminism and Dalit feminism is an important one over the centrality of intersectionality. Nivedita Menon, in her article 'Is Feminism about "Women"? A Critical View on Intersectionality from India', put forward several arguments rejecting the need of intersectionality in the Indian context, which has been responded to by Dalit feminist thinkers Mary E. John and Meena Gopal.

Menon suggests that intersectionality has originated in a Western framework based on *'western' experience* which is inapplicable in the 'non-West'.[23] Although accepting the possibility of concepts to travel across time, she questions application of intersectionality across space. Attempts to undermine the application of intersectionality to India is indicative of discomfort regarding the issue of caste. Mary E. John criticises Menon's blunt rejection of the application of intersectionality in India, demanding engagement with the concept, as it is 'an excellent candidate' facilitating us to attain gender justice.[24] She clarifies that salient issues of gender injustice that preoccupy Menon (as discussed in the previous section) are indecipherable via a class analysis alone. John writes:

> The term intersectionality ... certainly represents an advance over the more generic use of multiple axes of oppression, double and treble burdens and so on, and is a corrective to the commonly deployed notion of multiple identities. This way of alluding to the effects of 'race, class, gender' (or, in our context, 'class, caste, community, gender') is quite widespread, as I am sure readers are aware. The idea of being 'multiple' misleadingly suggests that identities are formed by adding together the various structures or axes that constitute them. In such a view, Black women's identities become a combination of being black and being women.[25]

Meena Gopal compounds Mary E. John's argument by pointing out that Menon raised several points as problematic regarding the relevance of intersectionality, but does not undertake to systematically clarify them.[26]

Second, Menon claims that the notion of 'double and triple burdens' adds nothing new to our feminist enterprise because a 'single axis framework' was 'never predominant or unchallenged in our parts of the world'.[27] The examples that Menon offers (on the Women's Reservation Bill and the Uniform Civil Code) in order to demonstrate the absence of single axis thinking in our context or the redundancy of intersectionality as an idea has been subjected to scrutiny. As Meena Gopal suggests:

> The 'homogeneity' versus 'heterogeneity' dichotomy simplifies the complex debates around the need for a civil code or the continuing pleas for gender-just laws that encompass not just relational arrangements and entitlements, but social security as well. Such simplification dehistoricises the trajectory of the women's movement and the sociopolitical context that shaped it and continues to do so.[28]

An intersectional analysis reveals that mainstream feminists have not given adequate attention to those who suffer 'double or triple burdens'. Mary E. John seeks to challenge this: 'We in India are up against the surprising tenacity of "single axis" agendas within the women's movement, and need to come up with adequate explanations for this'.[29]

Third, Menon asserts that 'woman' is an unstable category and the notion of caste is already involved in it; moreover, '[t]he presumed subject of feminist politics has been destabilised in India most notably by the politics of caste, religious community identity and sexuality'.[30] Menon argues that the questions of caste, religion or region 'destabilises' the political thrust of gender-based issues. Mary E. John asserts, however, that 'destabilisation alone is no guarantor of a more genuinely inclusive politics'[31] and thereby launches a further critique of Menon's position:

> There is no better instance of this than the term feminism itself, which has been repeatedly rejected for being Western and against 'Indian culture'. Indeed, the history of the ideas and frames of the women's movement in India offers extraordinarily complex instances of how feminists have charted a nuanced politics between false universals and equally false rejections of them.[32]

Fourth, Menon claims that intersectionality itself is an 'empty place' as a person bears only a single relevant identity at a given point of time.[33] In other words, at time T1 if one is being regarded as a woman, then at T1 she is not being regarded as Dalit, as labourer, as Muslim, etc. Pointing to the dynamics of power relations within these and similar groups, Menon believes that we should not further 'fracture' the 'woman'.[34] After all, Menon argues, associating a woman with identities other than gender weakens the feminist struggle.

Mary E. John opposes Menon here:

> If intersectionality is to have any genuinely liberatory potential it must be that it contributes to building solidarity across subjects that are recognised as otherwise getting lost between movements and agendas. A major (if less noted) aspect of the success of US hegemony in the intellectual field is its

heterogeneity, its capacity to house positions of opposition and to find space for immigrant differences.[35]

Meena Gopal supports Mary E. John's counterargument: 'Menon's account suggests there is a binary opposition between caste politics and feminist politics'.[36] Historically and practically, Dalit women have always been triply burdened subjects whose issues can thus only adequately be understood within an intersectional framework.[37]

Fifth, Menon claims that intersectionality poses a threat toward building solidarity-based feminist politics, serving instead as a tool to facilitate governmentalising and the depoliticising of gender by foregrounding other identities besides gender.[38] Mary E. John counters, however, that the arguments regarding the problems of governmentality and depoliticisation are posed too simply by Menon.[39] Such lax engagements with intersectionality pose a hazard to the sincere attempts to improve the tools available to feminism, tools that could otherwise be helpful in moving us forward toward a gender-just society.

Sixth, Menon argues that intersectionality originated in the context of jurisprudence, and that it is a truism within legal thinking that law is more just when it does not recognise differences. There are several problems with this criticism. Obviously, the context out of which a concept emerged does not necessarily condition the possibilities of its applicability for research in other areas or for understanding social realities. Also, the foundation for the existence of a legal discourse or notions of legal justice is the fact of injustice, including the inequalities prevailing across the world. Given this, if law remains blind to differences among individuals, it can scarcely provide justice. Menon's claims regarding the legal provenance of intersectionality run counter to the nature and functioning of law itself.

And finally, Menon argues that since each identity is unstable (be it caste, religion, queer, etc.) the subject of feminist inquiry must be 'people' and not Dalit, Muslim, Women, or other markers.[40] But, who are these people? Can there be people void of social, economic or political identity? Meena Gopal points out that Menon neglects to clarify 'whose feminist politics is being referred to'.[41] Gopal continues, '[d]espite the opening call to locate theory, there seems an urgency to theorise in response to global debates. This leaves us, even after going through the latter half of the essay, asking for more'.[42]

Menon's take on intersectionality is vague and seems to be self-contradictory: she accepts intersectionality at a global/international level but rejects it at the local level. Meena Gopal, thus, concludes that Menon's essay, opposite her intentions, 'opens up the possibilities of claiming intersectionality for one's own purposes'.[43] This Dalit feminist theory seeks to do.

The mainstream feminist standpoint on intersectionality is in some ways inscrutable. Why are Indian feminists so reluctant to seriously engage with the concept? It hints at their refusal to reflect upon their own caste-privileged status within Indian society. This endangers the potential for feminism to contribute to achieving the goal of gender justice for all.

To further contextualise how Dalit feminist theory uses intersectionality for its 'own purposes', we will turn to certain peculiarities about the nature of patriarchy in India; peculiarities all but ignored in mainstream Indian feminism.

The brahmanical nature of patriarchy[44]

The forms of patriarchy operating in India today are influenced by *brahmanical patriarchy*, a term coined by Dr B. R. Ambedkar.[45] This is a structural concept – also known as 'graded inequality' – which explains a specific modality of patriarchy by explicating a set of discriminatory levels constituting a hierarchical organisation of society based on caste, which is quite unique to the Indian subcontinent. Within this structure, implicit, insidious and seemingly impossible to challenge, 'upper'-caste men are most privileged, 'upper'-caste women are more privileged, 'lower'-caste men are more deprived, and 'lower'-caste women are most deprived.[46] All others find their place between these frames depending upon their caste and gender location within the system. 'Lower' caste women are most prone to violence as they face oppression at three levels:[47] (1) caste, as subject to caste oppression at the hands of 'upper' castes; (2) class, as labourers subject to class-based oppression, also mainly at the hands of 'higher' castes who form the bulk of landowners; and (3) gender, as women who experience patriarchal oppression at the hands of all men, including men of their own caste.

Dalit women face caste-based discrimination in the vertical structure of society and gender-based discrimination on the horizontal structure of society. Uma Chakravarti argues, therefore, that the gender issue cannot be comprehended without bringing in the caste question within the Indian social structure.[48] The logic behind this claim can be better discerned by considering the example of 'honour killing'.[49] There are generally two reasons for a couple/lovers getting murdered by their parents or elders or local authorities: one reason is that the lovers defied norms by choosing their own partners and pursuing marriage on their own; but the second, usually the catalyst, is that they chose partners outside of their caste. Caste is generally crucial in such murder cases.

It is important to observe that the concept of brahmanical patriarchy does not refer to the patriarchal practices followed by brahmin men; instead, it represents the multiform nature of patriarchy against women in India. Anyone, regardless of her caste or gender, who believes, practices, preaches or encourages any kind of discrimination based on this hierarchical structure would be considered a follower of brahminism by definition. Just as it does not require a man to practice misogyny, it is not necessarily brahmins who practice brahminism.[50] In his analysis of caste, Ambedkar calls patriarchy as the twinsister of brahminism.[51] As we will see later, he evidences that caste and gender are employed together to maintain endogamy (i.e., the absence of intermarriage), which is *raison d'être* to restrict women's sexuality.

Urmila Pawar and Meenakshi Moon argue that violence, especially sexual violence, against Dalit women is disproportionately public rather than domestic because working as labourers is peculiar to Dalit women's living. Violence against Dalits is a 'permanently existing threat'. It functions as a 'means to punish Dalit women and men' for asserting their rights against caste hierarchy.[52] Most of such violence (murder, gang rape, naked parade) torments Dalit women. This structure of violence makes them 'easy prey' for the lust and wrath of 'upper' caste men.

In her article 'Intersections of Gender and Caste', Sharmila Rege argues:

> In analysing the caste and gender matrix in Indian society, merely pluralising the term patriarchy is not enough. The task is to map the ways in which the category 'women' is being differently reconstituted within regionally diverse patriarchal relations cross-hatched by graded caste inequalities.[53]

The intersection of caste and gender produces a kind of experience not reducible to patriarchy alone, nor to caste oppression alone. A concrete example that may be useful for understanding this is the case of Bhanwari Devi (1992),[54] a Dalit *saathin* (i.e., social activist working at the ground level). Devi was campaigning against a one-year-old girl's marriage and consequently was gang-raped by five 'upper'-caste men related to each other (a man, his brother, his son, his son-in-law and son) in the presence of her husband. This brutal rape was intended to punish Devi for 'interfering' in their household, where child marriage was customary, and is indicative of the fact that caste-stratified society finds the assertions of a Dalit woman repugnant. Had she been from an 'upper' caste family, she would not be treated as *sexually available* by those men. Had she been a male activist, she might have suffered some other kind of violence but not rape. Had she not been from a lower class, options beyond working as a *saathin* would have been available. A single-axis framework for such a case renders a dysfunctional analysis. A merely additive evaluation of a Dalit woman's marginalisation is distorting, but adequately capturing their 'difference' can play a positive role for legislative as well as social justice. That is, in their experience, the difference is not of degree but of kind.

In summation, a case such as that of Bhanwari Devi exemplifies that mainstream Indian feminists fail to recognise that 'something unique is produced at the intersection point of different types of discrimination'.[55]

Therefore, Dalit feminist thought draws in this interconnected web of caste, gender and class together to challenge brahmanical patriarchy with a multi-axis approach. This is crucial, as Sharmila Rege, Mary E. John, Kalpana Kannabiran, J. Devika, *et al.* argue: in order to have a 'real feminism' there is a need to deal with gender-based issues keeping the caste question at the centre.[56] This takes us further on to the notion of 'Dalit difference'.

From difference to Dalit difference[57]

The present Reader aims to provide a complete picture of gender-based inquiry by addressing a theoretical gap in Indian feminism. It attempts to establish the need to recognise 'difference'; a 'difference' from Indian feminist philosophy arising from the caste perspective – a *Dalit* difference. It offers a departure point in feminist articulation based on the *difference* between the lives of mainstream and subaltern women. It seeks to develop a complete conceptual framework for Indian feminist thought by lodging the Dalit question into its core cluster of concerns.

Renowned feminists like Mary Wollstonecraft, Simone de Beauvoir, Judith Butler, *et al.* have widely discussed the nature and scope of feminist theory, wherein a significant juncture was completely glossed over. From the perspective of Black feminism, Kimberlé Crenshaw has criticised silence regarding the race element within First World feminism, and has introduced intersectionality as a tool to acknowledge the 'difference' to existent feminist philosophy.[58] 'Difference' has been understood within a unique kind of discrimination which Black women face due to their race-gender-class deprivations. Patricia Hill Collins has theorised this 'difference', placing it at the crux of feminist philosophy in order to resolve the race biases of First World feminists.[59] Through the lens of this 'difference', this race aspect, Collins democratises feminist thought, because gender justice bears no meaning if it does not entail gender justice for *all* women of all races.

So-called Third World feminists have adopted the idea of 'difference' as well as that of intersectionality based on their differences grounded in location. But the very idea of intersectionality, which is the theoretical ground for 'difference', has long been rejected in the works of mainstream feminists, who reject internal differences between Third World women even as they assert their own difference from First World feminists.[60]

Sharmila Rege offers a critique of 'difference' from a Dalit feminist standpoint position and argues that feminist 'difference' is incomplete unless the difference from a caste perspective, i.e., Dalit difference, is added to it.[61] Or, as Smita M. Patil has neatly captured it: 'Dalit feminist thought has the epistemic vantage location to challenge the authenticity of knowledge that is generated for the emancipation of the oppressed through pointing out the caste-cum-class privilege of the dominant intelligentsia and institutional histories'.[62]

Theorising Dalit difference

Writing in reference to the 2006 Khairlanji massacre of a Dalit family, paraded naked before being murdered, Sharmila Rege has asserted that, due to the lack of adequate focus on the caste-gender nexus, violence against Dalit women tends to be marked as 'either-or': either as *caste atrocity* or as *sexual atrocity*.[63] Critiquing this either-or from a Dalit feminist standpoint, she argues:

> In the absence of such critiques of Brahmanical, class-based hetropatriarchies, the political edge of sexual politics is lost. No politics committed to

caste-based society can overlook sexual politics. It is therefore important to revision it rather than give it up or pose the 'upper' caste women alone as the only needy constituents of such a politics.[64]

Rege argues that mainstream feminism does not capture the uniqueness of the marginalisation at the intersection point of different types of discrimination. That is, a woman faces a kind of discrimination at the intersections of her multiple identities which she may not face if she would belong singularly to any of the particular social, cultural, economic, political, or regional categories. Rege's perspective is inspired from Dr Ambedkar's understanding of the issue.

B. R. Ambedkar underlines the inadequacy of understanding the caste system in terms of the 'idea of pollution'[65] and argues instead that its fundamental characteristic is that of *endogamy* – the absence of intermarriage – which he calls its *essence*.[66] In order to maintain the numerical balance between the sexes in society, inhumane rituals like *sati pratha*,[67] enforced widowhood,[68] and child marriage were devised by brahmins.[69] Hence, controlling women's sexuality has been and remains as the essential way to sustain the caste system. Ambedkar thus regards patriarchy as the twin sister of brahminism. Ambedkar's analysis of caste reveals the inbuilt connection between caste and gender and consequently results in the innumerable social expressions with which we are all familiar: for example, the prevention of Dalit women's entry into Hindu temples; the phenomena of Devdasis, Muralis, Jogtinis and so on.

On the topic of Ambedkarite feminism, especially the frequent *ad hominem* critiques forwarded by mainstream feminists, Sharmila Rege responds to accusations that Ambedkar was not *feminist enough*, as he neglected to bring his wife into the forefront of his pursuit of justice, in contrast to Phule, for example.[70] According to Rege, these critics fail to appreciate the depth of his commitment for an overall just society, and criticise his contributions based on a 'selective and erroneous understanding of his personal sphere'.[71]

Along the same lines, Shailaja Paik writes:

> Phule, Ambedkar and Dalit women pushed caste out of the confines of the social, religious, and personal into the political. They debated it in public, in the spheres of constitutional law in state legislatures, and at national and international levels . . . . Dalit narratives turned rhetoric into powerful discourse that shaped Dalit woman's affect, behaviour, and subjectivity through their participation in collective action for education and empowerment.[72]

Paik concludes that though Phule seems more radical in this respect, Ambedkar has undeniably deeply influenced feminist progress in India.[73]

But back to the challenge of theorising Dalit difference. In her seminal article 'Dalit Women Talk Differently: A Critique of 'Difference' and Towards a Dalit Feminist Standpoint Position', Sharmila Rege revisits the historical evolution of feminist discourse starting from First World feminism, Black feminism, to the introduction of a Saidian[74] framework in feminism. She shows how white feminists had failed to capture the issues of Black women, and how racism turned out to be 'the sole responsibility of black feminists'. Black feminists thus criticised the established discourse on the grounds of the difference of their experience of combined discrimination based on race and gender. Analogously, Rege unfolds how the problems regarding caste become 'the sole responsibility of the Dalit women's organisations' in India. She argues for adding more difference (Dalit) to the (established) difference – she aims thereby to forward an ideological position for the unrecognised plurality of Indian women. She argues: 'It is imperative for feminist politics that 'difference' be historically located in the real struggles of marginalised women'.[75]

Based on the notion of *difference*, Rege further advocates for a Dalit feminist standpoint. Rege suggests that the ignorance of the category of caste within feminist discourse also manifests as distortions in other areas. For example, it leads to a limited perception regarding the violence against Muslim and Christian women, where it is assumed to arise only in relation to '*talaq*' and 'divorce', even though this facile assumption is routinely contradicted in survey reports. The latter reveal, on the contrary, a salient linkage between caste-determined professions and the violence against women involved in them. Hence, Rege reasserts that caste as a category plays a major role in 'the collective and public threat of rape, sexual assault and physical violence at the workplace and in public'; Dalit women suffer most in this regard.[76]

Political theorist Gopal Guru, in his article 'Dalit Women Talk Differently', put forward several arguments to show how Dalit women are more oppressed and victimised, which results in a difference in their way of talking and living. He asserts that Dalit women are more prone to patriarchal and structural violence. They talk differently because they suffer 'on the basis of external factors (non-Dalit forces homogenising the issue of Dalit women) and internal factors (the patriarchal domination within Dalits)'.[77] The phenomenon of talking differently is regarded as an act of dissent against their exclusion from both the brahmanical feminist politics as well as the dominant patriarchal culture.

Gopal Guru's claims open up the need to address further challenges to theorising Dalit difference, which we continue to explore in the next section in terms of articulation.

Articulation in contemporary Indian feminism

This section addresses two failures of the mainstream feminist approach, which serve to place hurdles toward the task of adequately theorising Indian feminism, and hint at its alienation from everyday women's patriarchal experiences. First is the legitimate challenge posed by the seeming impossibility of articulating a coherent theory of gender (taken up in Chapter 2). Second is the misconception about Dalit patriarchy (taken up in Chapter 3).

Susie Tharu and Tejaswini Niranjana highlight several problems in theorising gender. They suggest that there is a 'crisis in feminism', as the category 'woman' is not homogenous: there are well-known rubrics like Hindutva Woman, Women in the Mandal Movement, Women in the Chanduru Movement, Women in the Arrack Movement, etc. In this context, they point out various debates, such as that on chastity as a virtue, that on consent as a right, or on 'upper'-caste women's objectification as 'molestation' versus Dalit women's exploitation as 'custom'.

Tharu and Niranjana write:

> [A] whole range of issues that constitute the subjugation of women, and indeed their differential subjugation in relation to class, caste and community are marginalized in the 'woman' whose freedom and right to privacy is invoked and who becomes the bearer of the 'right' to chose.[78]

They argue that, although it is imperative for *us* as feminists to support Dalit movements, it is difficult to build alliances between feminism and *other political initiatives*. This characterisation of Dalit movements as 'other' to feminism would seem to pull the rug out from under the possibility of regarding Dalit feminism as itself a feminist initiative. Tharu and Niranjana provide a vast range of further difficulties in theorising Indian feminism, and they fail to offer any vantage point from which these difficulties may be resolved. It is our position, quite to the contrary, that intersectionality offers the tool through which the challenges that Tharu and Niranjana enumerate may be overcome. The evidence for this appears throughout the writings in Parts IV, V and VI (and in Chapter 14, some of the evidence comes from Tharu herself).

Another issue, far more insidious, misleading and dangerous, is the ever-increasing popularity of the concept of 'Dalit patriarchy'. A couple of decades ago, Gopal Guru had introduced the concept rather vaguely,[79] referring to the patriarchal dominance over Dalit women internal to their caste. Gopal Guru, in his usual exploratory and provocative way, was in no way aiming to launch a term that would snowball into a major, popular idea. But it has now, fostered and furthered by mainstream Indian feminists, emerged as a concept separate from brahmanical patriarchy, and regarded as supplementary to it. This is an ill-conceived and reactionary formulation that needs to be opposed.

Unfortunately, feminist sociologist V. Geetha uses this concept to refer to the patriarchal practices by (male) members of the Dalit community. She suggests that Dalit men, as part of their exploitation by 'upper'-caste men, also face taunts regarding their masculinity in terms of not being able to protect their women; this in turn results in their aggressive behaviour within their own families.[80] Uma Chakravarti, a well-known feminist historian, attempts to pluralise patriarchy by deploying the terms 'graded patriarchies' and 'Dalit patriarchy'[81] arguing that 'Dalit women experience patriarchy in a unique way'.[82] As Chakravarti writes, citing a Dalit poet in support of her claim:

> it is not as if patriarchies do not exist among the Dalit castes, or that Dalit women do not have to struggle against the patriarchies within their own communities. In the words of Swaroopa Rani,
>
> *When has my life been truly mine?*
> *In the home male arrogance*
> *Sets my cheek stinging.*

> *While in the street caste arrogance*
> Splits the other cheek open.[83]

But let us examine more closely Swaroopa Rani's poignant poem. In the first three lines, we see registered the phenomenon of *patriarchy* manifest as violence. In the latter two lines we see registered the phenomenon of caste arrogance, *brahminism*. The five lines, then, signal brahmanical patriarchy; they evidence Dr Ambedkar's formulation of the linkage between caste and patriarchy – brahmanical patriarchy. Where, how and why does Uma Chakravarti read in this the evidence of peculiarly Dalit patriarchy rather than brahmanical patriarchy? We must, it seems, clarify several misconceptions about the spurious concept of Dalit patriarchy here.

First, think back on V. Geetha's argument just mentioned. Hers is ostensibly an empirical claim. But where is the empirical evidence regarding the uniqueness in patriarchal practices followed by Dalit men? Similarly ambiguous, Chakravarti writes, '*whatever* might have been the differences between Dalit women's experience of patriarchy and that of 'upper' caste women',[84] indicating through the 'whatever' that the empirical claim is based on mere speculation. Whether or not Dalit men are mocked by symbolic 'emasculation', on what basis are we to conclude that they do not behave in more or less the same manner as non-Dalit men, or even to those who taunt them? In the absence of any evidence to the contrary, we must continue to assume that Dalit women experience brahmanical patriarchy. And indeed, the alleged 'emasculation' itself emerges from brahminism, not from within the Dalit community, and thus it is both empirically and logically more sensible to capture the issues under the concept of brahmanical patriarchy, instead of attempting to displace attention.

Secondly, if there is any truth to the empirical claim, then accordingly not just Dalit men but shudra men also would face such 'emasculation'. Shall we then develop the concept of OBC patriarchy? Given Ambedkar's assessment of the caste system as a system of graded inequality, we might equally speculate that the men of every caste face the threat of 'emasculation' from each above it, and perpetuate the same to the men of each caste below it – are we to proliferate patriarchies? Is it not, rather, that the entirety of the system, brahminism, has produced brahmanical patriarchy, which may manifest itself in different castes in different ways?[85]

What is at issue is brahmanical patriarchy, not some ambiguous and untenable concept like Dalit patriarchy. This dubious notion of Dalit patriarchy has also possibly been perpetuated as a mirror inversion of the earlier, equally dubious idea of Dalit egalitarianism; that is, the supposition that Dalit men do not oppress *their* women as much as 'upper'-caste men do, because Dalit men are cognisant of the pain of oppression, which they experience at the hands of 'upper' castes. It would be nice if it were true, but there is no empirical evidence beyond anecdotes.

Thirdly, the vague concept of Dalit patriarchy seems to arise from a misunderstanding of the concept of brahmanical patriarchy. Brahmanical patriarchy does not refer to the patriarchy followed by and perpetuated by brahmin men.[86] Rather, it represents the multiform nature of patriarchy-cum-caste in India, not necessarily perpetrated by brahmins or even by men. *Brahmanical patriarchy* explains a specific kind of patriarchy by explicating a set of discriminatory levels, which is unique to the context of the Indian subcontinent. On the contrary, feminists (and others) refer to Dalit patriarchy as the mode of patriarchy prevalent amongst Dalits, or perpetrated by Dalit men against 'their' women. Even if there is such a phenomenon – and as of yet there is no empirical evidence, although innumerable field studies are constantly undertaken, sponsored by 'upper'-caste researchers, that aims to uncover this evidence – it would logically need to be referred to as 'Dalit manifestations of brahmanical patriarchy'.

Fourthly, if 'Dalit patriarchy' has been conceived as a conceptual tool to further the work of Dalit feminism, then there is obviously some confusion about the meaning and scope of the latter. Dalit feminism in India has evolved for very much the same reasons as the emergence of Black feminism vis-à-vis First World feminism. Black feminism recognises the multiple deprivations of Black women based on race, class and gender. Similarly, Dalit feminism recognises the multiple deprivations of Dalit women based on caste, class and gender. If, then, there is a Dalit patriarchy, one would expect that there would have been forwarded an analogous concept of Black patriarchy. However, no such concept has been posited either within Black feminism or First World feminism in general. Such is, perhaps, the uniqueness of caste in India, and the cunning of brahminism, that here we have a proliferating discourse on the spurious concept of Dalit patriarchy, despite the lack of empirical evidence and the untenability of its logic.

In sum, mainstream feminists' attempt to coin a different term for the same practice, brahmanical patriarchy, is futile and misleading. Such an attempt is indicative of a certain irresponsibility of scholars who enjoy caste-class privilege and do not regard Dalit women's issues as central to feminism because Dalit women's issues are not *their* problem. For this and other reasons as well, we must encourage theorisation by those who live and share these experiences in an effort to honestly address caste-based issues in feminist discourse. This approach has been championed by Kanchana Mahadevan, among others, to whose position we now turn.

Dalit feminist theory against brahmanical feminism

The arguably brahmanical attitude of many Indian feminists places a hindrance for pursuit of a gender-just society. In mainstream Indian feminism's attempts to silence discussions on Dalit feminism, there have been several innovative tactics employed. These include attempts to reduce Dalit feminists to the status of 'informant';[87] to marginalise Dalit feminism as 'other political initiatives';[88] and, to reduce Dalit feminist conceptual production to mere works of 'poetry, short stories and other forms of writing',[89] as opposed to the *academic, intellectual, scholarly,* or *theoretical* works which contribute to knowledge production in Indian feminism. This 'us' (feminist scholars) versus 'them' (native narrators) dichotomy has been nicely represented in a different context through Gopal Guru's expression, 'theoretical brahmin and empirical shudra', which he had deployed while exposing the nature of *doing* social science in India.[90] Thus, Dalit feminist thought is subordinated by both a masculinist approach to theorising (the patriarchal nature of academia) as well as, ironically, by the mainstream Indian feminist community (the casteist nature of feminist discourse in India, thus leading us to characterise it as brahmanical feminism).

There have been a variety of ways that feminists have addressed the problem of what we are calling brahmanical feminism. Julie Stephens has identified a deep theoretical problem with Indian feminism. Stephens has argued that in numerous feminist movements today, the category of 'experience' is used as an important tool in the name of building 'international sisterhood'; however, this has been resisted by mainstream Indian feminists.[91] In other areas, marginalised women are emerging as a source of more comprehensively understanding gender-based problems; in India, however, feminist scholars *other* the marginalised women as mere objects under investigation. Thus, Stephens questions the status of 'experience', which is of course substantively different for the different women involved within feminist inquiry. She is led, then, to criticise the 'us'-'them' dichotomy prevalent in Indian feminism and charges mainstream feminists with the manipulation of 'experience', about which they are too conveniently selective.

Gopal Guru, along the same lines, had argued early on that since the reality of Dalit women is perceived from a specific social location, non-Dalit feminist theories fail to capture the reality of Dalit women. Consequentially, Dalit women's representation by non-Dalit women is 'unauthentic'.[92] Thus he has called for the articulation and addressing of Dalit women's issues by Dalit women scholars themselves. We subscribe to this project, but do not think it productive to be totalitarian about it. Well-wishers and fellow travellers must also be welcomed, as well as those who express sincere solidarity. But we cannot be glib; the risk of appropriation is serious and omnipresent.

These concerns have received studied attention in Kanchana Mahadevan's seminal essay 'Experience and Representation: Beyond Hierarchy'. Mahadevan crafts an alternative to the impasse posed by the dichotomies that we face. She proposes the idea of theorising by means of a collective, shared experience by those who live, share and articulate experience. Mahadevan cites de Beauvoir, who offers an onto-epistemic critique that helps to ground her innovation: '[T]he meaning of an object is not a concept graspable by pure understanding. Its meaning is the object as it is disclosed to us in the overall relation we sustain with it, and which is action, emotion, and feeling'.[93]

From the point of view of theory, in order to satisfy the minimal conditions of authenticity for a given analysis, the 'embodiment' of the analyst and the 'scholarship' of the subjects under investigation are both required to be recognised. Mahadevan does not regard experience as an 'incorrigible starting point' but rather as 'a dialectical process of collective articulation' by the persons belonging to conflicting social locations. She argues that '[e]xperience as a lived phenomenon is never solely owned or authored by an individual'.[94] On the contrary, '[e]xperience is both, objective and subjective, personal and collaborative, immediate and mediated, as well as singular and universal'.[95] This position, again, is coherent with de Beauvoir's approach, as may be discerned in Mahadevan's succinct depiction:

> The shared nature of experience allows for the researcher to take the point of view of the participant and vice versa. It is precisely such sharing – which presupposes embodiment – that allows feminists to undertake the emancipatory task of resisting caste privilege, which hinders feminist emancipation.[96]

Mahadevan's contribution is invaluable to the project of theorising beyond brahmanical feminism, offering an epistemic groundwork for feminist thought that may help prevent it from engaging in biased feminist enterprises, especially caste-biased enterprises in the Indian context. This approach pioneers an efficient and authentic way of doing feminist research, that also precludes the possibility of cynical appropriation. It advocates for an experienced researcher along with a trained narrator to progress towards authentic theory. This is how we conceive of Dalit feminist theory, and hence Mahadevan's chapter serves as a fitting close to this Reader.

Conclusion

The aim of this Introduction has not been to walk one-by-one through the chapters of the Reader, but instead to show the main reasons for the Reader's necessity. The 18 chapters that follow are organised into six parts, and each of the parts begins with a thematic note that introduces the main points of the chapters contained within them. The thematic notes also explain the rationale behind grouping the chapters together into parts. For more specifics on the individual chapters, therefore, you can turn to the six thematic notes.

For now, we hope that you will have caught a glimpse of why this Reader was conceived. It is a part of an ongoing effort to correct the errors and misdirection of contemporary Indian feminism. We offer it in the hope that one day gender justice can be achieved for all Indian women, irrespective of caste, class and other crucial markers of identity.

Notes

1 Thus Dalit 'womanist', as opposed to 'feminist', persuasions have emerged in recent times. See Cynthia Stephen's 'A Name of Our Own', *Journal of Dharma*, 36 (4), October–December, pp. 419–434.
2 We do not wish to enter into the complex #MeToo movement here; however, we would note that, as with a host of other issues, there are discernible differences between the ways that Dalit feminists understand #MeToo versus the mainstream Indian feminist take. For example, Dalit feminist Cynthia Stephens has pointed out that the #MeToo movement has been largely oblivious to the voices of Dalit women, and this – as Kanchana Mahadevan has pointed out – in spite of the fact that a Dalit feminist, Raya Sarkar, first brought the movement to attention in India.

3 Nivedita Menon, 'Statement by Feminists on Facebook Campaign to "Name and Shame"', *Kafila – 12 Years of a Common Journey*, October 10, 2017. Retrieved from https://kafila.online/2017/10/24/statement-by-feminists-on-facebook-campaign-to-name-and-shame/.
4 Terms like 'upper' and 'lower' assume a validity to the hierarchy of castes of a caste-stratified system, i.e., Brahminism. To discourage the assumed validity of the hierarchy, we place the terms in scare quotes wherever possible.
5 Sharmila Rege, 'Dalit Women Talk Differently: A Critique of "Difference" and Towards a Dalit Feminist Standpoint Position', *Economic and Political Weekly*, Vol. 33 No. 4, October 31–November 6, 1998, pp. WS39–WS46, WS43; Uma Chakravarti, 'Prologue', *Gendering Caste: Through a Feminist Lens*, Kolkata: Stree, 2013, pp. 1–2.
6 Wandana Sonalkar's Introduction to Pawar and Moon, *We Also Made History: Women in the Ambedkarite Movement*, translated and introduced by Wandana Sonalkar, New Delhi: Zubaan Academic, 2014, pp. 16–17. The ban was revoked due to protests by numerous women's organisations in Mumbai. The Supreme Court in 2019 has permitted dance bars to remain open, despite numerous challenges forwarded by the state of Maharasthra.
7 We do not pretend to exhaust all the various positions on the difficult bar dancing issue, and indeed only caricature the two main perspectives discussed. Our point is to mark the largely divergent positions arising in such debates between Dalit and Indian feminists. Sonia Faleiro (*Beautiful Thing: Inside the Secret World of Bombay's Dance Bars*, Black Cat, 2012) and Meena Gopal ('Caste, Sexuality and Labour: The Troubled Connection', *Current Sociology*, Vol 60 No 2, pp. 222–38) have written more extensively and precisely on these issues; the latter from a Dalit feminist perspective.
8 Nivedita Menon, *Seeing Like a Feminist*, New Delhi: Penguin India and Zubaan Books, 2012, p. 182.
9 Ibid., p. 180.
10 Ibid., pp. 180–82.
11 Ibid.
12 There is of course much more at stake in this complicated and long-standing debate between choice and dignity. There are questions of systemic exploitation, which makes a mockery of the liberal notion of choice, and the historical caste-based mandatory sex-work of Dalit women (devdasi, etc.). Thus, as Kanchana Mahadevan has pointed out, also at issue are recognition and stigma, not even getting into the wider socio-economic aspect of the commodification of the body and sex. Martha Nussbaum's, *Sex and Social Justice*, New York: Oxford University Press, 2000, and the ensuing debate between Nussbaum and Catherine MacKinnon are instructive in revealing the many issues at stake.
13 Sharmila Rege, *Against the Madness of Manu: B. R. Ambedkar's Writings on Brahmanical Patriarchy*, New Delhi: Navayana, 2013, p. 147. For details, see Janaki Nair, 'From Devadasi Reform Act to SITA: Reforming Sex Work in Mysore State, 1892–1937', *National Law School Journal*, Vol. 1, 1993, pp. 82–94.
14 Rege, *Against the Madness of Manu: B. R. Ambedkar's Writings on Brahmanical Patriarchy*, pp. 20–21.
15 B.R. Ambedkar, *Babasaheb Ambedkar Writings and Speeches*, edited by Vasant Moon, New Delhi: Dr. Ambedkar Foundation, Govt. of India, January 2014, first published in 2003, Vol. 17, Part 3, pp. 150–51.
16 Ibid., p. 150.
17 Ibid., p. 151. Emphasis added by Rege in *B. R. Ambedkar's Writings on Brahmanical Patriarchy*, p. 146.
18 Within this context, Ambedkar is also referring to traditional practices of *Devadasis*, *Muralis*, and *Jogtinis*, according to which young women from untouchable communities were sent into religious consecration to stay in temples, abandoning their families and houses; they were required to be sexually exploited by the priests of those temples. This is also known as 'religious prostitution' because religion becomes the original cause for many untouchable women's entry into prostitution.

19 Ibid., p. 146. In support of her argument, Rege mentions poet Namdeo Dhasal's works, who has competently described the life of Kamatipura's women.
20 Sharmila Rege, 'The Hegemonic Appropriation of Sexuality: The Case of the Lavani Performers of Maharashtra', *Contributions to Indian Sociology*, Vol. 29 No. 1–2, cited in Rege, 'Dalit Women Talk Differently', p. WS-44.
21 Wandana Sonalkar's Introduction to U. Pawar and M. Moon, *We Also Made History: Women in the Ambedkarite Movement*, translated and introduced by Wandana Sonalkar, New Delhi: Zubaan Academic, 2014, p. 18. Again, see the caveat in Note 12.
22 Chapters 1 and 15 offer detailed discussion on this theme.
23 Nivedita Menon, 'Is Feminism About "Women"? A Critical View on Intersectionality from India', *Economic and Political Weekly*, Vol. L No. 17, April 25, 2015, p. 37.
24 Mary E. John, 'Intersectionality: Rejection or Critical Dialogue', *Economic and Political Weekly*, Vol. L No. 33, August 15, 2015, p. 6.
25 Ibid., p. 2.
26 Meena Gopal, 'Struggles around Gender: Some Clarifications', *Economic and Political Weekly*, Vol. L No. 33, August 15, 2015, p. 77.
27 Menon, 'Is Feminism About "Women"?', p. 38.
28 Gopal, 'Struggles Around Gender', p. 77.
29 John, 'Intersectionality', p. 4.
30 Menon, 'Is Feminism About "Women"?', p. 38.
31 John, 'Intersectionality', p. 1.
32 Ibid., p. 5.
33 Menon, 'Is Feminism About "Women"?', p. 40.
34 Ibid., p. 39.
35 John, 'Intersectionality', p. 6.
36 Gopal, 'Struggles Around Gender', p. 77.
37 Accordingly, this Reader will treat of the historical perspective in Part II (in terms of the predecessors of Dalit Feminist Theory), and of the practical aspect in Part III (in terms of Dalit women's lived experience).
38 Menon, 'Is Feminism About "Women"?', p. 42.
39 John, 'Intersectionality', p. 1.
40 Menon, 'Is Feminism About "Women"?', p. 40.
41 Gopal, 'Struggles Around Gender', p. 78.
42 Ibid., p. 78.
43 Ibid.
44 Chapters 7, 13 and 14 offer elaborate analysis on this theme.
45 B. R. Ambedkar, *Babasaheb Ambedkar's Writings and Speeches*, Vol. 17, Part 3, pp. 150–51.
46 Uma Chakravarti, *Gendering Caste: Through a Feminist Lens*, Kolkata: Stree, 2013, p. 141.
47 Ibid., pp. 142–43.
48 Uma Chakravarti, 'Conceptualising Brahmanical Patriarchy in Early India: Gender, Caste, Class and State', *Economic and Political Weekly*, April 3, pp. 579–85.
49 'Honour killing' is a term used for murders when people believe that they are protecting their 'honour' by killing.
50 'The understanding of social stratification cannot be limited to ranked gradations whether they be of power or wealth, status, purity, pollution, or colour . . . because such ranks tell us only about the order and very little regarding the potentialities for social mobility and changes within and of that order' (Dipankar Gupta, 2000: 20).
51 B. R. Ambedkar, *Babasaheb Ambedkar's Writings and Speeches*, Vol. 1, p. 14.
52 As Wandana Sonalkar presents it in her translation and introduction to Urmila Pawar and Minakshi Moon, *We Also Made History: Women in the Ambedkarite Movement*, pp. 13–14.
53 Sharmila Rege, J. Devika, Kalpana Kannabiran, Mary E. John, Padmini Swaminathan and Samita Sen, 'Intersections of Gender and Caste', *Economical and Political Weekly*, Vol. 48, No. 18, May 4, 2013, p. 36.
54 Zia Mody, *10 Judgements that changed India*, Delhi: Penguin, 2013, p. 190.

55 'Intersectionality: A Tool for Gender and Economic Justice', *Women's Rights and Economic Change* No. 9, August 2004, p. 3.
56 Rege, et al, 'Intersections of Gender and Caste', pp. 35–36.
57 Chapters 4, 5, 6, and 12 elaborate diversely on this theme.
58 Kimberlé Crenshaw, 'Demarginalizing the Intersection of Race and Sex: A Black Feminist Critique of Antidiscrimination Doctrine, Feminist Theory and Antiracist Politics', *University of Chicago Legal Forum*, Vol. 1989 No. I, Article 8, pp. 140–67.
59 Patricia Hill Collins, 'The Social Construction of Black Feminist Thought', *Signs: Journal of Women in Culture and Society*, Vol. 14 No. 4, Common Grounds and Crossroads: Race, Ethnicity, and Class in Women's Lives, Summer 1989, University of Chicago Press, pp. 745–73.
60 See Julie Stephens, 'Feminist Fictions: A Critique of the Category "Non-Western Woman" in Feminist Writings on India', in Ranjit Guha (ed.), *Subaltern Studies VI: Writings on South Asian History and Society*, New Delhi: Oxford University Press, February 1, 1994, pp. 92–125.
    Compare, Menon, 'Is Feminism About "Women"?', pp. 37–44.
61 Rege, 'Dalit Women Talk Differently', pp. WS39–WS46.
62 Smita M. Patil, 'Revitalising Dalit Feminism: Towards Reflexive Anti-Caste Agency of Mang and Mahar Women in Maharashtra', *Review of Women's Studies, Economic and Political Weekly*, Vol. XLVIII No. 18, May 4, 2013, p. 43.
63 Rege, *Against the Madness of Manu: B. R. Ambedkar' Writings on Brahmanical Patriarchy*, p. 20.
64 Sharmila Rege, "Real Feminism' and Dalit Women: Scripts of Denial and Accusation', *Economic and Political Weekly*, Vol. 35, No. 6, February 5–11, 2000, pp. 492–495.
65 B.R. Ambedkar, *Babasaheb Ambedkar's Writings and Speeches*, Vol. 1, p. 7.
66 Ibid., p. 9.
67 *Sati pratha* is a ritual prescribed by Brahmins according to which a widow has to immolate herself at the funeral pyre of her husband.
68 Enforced widowhood describes the practice according to which a widowed woman has to alienate herself from all kinds of colours, festivals, delicious food, wedding ceremonies, deity worship functions, etc. and she is never allowed to marry any other man.
69 B.R. Ambedkar, *Babasaheb Ambedkar's Writings and Speeches*, Vol. 1, p. 14.
70 Sharmila Rege, 'Introduction' of Ambedkar, B. R. *Against the Madness of Manu: B. R. Ambedkar's Writings on Brahmanical Patriarchy*, Selected and Introduced by Sharmila Rege, New Delhi: Navayana, 2013, p. 23.
71 Ibid., p. 24.
72 Shailaja Paik, 'Forging a New Dalit Womanhood in Colonial India: Discourse on Modernity, Rights, Education, and Emancipation', *Journal of Women's History*, Vol. 28 No. 4, Winter 2016, pp. 14–40, Johns Hopkins University Press, p. 33.
73 Ibid., p. 35.
74 Saidian refers to Edward Said (1935–2003), Palestinian American literary theorist and public intellectual who helped found the field of postcolonial theory.
75 Rege, 'Dalit Women Talk Differently', p. WS-39.
76 Ibid., p. WS-43.
77 Gopal Guru, 'Dalit Women Talk Differently', *Economic and Political Weekly*, Vol. 30 No. 41/42, 1995, p. 2548.
78 Susie Tharu, 'Problems for a Contemporary Theory of Gender', in Shahid Amin and Dipesh Chakrabarty (eds.), *Subaltern Studies IX: Writings on South Asian History and Society*, New Delhi: Oxford University Press, p. 247.
79 Guru, 'Dalit Women Talk Differently', p. 2549.
80 V. Geetha, *Patriarchy*, Kolkata: Stree, 2009, p. 108.
81 Uma Chakravarti, 'Graded Patriarchies', in *Gendering Caste: Through a Feminist Lens*, Kolkata: Stree, 2013, first published in 2003, p. 86.
82 Ibid., p. 88.

83 Ibid.
84 Uma Chakravarti, 'Graded Patriarchies', p. 87, emphasis added.
85 Cf. Anupama Rao, who would seem to posit the need for a Maratha patriarchy, in supplement to Brahmanical and Dalit patriarchy, in her 'A Study of Sirasgaon', in Rajeswari Sunder Rajan (ed.), *Signposts: Gender Issues in Post-Independence India*, New Delhi: Kali for Women, 1999, pp. 209–10.
86 Rege, *Against the Madness of Manu: B. R. Ambedkar's writings on Brahmanical Patriarchy*, p. 22.
87 Uma Chakravarti, 'In Her Own Write: Writing from a Dalit Feminist Standpoint', *India International Centre Quarterly*, Vol. 39 No. 3/4, Winter 2012–Spring 2013, p. 137.
88 Susie Tharu and Tejaswini Niranjana, 'Problems for a Contemporary Theory of Gender', pp. 232–60.
89 Chakravarti, 'In Her Own Write', p. 143.
90 Gopal Guru, 'How Egalitarian Are Social Sciences in India', *Economic and Political Weekly*, Vol. 37 No. 50, December 14–20, 2002, p. 5009.
91 Stephens, 'Feminist Fictions', pp. 111, 115.
92 Guru, 'Dalit Women Talk Differently', p. 2549.
93 Kanchana Mahadevan, 'Experience and Representation: Beyond Hierarchy', *Labrys, etudes feminists/ estudos feministas* No. 27, January–June 2015, pp. 1–20. Retrieved from http: www.labrys.net.br, pp. 11–12, citing Simone de Beauvoir 2004, 270.
94 Ibid., p. 12.
95 Ibid., p. 13.
96 Ibid.

PART I
Indian feminism vs Dalit feminism

As explained in the Editors' Introduction, the present Reader attempts to correct defects within Indian feminism by introducing the category *Dalit* into the heart and centre of Indian feminist thought. Mainstream feminists fail to reflect closely upon a key aspect of the Indian patriarchal system, due to their refusal to acknowledge the centrality of the caste-based social order peculiar to India. Thus, they lose the important insight that caste-based feminist inquiry is the only way to comprehensively resolve gender-based injustices, and to facilitate us (*all* of us) in theorising Indian feminist discourse.

Part I presents three different challenges to theorising feminism in India along the lines indicated earlier. These challenges are posed not by just anyone but by foremost feminist theorists of India. Take for example Nivedita Menon, a leading Marxist feminist, who identifies capitalism as the most salient perpetuator of patriarchy in the South Asian context, and expresses strong resistance to intersectionality, which she dismisses as a tool for governmentalising and depoliticising gender (Chapter 1). Although they fully support efforts toward cultivating a Dalit feminist theory, a serious intellectual obstacle is nevertheless posed by Susie Tharu and Tejaswini Niranjana. The authors forward a major hurdle for theorising gender as such, arguing that the primary subject of feminist inquiry, i.e., *woman*, is not a homogeneous category, due to its substantive linkage with caste, class and community factors (Chapter 2). As Tharu and Niranjana provide no clues for how this challenge may be faced (though Tharu will later take some steps in Chapter 14), we thus encounter here a pessimistic approach towards theorising Indian feminism that Dalit feminists must themselves set out a course to overcome. Third, from an internal critical standpoint Gopal Guru has introduced a new notion 'Dalit patriarchy', and Uma Chakravarti and V. Geetha have furthered such deeply irresponsible concepts into mainstream feminist discourse; that is, 'graded patriarchies', and especially, 'Dalit patriarchy' (Chapter 3). These misleading concepts have been appealed to without offering empirical evidence, or logical coherence, or even theoretical necessity. Misdirection of just this sort serves to give credence to the increasingly posited ascription of mainstream Indian feminism as a savarna feminism. That is, as a sort of feminism that privileges dominant caste Indian women, both in theory and in practice.

The selection of texts in Part I reveals something further about mainstream Indian feminism. That is, that again seemingly true to its characterisation as savarna feminism, mainstream Indian feminism tends completely to ignore the Dalit feminist insights forwarded over the last century by pioneers like Dr B.R. Ambedkar, Jyotiba Phule and Pandita Ramabai, and carried forward by their successors (Rege, Pawar, Moon, Paik and others). Such insights have been a source of sensitising and reforming the Indian social system by taking up the issues of *all* Indian women. Unfortunately, Indian feminism has stopped its ears to this long and productive history of Dalit feminism, and has instead relegated Dalit feminist interventions to the status of mere informants, or dismisses it as being constituted simply by works of poetry and short stories, or 'others it' by characterising it always as the *et cetera*, in phrases like 'feminist theory *and other* political initiatives'.

Beyond ignoring or othering its predecessors (the area of focus for Part II of the Reader), mainstream Indian feminism has also exhibited its savarna privilege by choosing to turn away from the well-documented experience of Dalit women's lives, which has long revealed unique forms of vulnerability to violence due to intersectional caste, gender and class disadvantage. As Part III will explore in greater detail, Dalit women's representation as objects of lust and servitude, as symbols of impurity and evil, and other peculiar patriarchal and misogynistic modalities of representation of Dalit women, have not been brought into the purview of mainstream feminist discourse, or has been dumped onto the shoulders of Dalit feminists as their own burden and responsibility. The misfortunes of Dalit women's everyday experiences have never been challenged by caste-privileged 'Indian' feminists because it is not *their* problem.

For these reasons, the mainstream approach to Indian feminism tends to pose a hindrance for the flourishing of gender justice for *all* Indian women. Irony of ironies, Indian feminists seem to be as brahmanical as the patriarchal system they seek to dismantle.

1
A CRITICAL VIEW ON INTERSECTIONALITY[1]

Nivedita Menon

In this second decade of the twenty-first century, we all know that feminism is not in fact about 'women' but about recognising how modern discourses of *gender* produce human beings as exclusively 'men' *or* 'women'. In other words, feminism requires us to recognise that 'women' is neither a stable nor a homogeneous category. But nor are caste, race or class stable or homogeneous categories.

Does intersectionality as a universal framework help us to capture this complexity? I argue that it does not. In this chapter, I will address this question through the intricacies of the terrain that feminist politics must negotiate, using the Indian experience to set up conversations with feminist debates and experiences globally.

Theory must be *located* – we must be alert to the spatial and temporal coordinates that suffuse all theorising. When we in the non-West theorise on the basis of our experiences, we rarely assume that these are generalisable everywhere, unlike theory arising in the West. But we do believe that comparisons and engagements with other feminisms are not only possible, but unavoidable. I assume and address therefore, the lively global feminist voices that surround us.

Two sets of questions

The first set of questions we come up against when engaging with the idea of intersectionality circulate around the imperialism of categories, and the manner in which concepts developed in the global North are assumed to have universal validity. Even when *an understanding of politics* in the global South predates *a name for a similar understanding* developed in the Western academy, it is the earlier conception that will be named after the later. For instance, in a paper on Ram Mahohar Lohia, a Socialist activist and thinker of mid-twentieth-century India, who tried to link caste, class, gender and the politics of language (English versus Hindi) in his life and work, the twenty-first-century writer of the article explicitly uses the framework of intersectionality.[2] The point here is not about anachronism, and whether or not concepts can be made to travel across time, because I believe this is possible. Rather, I am suggesting that the tendency when studying the 'non-West' is to test the applicability of theory developed through 'western' experience, rather than entering into the unfamiliar conceptual field opened up by thinkers and activists in the former.

The assumption is that the concepts emerging from Western (Euro–American) social philosophy necessarily contain within them the possibility of universalisation – the reverse is never assumed. Can, for instance, Julius Nyerere's concept of Ujamaa or the trope of Draupadi as the ambiguous figure of assertive femininity ever be considered relevant to analyse Euro-American experience? But Antigone can be made to speak about women and war everywhere.

The second set of questions has to do with the power of international funding to promote certain concepts. The concept of intersectionality has by now travelled very widely globally, being attached to funding, United Nations (UN) funding in particular. Nira Yuval-Davis tracks the introduction of the concept in the UN to the preparatory session to the World Conference against Racism (WCAR) in September 2001, at which Kimberlé Crenshaw, the originator of the concept, was invited to speak.[3] As a result, in India too, non-governmental organisation (NGO) documents and activists have started to use it quite unproblematically. What are the implications of this kind of 'facilitated travel' of concepts, and do funding agendas depoliticise initially radical concepts?

It has been argued even for the country of its birth that the spread and dominance of the intersectionality framework, which has made intersectionality a buzzword, has obscured the fact that different feminist perspectives, from feminists-of-colour to poststructuralist, have long held the notion, as Jennifer C. Nash puts it, that identity is formed by 'interlocking and mutually reinforcing vectors of race, gender, class, and sexuality', that 'woman' itself is 'contested and fractured terrain', and that the experience of 'woman' is always 'constituted by subjects with vastly different interests'. In this sense, Nash argues, 'intersectionality has provided a name to a pre-existing theoretical and political commitment'.[4]

This is even more the case in India, but here it is not simply a question of giving a name to a pre-existing perspective.

'Woman' in Indian feminism

The first set of questions I outlined earlier, around the 'imperialism of categories', leads us to think about how 'Woman' has come to be constituted and reconstituted in feminist politics in India. Generally, the term intersectionality when used in India expresses one of two familiar feminist ideas – 'double and triple burdens', or that 'Woman' must be complicated by caste, religion, class. When used in this sense, the term has no particular purchase, and adds nothing new to our understanding. This is because the politics of engaging with multiple identities, their contradictions and interrelations, goes back to the early twentieth century and the legacy of anti-imperialist struggles in the global South.

Whether Mahatma Gandhi and Bhimrao Ambedkar in India or African socialists like Nyerere and Kwame Nkrumah, most nationalist leaders constructed national identities, not through the idea of individual citizenship but through that of communities – caste, religious, ethnic groups. Their language of politics remained non-individualistic even as the idea of the individual entered these societies via colonial modernity. So there remained always a tension in postcolonial democracies between the individual and the community defined in different ways, as the bearer of rights. This tension is evident in the Indian Constitution, for instance, where the Fundamental Rights protect the rights of both the individual and of the religious community. Sometimes this leads to contradiction between the two – as when equal rights for women as individuals come into conflict with religious personal laws, all of which discriminate against women. Similarly, the demand for reservations in representative institutions on the basis of group identity – women, castes or religious communities – fundamentally challenges the individualist conception of political representation at the core of liberal democracy. We will return to these two issues later.

Women's movements in the global South thus never started with the idea of some subtract Woman that they later needed to complicate with more and more layers. This identity of Woman was from the start located within Nation and within communities of different sorts.

The term intersectionality, coined by legal scholar Kimberlé Crenshaw, emerged, in the words of Jennifer C. Nash:[5]

> In the late 1980s and early 1990s from critical race studies, a scholarly movement born in the legal academy committed to problematising law's purported colour-blindness, neutrality, and objectivity. From its inception, intersectionality has had a long-standing interest in one particular intersection: the intersection of race and gender. To that end, intersectionality rejects the 'single-axis framework' often embraced by both feminist and anti-racist scholars.

Crenshaw drew attention, instead, to 'the various ways in which race and gender interact to shape the multiple dimensions of Black women's experiences'.[6]

My argument is that the 'single axis framework' was never predominant or unchallenged in our parts of the world. New identities continually arose then, and do now, from different contexts, forcing recognition on our part that all political solidarities are conjunctural and historically contingent.

I refer here to feminist politics on the ground and to feminist scholarship. We will address later in the chapter the place and understanding of the category of 'women' in funded activism of NGOs and in the governmentalising practices of the state.

The instability of 'woman'[7]

The presumed subject of feminist politics has been destabilised in India most notably by the politics of *caste, religious community identity* and *sexuality*. The politics of caste and religious community identity insistently pose a question mark over the assumed commonality of female experience, thus challenging the identity of 'woman', the supposed subject of feminist politics; while the politics of sexuality throws into disarray the certainty of recognisably gender-coded bodies, the male-female bipolarity, the naturalising of heterosexual desire and its institutionalisation in marriage.

The growing visibility and militancy of caste politics over the 1990s has increasingly forced the recognition that Woman is not simply an already existing subject which the women's movement can mobilise for its politics. This is most clearly revealed by the debate that has been underway since the late 1990s around reservations for women in Parliament. The opposition to the proposed legislation cannot simply be categorised as patriarchal, it comes from a particular caste location that includes women, which expresses the legitimate apprehension that a blanket reservation of 33% for women (the current proposal being debated), would simply replace 'lower'-caste men with 'upper'-caste women. The democratic upsurges of the 1980s transformed Parliament from a largely upper class and upper caste, English-educated body to one that more closely resembles the mass of the population of India in terms of class, caste and educational background. Today an immediate conversion of one-third of the existing seats into ones reserved for women is likely to bring into the fray largely those women who already have the cultural and political capital to contest elections, and in an extremely unequal society like India, these are bound to be elite women.

It may be noted that the opposition to the legislation in India is not that the category of citizen is universal and should remain 'unmarked' by any other identity, that its universalism should not be fractured by introducing gender identity. Rather, the opposition to it is in the form of insisting that *more* identities and differences (caste/community) should be inserted into that of gender – the 'quotas within quotas' position. Here a comparison to a similar move in France is instructive.

The parity movement in France, which emerged in the 1990s, was a demand for complete equality, that is, numerically equal representation for women and men in decision-making bodies, especially elected assemblies. However, the debates over the issue played out very differently in France than in India. In France the recognition of gender in citizenship was seen as antithetical to democracy, to universal citizenship in which no difference should be recognised; while those who defended parity too, claimed the universal position – that citizenship would be more truly universal only when gender was recognised. Thus, all arguments in France on the issue of parity – both feminist pro- and anti-parity positions as well as anti-feminist denunciations of parity – were largely in terms of different kinds of reassertion of the universal. In India as we have seen, on the contrary, the critique was that the universal of 'woman' was not fractured *enough*.

It is clear that the distinctive historical trajectories of the two democracies have created different sets of concerns about citizenship and representation – France having undergone a 'classic' bourgeois democratic revolution in the eighteenth century, and India a postcolonial democracy that came into being 200 years later, where the ideal of the abstract and individual citizen as the basis for democracy was never unambiguously enshrined as it was in the European context. Thus, feminist politics must always be sensitive to the significance of different locations, different in terms of both time period and geographical location.[8]

The challenges to feminist politics from caste politics erupt also in other contexts. A revealing moment of tension was manifested at the National Conference of Autonomous Women's Groups in Kolkata (2006), between the newly politicised bar dancers of Mumbai and Dalit feminist groups, who found it impossible to support bar dancing as a profession. Dalit feminists argued that such forms of 'entertainment' are not only patriarchal, but also casteist, since many Dalit women come from castes that are traditionally forced into such professions. Thus, the discomfort of Dalit feminists with sex-work and professions seen to be related to prostitution (such as dancing for male audiences in bars) cannot be seen only in terms of conventional morality. There are sharply political and equally feminist positions ranged on both sides, and the opposition between them is not easily amenable to an elite/subaltern division since often both identities, as in this case (Dalit/bar dancer), are equally subaltern, and there are Dalit women on both sides of the debate.

At another level, there is a general suspicion of mainstream Indian feminism among Dalit women, who see it as dominated by privileged dominant caste, upper class, urban feminists and their issues. This too, is a site that is simultaneously acrimonious and productive.

Uniform Civil Code

The politics of religious community identity is best exemplified by the debate over the Uniform Civil Code (UCC).

The debate over the UCC arises from the tension in the Fundamental Rights assured by the Constitution that pits rights of women as individual citizens against rights of communities that have the right to their personal laws. Since these personal laws cover matters of marriage, inheritance and guardianship of children, and since all personal laws discriminate against women, the women's movement had made the demand for a UCC as long ago as 1937, long before independence. However, the UCC has rarely surfaced in public discourse as a feminist issue. It has tended invariably to be set up in terms of National Integrity versus Cultural Rights of Community. In other words, the argument for a UCC is made in the name of protecting the integrity of the nation, which is seen to be under threat from plurality of legal systems and from the very existence of difference from the Hindu/Indian norm; while the UCC is resisted on the grounds of cultural rights of communities. Thus a party that stands unambiguously for a UCC is the Hindu right-wing Bharatiya Janata Party (BJP), for underlying its national integrity argument is the claim that while Hindus have willingly accepted reform, the 'other' (minority) communities continue to cling to diverse and retrogressive laws, refusing to merge into the national mainstream.

Thus, there always circulates in the public domain some version of the argument that to be truly secular, India needs a UCC, while from a feminist point of view, the idea of a UCC is less about 'secularism' – the relationship between religious communities and the state – and more about gender-injustice – that is, the constitutionally enshrined inequality between men and women.

The women's movement has moved from a strong demand for a UCC, expressed since the 1930s, to a suspicion of uniformity by the 1990s, taking a hint from the support for a UCC from the Hindu right. This disavowal of uniformity by the women's movement in the 1990s is significant in that it marks the recognition of the need to rethink the nation and religious communities as homogeneous entities. Each religious community is a heterogeneous one, and 'Hindu', 'Muslim' and 'Christian' practices differ widely from region to region of India, from sect to sect. Some of these practices are better for women than others, and intra-community drives towards homogenising are as problematic as when such moves are inter-community.

For the women's movement then, the focus now is on gender-just laws. When reform is initiated 'top-down' by the state in the overall atmosphere of anti-minority politics that India sees today, the fear of minority communities is that reform of personal laws is only a pretext for eroding their identity. This is why ongoing reform initiatives from inside the communities themselves have a better chance of succeeding.

Queer politics

Queer politics has produced a public discourse that insists on the potential fluidity of sexual identifications and the linking of sexuality to other forms of identities, as a politically productive stance. In this context, the term 'queer' is increasingly gaining currency among activists familiar with academic and political work in the Anglophone world, although the term may be taking somewhat different forms and directions in India.

The term queer has from the beginning in India gone beyond sexuality. Queer politics sees itself as complicated at its point of origin by class, caste and community identity, and is self-critical to the extent it is unable to engage with this complication. For example, in an intense and introspective essay, Sumit Baudh, a Dalit gay man, ruminates on living with these two marginal identities. His upwardly mobile parents hid his Dalit identity from him, and gave him a fictitious surname to pass as a caste Hindu. In an intensely caste-defined society such as India, such 'passing' is rare, as one's caste identity is the first thing made evident by any Hindu name. Baudh writes therefore 'Thus, I remained a closet Dalit all through school and college'.[9] In an odd (queer?) reversal then, he begins first by 'coming out as Dalit' (a contradiction in terms under normal circumstances in India) and only later as gay.

Queer politics in India engages with the question of biology critically, treating sexuality as fluid, not a biological or genetic given. (Here I refer to explicitly political stances; at an existential level, hijras and many transpeople invariably speak about 'feeling like/being women/men in the wrong body'.) Also, it does not attempt to produce a new universal, within which all sexual identities will be submerged. Rather, it sees 'queer' as a political and in some ways unstable term, enabling the continuous challenge to heteronormativity, whether through gay/lesbian/transgender, feminist or other identities.

The politics of caste/community identity and sexuality thus prevents the full constitution of Woman as the stable subject of feminist politics. With this challenge, I suggest that they offer us the potential to explore new ways of being feminist and doing feminist politics. How does intersectionality figure in this analysis?

Intersectionality, identity, law

Crenshaw developed the intersectionality framework to address a problem she saw with identity politics, that is, its inability to address internal heterogeneity. Intersectionality claims to do this by recognising gender in race and race in gender, thus breaking up the assumed homogeneity of both 'women' and 'blacks', while acknowledging the importance of asserting group identity.

However, in my rendering of how caste, religious identity and sexuality travel through and refigure 'woman', each of these identities is fundamentally unstable. Each identity emerges or rather, is called into being, in particular contexts in such a way that at that moment it is not simply an intersection of two or more identities but an unstable configuration that is more than the sum of its parts – recall here the figures of the Muslim/Woman in the UCC debate, the Dalit/bar dancer and Dalit/queer that we encountered previously.

It is also important to remember that Crenshaw developed the idea of intersectionality in the context of the law, and its inability to recognise multiple identities. If the intention is to make the law sensitive to these different registers, I have argued earlier that in fact the law is most 'just' when it does *not* recognise multiple identities. The functioning of legal discourse tends to subvert the ethical impulse of subordinate groups and to reassert dominant values. Recognising that categories of identity do not 'naturally' exist, but are constructed by our political practice, we need to surrender the belief that they can be given the meaning and force we desire through the validation of the law.[10]

At the same time, the only permissible identities in modern democracies are those put in place by the law. We are inextricably implicated in state and legal procedures – every aspect of my identity is legally established – as woman, as Hindu, as upper caste. But precisely for this reason, because the regulating and defining force of the law is directed towards the creating and naturalising of specific, governable identities, it is a failed project to turn to it to reflect our own complex ethical positions.

For instance in 2002, two high court judgements set aside the election of two hijras from posts reserved for women. They were criticised by queer and democratic rights groups on the grounds that they implied that one cannot choose one's sex and that one should remain within the sex into which one is born.

However, the questions that arise here are more complicated. The judgements were not reflecting on identity itself, but on the even more fraught question of the *political representation of identities*. What is at stake here is the claim to represent a particular identity. Hijras continue to hold elected posts in general (unreserved) seats, and these judgements did not affect them. The identity of hijras is not in question here. Nor is the fact that hijras today are among the most marginalised of communities in India. The question is – *can hijras represent women in constituencies reserved for women?*

The point at issue, therefore, is not whether one can *biologically* become a woman at any point in one's life, but whether *experiences* of 'women' of different 'classes' and 'castes' can somehow be written into parliamentary discourses. Thus, if we are to think of ways in which the experiences of hijras, among other identities, are to be similarly written in, then we must think of more radical alternatives than to divide representation simply between 'men' and 'others'. The experience of oppression that 'hijras' have is not reducible to the experience of 'women'.

A more promising strategy is the demand by hijras to be recognised as a third gender. The recognition of several genders and of multiple and shifting ways of being constituted as political entities may be able to help generate new ways of thinking about representative institutions in a democracy. But the intersectionality framework, especially within the governmentalising practices of the law, cannot engage with the fact that there are multiple foci around which identities form and dissolve.

There have been earlier attempts, unrelated to the intersectionality framework, to confront the tendency of the law to fix meaning. In the Indian context, Marc Galanter's is one of the most notable such endeavours, in which he tries to build into the law a conception of identity, not as a fixed, natural or inherent quality, but as something constituted by interaction and negotiation with other components of society. It is Galanter's view that this understanding of identity would require courts to adopt an 'empirical' as opposed to a 'formal' approach. The formal approach sees individuals as members of one group only, and therefore, as having only the rights to which that group is entitled. Thus, for example, one who attains caste status loses tribal affiliation as far as the law is concerned. The empirical approach on the other hand, does not attempt to resolve the blurring and overlap between categories and accepts multiple affiliations. It would address itself to the particular legislation involved and tries to determine which affiliation is acceptable in the particular context.[11]

What one notes is that all such projects, Galanter's as well as the intersectionality framework included, apply the understanding of identity as relative and shifting *only* to 'people', and *not* to 'courts' or 'government'. The latter are assumed to be outside grids of affiliations, to have an external and superior understanding of affiliations 'people' have, and to be capable of choosing the 'correct' perspective, empirical or formal. Such attempts to contest law's rigid codifying procedures are based on the erroneous assumption that the state and law constitute a unified and self-transparent agency that will interpret, correctly or incorrectly, the multiplicity of identities around it.

Even within the global North, there has been considerable queer and feminist rethinking on the value of 'intersectionality' in the law. Emily Grabham, for instance, points out that 'Within the disciplinary system of law, focusing on the 'intersections', between categories merely leads to the production of 'more' categories thereby supporting the law's propensity to classify'.[12] Grabham argues that 'not only does intersectionality analysis in law fail to challenge categories . . . it actually deepens and extends the law's impetus towards the regulatory production of identities'.[13]

Governmentalising gender[14]

The second set of questions about the governmentalising of intersectionality, and its attachment to funding-driven agendas and policy for the global South, is a feature parallel to the governmentalising of the term 'gender' itself. Many feminists and women's movement activists in India have been struck by the general acceptability of the word 'gender' in the corridors of state power since the 1990s. The term has been domesticated and has become a synonym for 'women' – that is, women as they already are in patriarchal society. While in feminist vocabulary the term 'gender' has deeply destabilising potential, relocated within the vocabulary of 'governance', it acquires quite another meaning. The concept of 'governance' or 'good government' has been made popular by the World Bank since 1992. Major donors and international financial institutions are increasingly basing their aid and loans on the condition that governments carry out reforms that ensure 'good governance'.

A well-known dissection of the concept is that of John Harriss, who demonstrates that 'governance' is a powerful tool for the refashioning of the agenda of corporate globalisation, in the face of the recognition that structural adjustment will not succeed without 'a human face'.[15] Closely tied to governance are the terms 'gender sensitivity' and 'engendering development', which are about using 'women' to regulate development which in essence is corporate globalisation.

The development process undertaken by the Indian state is ecologically unsustainable, further marginalises already deprived communities, and since the 1990s, involves the state acquiring agricultural lands from peasants cheaply and invariably by force, to be handed over to private corporations to develop special economic zones (SEZ). Mainstreaming gender or adding a 'gender component' to development programmes planned within this agenda essentially means using women's specific skills and experience produced by their location within patriarchal society (that is, precisely by the sexual division of labour), to make development programmes successful. Making gender a component of development depoliticises feminist critique, both of patriarchy as well as of development and of corporate globalisation and essentially 'empowers' women to act as agents within the overall development agenda of the state.

Women are leading the massive and widespread struggles in India against ecologically unsustainable and unjust capitalist development, against nuclear energy and land acquisition for corporations. It is these enormous and militant waves of struggle that the state seeks to tame though 'engendering development'. In international human rights discourses, intersectionality helps perform the function of governmentalising and depoliticising gender, by assuming a pre-existing woman bearing multiple identities. According to Yuval-Davis, the very purpose of the introduction of intersectional analysis to human rights discourse is to contribute to 'gender mainstreaming', so that 'the full diversity of women's experiences' can be considered in order 'to enhance women's empowerment'.[16]

The critique I offer here of governmentality must be differentiated from Nancy Fraser's anxiety that feminism has become the 'handmaiden to capitalism' because neo-liberalism uses gender to undermine class.[17] Fraser's argument reveals ignorance of the heterogeneity of feminist politics and scholarship in what we may call 'the rest of the world' – which this chapter gestures towards – through its problematic assumption that one kind of UN-driven privileged feminism is the only kind there is. But more importantly, it is naïve in its assumption that 'feminist' or 'left' categories are in themselves, pure and if they are co-opted by power or governmentalised, their purity itself is in question. After all, capital in the global North used labour rights arguments to limit – through the 'social clause' – the trade advantage for India and China arising from their lax labour standards.[18] (This was before the North moved its labour-intensive components to the South to take advantage of that same 'cheap labour'.) Did support for the social clause make labour rights advocates in the South 'handmaidens' of Northern capital?

We need to recognise that destabilising trends have as much potential to be drawn into governmentalising modes as stabilising ones have to produce sites of instability and resistance.

Thus, the politics of sexuality, arising as it does from the imperatives of HIV/AIDS control and the funding generated by it, can be extremely state-centric and funding imperatives can tame radicalism. Similarly the politics of caste can get narrowly restricted to the politics of 'reservations', leading to internal competitiveness among deprived groups for a larger share in the small part reserved for them. The sharp challenge that Dalit and non-upper-caste feminist perspectives pose to the upper-caste orientation of Indian feminism can get mired in a fruitless debate on 'primary contradiction' – is caste the primary contradiction or is gender? – thus solidifying the boundaries of both rather than productively opening them up. The challenge of course, for both feminist and Dalit politics, is to recognise that in different contexts the salience of gender and caste will vary, requiring both to proceed tentatively, each prepared to be destabilised by the other.

Conversely, government programmes can produce new solidarities among women drawn into them, and radicalise women hitherto unexposed to public activity despite the fact that this is not the goal of such programmes. For instance, one of the most militant and proud faces of the Indian women's movement against sexual violence is that of Bhanwari Devi, who was raped by upper-caste men of her village to punish her for trying to implement the law against child marriage in her village, as an employee of a government programme.

Foucault explains these interrelated moves of power and resistance in a famous interview, using the example of the revolt of the sexual body against the 'encroachment' of power on the body. As power produces appropriate bodies – the bodies of children, soldiers, healthy bodies, clearly gendered bodies and so on – in counter-response: 'emerge . . . claims and affirmations, those of one's own body against power, of health against the economic system, of pleasure against moral norms'.

But in return power responds precisely to this revolt, for instance, economically and ideologically by exploiting eroticisation, by selling everything from suntan products to pornographic films. Power begins now to: 'control by stimulation. "Get undressed – but be slim, good-looking, tanned!" For each move by one adversary, there is an answering one by another . . . . One has to recognise the indefiniteness of the struggle'.[19] Fraser's 'handmaiden to capitalism' argument fails to recognise the complex nature of the political field that we do in fact inhabit.

Reconsidering intersectionality

How useful is intersectionality if we read feminist politics in the way this chapter does?

Is the intersectionality framework universally fruitful now, regardless of when and where it arose?

We have seen how it functions very well within governmentalising frames, but is this concept useful to frame a feminist politics of solidarity across identities?

Let me highlight two issues that for me are problematic. One arises from a certain kind of interpretation of Crenshaw's famous example of the traffic intersection. Based on a presentation by Crenshaw at the WCAR in 2001, a report of a UN meeting interpreted intersectionality in this way:[20]

> Intersectionality is what occurs when a woman from a minority group . . . tries to navigate the main crossing in the city. . . . The main highway is 'racism road'. One cross street can be Colonialism, then Patriarchy Street. . . . She has to deal not only with one form of oppression but with all forms, those named as road signs, which link together to make a double, a triple, multiple, a many layered blanket of oppression.

This reading of intersectionality is indeed the prevalent one. In this, the image is of a (marginalised) individual bearing many marginalised identities, one of which is primary ('the main highway is racism road'). One of the problems with this image that has been addressed in intersectionality studies is that intersectionality theory has

> obscured the question of whether all identities are intersectional or whether only multiply marginalised subjects have an intersectional identity. While

some feminist scholars insist that intersectionality refers to all subject positions (which are all fundamentally constituted by the interplay of race, gender, sexuality, class, etc), the overwhelming majority of intersectional scholarship has centred on the particular positions of multiply marginalised subjects. This unresolved theoretical dispute makes it unclear whether intersectionality is a theory of *marginalised subjectivity* or a *generalised theory of identity*.[21]

I see a different problem from the perspective of the global South, where, as we saw, individualism never became the uncontested core of identity. The idea of *intersection* – in a general sense, not related to 'intersectionality' – makes more sense when we think of identities as provisionally forming at the intersection of two or more axes. Not all of the potential identities available in a society to a person or a group may be relevant at all times for them. Rather than a Black woman being both Black and a woman, she may at times be only Black, and at others, only woman. The intersection itself is an empty place.

The subject of feminist politics has to be brought into being by political practice. In other words, there are not pre-existing 'women' who may be Hindu or Muslim, upper caste or Dalit, white or Black – rather, there are 'people' who may respond to different kinds of political challenges as 'Dalit' or 'Muslim', or as 'women'. The success of feminism lies precisely in its capacity to motivate 'people' to affirm themselves *as* feminists in different kinds of contexts.

The key notion central to European modernity was the putting in place of the notion of the individual – that 'I' am this body and that 'my self' stops at the boundaries of my skin. Although this seems an entirely natural identification to the modern mind, it is in fact only about 400 years old and has specific cultural moorings in the experience of the West. In non-Western societies this notion of the individual, separate from all other individuals, as the unit of society, is still not an uncontested one. At every level in non-Western societies then, there remains a sense of self that is produced at the *intersection* of individuated bodies and collectivities of different sorts. Individuation then, that is, the process of recognising oneself as primarily an individual, is as much a process of identity formation as the process of recognising oneself as Black or Dalit or a woman, and is always a process *in the present continuous* in our parts of the world. Identity is not something taken on by pre-existing individuals. All politics then is 'identity politics' – whether based on class or on liberal individualism.

It is against this backdrop that we must ask the question – was even sex/gender a *universally* relevant criterion of social differentiation at all? That is, did all societies at all times and in all places make male/female distinctions that sustained themselves over stable bodies?

This question is raised frontally by Nigerian scholar Oyeronke Oyewumi, who challenges the universality of gender as a social category. She argues that Western anthropologists, even feminists, failed to understand African society in its own terms, because they assumed that gender identities and hierarchies were universal: 'If the investigator assumes gender, then gender categories will be found whether they exist or not'.[22]

Oyewumi argues that the emergence of patriarchy as a form of social organisation in the West is rooted in particular assumptions that emerged with modernity in the West – the gradual privileging of gender difference as the primary difference in society, and locating this difference in certain visual cues. Oyewumi thus makes the radical suggestion that 'gender' as a category did not operate in any significant way in pre-colonial Yoruba and many other African cultures.[23] Even with the sweeping transformations brought about by colonial modernity in these societies, countermemory continues to circulate around bodies and identities even to this day.

What I find revealing in debates on intersectionality, even among its critics, is the total lack of engagement with literature outside the Euro-North American (at most Australian) academy. Even a thoroughgoing analysis such as that of Yuval-Davis cites just one scholar from the global South – misspelling both his names (Ashis Nandy becomes Ashish Nandi) – when entire libraries can be filled with feminist theorising available in English, precisely of multiple identities, from South Asia, Africa and Latin America.[24]

The second problem arises from the key idea in Patricia Hill Collins that the intersectional paradigm views race, class, gender and so on as '*mutually constructing* systems of power. Because these systems permeate all social relations, untangling their effects in any given situation or for any given population remains difficult'.[25]

Hill Collins' idea of 'mutually reinforcing vectors' as remaining within the framework of double and triple burdens borne by already existing 'women' has been criticised for its essentialised notion of identity and for its additive character. For instance, Yuval-Davis, tracking the gradual entry of 'intersectionality' into UN documents, notes the continuous collapse of intersectionality to 'identity' even when more complex arguments are being outlined.[26] She points out that too often intersectionality analysis

> does not attend to the differential positionings of power in which different identity groups can be located in specific historical contexts, let alone the dynamics of power relations within these groups. Nor does it give recognition to the potentially contested nature of the boundaries of these identity groupings and the possibly contested political claims for representation of people located in the same social positioning.[27]

Global perspective

However, it is imperative for us as feminists to make another kind of critique too. I would argue that we need to see these structures not as necessarily mutually reinforcing but as often working against one another and weakening one another. Capitalist globalisation undermines traditional patriarchies and caste hierarchies, and globalisation of capital also leads to globalisation of dissent and struggle. Dalits abandon traditional occupations and enjoy the new anonymous worlds that replace the 'old worlds' the loss of which ecological frameworks mourn. Women get work – exploitative work – in sweat shops, and they become the main earners of their families, challenging internal family hierarchies of age and gender, while many of them also learn to organise against capital itself.

Sometimes some of this comes together in resistance, sometimes different subaltern positions are in conflict with one another, as we have seen throughout this chapter.

Patriarchy, capitalism, caste – none of these are closed orders. Their borders are porous, the social order fragile and every structure is constantly destabilised by another outside of it. Like any other structure of power then, patriarchy too has an 'outside', as has capitalism, and caste and race, which is what makes possible the different kinds of recalcitrance we have seen, that constantly undermine them.

In conclusion

I am far from attempting to produce another universal framework to replace intersectionality, and nor am I arguing that the term has no relevance anywhere. I am suggesting rather, that (1) Feminist solidarities as well as disjunctures in solidarity must be seen as conjunctural, fluid and radically negotiable. No universal framework can capture this conjunctural nature of political engagement; and (2) I suggest that as we saw with the governmentalisation of gender, the easy acceptability of intersectionality for international funding agencies should give us pause. The term intersectionality seems to work not for *feminism*, but for *states and international funding agencies*. As Mrinalini Sinha has pointed out, to 'bring a global perspective to gender' means not seeing the world through a universalising perspective, but 'taking theoretical cognisance of the local and empirical', thus producing a 'dense contextual analysis'. This move would protect us against two tendencies – 'false analogies between different historical formations', and naturalising the present, thus limiting the possibilities of the future. It would also open us to a feminist politics 'whose concepts and strategies are flexible enough to respond to changing conditions'.[28]

Feminism is heterogeneous and internally differentiated across contexts. This recognition makes it impossible to articulate a simple 'feminist' position on any issue, and alerts us to what Walter Mignolo has termed 'diversality' – the recognition of diversity as a universal condition (2000). Analyses that begin with the assumption of a unified and homogeneous category of 'woman' may well be productively opened up to other identities by the intersectionality framework; but analyses that begin with the understanding that identity is provisional and conjunctural, would find, I have argued, that the intersectionality framework freezes notions of pre-existing individual, woman and other identities. Attention to diversality teaches us that universal frameworks generally flow from the North to the South, that the direction of this flow this is not simply coincidental and that close attention to specificities of time and place would reveal the inadequacy of universal paradigms.

Notes

1 This chapter has appeared as an article entitled 'Is Feminism About "Women"? A Critical View on Intersectionality from India', *Economic and Political Weekly*, Vol. L No. 17, April 25, 2015, pp. 37–44. Used with permission.
2 Anand Kumar, 'Understanding Lohia's Political Sociology: Intersectionality of Caste, Class, Gender and Language', *Economic & Political Weekly*, Vol. XLV No. 40, October 2, 2010.
3 Nira Yuval-Davis, 'Intersectionality and Feminist Politics', *European Journal of Women's Studies*, Vol. 13 No.3, 2006, p. 193.
4 Jennifer C. Nash, 'Re-thinking Intersectionality', *Feminist Review*, Vol. 89 No.1–15, 2008, p. 3.
5 Ibid., p. 2.
6 Kimberlé Crenshaw, 'Mapping the Margins: Intersectionality, Identity Politics and Violence against Women of Color', *Stanford Law Review*, University of Chicago Legal Forum, 139, Vol.43 No.6, 1991, p. 1244.
7 This section draws on my paper 'Sexuality, Caste, Governmentality: Contests over 'Gender' in India', *Feminist Review*, Issue 91, 2009 and my book *Seeing Like a Feminist*, New Delhi: Penguin India and Zubaan Books, 2012.
8 Nivedita Menon, *Recovering Subversion: Feminist Politics Beyond the Law*, Ranikhet: Permanent Black and University of Illinois Press, 2004.
9 Sumit Baudh, 'Reflections of a Queer Dalit', *In Plain speak* No. 3, 2007, p. 33.
10 Menon, *Recovering Subversion*.
11 Marc Galanter, *Competing Equalities: Law and the Backward Classes in India*, New Delhi: Oxford University Press, 1984, p. 357. For a more detailed discussion of this point, see Menon's, *Recovering Subversion*.
12 Emily Grabham, 'Intersectionality, Traumatic Impressions', in Emily Grabham, Davina Cooper, Jane Krishnadas and Didi Herman (eds.), *Intersectionality and Beyond: Law, Power and the Politics of Location*, London: Routledge-Cavendish, 2008, p. 186.
13 Ibid., p. 193.
14 This section draws on my paper 'Sexuality, Caste, Governmentality'.
15 John Harriss, *Depoliticising Development: The World Bank and Social Capital*, New Delhi: Left Word Books, 2002.
16 Center for Women's Global Leadership 2001, cited by Yuval-Davis, 2006, p. 204.
17 Nancy Fraser, 'How Feminism Became Capitalism's Handmaiden – and How to Reclaim It', *The Guardian*, Monday, October 14, 2013.
18 Aditya Nigam, 'Radical Politics in the Time of Globalisation', in Niraja Gopal Jayal and Sudha Pai (eds.), *Democratic Governance in India: Challenges of Poverty, Development and Identity*, New Delhi: Sage Publications, 2001.
19 Michel Foucault, 'Body/Power', in *Power/ Knowledge, Selected Interviews and Other Writings 1972–77*, New York: Pantheon Books, 1980, pp. 56–57.
20 Cited by Yuval-Davis, 'Intersectionality and Feminist Politics', p. 196.
21 Nash, 'Re-thinking Intersectionality', pp. 9–10, emphasis added.
22 Oyeronke Oyewumi, *The Invention of Women: Making an African Sense of Western Gender Discourses*, Rochester: University of Minnesota Press, 1997, p. 16.
23 Ibid.
24 Yuval-Davis, 'Intersectionality and Feminist Politics'.
25 Patricia Hill Collins, *Black Sexual Politics*, New York: Routledge, 2005, p. 11.
26 Yuval-Davis, 'Intersectionality and Feminist Politics', pp. 196–97.
27 Ibid., p. 204.
28 Mrinalini Sinha, 'A Global Perspective on Gender, What's South Asia Got to Do with It?' in Ania Loomba and Ritty Lukose (eds.), *South Asian Feminisms*, Durham: Duke University Press, 2012, pp. 370–71.

2

PROBLEMS FOR A CONTEMPORARY THEORY OF GENDER[1]

Susie Tharu and Tejaswini Niranjana

I

Suddenly 'women' are everywhere. Development experts cite 'gender bias as the cause of poverty in the Third World'; population planners declare their commitment to the empowerment of Indian women; economists speak of the feminisation of the Indian labour force. In 1991–92, for instance, the People's War group of the CPI (M-L) found themselves drawn increasingly into women's campaigns against sexual and domestic violence, dowry and the sale of arrack or country liquor. Upper-caste women thronged the streets in the anti-Mandal protests; women are among the best-known leaders of the Ramjanmabhoomi movement; the BJP have identified women and Dalits as the principal targets of their next election campaign. Film after film features the new women, who also figures prominently in Doordarshan programmes. In overwhelming numbers, women joined the literacy campaigns in Pondicherry and parts of Andhra Pradesh. The anti-arrack movement initiated by rural women destabilised the economy of Andhra Pradesh.

How might we 'read' the new visibility of women across the political spectrum? What does it represent for gender theory and feminist practice today? For all those who invoke gender here, 'women' seems to stand in for the subject (agent, addressee, field of inquiry) of feminism itself. There is a sense, therefore, in which the new visibility is an index of the success of the women's movement. But clearly this success is also problematic. A wide range of issues rendered critical by feminism are now being invested in and annexed by projects that contain and deflect that initiative. Possibilities of alliance with other subaltern forces (Dalits, for example) that are opening up in civil society are often blocked, and feminists find themselves drawn into disturbing configurations within the dominant culture. We attempt in this chapter to understand the implications of this phenomenon. We feel our task is all the more urgent since the crisis in feminism is clearly related to the crisis of democracy and secularism in our times.

In the 1970s and 1980s, an important task for feminist theory was to establish 'gender' as a category that had been rendered invisible in universalisms of various kinds. In Hyderabad, for example, the campaign against 'eve-teasing' taken up by women students in the early 1970s brought into the open the hostile and sexually threatening conditions all women had to deal with everyday, not only in the university, but also on the streets and in every kind of workplace. Through public interest litigation, as in the cases of injectable contraceptives (Net-Oen) and police rape, and appeals against a variety of judgements – on custodial rape, family violence, restitution of conjugal rights – we demonstrated the asymmetries and inequalities in gender relations that underwrote the notion of rights and the legal process. We demanded changes that would make the law more sensitive to the cultural and economic contexts of women's lives. Women's groups investigating 'dowry deaths' demonstrated how the designation of the family as private domain restricted women's access to protection against domestic violence. They exposed the collusion of the law, police, medical system and the family in classifying these deaths as suicides. Feminist scholars worked to salvage gender and women's issues from being subsumed by class analysis, sought to extend the Marxist understanding of labour to include domestic production, and pointed out the marginality and vulnerability of women in the workforce; disciplinary formations such as history or literature were critically discussed, and alternative narratives produced that foregrounded women. We demonstrated gross inequalities in women's access to health care systems or to 'development', and examined patriarchal ideologies as they worked across a wide range of institutions. These initiatives extended our understanding of the micropolitics of civil society, showing how pervasively mechanisms of subjugation operated, and how processes of othering functioned in relation to women.

In the late 1980s and the early 1990s – the Mandal/Mandir/Fund-Bank years – however, we face a whole new set of political questions.[2] Entering into new alliances we have begun to elaborate new forms of politics. These have demanded engagement with issues of caste and religious affiliation/community and with new problems emerging from the 'liberalisation' of the economy, creating contexts in which the contradictions implicit in earlier initiatives have become increasingly apparent. For example, feminists calling for a uniform civil code in the context of the Shah Bano case soon realised the difficulty of distinguishing their position from that of an aggressively anti-Muslim lobby, and began to downplay the demand as 'Shah Bano' became the rallying cry for Hindutva. Similarly, in Chunduru, sexual harassment was cited as justification for the punishment meted out to Dalits by upper-caste men. More recently, leftist women's organisations in Hyderabad were placed in a dilemma about joining in a protest against the arrest and torture of a Muslim student accused of 'eve-teasing'. Debates around the introduction of hormonal implants and injectables into the national family planning programmes reveal analogous contradictions that underlie notions such as women's freedom, self-determination, or their right to choose. We feel that the kind of contradictions that confront gender analysis are structurally similar to those that face class analysis, caste initiatives and, more broadly, democracy and secularism today. In this chapter, our concern is to investigate the relationship of these contradictions to the gender, caste, class and community composition of the 'subject' in the dominant order. Historically, this citizen-subject has been underwritten, and naturalised, by the 'humanism' that presents it as politically neutral.

II

Gender analysis, like class analysis, had revealed how the humanist subject and the social worlds predicated onto it functioned in such a way as to legitimise bourgeois and patriarchal interest. What has never been really apparent, however, is the way in which both Marxist and feminist politics continue to deploy other dimensions of a hidden structuring (such as caste or community) of the humanist subject, as well as the premises of secularism-democracy invoked by it. We have been unable, therefore, to critically confront inequalities of caste or community implicit in that subject or its worlds. We have also found it difficult to radicalise the concepts of secularism and democracy to meet the political requirements of our times. We shall be arguing in this chapter that these tasks call for an investigation and critique of the humanist premises that not only underwrite the politics of dominance but also configure the 'subject of feminism'.

The notion of the 'human' as it appears in political theory, and more importantly in humanist common sense is inextricable from what has been termed the metaphysics of substance. Framed by this metaphysics, the human appears as a substantive base that precedes and somehow remain *prior* to and outside of structuring of gender, class, caste or community. In liberal political theory, it is this human core that provides the basis for legal personhood. Humanist Marxism offers a critique of the class investments of liberal individualism, but preserves the normative idea of a human essence, principally in the concept of alienation and in teleological notions of history but also in the notion of ideology as false consciousness. Humanist feminism, too, is predicated on notions of female alienation from a putative human wholeness. Even across significant political and theoretical divides, the notion of a human essence that remains resolutely outside historical or social coding continues to operate as 'common sense'. It is not difficult to see that these theories, and their politico-legal derivatives, actually produced what they claim to recognise. For example, by basing the *rights of the individual* on the fiction of substantive human core,[3] the law creates that core, or more precisely, a core effect; the idea of *alienation* gains force only as it measures itself against a human fullness; *teleological narratives of history* find resolution only in a fully and recognisably human world.

Thus produced, this human subject, on whom the whole question of 'rights' is predicated, was imagined as the citizen-subject and the political subject. This imagining, (1) articulated gender, caste and community (and initially even class) only in the realm of the social; (2) marked these as *incidental* attributes of a *human* self; and, (3) rendered invisible the historically and social/cultural structuring of the subject of politics. The shaping of the normative human-Indian subject involved, on the one hand, a dialectical relationship of inequality and opposition with the classical subject of Western liberalism and, on the other, its structuring as upper-caste, middle-caste, Hindu and male. The structuring was effected by *processes of othering/ differentiation such as, for example, the definition* of upper-caste/class female respectability in counterpoint to lower-caste licentiousness, or Hindu tolerance towards Muslim fanaticism, and by a gradual and sustained transformation of the institutions that govern everyday life.[4] Elaborated and consolidated through a series of conflicts, this structuring became invisible as this citizen-self was designated as modern, secular and democratic.[5]

Our strategy in this chapter will be to examine certain 'events', such as Mandal or the rise of Hindu Right, in which contemporary feminist analysis is coming up against certain impasses. These impasses indicate, on the one hand, a fracturing of the humanist consensus that has been the basis of left- as well as right-wing politics and, on the other, an opening up of possibilities for new political alignments and initiatives. These events, it seems to us, characterise the moment of the contemporary and might be investigated as metonyms of gender in which cultural meanings are being contested and refigured.

Obviously, each of these metonyms has a separate and particular history. But since our focus here is on the contemporary moment, we are concerned less with the emergence of these 'events', more with the impress of history on the present. In a strict sense, then, our approach is genealogical. We wish to explore historical conflicts as they structure everyday life and affect political initiatives in our time. The aim is to initiate a polemic that *will render visible the points of collision and the lines of force* that have hitherto remained subterranean, and construct instruments that will enable struggles on this reconfigured ground.

III

Our first metonym is Mandal-Chunduru, where we investigate the articulation of the gender question in the hegemonic culture of the 1990s. In both Mandal and Chunduru, 'women' were foregrounded, although in different ways. 'Women' came to be invoked here as, in a sense, feminist subjects: assertive, non-submissive, protesting against injustice done to them *as women* (Chunduru) or *as citizen* (the anti-Mandal agitation). An examination of the hidden structuring of this feminist subject would, we believe, reveal its similarities with the subject of humanism, marked – in a way that requires the occlusion of the marking – by class, caste and community.

Mandal

The background is one familiar to most of us. The then Prime Minister V.P. Singh's announcement on August 7, 1990, of the implementation of the Mandal Commission recommendations for reservations of 27% for Backward Caste, apart from 22.5% for SC/STs in government service and public sector jobs, sparked off student riots, primarily in North India but also in Hyderabad and a few other places. The methods of protest ranged from street-cleaning and boot-policing to self-immolation; the discourses deployed most significantly were those of Unrewarded Merit and the Salvation of the Nation.[6] The actual course of events is too well-known to require recounting here. What we would like to focus on is the imaging of women in the anti-Mandal agitation, preceded by a brief discussion of the way in which the agitation itself was represented in the media.

Indian Express editor Arun Shourie, rousing the upper-caste youth to action in his editorials, spoke of 'the intense idealism and fury' of the students.[7] A well known intellectual denounced the reservations for OBCs as a 'transgression of moral norms' and as a political practice that would 'destroy the structure of democratic politics'.[8] She spoke of the 'hidden despair' of the 'youth', and the government's refusal to recognise that 'people' 'may be moved by utopias, not interests'. The media's invocation of *students, youth* and *people* was marked by a strange consensus on usage – these terms were obviously unmarked, yet referred only to those who were upper caste or middle class. An editorial in the *Independent* bemoaned the fact that the middle class have no place in India, suggesting that somehow they were the only legitimate political subjects/actors in a democracy.[9] Only the subject of humanism could claim the utopias of the Enlightenment.

The Nation was a central figure in the anti-Mandal discourse. Claiming the heritage of Jawaharlal Nehru (a 1950s speech of Nehru's that was widely circulated, asserting that reservations would produce a 'second-rate' nation), the anti-Mandalites saw themselves as the authentic bearer of secularism and egalitarianism. Equality, they argued, would be achieved by a transcendence or a repudiation of caste, community and gender identifications. For feminists who had struggled for years to inscribe gender into the liberal model, the Mandal issue posed a difficult question. Young middle-class women began to declare that they were against the reservations for women that had been announced in Andhra Pradesh for instance, as well as against the idea of reserving seats for women in public transport. Reservations (like subsidies) were *concessions*, and would make women 'soft', they said, reducing their ability to be independent and strong. In the anti-Mandal protest, women often appear not as sexed beings but as free and equal citizens, as partners of the rioting men, jointly protesting the erosion of 'their' rights. The nearly unanimous media celebration of the upper-caste students framed them within a nonsectarian nationalism and humanism; these young men and women were truly egalitarian and therefore anti-Mandal, whereas pro-Mandal groups were accused of supporting a resurgent casteism.

We asserted earlier that 'the Indian' comes into being in a dialectical relationship of inequality with the Western subject of humanism. In the first two decades or so after Independence, the postcolonial 'Indian' lays claim to a more egalitarian liberalism than that produced in the age of empire and in the heart of empire. Nehruvian socialism takes shape after the Soviet example of state planning, although allowing for a 'mixed' *economy that retains large number of middle-class professionals* in the public sector. In the global configuration that has emerged after the collapse of the second world, in the context of economic 'liberalisation' in India and the gradual erosion of the public sector, the neo-nationalist Indian subject proclaims its Indianness even as it internationalises itself. Now claiming equality with the Western subject of humanism on the latter's own terms, the 'Indian' aggressively demands the rejection of everything that would come in the way of its achieving an equal place in the new world order.

Whereas in the Nehru years the retarders of progress were seen as casteism, fundamentalism, or feudalism, and the role of the state was to help overcome these, in the Fund-Bank years these 'evils' are imaged as being located in welfarism and in the state-controlled public sector itself. The 'failure' and 'inefficiency' of the public sector is seen primarily as the outcome of the reservations policy; if becoming 'efficient', therefore, is the only way of integrating India into the world economy, then the obvious means of achieving this is to abolish reservations and establish a meritocracy. The sociologist Andre Beteille argued that no one wants to defend a caste hierarchy today;[10] but what he did not add was that the new secular hierarchy – a meritocracy premised on efficiency – refigures, transforms and redeploys caste. In an article written during the anti-Mandal agitation, BJP leader K.R. Malkani mentioned 'a vice president of the IBM' who 'joked that they have so many Indians, and they are so good, that they in the IBM have decided not to employ any more, since they could just take over the IBM! Read the Brahmin for the educated Indian, and you have some idea of our wealth and brain power'.[11] After the self is marked upper class/upper caste, the process of marking, as we have already suggested, becomes invisible. The recomposition of the middle class, the secular class that stands in for the nation, is thus predicated on the redeployment and othering of caste.[12] Professing secularism enables a displacement of caste (and also community) from the middle class sphere, so that it gets marked as what lies *outside, is other* than, the middle class. In the consolidation of the middle class and in the othering of caste, 'women' play a crucial role.

Not only were women visually foregrounded by the media during the agitation, they also took part in large numbers in the struggle to do away with reservations for backward castes and Dalits. A report in the *Free Press Journal* says: 'The girls of Jadavpur University were the most militant and wanted to blockade roads and defy the law'.[13] In many cities, hitherto 'apolitical' women students participated enthusiastically in demonstration and blockades, mourning the 'death of merit' and arguing the need to save the nation. Wives of IAS officers demonstrated in the capital on behalf of their children, who they claimed were being denied their rightful share in the nation. The fact of women 'taking to the streets' became in the hegemonic culture iconic of an idealism that recalled the days of the freedom struggle. The marking of 'women' as middle class and upper caste has a long genealogy that, historically and conceptually, goes back into nationalism as well as social reform.[14] Marked thus, 'women' are seen as morally pure and uncorrupted – hence the significance of their protest, which becomes a 'disinterested' one since they have no place in the organised political process.[15] However, as a powerful strand of nationalism asserts, it is women who are entrusted with the task of saving the nation. In actually, the nation is frequently imaged as 'woman' (Bharatmata, Mother India).

The re-emergence of women in the public sphere as claimants to the nation and to citizenship results in a masculinisation of the lower castes. To rephrase the title of a well-known feminist book, in Mandal-Chunduru, all the women are upper caste (and, by implication, middle-class Hindu) and all the lower castes are men. As we argued earlier, in the anti-Mandal agitation, 'women' featured as citizens and not necessarily as gendered beings. But the representation in the media of their well-nourished faces and fashionable bodies visually defined the lower castes as Other. The photographs of the anti-Mandal women suggested that caste (read lower caste) is defined against 'women', and against the assertive and articulate humanist-feminist subject. As Sangari and Vaid have argued, 'the description and management of gender and female sexuality is involved in the maintenance and reproduction of social inequality'.[16] Sexuality was a *hidden* issue in Mandal, as an interview with an anti-Mandal woman student suggested. The student had held in a demonstration a placard reading: 'We want employed husbands'. When asked why, she said that reservations would deprive their men of employment. In that case, why should they not marry 'backward' boys? 'But how can that be . . .', her voice trailed off.[17] The anti-Mandal women had learned to *claim* deprivation and injustice, now not as women but as *citizens*, for to ground the claim in gender would pit them against middle-class men. The claiming of citizenship rather than sisterhood now not only set them against Dalit men but also against lower-caste/class women.

Chunduru

Interestingly, it is the claim to sisterhood that accomplishes the same effect in Chunduru. To sketch the context: in the culmination of a series of hostile encounters spread across at least two to three years, on August 6, 1991, in the village of Chunduru in coastal Andhra Pradesh, 13 Dalits were murdered by upper-caste Reddys. The catalysing 'event' appeared to be the incursion into the cinema hall space reserved by tradition for members of the upper castes by a young Dalit graduate, who was later beaten up, forced to drink liquor and marched to the Chunduru police station, where he was 'accused of harassing upper-caste women in an inebriated condition'.[18]

After the carnage of August 6, the mourning Dalits organised a funeral procession, during which some haystacks and thatched roofs were set on fire. Most of the Reddy males had left Chunduru to avoid arrest. The upper-caste women who stayed behind complaint loudly of harassment by the Dalits, suggesting that their present accusations stemmed from a long history of grievances against Dalit men. The woman claimed that they had been tied to trees and kerosene poured over them, and only the arrival of the police saved them from death.

Shortly after, the Reddys of the region formed a 'Sarvajanabhyudaya Porata Samiti' along with the Kammas, Brahmins, Kapus, Rajus and Vaishyas, and organised processions, *dharnas* and roadblocks to protest their 'oppression' at the hands of Dalits.[19] The upper-caste women, they contented, had been systematically harassed by

Dalit men. Accusations of eve-teasing and assault multiplied, post-Chunduru. On August 13 in Kollipara village near Tenali, a Dalit boy was beaten up by upper-caste boys for teasing 'a schoolgirl'; a report dated August 11, 1991, said that earlier in the month, a Dalit student was stabbed on the pretext that he had teased 'three girls'. The original cinema hall story was recorded as one about 'a Harijan youth putting his feet up on the seat in front in the cinema hall occupied by a caste Hindu girl'.[20] In Chunduru itself, the story went, just before August 6, when Dalit labourers were no longer employed for transplantation and women from the landlords' family had undertaken the task, Dalit men were supposed to have accosted the women one day, quarrelled with them, stripped them naked, and forced them to remove the transplanted seedlings and re-plant them. Enraged upper-caste women attacked the convoys of Chief Minister Janardhana Reddy and former Chief Minister N.T. Rama Rao, blaming the state for not providing them protection from the Dalits.

Years of sexual abuse of Dalit women by upper-caste men appear under the sanction of 'custom' while the alleged 'eve-teasing' of upper-caste women by Dalit men invokes the horrors and prohibitions/punishments of major transgression, the penalty of death. Chunduru drew the attention of urban women's groups, but especially for those feminist who had refused to be part of the anti-Mandal agitation and were attempting to build fragile alliances with Dalit organisations, the hegemonic articulation of the gender issues as one of 'molestation' (of upper-caste women) was deeply problematic. But to counterpose this against the molestation of Dalit women was equally problematic.

Feminists can grapple with this problem only by addressing the key role played by caste in the making of the middle-class woman. In the nineteenth-century *bhadralok* campaigns against Vaishnav artists, as much as in the anti-nautch initiatives in Madras Presidency, the virtue and purity of the middle-class woman emerged in contrast to the licentiousness of the lower-caste/class woman. It is a logic that continues to operate, as for instance in cases of Rameeza Bee and the Birati rapes: the women crying rape were 'prostitutes' and therefore had no right to complain of sexual harassment.[21] A woman's right over her body and control over her sexuality is conflated with her *virtue*. So powerful does this characterisation become that only the middle-class woman has a right to purity. In other words, only *she* is entitled to the name of woman in this society. Again we see, as in Mandal, the masculinisation of the lower caste – the Dalits only male, the women only upper caste. The category of 'woman', and therefore in a very important sense the field of feminism as well as the female subject, emerge in this context by obscuring the Dalit woman and marking the lower caste as the predatory male who becomes the legitimate target of 'feminist' rage.

IV

Hindutva women

Women on the Right have also opened up a space that might in many ways be regarded as feminist. As Tanika Sarkar points out in a study of the Rastrasevika

Samiti (the women's wing of the RSS), women are 'active political subjects' not only in the Samiti, but also more generally in the domain of communal politics.[22] The women leaders of the BJP are not daughters, wives, or mothers of deceased male leaders. They are there in their own right and seem to have carved out distinctive political roles and identities for themselves. Equally significant is the articulate and often passionate involvement of women who otherwise seem to have little interest in public life in issues such as reservations, the appeasement of Muslims, or corruption in the bureaucracy. Riots now have a new profile, with women, sometimes even middle-class women, actively participating as in Bhagalpur in 1989, Ahmedabad in 1990 or Surat in 1992. News photographs showed a sizeable number of women among those arriving for the 1992 Ayodhya *kar seva*. Several papers carried reports of Sadhvi Rithambara and Uma Bharati cheering on the crowd that tore down the Babri Masjid.

More striking – and in some ways more disturbing – than the appearance of this militant individual on the public battlefields of Hindutva is her modernity and indeed her feminism. The new Hindu woman nearly always belongs to the most conservative groups in Indian society – upper-class/caste, middle-ranking government service or trading sectors – but she cannot be regarded as traditional in any simple sense of the term, any more than Hindutva can be read as fundamentalist.[23] There is very little talk of going back to tradition. The focus is on injustice, for which the Babri Masjid serves as symbol. At issue in the war of Hindutva, which is defined after Savarkar as love for the motherland, is not Hinduism, but the Indian nation.

Predictably, self-respect is an important theme. However, hitched into women's aspirations for self-respect is the idea of Hindu self-respect. One account of the origin of the Samiti is that Lakshimibai Kelkar founded it after she saw *goondas* (interestingly not Muslims) raping a woman in the presence of her husband. Since Hindu men (who are in this story both lustful and weak) could not protect their wives, Hindu women had to train to do so themselves.[24] As in authoritarian politics the world over, the emphasis is on discipline and on purging or cleaning the social body of corruption, using force if necessary. While the immediate object appears to be Indian society, the Muslims enemy is very close to the surface here. In the RSS/VHP/BJP imaginary, the *matrabhumi* is presented as a repeatedly raped female body and the myth of the enemy within and of Muslim lust play key structural roles. Thus, for Muslims *'aurat matrabhumi nahin hai, bhog bhumi hai'* (Woman is not the motherland, but the earth to be enjoyed).[25] The violence women experience and their need to fight against and gain respect within their own society is all but obscured as the well-made enemy steps in, suggesting that self-respect is best gained in the protection of the motherland. The fact that in the projected Hindu *rashtra* Muslims would not be allowed four wives was regarded by *karsevikas* at Ayodhya as index of the respect women would receive in the utopia.[26]

Like the anti-Mandal agitation, Hindutva would seem to have enabled an articulate, fighting individualism for women and for men. Its power is productive in the Foucauldian sense, inciting its subjects to speak out, act, to become independent, agentive, citizen-individuals. One notices increasingly the confident exponents of Hindutva (students, otherwise unremarkable middle-class men and women) who intervene at seminars and public meetings. These subjects are marked as authentically Indian and as having found an ethos within which their natural – and national – expressive selves can emerge and be sustained.

It is important to understand that though this new Hindu self is represented as discriminated against the embattled, it has the confidence of occupying a 'neutral' ground that provides the basis for a new moral authority. Hindutva, for example, is represented as a potential national ethos within which all other religions and communities might be justly housed. The claim is commonly backed by two arguments. One, a redeployment of nationalist versions of Indian history in which Hinduism is represented as having a long tradition of tolerance; the other an invocation of Western nation-state and their endorsement of dominant religious traditions in the secularism they practice. The history of violence through which those national bourgeoisies established authority is never discussed. The new Hindu subject speaks the voice of a reason that opposes false dogmas (such as Western theories, pseudo-secularism), challenges the bias of existing institutions (the courts, the constitution) on the ground that they are not sensitive to the desires of the majority and appeals to truths that was self-evident to genuine Indians. Thus Girilal Jain writes about the 'bloated rhetoric of secularism, constitutionalism and the law',[27] while Swapan Dasgupta comments after the demolition of the Masjid:

> In effect the *kar sevaks* presented Hindu society with a *fait accompli*. They could either disown the illegal act on account of both politics and aesthetics. Or they could come to terms with their own assertiveness, equate it with the storming of the Bastille and the collapse of the *ancient regime*, and prepare to face the consequences.[28]

In moves that are surprisingly quickly effected and apparently hold conviction for increasingly large numbers of Indians, the virulent anti-Muslim history of Hindutva, a political agenda focused on pulling down a mosque and building a temple, and a record of communal violence, is gilded over the legitimised as Hindutva reoccupies the discourses in which bourgeois nationalism established authority in its European birthplace – and, more important from the point of view of our argument in this chapter, the forms of subjectivity that emerge in tandem with it. Thus L.K. Advani (invariably represented in the press as mature, soft-spoken and charming) insists that his is actually the only 'secular' party. The demolition of the Babri Masjid is only a 'temporary setback'. A.B. Vajpayee (honourable, reasonable, cultured) exonerate the real BJP by locating communalism only in its 'young and overenthusiastic party workers'.[29] The angle on neutrality that appears in the context of the gender question is more telling. Members of the Rashtrasevika Samiti distinguished their position from that of other women's organisations by saying, 'when we arbitrate we do not always take the women's side. We are neutral . . . . *Ham ghar torne-wale nahin hain*', (We are not home-breakers).[30] Similar evidence of 'neutrality' in relation to caste or class is not difficult to locate.

The politics of this neutrality-effect demands closer scrutiny. The BJP/VHP/RSS combine are pressing in on a whole set of existing figures, logics and institutions as they lay claim to the nation and to neutrality. As their allusions to European history and to First World nationalism also indicate, a figure that is repeatedly referenced is the bourgeois citizen-subject and the world that was 'legitimately' – and ruthlessly – recast in his interest and in his singular image. Closer home in the neutrality of the Neharuvian state and of planned development in which the 'social' problems of caste, class and gender, and colonialism are addressed and analysed by scientific planners and handed over to the bureaucracy for redress. The problems, briefly summarised, is that though this state acknowledges social disbalances and accepts responsibility for righting them, it functions on the basis of an executive centrality in which the state is authorised to speak and act for the people. It is becoming increasingly clear that the task of shaping this executive centrality and a social imaginary that authorised it, dominated cultural politics in the immediate post-Independence period. Identities that had taken shape in major pre-Independence class, caste and gender struggles, and which might have provided the basis for another social imaginary of the nation, were fractured and disorganised as they were rewritten into narratives of humanity and citizenship. The task, however, is an ongoing one, for hegemony is continuously under threat. Films, novels, histories, television programmes, the press in general, the curricula and a range of their institutions of civil society address potentially rupturing questions of caste, gender or community and rework them into narratives that legitimate the middle-class, upper-caste Hindu, patriarchal and internationalist markings of the hegemonic subject.

As a result of this alliance with the subject of humanism, the common sense of the new Right has a much greater hold than the formal/electoral support received by the BJP might suggest. Thus, whether one looks at the mainstream press or at the apparently non-political programmes put out by Doordarshan (the morning chat show, the evening serials, the children's programmes, the afternoon women's programmes), or ways of thinking, feeling, reasoning and arriving at conclusions that govern the daily lives of the growing consumer population, Hindutva seems well set to becoming hegemonic. Powerful new discursive articulations are thus effected between this individualism and organic-conservative themes of religion, tradition, nation, family, personal integrity, order and discipline. The discussion on minoritism, injury/appeasement, pseudo-secularism and nationalism have brought these subjects into focus in a virulently anti-Muslim frame and as it feeds directly into a genealogy of modern Indian womanhood that marks it not only as Hindu, but as upper caste/class, the Muslim woman is caught in a curious zero-zero game. Either way she loses. She cannot really be woman any more that she can be Indian. As woman and as Indian, she cannot really be Muslim. As for the women on the Right, they are indeed empowered by these new movements, but in a way that sets up the feminist project as one that endorses caste/class hierarchies and the othering of Islam.

V

We have been arguing that the hegemonic articulation of the gender issue sets up the feminist subject in an antagonistic relationship with, for example, class-caste (Mandal-Chunduru), or religious identity (woman on the Right), and in such a way as to aid the reabsorption of this subject into consumer capitalism. We now turn to our last metonym, the anti-*arrack* movement in Andhra Pradesh. The various ways in which the movement has been interpreted and 'women' have been represented seem to work in such a way as to erase and delegitimise earlier feminist initiatives. The process is not a simple one, and we do not claim that we have been able to map all – or even most – of its complicated strategies and effects. Media depictions of the anti-arrack movement annex its initiative into a variety of contemporary discourses about the nation, its women and the purification of the former by the virtue of the latter. Feminist theory and practice are caught in a curious set of contradictions. The portrayal of the anti-arrack women as the only authentic feminist, paradoxically also involves, (1) a denial that their struggle is concerned specifically with *women's issues* and (2) a reinscription of it as an anti-feudal struggle, or as a struggle to cleanse the body politic and save the nation. What seems to enable both the denial and the reinscription is the invoking to the anti-arrack woman as the subject of humanism. Interestingly, in terms of the positions offered to the female/feminist subject, there is little to distinguish the articulators of the women's issue in a conservative, high nationalist mode from those who invoke it as part of the class (or specifically anti-feudal) struggle. As these diverse writers seek to separate the anti-arrack movement from historical feminism, they obscure crucial dimensions of the radical egalitarian potential of actually existing feminism. At the same time, they make invisible dimensions of the anti-arrack movement that find resonance with other feminist initiatives.

What are the facets of the anti-arrack struggle that become visible as we contest these dominant representations of it? What implications do they have for contemporary feminist practice and gender theory? We begin with a brief narrative of the movement.

A series of struggle centred around government-backed sales of arrack (*sara* in Telugu) have been taking place over the past decade or so in various regions of Andhra Pradesh. In each region, different local configurations have sustained arrack as an issue; while in the Telangana region and in a few other districts the CPI(M-L) groups have initiated or supported the agitation, in some the coastal Andhra districts that movement seems to have emerged in conjunction with other events, such as the adult literacy programme. Women all over rural Andhra Pradesh attacked excise department jeeps and police, burned arrack packets, punished arrack sellers and fined the men who continued to drink. After September 1992 the movement appears to have gathered rapid momentum, spreading from village to village in a manner that no organised political party has been able to predict or control.

The Andhra Pradesh government announced a ban on arrack in Nellore District from April 15, 1993, and throughout the state from October 1, 1993. The ruling

Congress-I claimed the ban as a pro-people initiative on its part. Enormous coloured hoarding depicted the evils of arrack, portrayed smiling rural families freed from the menace, and Chief Minister Vijayabhaskara Reddy gazed benevolently on the scene from gigantic cutouts towering above hoardings, which were put up at major intersections in the capital city of Hyderabad.[31] The audio-visual publicity machinery of the government ventured into remote areas of Andhra Pradesh to spread propaganda about the need to stop drinking arrack. In the Assembly elections of November 1994, the Congress suffered a major defeat, and the Telugu Desam Party (which had earlier introduced the government-sponsored distribution of arrack) returned to power. The new Chief Minister, N.T. Rama Rao, declared within minutes of taking office that prohibition of all liquor would immediately come into force in the state. He was only acceding, he said, to the demand of the sisters who had voted for him.

Each political organisation, however, seemed to appropriate the *sara* women, laying claim to their struggle, and configuring them as the true subjects of feminism. The range is an astonishing one: from the Gandhians to the Lohiaits to the Telugu Desam to the BJP/RSS; from the Marxist-Leninist parties to the traditional Left (CPM and CPI) to the Dalit Mahasabha; not to mention women's organisations across the spectrum: from the Arya Mahila Samiti to the socialist Mahila Dakshata Samiti, from the A.P. Mahila Sangham to the two Progressive Organisations for Women backed by different M-L parties. The woman in the anti-arrack struggle appeared as a Romantic subject, and predicated onto her were an assortment of complex narratives of which she was sole heroine.[32]

The BJP MP, Uma Bharati, praising the anti-arrack women, wanted 'women' 'also [to] campaign against dowry, craze for foreign goods and corruption'; she felt they should 'help create national awakening (*swadesh jagran*)'.[33] The BJP in Nellore District where the movement was very strong are said to have named the women as Shakti, Kali and Durga, just as the all-India vice-president of the BJP, Jana Krishnamurthy, declared that '*matru shakti*[mother's power] had caused others to fall in line'.[34] Taking a slightly different but related stand, Dalit-bahujan theorist K. Ilaiah spoke of the movement as asserting 'the mother's right to set the family right'.[35] Vavilala Gopalakrishnaiah, an elderly freedom fighter, argued that the anti-arrack movement was 'similar to the freedom movement' and that 'care should be taken to see that it will not be politicized'.[36] 'Mother with babies in their arms walk miles to come for demonstrations, wrote Vimala of the POW.[37] The imagery was that of women 'who has come out into the street [*veedhiloki vacchindi*]';[38] and, as in the anti-Mandal agitation, or in the nationalist movement, this woman became the icon of purity and idealism.

In trying to explain why women were out on the streets, writers seem to obscure many factors that might have enabled the rebellion to find articulation, such as the withdrawal of the rice subsidy, the carefully planned increase in arrack sales, the literacy classes and the stories about arrack in the literacy primers. What is offered instead is the picture of the village women's eternal tears and suffering, and how *sara* 'sucks the blood of the poor'.[39] When driven to extreme despair, suggest the dominant narratives, the woman's human essence asserts itself and allows her to claim the status of citizen-subject.[40] Interestingly, the assertion of her 'civility' is premised on her being wife and mother, on her concern for her children and husband. What the woman desires, as Sharada would have it, is 'happiness in the family'[41] and that the auspicious marks of her marriage (*paspu-kumkumam*) not be taken from her. This refiguring of the authentic subject of feminism seems to be an implicit critique, for example, of urban feminists as they are customarily imagined in the dominant cultural representations. This authentic feminist subject is characterised by a retired judge as a rural woman with 'a specific nature of her own'; 'she lives as a slave to custom as long as she can, and when she cannot tolerate that life any more and begin to break barriers, neither men nor the urban women can imagine the manner in which she will struggle. She has nerve'.[42] The woman's militancy is coded as that spirit which makes her a good wife and mother; the true *sati* demonstrates her *pativratya* or devotion not by being passive but by acting aggressively to save her husband from an untimely death.

By emphasising the 'familial' impulse behind women's militancy, dominant explanatory narratives deny the status of the *political* to their actions and seek to contain their scope. Celebratory report in *Indian Express* described the anti-arrack issue as 'a burning social question';[43] N.T. Rama Rao of the Telugu Desham Party invoked the memory of Gandhi's desire to impose prohibition and his (Gandhi) opinion that 'only womenfolk could bring about this social change'.[44] Ramoji Rao, editor and publisher of *Eenadu* Telugu daily that gave extensive coverage to the *sara* struggle, said: 'Every individual who keeps trust in the value of social life should wholeheartedly welcome the Great Movement [*Mahodyamam*] .... Everyday with flesh and blood, who has a sense of shame, and humanism, is cheering the struggle'.[45] Analyst on the Left seemed to veer between interpreting the movement as one for social reform[46] and seeing it as 'part of the anti-feudal struggle'.[47] That the movement was perceived by some as 'leaderless' helped to push towards a characterisation of it as 'non-political'. As Ramoji Rao put it in an editorial, the movement had 'transcended caste, religion, class and party' although after it had gathered momentum various 'political parties and women's organizations are now hurrying after it'.[48]

The obverse of the refusal to image the women as political actors is the bestowal on them of a social role, that of rescuing not only their families but also 'saving the nation'. The hegemonic narratives *authorise* the women, give them 'moral authority' to *cleanse* a body politic 'stinging of *sara*'.[49] Once again, the consensus in terms of analysis and solution is stunning. Across the political spectrum, writers set up an elaborate demonology in which the valiant women battle the forces of evil, represented by the politicians, the arrack contractors, government officials, industrialists and the whole 'corrupt' apparatus of state and civil society.[50] The meaning of *sara* (K. Balagopal calls it the 'obscene fluid') here becomes that which is unnameable and disgusting beyond belief, stands for the 'uncivilised politics'[51] abhorred by enlightened secular humanist. Repeatedly, *sara* is evoked not only as being 'responsible for all the violence and atrocities on women'[52] but also as signifying the source of all evil and corruption; and it is rural women who are 'blowing the conchshell of battle to destroy the atrocious *sara*demon'.[53] As K. Balagopal puts it, 'The supreme courage and tenacity of thousands of rural women has pitted itself against the abysmal humbug of the state's rulers ... [and the women] have taken up sickle and broomstick to drive the obscenity out of all our lives'.[54] The anti-arrack movement will 'cleanse us of corruption' (A CPM supporter, in personal conversation); a polity that has fallen away from the idealistic days of nationalism will have its moral impurity washed away by the *sara* women.

What other readings might be possible both of the problem and the struggle? We would want to contest the dominant representations, for example, by suggesting that the *sara* movement is a significant elaboration of the politics of everyday life, and that in such a reading questions of gender, class, caste and community come into a radically different configuration, where the emphasis shifts from moral purity to economic exploitation or the aspiration for physical well-being.

The observations that follow, necessarily impressionistic, are based on our visit to 12villages in three *mandals* of Nellore District in November 1992.[55] While the women's success in reducing or even preventing arrack sales directly affected the state and can be seen without much effort as a 'political' action, the movement also seemed to have resulted in a reconfiguring of power – and gender relations – within villages. Women did not usually confront individual men in their homes but attacked the local *sara* shops and the excise jeeps that supply liquor. The women also seemed to articulate many domains of their life in political terms or as political issues (even areas that class analysis would see as 'economic'). As Kondamma of Thotlacheruvupalli put it: 'Why does the government send us *sara*? Let them give us water instead, and we could have two crops a year. Now we have nothing'. Commenting on the state's indifference to their lives, she pointed out that while they had 'home delivery' of arrack they had to go nearly 20 miles to the nearest town to treat a simple case of diarrhea. In this village (Udaygiri Mandal, Nellore District), the women had pulled down the arrack shop and collected donations to build a stone platform over it which they used for public meetings. 'Why should we care', said Kondamma, 'if the government is losing money on *sara* because of us. When they had profits, did we see any of it? If the government has losses, let them cut *your* salaries'. Marveling at the state's obtuseness, she remarked: 'You should feed a buffalo before you milk it, otherwise it'll kick. And we've kicked'. 'This year we won't vote for anyone', she continued. 'They are all the same. And if our men want to vote, there'll be war between us'.

Other women, in the village of Kacheridevarayapalli (Anantsagar Mandal, Nellore District), drew up a figurative balance sheet that assigned a different set of meanings of *sara*. The *cost* of the government's Rs 850 crores of excise revenue was death (caused by the men's drunkenness – the deaths were those of themselves as well as of the women, the latter often suicides), hunger, ill-health, lack of education for the children, constant debt, their belongings – all the pots and pans and all their clothes – pawned for buying *sara*, their mental anguish. When they got rid of *sara*, said the women, they began to eat twice a day, the village streets were clean ('no drunks vomiting all over the place') everyone's health improved ('the men are getting fat and contended'), they had peace of mind (*'ippudu manasushanti undi'*), freedom from abuse, and solvency. The village landlords expressed the fear that labourers who had stopped drinking *sara* and were now able to save a little would not come to them for loans. Agricultural wages would now have to be paid in real money rather than partly in packets of *sara* obtained at a discount. Women's growing control over wages was beginning to undermine long-standing structures of dependency. What is seldom noted in the celebratory account of the origin-stories of the anti-arrack movement is the Congress government's withdrawal of the rice subsidy for low-income families. The movement could be seen then as a critique, in a sense, not only of the state but also of the priorities of the globalising economy and the effects on everyday life of structural adjustment and the contemporary reorganisation of markets.

Many of the women in the movement spoke of the significance education, or literacy, has for them. One of the stories we heard about the beginnings of the movement was about an inaugural function in Ayyavaripalli village for the government-initiated Akshara Deepam programme designed to eradicate illiteracy. The function, attended by a state Cabinet Minister and the District Collector, was disrupted by some drunken men. The women of the village, as in all other villages the only ones who attended the night classes, demanded the closure of the local *sara* shop so that their classes could be held in peace. Willing to promise anything to ensure the success of the literacy programme, the officials complied. This and other narratives about women's achievements were written into the post-literacy primers; story such as the one about Dubagunta village (*'Adavallu Ekamaithe'*–If women unite) where three drunken labourers lost their way and drowned in a tank. A hundred women first stopped the local arrack cart from entering the village; then they turned back 'a jeep full of *sara* packets'; after this, the lesson goes, the police arrived to enforce the right of the contractor to sell arrack. The women stood their ground, saying they would go to the Collector if necessary. 'This year', the lesson concludes, 'no one came forward to bid for arrack in our village'.[56] Women also spoke of other lessons, charts and topics for discussion in their literacy primers, such as 'seethamma Katha', 'Unity', and 'Who's Responsible for this Death?', which inspired them to join the struggle against arrack. 'We want our children to go to school', said Kondamma of Thotlacheruvupalli. This claiming *from below* of the right to education makes evident one of the most important agendas of the anti-Mandal agitation, the denial of education to the lower castes.[57] The upper-caste anxiety about educated Dalits, as in Chunduru, is to prevent them from occupying the space of the modern as it has been marked out in the postcolonial nation. The *sara* women's claiming of education seemed to recognise this logic and challenge the exclusions of modernity itself. The Dalit and Muslim women engaged in the struggle seemed to be articulating a claim on the rights of the citizen, from a critical perspective not necessarily predicated on their 'human essence'.

In spite of the fact that the women in the movement were predominantly from the Scheduled Caste, Backward Caste and Muslim communities, their jointly undertaken efforts to stop the excise officials received the tacit support of the upper-caste women of their village. Although it is an understanding obtained from the women's perspective that allowed them to claim *sara* as 'their' issue, the movement seldom pitted them against individual men, or against women from other castes/communities.

A unique feature of the anti-arrack movement was the refusal of the women to take up initiative beyond their village. As Mastan-bi of Kacheridevarayapalli put it, 'Are the women of the other villages dead? Why should *we* go there to fight against *sara?*'in relating their initiatives to the specificity of their location (their slogan is *Maa ooriki sara vaddu* – 'We don't want sara in our village'), in demarcating a domain over which they can exercise control, the anti-arrack women seem to be envisaged, and engaged, in a politics of the possible.[58]

VI

It seems to us that the early 1990s represent a turning point for Indian feminism. Each of the metonyms we have chosen for analysis focus on hegemonic mobilisations of a 'feminist' subject. Each displays the contradictions that emerge within feminist politics and the challenges that confront gender analysis in the context of the refiguring of dominance in a rapidly globalising Indian economy. Clearly the metonyms evidence an undertow in existing Indian feminism of structures of domination. Yet the anti-Mandal agitation, the politics of contraceptive choice, the feminism of Hindu Right, or the representations of the anti-arrack movement provide us also with configurations that crystallise and precipitate the possibilities of new and more radical alliances. This chapter has been primarily concerned with the exploration of factors that disable alliances between feminism and other democratic political initiative, but we regard this as a crucial first step in the shaping of feminism capable of a counter-hegemonic politics adequate to our times.

It is possible that in this essay this concern has not allowed us to focus richly enough on the democratic potential of actually existing feminism. Yet it is clearly this potential that both demands and empowers the kind of critical engagement evident in our argument. It is also precisely this democratic potential that has enabled us as feminists to support Dalit movements or take part in anti-communal initiatives today. By confronting the specific genealogy of the woman-subject and its impress on contemporary politics, we have tried also to open up for investigation the subject of democracy-secularism in India.

Notes

1. This chapter has appeared as an article entitled 'Problems for a Contemporary Theory of Gender', in Shahid Amin and Dipesh Chakrabarty (eds.), *Subaltern Studies IX: Writings on South Asian History and Society*, New Delhi: Oxford University Press, 1996, pp. 232–60.
2. We use 'Mandal' to refer to the anti-Mandal (anti-reservation) agitation, 'Mandir' to refer to the Ramjanmabhoomi movement to build a Ram temple in Ayodhya-Faizabad, and 'Fund-Bank' to refer to the era of structural adjustment policies promoted in India by the International Monetary Fund and the World Bank.

3 For a relevant discussion of the metaphysics of substance and the question of rights, see Mary Poovey, 'The Abortion Question and the Death of Man', in Joan Scott and Judith Butler (eds.), *Feminists Theorize the Political*, London: Routledge, 1991.
4 The historical emergence of the citizen-subject in India has been explored in the impressive work of scholars like Kumkum Sangari, Uma Chakravarti, Lata Mani, Partha Chatterjee, Gyanendra Pandey, and others. See Kumkum Sangari, 'Relating Histories: Definitions of Liberty, Literature, Gender in Nineteenth-Century Calcutta and England', in Svati Joshi (ed.), *Rethinking English: Essays in Literature, Language, History*, New Delhi: Trianka, 1991; K. Sangari and Sudesh Vaid, 'Introduction', in K. Sangari and S. Vaid (eds.), *Recasting Women: Essays in Colonial History*, New Delhi: Kali for Women, 1989; Uma Chakravarti, 'What Happened to the Vedic Dasi? Orientationalism, Nationalism and Script for the Past'; Lata Mani, 'Contentious Traditions: The Debate on Sati in Colonial India'; Partha Chatterjee, 'The Nationalist Resolution of the Women's Question', all in *Recasting Women*; Gyanendra Pandey, *The Construction of Communalism in Colonial North India*, New Delhi: Oxford University Press, 1990.
5 For fine account of how Satyajit Ray effects the consolidation of this human, citizen-subject in the freshly minted realism of the Apu trilogy, see Geeta Kapur, 'Cultural Creativity in the First Decade: The Example of Satyajit Ray', *Journal of Arts and Ideas*, Vol. 23 No. 4, January 1993, pp. 17–50.
6 These activities were designed to signify that meritorious men and women, who would otherwise occupy white-collar positions, would be forced as a result of the reservations policy to earn a menial's livelihood.
7 *Indian Express*, September 29, 1990.
8 Veena Das, *Statesman*, September 3, 1990.
9 *Independent* editorial, October 4, 1990.
10 In a public lecture on caste in modern India, delivered at the University of Hyderabad, January 1992.
11 *The Daily*, October 11, 1990.
12 The media always uses the term 'caste groups' or 'caste organisations' to refer to lower-caste groups. As K. Satyanarayana has pointed out, 'caste' usually refers only to lower caste.
13 *Free Press Journal*, October 15, 1990.
14 Seethe articles in *Recasting Women* by Partha Chatterjee and Uma Chakravarti, as well as the introduction to Susie Tharu and K. Lalitha (eds.), *Women Writing in India: 600 BC to the Present*, Vol. II, New York: Feminist Press, 1993.
15 That 'this student movement' 'articulates political processes that lie outside the domain of organized politics' was Veena Das's characterisation of the anti-Mandal agitation in 'A Crisis of Faith', *Statesman*, September 3, 1990.
16 Sangari and Vaid (eds.), *Recasting Women*, p. 5.
17 Jyoti Malhotra, *The Independence*, August 23, 1990.
18 We base this narrative of the events on Samata Sanghatana's report, published in *Economic and Political Weekly*, Vol. XXVI No. 36, 1991, pp. 2079–84.
19 For this information, we are indebted to K. Balagopal's report, 'Post-Chunduru and Other Chundurus', *Economic and Political Weekly*, Vol. XXVI No. 42, 1991, pp. 2399–405.
20 *Statesman*, August 9, 1991.
21 See Report of the Commission of Inquiry into the *Rameeza Bee and the Ahmed Hussain Case*, Government of Andhra Pradesh, 1978, and Tanika Sarkar, 'Reflections on Birati Rape Cases: Gender Ideology in Bengal', *Economic and Political Weekly*, Vol. XXVI No. 5, 1991, pp. 215–18.
22 Tanika Sarkar, 'The Women as Communal Subject: Rashtrasevika Samiti and Ram Janmbhoomi Movement', *Economic and Political Weekly*, Vol. XXVI No. 35, August 31, 1991, p. 2062. Henceforth cited as TS.
23 Each one of the office bearers of the Rashtrasevika Samiti, Tanika Sarkar points out, denounced sati. What about voluntary sati? 'A young activist said with genuine revulsion: *Who ho nahin sakta. Aur jalengi Kyun?*' (That can never happen. Why would a woman burn herself?) Shakha members do not use their caste names and everybody eats together. The

Samiti is not against inter-caste or even inter-community marriage – provided the families agree (ibid.).
24 TS 2061.
25 Pradip Datta, Biswamoy Pati et al., 'Understanding Communal Violence: Nizammuddin Riots', *Economic and Political Weekly*, Vol. XXV No. 45, November 10, 1990, p. 2494.
26 TS 2062.
27 *Times of India,* December 12, 1992.
28 *Sunday,* December 20–26, 1992, p. 9.
29 *Indian Express,* December 26, 1992. The Left Front government in West Bengal distinguished itself at the time of the Bantala and Birati rapes by very similar evasions. See Sarkar, 'Reflections on the Birati Rape Cases'.
30 TS 2062.
31 Government Order (G. O.) No. 402 dated April 24, 1993. Announcing the ban, Vijayabhaskara Reddy said that total prohibition was the 'policy of the Congress Party right from the start' and the ban had nothing to do with the crusade launched by the Telugu Desam.
32 They use the word 'Romantic' as shorthand for the free, agentive, expressive, spontaneous rebel subject typical of the nineteenth-century literary-cultural movement of Romanticism.
33 *The Hindu,* October 20, 1992.
34 *The Hindu,* October 12, 1992.
35 Kancha Ilaiah, 'Andhra Pradesh's Anti-Liquor Movement', *Economic and Political Weekly,* Vol. XXVII No. 43, 1992, p. 2408.
36 *The Hindu,* October 16, 1992. There are interesting parallels with the anti-Mandal agitation, which many intellectuals acclaimed as a manifestation of nationalism, the same time warning against any attempt to 'politicise' it.
37 *Nalupu,* October 1–3, 1992.
38 Film actress Sharada, in *Eenadu,* October 5, 1992.
39 *Nalupu,* October 1–31, 1992.
40 'The tears of thousands of families are pushing them into the struggle', says the actress Sharada, in *Eenadu,* October 5, 1992.
41 *Eenadu,* October 5, 1992.
42 Justice Arula Sambasiva Rao, in *Eenadu,* October 6, 1992.
43 *Indian Express,* October 13, 1992.
44 *Indian Express,* October 15, 1992.
45 *Eenadu* editorial, October 25, 1992.
46 Based on personal conversation with CPM members.
47 *Nalupu,* November 1–15, 1992.
48 *Eenadu* editorial, September 13, 1992.
49 Ibid.
50 See, for instance, civil liberties activist K. Balagopal's, 'Slaying of a Spirituous Demon', *Economic and Political Weekly,* Vol. XXVII No. 46, 1992, pp. 2457–61.
51 The phrase is from the AP Civil Liberties Committee press statement, issued by K. G. Kannabiran and K. Balagopal, *Eenadu,* September 18, 1992.
52 Suman Krishna Kant, Mahila Dakshata Samiti chair, in *Eenadu,* October 3, 1992.
53 *Eenadu* editorial, October 25, 1992.
54 K. Balagopal's, 'Laying of a Spirituous Demon', *Economic and Political Weekly,* November 14, 1992, p. 2457.
55 We were part of a team sent to Nellore by Anveshi Research Centre for Women's Studies, Hyderabad. Our account of the movement draws heavily on the Anveshi report of the visit.
56 *Chanduru Velugu* and *Akshara Deepam* literacy primers. We are grateful to T. S. S. Lakshmi and K. Sajaya for providing translations of the lessons.

57 A popular anti-Mandal refrain was that educational opportunities for lower-caste people would wean them away from their traditional occupations, turn them into clerks, and thereby destroy the handcrafts and textiles that symbolised Indian culture.
58 We take this phrase from Kumkum Sangari's well-known article, 'The Politics of the Possible', reprinted in Tejaswini Niranjana, P. Sudhir, and Vivek Dhareshwar (eds.), *Interrogating Modernity: Culture and Colonialism in India*, Calcutta: Seagull Books, 1993.

3
INDIAN FEMINISM AND 'DALIT PATRIARCHY'

Dalit patriarchy: excerpted from 'Dalit Women Talk Differently'[1]

Gopal Guru

Besides th[e] external factors, there are certain internal factors that have prompted Dalit women to organise separately *vis-a-vis* Dalit men. In the post-Ambedkar period, Dalit leaders have always subordinated, and at times suppressed, an independent political expression of Dalit women. This political marginalisation has been openly condemned by Dalit women at the regional conferences of Dalit women and at the Delhi meet.[2]

It is not only in the political arena that Dalit women face exclusion. In the cultural field, for instance, Dalit women have criticised their male counterparts for dominating the literary scene. Dalit writers do not take serious note of the literary output of Dalit women and tend to be dismissive of it. Dalit women rightly question why they are not considered for the top positions in Dalit literary conferences and institutions. This dissent brings three things to the fore: (1) It is not only caste and class identity but also one's gender positioning that decides the validity of an event; (2) Dalit men are reproducing the same mechanisms against their women which their high caste adversaries had used to dominate them; (3) the experience of Dalit women shows that local resistance within Dalits is important. The whole situation compels us to defend the claim that Dalit women talk differently.

Firstly, defended independent assertion of Dalit women should not be viewed by Dalit men as divisive; instead, it ought to be seen as carrying positive emancipatory potential. It can lead to a meaningful engagement of their creative energies. Secondly, the autonomous mobilisation of Dalit women can also be understood from an epistemological standpoint. This perspective maintains that the less powerful members of a society have a more encompassing view of social reality than others because their disadvantaged position grants them a certain epistemic privilege over others. It has to be noted that though there are some non-Dalit women activists sensitive to the caste dimensions of women's exploitation, their stand has remained ambivalent regarding the critique of caste.

§

Dalit patriarchy: excerpted from *Gendering Caste: Through a Feminist Lens*[3]

Uma Chakravarti

Other Dalit thinkers have also argued that women are less oppressed within the Dalit castes because there is less of the burden of the pativrata ideology among Dalit women who do not regard their husbands as 'hounoured' beings who must be respected at all times. Upper-caste women's own respect is derived from the respectability of their men, whereas Dalit women have less of a derivative position. Codes of *izzat* – honour, respect and shame – imply further that upper-caste women cannot really reveal the experiences of oppression that they may have to live with. Such codes of maintaining a discreet silence, no matter what is happening inside the family, do not have the same bearing among Dalit women. However, it is not as if patriarchies do not exist among the Dalit castes, or that Dalit women do not have to struggle against the patriarchies within their own communities. In the words of Swaroopa Rani,

> *When has my life been truly mine?*
> *In the home male arrogance*
> *Sets my cheek stinging,*
> *While in the street caste arrogance*
> *Splits the other cheek open.*[4]

§

Dalit patriarchy: excerpted from *Patriarchy*[5]

V. Geetha

There have been other attempts to think through caste and gender, notably the idea of 'Dalit' patriarchy. There are two different arguments here: the one notes that Dalit men have as much a stake in masculinity as other men. A notable feature of the exploitation of Dalits has been the humiliation of Dalit men: in the course of the power that upper-caste men exert over their labour, they also taunt them about their masculinity. They claim that Dalit men can never hope to protect their women, who are considered 'easy prey' by upper-caste men. Such symbolic 'emasculation' of Dalit men results in their feeling beleaguered in specifically gendered ways, which results in their exerting prowess in their families. The second argument accepts the premises of the first, but notes that apart from remaining 'masculine' within, Dalit men also seek to express their covert anger at the humiliation they are forced to endure by seeking to tease upper-caste women.

Whatever might have been the differences between Dalit women's experience of patriarchy and that of upper-caste women, the process of sanskritisation or 'jatikarana' – intensified castification – led to upper-caste norms and upper-caste patriarchal practices percolation into the lower-caste ranks too. Dalit women experience patriarchal oppression in unique as well as in shared ways. Given that the oppressions of both caste and patriarchy mark the lives of Dalit women in particular ways, it is not surprising that this situation has led Dalit women to take the position that they need their own women's organisation. In furtherance of this objective the Dalit Women's Federation, a national-level organisation, was set up in the 1990s.

Notes

1. An excerpt from the article 'Dalit Women Talk Differently', published in *Economic and Political Weekly*, Vol. 30 No. 41/42, October 14–21, 1995, pp. 2548–550, 2549.
2. National Federation of Dalit Women was formed on Aug 11, 1995, following the Beijing conference.
3. An excerpt from *Patriarchy*, Kolkata: Stree, 2009, pp. 108–9.
4. An excerpt from *Gendering Caste: Through a Feminist Lens*, Kolkata: Stree, 2013, first published in 2003, pp. 83–88.
5. Challapalli Swaroopa Rani, 'Dalit Women's Writing in Telugu', *Economic and Political Weekly*, Vol. 38 No. 17, 1998.

PART II
Predecessors of Dalit feminism

Part II includes three chapters presenting foundations for Dalit feminism from the history of India, with a focus on their contemporary relevance. The feminist pursuits of B.R. Ambedkar, Jyotiba Phule and Pandita Ramabai offer mechanisms to achieve the goal of social justice by emphasising gender justice. Although located in different social identities and time-frames, each of them realised that our aspirations to develop an overall gender-just society can never be actualised unless and until we bring the caste question into view. They paid specific attention to *Dalit* women's upliftment in order to promote the base of an empowered womanhood within highly patriarchal Indian society. Such insights not only make feminist efforts fruitful but also establish a paradigm for later generations of feminists to learn from their pursuits.

Unlike the representatives of dominant Indian feminism who lexically prioritise gender over caste, Ramabai-Phule-Ambedkarite feminist approaches seek to unearth the roots of patriarchal practices from within broader Indian culture and history. In doing so, they exposed the brahmanical nature of Indian patriarchy. Much of their work reflects upon and combats brahminism precisely as an effort to resolve the peculiar problems of gender injustice in India. In this more expansive project, they observed that the core of brahminism is to keep knowledge far from women and Dalits, and to reserve it for male brahmins, in order to stabilise the hierarchical social system. This is why Ramabai, Phule, Ambedkar and other predecessors emphasised the education and learning of *all* Indian women as a precondition for them to flourish as intelligent, independent, confident, assertive and active agents. They believed that such an empowered womanhood was necessary for building the foundation of an overall just-society, one where no woman of any caste would get systematically left behind.

Evincing that Dalit feminism has long been an important part of Indian history, Shailaja Paik (Chapter 4) attempts to forge a new 'Dalit womanhood' by fusing

64 Predecessors of Dalit feminism

the Phule-Ambedkarite feminist perspective with contemporary Dalit women's assertive agency. Wandana Sonalkar (Chapter 5) presents the history and evolution of the Dalit feminist standpoint by rethinking the feminist approaches of Ramabai and Ambedkar specifically in terms of highlighting the participation of Dalit women within their activism. Sharmila Rege (Chapter 6) champions the utility and significance of Ambedkarite feminism in the present context, cautioning against mainstream feminists' appropriation of the caste question in gender pursuits hinting at 'brahmanical surveillance'.

We must keep Rege's caution clearly in view today, as 'Indian feminists' launch on the project of including caste within their feminist enterprises. As mainstream Indian feminists treat more and more issues such as caste-based politics, debates over the practices of bardancing, prostitution and 'unorganised' labour, we should keep in mind that the women whose experiences are being theorised and whose fate is being determined are predominantly Dalit women. Hence we must ensure that we consistently scrutinise the methods and approaches of such articulation.

4

DALIT WOMEN'S AGENCY AND PHULE-AMBEDKARITE FEMINISM[1]

Shailaja Paik

Dalit women's modern and strategic subjectivity and agential capacities emerged out of the exigencies of the immense, discontinuous and shifting political situation, and from their complex everyday negotiation with Dalit men's ambivalences and civilisational and cultural anxieties as well as with elite feminism's discourse and power of exclusions, erasures and repressions. It is their historical experience of the modern: of life's possibilities and pitfalls, the socio-economic developments as well as the momentous subjective transformations that shaped their lives on the individual and group levels and concomitantly thwarted their creative potential. In a sharp contrast to the upper-caste elite agenda for education to embellish the 'softer' virtues of beauty, submission, compassion and kindness in women and to instruct them in self-refinement, Phule, Ambedkar and the larger Dalit community urged women to gain every possible educational qualification to develop self-esteem, self-confidence, determinacy and daring in order to channel their agency effectively towards cleansing the community as well as striking at the roots of caste and gender oppression.

Ambedkar did not conceive of a struggle for Dalit rights and uplift that did not involve women's education and emancipation. Tackling Dalit patriarchy was an integral part of this battle for women's self-development. Yet there were complications, because these male-centred efforts were also contradictory and ambiguous. Paradoxically, while Dalit radicals attempted to restore agency and dignity to Dalit women, they also restricted them to an extent by emphasising their central role in the family. Nevertheless, on the whole, these articulations and practices enabled Dalit women's individual and collective agency.

We see that Dalit women fought the contradictions between the rhetoric of elite, brahmani agenda of education as well as liberal feminism and their practices and forged a new political consciousness. This chapter deepens it further by dealing with the politicisation around gender reforms and education within the

Dalit community itself. There were significant connections as well as contradictions between Dalits and upper castes. Dalits' cultural anxiety, combined with the agenda of modernity and education, embraced upper-caste, middle-class ideas and practices to an extent, yet also radically departed from them in many different ways. Instead of dwelling on merely modernising, Dalits actually sought to deeply democratise; that is, to emphasise egalitarian gender relations and undercut privilege.

How then did Dalit radicals resolve the actual 'Dalit woman's question'? How did they negotiate their contradictions between confining women to the private sphere and pulling them into the public sphere? How did Dalit women make sense of their communities' and their own identities and educational experiences, and understand their beliefs about civic inclusion through educational opportunities? How did they live at the intersection of vast systems of power, patriarchy, caste and colonialism? In these processes, what did Dalit women gain and lose?

I answer these questions by investigating the kinds of uncertainty, anxiety and authority that underwrote Dalits' experiments in achieving a certain modernity. Dalits negotiated with the liberal-rationalist version of modernity and transformed its meaning to serve their own purposes relevant to their specific circumstances. However, by emphasising equality between different castes and male and female genders they engaged in practices of democratisation and went beyond merely modernising and creating a 'liberal' space for middle-class women. As a result, Phule and Ambedkar appropriated forces of modern power and sought to arrange and rearrange social and political conditions (both discursive and non-discursive) so as to oblige Dalit women to reform their subjectivities, make choices within constraints and transform themselves for *sudhaaranaa* (improvement). In the process, the micro-technologies of governmentality and power polished, disciplined and 'civilised' Dalit women while simultaneously restricting them.

By illustrating how Dalit political and cultural anxieties coalesced particularly around the bodies of Dalit women, I reveal that Dalits' struggle for education, equality, freedom and power became intimately connected with the politics of radically remaking Dalit women as historical subjects and transgressive agents of social reform. This 'self-making' of Dalit women was not like the 'recovery' of women's subjectivities that some feminists have rehearsed well in the context of upper-caste, elite women.[2] Moreover, Dalit women were also not merely 'humble interpreters of a supernatural leader's vision', as the historian Pandey has recently suggested.[3]

I challenge the dominant renderings of mainstream historiography of both India and the women's movement, which cast Dalit women as the 'labouring poor' or 'unfortunate and lowly'. Scholarship is divided on interpreting Dalit women's lives: they are either looked upon as those 'broken', 'terribly thrashed' or who have 'smash(ed) the prisons'.[4] I prise open the gap between the two sets of scholarships and dichotomies to emphasise how Dalit women cannot be confined to such linear readings. Rather, I focus on the complexity of Dalit women's subjectivities as both victims and agents: their struggles against victimhood shaped their selves and agency. Unlike middle-class, upper-caste women, Dalit women have never figured as subjects or agents in historical accounts of either anti-colonial nationalist struggle or of gender reforms. Some historians and feminist scholars have worked on the theoretical and compounded nature of caste and gender (for example, Gail Omvedt, Uma Chakravarti, Pratima Pardeshi, Sharmila Rege, Anupama Rao and Wandana Sonalkar); however, they have yet to study how these entangled oppressions affected the lived and everyday experiences of Dalit female entrants in schools. Moreover, by dealing with the shaping of Dalit women's ideas of family and wider society, I examine the intricate processes of the construction of ordinary Dalit women's subjectivities.

I emphasise Phule's and Ambedkar's creative roles in radically democratising gender norms. As a result, gender emerged as a generative process to imagine 'new' forms of public emancipation. The two leaders reconceptualised the shifting, porous and entangled nature of public and private realms, and pioneered struggles for women's education, rights and status within both the community and the wider society. They articulated interlocking technologies of education, caste, gender, community, moral reforms and sexuality in a particular historical and political conjuncture. While it is tempting to read the two radical men as feminists,[5] we need to also look at the ways in which they are indeed analysing gender deeply rather than confining it to a narrow feminist agenda. The feminism of colonial times, especially of the early twentieth century, was a constrained project that focused on granting women limited access to the public sphere, education and political participation. Like Phule and Ambedkar, many imperial and indigenous feminists and upper-caste men worked to dismantle hegemonic structures; however, unlike the former, the latter did not seek actual parity with men.[6] In the fraught process of challenging some inequities, some reformers actually produced them anew.

Moreover, Phule's and Ambedkar's work for women's education attracts far less scholarly interest than that of brahmin educators like D.K. Karve or Pandita Ramabai.[7] Scholars have also done little to study the potential connections between public institutions such as education and private realms like the family, gender, marriage and sexuality in the context of the Dalit community.

Formal schools not only trained Dalit men and later women, but refashioning women became the reason for making education central. Dalit women's construction as 'custodians' of the community also reinforced their creative social role as 'subjects' of social reform. The question of women's liberation was central to Dalit political and social programmes. By centring on women's education and self-making, Dalits departed from elite, brahmani norms, which were initially against women's education. Even later, when education was extended to women, brahmins restricted it and prescribed an instrumental agenda of education. Yet Dalits imitated some brahmani patriarchal norms. However, these processes were fractured. Dalits' insistence on patriarchal values was complicated and shifting because they negotiated, and only selectively appropriated, bourgeois values. At the same time, by constructing Dalit women as historical agents with real and political, not just symbolic, value (such as in the Hindu nationalist gender discourse), Dalits radically departed from caste-Hindu norms. Nonetheless, in the process, Dalit radicals seemed to tighten patriarchal restrictions on women; this held unsettling implications for Dalit women, whose place in the body politic remained contested and uncertain. Due to the numerous tensions and shifting combinations of acceptance and rejection of caste and gender hierarchies, Dalit women were (and are) burdened by male reformers' anxieties and contradictions around gender.

In this chapter, I analyse the historically contingent discursive practices that shaped Dalit women's political consciousness from the early decades of the twentieth century. The first section deals with Phule's articulation of the interlocking technologies of knowledge, caste and gender as they operated on bahujan (non-brahmin and Dalit) women's bodies. The second focuses on education, gender and moral reforms from 1880 to 1920 to unravel Dalit radicals' anxieties about female sexuality. In their battle for higher social status, Dalit reformers also sought the authority to control the sexuality of stigmatised women, as we see in the murali reform. Finally, the last section focuses on Dalit women's radical and effective activism and its constraints.

I want to reiterate that, unlike upper-caste elite women, Dalit women did not write for or publish magazines of their own during that period. Most of the time, I have had to understand their views and lives through the vision and ideas of male reformers who wrote regularly for printed Dalit newspapers and periodicals. Women had only begun to express themselves in writing and did not systematically publish their views.

Phule's *Trutiya Ratna*: contesting knowledge, caste and gender differences

Phule forcefully attacked the interconnectedness of knowledge, human rights, untouchability, caste and gender by starting schools for both: untouchables in 1848 and widows' homes for brahmin women in 1854. In contrast with the upper-caste agenda of producing modest helpmeets, Phule sought to identify knowledge as the trutiya ratna (literally the 'third jewel'). In his first political play, titled *Trutiya Ratna*,[8] Phule deployed the jewel as a metaphor for the third eye, which would help knowledge-seeking women to examine oppressive social relations and the multiple operations of brahmani hegemony.[9] Thus the ratna would be an important weapon especially for non-brahmin and Dalit women and men to strike at the roots of caste, gender and educational oppression. It would also help bahujan women to fight against double patriarchy, both within their homes and outside. Towards this end, and to challenge the brahmin monopoly on education, Phule opened his first school for low-caste girls in 1848 in Pune, the orthodox seat of power.

Reinforcing Jotirao's efforts, his wife Savitribai Phule devoted her life to working for women's education and against caste practices. Along with her husband, Savitribai underscored the significance of challenging caste endogamy and also suggested an anti-caste, bahujan alliance of all women and Shudras and Ati-Shudras against brahminism. The Phules thus challenged brahmani practices as they discriminated against lower castes and restricted the sexuality of upper-caste women. Advancing her teacher's efforts, Muktabai Salve, a 14-year-old Mang girl in Phule's classroom in 1855, wrote about the 'Grief of Mang-Mahars'. In her essay Muktabai exposed the deep social stratification in society and criticised brahmani domination. She also questioned God's deployment of caste differentiation: 'You have given the Vedas to Brahmans and nothing to us?'[10] She further examined the kroor (cruel) attitude of brahmins towards Mang-Mahars, using 'Mang-Mahars' as a combined community.

Most significantly, Muktabai lamented lower castes' exclusion from specific forms of textual knowledge. In fact, she ended her essay by pleading to Mang-Mahars to study hard in order to open their trutiya ratna. Trutiya ratna, the tool of critical thinking, would help them to analyse their oppressed lives under brahmani hegemony as well as patriarchy. Seeking education was akin to building critical consciousness in women to bring about social change. Like her teacher Phule and other Dalit women, Muktabai insisted that education would end brahmins' ill treatment of Shudra-Ati-Shudras.

While comparing the reproductive labour of Dalit and brahmin women, Muktabai underscored the particularities of the experiences of Dalit women: 'Our women give birth to babies and they do not even have a roof over their heads. How they suffer rain and cold! Try to think about it from your own experiences'.[11] In other words, Muktabai asked, 'Aren't Dalit women 'women' who suffer the pains of womanhood?', thereby implicating the reader. Muktabai thus subverted the strategies of both nationalists and elite women who passed the burden of eradicating untouchability and caste oppression on to Dalit women alone. Rather, by making a moral and political appeal to upper castes, she, like Ambedkar and Gandhi, attempted to return the burden of caste to them. Her particularly powerful script teaches us to connect the personal details of experiences with structural oppressions in gender and caste politics in order to analyse the specific hurdles of Dalit women. Significantly, Muktabai revealed the contradiction between the ideological myths of genteel (Hindu) womanhood and the particular realities of Dalit women's everyday struggles. We can not afford to ignore how she theorised her ordinary personal experiences of pain by tying them to systemic phenomena: the anatomy of caste, class, knowledge and gender hierarchies, local economy and power relationships. In a similar vein, Phule critiqued upper-caste brahminism, articulating brilliantly the overlapping and graded ways in which brahmani patriarchy exploited women of different castes.[12] Moreover, by analysing how interlocking technologies, or the matrix of caste and gender oppressions, interacted to shape the multiple oppressions of non-brahmin, labouring Kunbi and Dalit women, Phule's analysis introduced a feminist framework of 'intersectionality'.[13] He analysed that the fundamental differences between lower- and upper-caste women sprang from possession of material resources – the burden of work and the particular difficulties – of Dalit-Bahujan women, in contrast with the (brahmin) Bhat women who had servants to attend to their needs.[14] However, to him, the brahmin woman was also oppressed by the brahmin man. Hence, although gender seemed the fundamental basis for women's oppression, its entanglement with caste created severe problems for lower-caste women.

Most significantly, in his *Sarvajanik Satyadharma Pustak* (Book of the Universal Philosophy of Truth), published in 1891, Phule addressed *sarva ekandar streepurush* (that is, all women and men together), and analysed the material aspects of women's oppression. He declared that women were indeed *sreshtha* (superior) to men.[15] He questioned:

> Have you ever heard of a Brahman widower performing sataa? They can marry many times, [but] the same is not allowed to women. When a married woman dies, her old, worn-out, decrepit widower marries ignorant maidens and ruins their youth. However, men have produced strict strictures and practices not to allow girls to re-establish marital relations for the second time. If you [men] do not like women's practice of marrying two to three times, how will women accept such filthy behaviour from men? Because women and men are capable of enjoying all *maanavi adhikaar* [human rights], it is discriminatory to have different standards for women and for *dhurt* [cunning] and *dhaadasi* [bold] men. As a result, women's rights are usurped by men, and of course the reverse will not apply. This has happened due to some daring men's selfish fabrications of the religious books. The other castes [like sonaars, goldsmiths] also follow the Brahmans and subject women to the same miseries.[16]

Thus, Phule emphasised the double standards of brahmin men and their religion as well as the reproduction of women's oppression among non-brahmins. He argued that while men frolicked with prostitutes and mistresses, they enforced fidelity for women. He further explained that the causes of the secondary position of women and untouchables were not their naturally inferior physical strength (as some upper castes believed),[17] but because they were not as *dhaadasi* (bold) as the *lobhi aani dhurt Aryabhat* (greedy and cunning brahmin) men, as well as their lack of knowledge. According to Phule, it was due to the '*kavebaji* [cunning] of Aryabhat Brahmin [men] who do not allow Shudra-Ati-Shudras to even look at or listen to their granths'.[18]

Phule diagnosed the situation of women in similar terms, using the term *streejaat*, which combines the roots *stree* (woman) with *jaat* (caste):

> Since *streejaat* (woman-caste) is very *abalaa* [lacking strength and vulnerable], *lobhi* [avaricious] and *dhaadasi* [daring] men with great cunning have never consulted women, and in general all men have always dominated them. Since they did not want them to understand *maanavihakka* [human rights], they denied them *vidya* [knowledge]. Due to this all women are oppressed.[19]

In this manner, Phule affirmed that crafty brahmin men conspired to exclude women from education and human rights, and poured *julum* (tyranny) on them. Moreover, they reproduced a similar strategy and denied knowledge to Shudra Ati-Shudras in order to maintain their dominance.[20] History shows how they have established their claim to 'purity' by 'othering' women. Yet, as we see, some brahmin women consented to and supported brahmin men. Hence, for Phule, if women and untouchables wanted real *sattaa* (power) they would have to seek education and fight brahminism. His agenda was reinforced and revised in Ambedkar's programme of education in the twentieth century.

Phule was the first revolutionary to insist on using the term *streepurush* (women-men). He thus underscored women and men's equality and their claims to common human rights as well as emphasising gender differentiation instead of a gender-neutral unity, as underscored by upper-caste elites. In a sharp contrast to the upper-caste agenda of schooling women in traditional patriarchy, proper deportment, correct ritual, and domestic practice and *sanskruti* (culture), Phule's and Ambedkar's radical technologies underlined the construction of intellectual and moral superiority. They thus challenged the idea of the natural endowment of mental faculties on brahmins. They also instilled in women the agency to dismantle hegemonic control and consent. Middle-class Hindu and Muslim men were ambivalent about higher education for women and allowed limited agency for them to function in a well-marked domestic sphere while upholding brahmani hegemony. Unlike them, however, Dalit radicals supported Dalit women's pursuits in higher education and advertised their academic achievements widely.

Although some women thus challenged brahmani patriarchy, many brahmin women, like Anandibai Joshi and Ramabai Ranade, also implicitly consented to it by agreeing with male reformers' ideals of companionate wives and the patriarchal practices laid down for them. Women were to be modern, but modest and mellow. Although Pandita Ramabai challenged both reformist and nationalist patriarchal agendas, which robustly reinforced each other, her object of reform remained the high-caste Hindu woman. She was a pioneering feminist who attacked the alliance between local patriarchal elites and their colonial counterparts, but at the same time she also borrowed to an extent from the discourse of dominant Hindu nationalism.[21] Yet Phule supported her and asserted her rights because she challenged brahmani orthodoxy by converting to Christianity in 1883.[22]

Phule envisioned an emancipatory *Bali rajya*, the kingdom of the non-brahmin king Bali, which was grounded in equality, dignity and freedom and included all humans, whatever their gender or caste.[23] He also revised marriage rituals and underscored a Satyashodhak marriage ceremony that called upon men to be considerate of a woman's need for knowledge, dignity, respect and freedom, and bound them with a *pratidnya* (oath and agreement).[24] He challenged practices of child marriage and enforced widowhood.[25] Thus Phule consistently attacked the dominance of men and of brahmani social structures, and emphasised male-female equality because he was concerned with the position, rights, identity, desires and emotions of women. The conversations and debates around the 'woman's question' grew sharper in the early decades of the twentieth century, when Dalits encountered modernity in multiple ways.

Morality, modernity and reform before 1920

Dalit activists challenged both external colonial rule and upper castes' internal colonialism. When the nationalists were increasingly working to incorporate the 'others' (lower castes, women, Muslims), upwardly mobile non-brahmin and Dalit radicals critiqued brahmin power and hegemony, which they argued had stunted their *vyaktivikaas* (individuated advancement). While both non-brahmin and Dalit radicals vied for educational and employment opportunities, they also emphasised their families' education, health and moral discipline. Dalit radicals interrogated false dichotomies like public versus private and masculinity versus femininity and transcended them by organising women and asserting their autonomy. The household was an economic and domestic realm, but it was also tied to the interests of the community. Hence, it was impossible to show where 'private' relations ended and 'public' relations began, since both were imbricated in the same total context. Dalit streepurush were helpmeets in private as they had been in public. In the process, the imagination of family with its affective and social and political relations, making the home a political space and reforming women and gender was critical to the discourse of Dalit emancipation. Thus, unlike upper castes, Dalit radicals centred their efforts on a double task: refashioning Dalit women and building their self-confidence as well as uplifting the community.

Non-brahmins and Dalits were indeed torn between emulating brahmani social and religious values and rejecting them to an extent. Similar to Hindu nationalists, they simultaneously exalted and subordinated women. They sought to challenge brahmani caste ideology along with importing and reproducing certain novel and even harsher patriarchal practices into their own households. Yet Dalits' insistence on patriarchal values was not as automatic as it might seem. Dalits were not involved in simple mimicry of upper-caste values practices, as some scholars believe. In fact Dalits 'negotiated' strategically every day; they selectively appropriated certain brahmani values, reshaping them constantly to produce spaces for themselves within the colonial Victorian and brahmani order.[26] This complicated, contingent and intentional everyday negotiation involving the dialectic of appropriation and subversion operated at every moment in the social, cultural, educational and political realms. The Dalit community was constantly in a process of making micro transformations through everyday negotiations.

In general, and due to the emergence of the 'new woman' paradigm of patriarchal nationalism in particular, elite women and men had always-already ostracised Dalit women as 'unrespectable', 'unruly' and 'other'. To attack such social constructions and stereotyping, Dalit radicals insisted on middle-class bourgeois respectability and honour: correct, 'cultured', decent manners; proper, full attire; propriety of behaviour; and sexuality standards that were stricter for women than for men. In an effort to decentre upper castes, Dalits embraced to an extent the gendered discourse of morality; women emerged as the principal means of asserting the rhetoric of moral superiority. Thus, echoing nationalists, the metaphoric deployment of womanhood and domesticity was tied to fashioning Dalit modernity, and women bore the burden, as icons or status markers of the community. Unlike the nationalists, however, women were agents to remake themselves and uplift the community. Although these tenuous processes were fractured, by emphasising the constitutive role of women and gender in its construction, Dalit radicals sought to politicise the community through a reform of education, family and female subjects. To gain bourgeois respectability they sought to control sexual relations and denounced the immoral lives of some *baatalelya* (stigmatised) women like muralis and prostitutes. By emphasising their prurient interests, they expressed an anxiety about women's sexuality. Dalit radicals also underlined that Dalit women's sexual violation continued due to communities' prevalent 'customs' of abandoning Dalit girls as muralis and jogtinis in the name of God.

As a result, in 1909, Shivram Janaba Kamble of Pune and other reformers petitioned the British government to intervene in the murali matter, to end the practice of dedicating Mahar-Mang girls to the god Khanderao (or Khandoba) as muralis (Government of Bombay 1909, 1913). Muralis married to God were obligated to provide sexual services to men of all castes. Dalit reformers thus expressed their cultural anxiety over unbounded female sexuality by starting a criminalisation campaign. Their disciplinary tone underscored monogamous marriage and sex within marriage as the norm. Anything outside the institution of marriage was 'deviant' behaviour and potentially criminal, to be punished by law. Many non-brahmins had already criticised the morality of upper-caste women as a strategy of resistance. Dalit radicals also negotiated with upper-caste hegemony by attempting to claim through gender reform the power denied to them by caste hierarchy, and valorised marriage and monogamy.

By adopting the popular medium of *jalsaa, powaadaa* and *tamaashaa*, Dalit troupes toured remote villages and modern cities and engaged in singing and music to bring about social change. In the process, however, Dalit radicals also sought to restrict celebration of the *jalsaa* to men so as to counter practices that they now considered immoral and degrading. They believed that by acting in such roles, Dalit women degraded the status of the Dalit community as a whole. Driven by a desire to 'modernise' their practices, they decried performance that they now considered 'backward'. In their battle for higher social status, Dalit reformers and the colonial state also sought the authority to control the sexuality of stigmatised women and criminalise their lifestyle, as we see in the *murali* reform of 1909. They thus sought to discipline and control the women of the Dalit community and thus one expression of their sexuality. This gave rise to a tangled politics of caste, untouchability, gender and moral reform in the colonial context. The logic of legal, bureaucratic and caste communities' regulation of *murali* sexuality was rooted in restructuring the self and based on modern middle-class sexual ethics.

Challenging the public redress and heavy and indignant censure from the press as deployed by Dalits and the colonial government, *muralis* like Shivubai Lakshman Jadhav provided in turn an internal critique by challenging the double standards of Dalit men. Shivubai declared that '*aamchyaavar tikaa karun haa prashna sutanaar naahi* [this question cannot be resolved by criticising us]'.[27] She in fact held fathers responsible for the continuation of such 'evil' practices and for *muralis*' lives of shame, something ignored by male reformers. Shivubai called for a campaign against Dalit fathers, arguing that their superstitious beliefs and ignorance pushed their daughters into such caste-based sexual labour.

However, Dalit streepurush continued to inspire eloquent exercises in shame and sexual morality by arguing for chaste and respectable Dalit womanhood to maintain the pride of the community. To them, muralis stigmatised the entire community. Hence, women like Anusayabai Kamble from Rasta Peth, Pune, for example, called upon the community 'to provide every small assistance to *muralis* and *bhutyas* for their remarriage and resettlement'.[28] Kamble saw marriage as the only 'respectable' option for muralis. Dalit women's self-disciplining and monitoring of the sexual subject would thus constitute a respectable and powerful Dalit identity, most significant for a degraded community. In the process, however, Dalits also reintroduced gender hierarchies because, unlike women, men could get away with wrongdoing. The construction of family oriented and chaste Dalit womanhood may, however, be read as Dalit radicals' effort to reclaim the morality of the community.

Historians have observed how the British constructed Indian men as 'weak' and 'lacking in manliness', even 'like women'. Indian elites challenged the colonial standpoint by arguing about Indian masculinity. Yet, while appropriating masculinity and historical subjectivity for themselves, upper-caste males in pre-colonial and colonial times deployed their internal colonialism within the colony by excluding Dalits (peasants, women, tribals) from history. They often stereotyped Dalit men as 'weak', 'stupid' and 'lacking self-discipline, intelligence, and manly virility'.[29] They also systematically disparaged and demonised low-caste Dalit women's sexuality to justify the nationalist movement, colonialism, casteism and racism. Both colonial and elite discourses and practices drew upon brahmani frameworks of patriarchal hegemony (and strict surveillance of upper-caste women's sexuality) to create a dichotomy between the (upper-caste) goddess and the (lower-caste) whore. They also constructed Dalit women as public property and legitimised upper-caste men's access to the sexual labour of Dalit women, thereby socially constructing female Dalit sexuality. Due to caste practices of distinction between *anuloma* (hypergamous) and *pratiloma* (hypogamous) marriages, brahmin and upper-caste men constructed dominant discourses which strengthened connections between upper castes and chastity. In the process, upper-caste men always-already had open access to lower-caste women, whereas upper-caste elite women were a sign of power, a guarded possession. As the feminist Gayle Rubin has argued, discourses of 'sexual morality [have] more in common with ideologies of racism than with true ethics [because they] grant virtue to already dominant groups'.[30]

In this manner, upper-caste men crafted differentiations of gender, caste and sexuality, and amplified their morality and caste power. They accused the brutalised Dalits of 'loose' sexuality and through their practices forced many Dalit women to provide sexual services to them as muralis. Thus there was/is a chasm between upper- and lower-caste morality and the concept of womanhood: purity as opposed to promiscuity and desire, normality as opposed to deviance, superiority as opposed to subservience, order as opposed to disorder. Dalits were aware of these discontinuities and the ensuing tensions. Neither were non-brahmins silent; they publicly criticised the morality of brahmin women as a strategy of resistance. Continuing to assert their morally superior public face and to challenge these brahmani codes, as well as to underscore normative conjugality, Dalit radicals strategically sought to withdraw some Dalit women from the sex market. For them, such 'unchaste' women represented the backwardness of Dalits; they attempted to assert their superiority over brahmins on this issue and to challenge their powerlessness.

Dalits negotiated with an upper-caste agenda of controlling women's sexuality and entrenching patriarchy by foregrounding institutions like family, marriage and chastity; yet they radically departed from it by interrupting upper-caste men's open access to Dalit women's sexual labour. Some scholars have argued that the impact of 'sanskritisation' entailed fresh restrictions for Dalit women as markers of higher social status.[31] Yet, as I have just revealed, this would be too simplistic an argument that obliterates Dalits' intentionality. Indeed, Dalit politics emerged out of negotiating the historically contingent and contrary experiences that required Dalit subjects not to imagine the succession of the past but to recognise unprecedented changes in their present and to build their future. In their struggle to appropriate modernity, at times they adopted strategies of sanskritisation without much success, but also refused to be its prisoners and confronted the uncontested assumption of the sexual availability of Dalit women. They subverted their disadvantages through movements for self-respect and political empowerment as well as engendering cultural transformation. They thus twisted and turned the master narrative of modernity by reformulating their positions and pasts within Indian society and politics.

Significantly, in these entangled processes, there were no binaries; Dalits were thus dominated and dominating at the same time. Dalits emphasised marriage and sexual monogamy. With this strategy of elevating Dalit women's chastity, however, they limited the earlier flexibility of Dalit women's domestic arrangements. Such strategies were significant to protect Dalit personhood and social progression, to protect their crumbling woman/manhood or even human rights, as well as to build the confidence and dignity of women and the community as a whole. Thus control of sexuality was related to practices of Dalits' social regulations and was important in regenerating and modernising their society. This was a means of asserting a morally superior face to the upper castes, but of course, this strategy came with costs.

In the 1920s and especially the 1930s, the 'woman question' penetrated the Dalit public sphere. Dalit women represented the most symbolic and guarded possession of some Dalit elites. They associated women's status and *ijjat* and *aabru* (honour, respectability) with that of the community. Their strategy was perhaps similar to Victorian/imperial feminists', to upper-caste ideologies and reform around the woman question in the late nineteenth and early twentieth centuries, and to the universal agenda of women's work for the community and the nation. In the last decades of the nineteenth century, imperial feminists authorised a redemptive role for women in both the private domain of the family and public work. In this debate they used the trope of women as the 'producers' of the nation; their moral superiority and responsibility was extended from domestic to national functions.[32]

To an extent, Ambedkar also shared the emancipation ideology of feminist debates and upheld Dalit women's gender roles as caretakers, transmitters of culture, class socialisers and civilisers of Dalit community. Similar to the nationalist and imperialist projects, he celebrated Dalit women's values of purity or chastity, honour, integrity and duty. Yet his construct of 'Dalit woman' both fits into this framework and radically departs from it in its attack on patriarchy within Dalit and non-Dalit communities. Most significantly, he challenged Dalit women through his writings, speeches and public activities, created possibilities, and worked for their individual and collective agency in order to be independent, organise effectively, uplift themselves and emancipate the Dalit community. In the process, Dalit women found a way to create agency, womanhood and a full humanity denied to them by both upper-caste elite nationalists and liberal feminists; they enacted their choices within constraints, and gained more, rather than less.

Dalit women's radical and effective activism

The arrival of modernity and process of democratisation among Dalits was both enabling and constraining. Women actively participated in the public political sphere at different levels. Chandrikabai Ramteke, Jaibai Chaudhari and Sulochanabai Dongre were fearless leaders in the All India Dalit Mahilaa Congress. In 1945 Jaibai was also a major activist of the Scheduled Caste Federation. She attended men's meetings, put forth her views candidly and counselled women on many topics.[33] Laxmibai Naik established an Untouchable Women's Society in 1921 in Amravati. Dadasaheb Gaikwad's daughters Seetabai, Ramabai and Geetabai were in the forefront of the Nasik's Kalaram temple-entry satyagraha of 1930. Ratibai Puranik was responsible for organising the first Sisters of the *Bahishkrut Bharat* Conference and worked for the wider distribution of Dalit journals.[34] Geetabai Pawar, an educated activist of the Matang community, and a teacher, along with Madhalebai and Mainabai, started a mahilaa mandal in 1932 and spread Ambedkar's message in Bheempura, Kamathipura and the Range Hill area in Pune. She clearly remembered her first speech trials at Seva Sadan, when Vitthal Ramji Shinde urged her to speak: 'I did not quite know what I was saying, but I could hear the sound of Modern Dalit women as agents clapping. Shinde patted me on the back'.[35] She took part in inter-caste common meals and believed in Ambedkar's movement and leadership. Mukta Sarvagod organised women in Mumbai's BDD chawls and established 19 women's associations. Anjanibai Deshbhratar organised a conference of untouchable girl students from Berar in the Nagpur Cotton Market from May 21 to 25, 1936. She was also instrumental in founding a hostel for Dalit girls. As a teacher she continued her participation in the liberation movement.

At this historical conjuncture of the 1930s, when the debate on separate electorates for Dalits was contested between Dalits, elite nationalists and the colonial government, another crucial question emerged on the issue of representation: who actually represented the Dalits? Contesting Gandhi's claim as the 'true leader of Dalits', Anjanibai and Radhabai Kamble attended a meeting held by the Untouchable Women's Reform Association at Imamwada on April 26, 1936, and resolved: 'Dr. Babasaheb Ambedkar is the true leader of the untouchable community, and we untouchable women will follow his footsteps and undertake reforms; this is our resolve'.[36] Women articulated their claims and made critical choices. Yet Ambedkar's claim to truly represent Dalits electorally was thwarted by Dalit sub-castes like Chambhars and Mangs, who contested his authority (as a Mahar) to represent the entire Dalit community. Thus the processes that sought to construct a united Dalit identity were also fractured along jati lines.

Indirabai Patil (1919–64) was general secretary of the All India Untouchable Women's Council when it held its annual conference on July 20, 1942. About 25,000 women attended. Dongre and Shantabai Dani were presidents of Women's Conferences of the All India Scheduled Castes Federation (AISCF) and enjoyed power, however limited. Dongre gave an inspiring speech in front of 25,000 women assembled from different parts of the country. She also attended the Women's Conference in Kanpur in 1944. Dani was also the chairperson of the Women's Council of the AISCF held in Kanpur in 1944 and was secretary of the SCF in Bombay Presidency.

Women thus gained political consciousness due to their direct and indirect involvement in campaigns, protests, demonstrations, satyagrahas, political debates, mahilaa mandals and social reform movement activities, for example, via the Bahishkrut Hitakarini Sabha. In 1946 the SCF candidate was Radhabai Kamble, who emerged as a workers' leader from Bardi. Although educated only until the fourth grade, she was adept at standing in front of thousands of people and delivering provocative and strong speeches. Once she also declared, 'We will win our rights whatever happens. If they don't give them to us we will grab them, take them by force, and snatch them away'.[37] While working in the ginning mill in Nagpur, Radhabai would stop the men and women as they came out of the gate and hold meetings outside the mill. Everyone would stand still and listen to her fiery speeches. Women held processions when there was injustice or violence against Dalits and shouted slogans such as 'The blue flag of the Dalits is dear to us and we want to become a ruling community'.[38] By participating in public meetings, women improved their confidence. Such a collective struggle allowed them to identify and support the larger Dalit community actively, particularly when the issue of separate electorates erupted. Parbatabai Meshram agreed that they 'gained knowledge of the outside world, they became aware of injustice, oppression, and insult, and a sense of identity awakened in them. They preferred to work for the society instead of sitting around and gossiping'.[39]

Dalit women also participated in the activities of the Samataa Sainik Dal (Army of Soldiers for Equality, SSD), formed in 1927. Ambedkar instituted the SSD, a disciplined youth wing, as a volunteer corps that initially organised meetings, rallies and conferences, house-to-house publicity campaigns, engaged in physical and psychological training, and sought to protect Dalits from physical attacks and intimidation. But after 1942 it took up a broader programme of confronting and resisting injustice, inequality and atrocities. The Sainiks wore red shirts and khaki pants and followed military discipline. Some Dalit radicals rhetorically questioned women about their contribution to the struggle and also requested that they participate in the Samataa Mahilaa Sainik Dal (Army of Women Soldiers for Equality, the women's wing of the SSD):

> Both men and women should work toward the progress of the community. Like men have volunteered enthusiastically, so should women, in order to bring about unnati (advancement). Women should be more organised than men. Times are changing and cultured men understand that women can equally contribute to the struggle. You have strength of character, patience, perseverance, and toughness, and the movement needs your contribution. Women should remember that it is time to show their stellar qualities and fight for their rights themselves. Similar to the Samataa Dal, women should also have a sainik dal. Women in other countries are progressing and so should Dalit women. Abandon the 'Untouchable' feeling that you are *heen* [deficient/inferior] and by *dhadaadi* [undertaking daring feats] you should resolve to assist Babasaheb's efforts. We are struggling for human rights, we should be able to get them and we should have the *paatrataa* [ability] to preserve them too. It is our duty to build that ability. Since we are fighting for our rights we should work on advancing our *yogyataa* [fitness/aptitude] to possess them and for this an organisation is needed. Why can't women volunteer with *utsaah* [enthusiasm] and *svayamsphurti* [self-motivation]? I ask all Untouchable women: don't sleep. Wake up. Throw away your old ideas and imaginations. Organise and reinforce the movement. On Babasaheb's next birthday he should be gifted with a magnificent salute by the Samataa Mahila Sainik Dal. Nischyane, chikaatine karyaas laagaa [start working resolutely and consistently], *kartutva gaajavaa* [make big achievements], and you will find yash [victory].[40]

Thus femininity and masculinity were (and are) shifting and unstable categories. At one level, by feminising patience, perseverance and toughness, Jangalgop almost reinforced Gandhian gendered attributes. Yet, like Ambedkar, he also wanted women to work in a masculine fashion by using resoluteness, dhadaadi, dhamak and nischay to their fullest abilities. As a result, more than 500 women marched 'in martial array like disciplined soldiers' at the start of the Nasik Satyagraha of 1930.[41]

Many women also actively supported the Hindu Code Bill. Women were the central core of the bill through which, by proposing reforming laws on property, marriage and divorce, Ambedkar sought to question the prevailing Hindu laws which were patriarchal, and denied women certain fundamental rights. Nalini Ladke, a teacher, was the chairperson of a Dalit women's conference held on February 29, 1949. Lakshmibai Naik, Arunadevi Pise and Hirabai Meshram made speeches at this meeting and also passed a resolution supporting the Hindu Code Bill. They challenged some brahmin men and women who opposed the bill[42] and resolved that hostels be set up for Dalit women and that they be provided with free education.[43] Women thus contested elections, participated in school committees, fought for landless labour, joined the Naamaantar movement to change the name of

Marathwada University to Dr Babasaheb Ambedkar University, and continuously challenged the hegemonic ruling communities and the state.

In this manner, Ambedkar challenged patriarchy in the everyday lives of women, yet he and his followers were also limited in creating a new anti-patriarchal consciousness. While many women played leading roles, others faced certain restrictions. Chandrika Ramteke recounted that, taking into account her public work for the movement, her husband shamefully accused her of going out '*navare karayala tithe*' (to make many husbands there).[44] Women faced enormous resistance from the men if they undertook organisational tasks. Sindhutai Pagare, Sushila Jadhav and Bhagatai Kaasare reported:

> We merely participated in programmes outlined by men. We were never *karyakarinichaa sadasyatva* (members of executive committees) or decision-makers and remained subservient to men in Dalit organisations like the Bauddhajan Panchayat Samiti, the Republican Party, and the Dalit Panthers [in post-Ambedkar times].[45]

Thus women complained that their roles were limited to preparing other women to participate in organisations, collecting dues, leading demonstrations, or *purushanna ovalanyapurtich* (honouring men).[46] The last act was a type of offering in which women waved a platter with light wicks around leaders' heads (to remove all troubles and evil) and garlanded them. Some women did not gain significant positions in male-dominated political spaces. The prescription of the 'mother model' entered the public domain and the workplace and curtailed the mobility, as well as equal opportunity and equal treatment, of women. In a move similar to an extent to imperial feminists and upper-caste nationalists, Ambedkar emphasised that *streejaat samajacha alankar aahe* (the woman-caste was a jewel of the community) and used the power of Dalit women.[47] He also maintained that 'educated women were to protect their *sheel* [virtues], understand their *kartavya* [responsibility], and work toward the community's advancement'.[48] To an extent, like Hindu nationalists, he constituted them as symbols of the modernisation of the Dalit community as a whole, yet he clearly departed from this characterisation to deploy them as agents, as levers to uplift the community.

Dalit radicals made women the guarantors of the transformed home, with the responsibility to protect and build a confident, masculine Dalit womanhood. Ambedkar and other Dalit activists had grasped the crisis that was emphasised by social stereotypes and colonial perceptions. In order to challenge the stereotypes about themselves, women and men resorted to asserting their masculinities in different ways: political activities, making demands in public spaces, cultural performances, and so on. Unlike Tilak and Gandhi, who were uncomfortable with women assuming high-profile public roles and assigned them jobs they saw as more suited to their feminine nature, Dalit radicals wanted women in the forefront of their struggle.

Dalit radicals thus continuously challenged upper castes and worked to destabilise their firm faith in their existential superiority over Dalits. Through these actions they attempted to keep their distance from Dalitness, which was associated with marginality, vulnerability and subordination. Dalit radicals' rhetoric, actions and efforts were important for restoring svaabhimaan and svaavalamban – that is, dignity – to Dalit women and the community as it attempted to fashion a new, modern self in the present and the future. Dalit affective narratives turned rhetoric into powerful discourse that shaped Dalit women's affect, behaviour and subjectivity through their ritualistic participation in the collective action for education, citizenship and empowerment.

Describing the achievements of such a Bhimvaaraa (winds of change, inspired by the Ambedkar movement), Baby Kamble, a feminist who shares her aunt's passion for justice, records the impact of Ambedkar's speeches on the community, noting that after his speech at Jejuri:

> My father's aunt Bhikabai ascended the stage and stood in front of Baba to address the gathering. She said, 'What Bhimrao Ambedkar says is very true [*khara*]. We should educate our children. We will not eat carcasses. We shall reform the society. We shall take oaths with Ambedkar to fight. Let anything happen, but I am telling you all to follow him'.[49]

By participating in many *sabhaas* (conferences), Bhikabai had gained immense confidence. She supported Ambedkar, who reminded women of their pivotal role in the Dalit revolution and called upon them to usher in a new era. Ambedkar, like Periyar, did not limit participation to domestic matters, but extended it firmly into the sphere of politics and provided novel ways to link personal and political struggles. As Shantabai Dani aptly sums up:

> We Untouchables took every word of Babasaheb's speeches as an inspiration. His words gave us identity, self-respect, independence, and the strength to fight against injustice. We can say that his words shaped our minds and our personalities.... I was living the life of an ordinary school teacher, an ordinary woman, but Baba's work made me a social activist. The change I underwent surprises me even now.[50]

Dani's emotions are reinforced by Babytai: 'Thanks to Babasaaheb, the Mahar retrieved their souls and changed their situation radically and for the better'.[51] Although women like Dani and many others cite Ambedkar as their source of energy and inspiration, conceal themselves behind the male figures of their families or communities and minimise their own contributions, I need to reiterate, with many feminists, that this is a universal feature of women's writings and is not specific to Dalit women. What is, however, more important is that women's emotional subjectivity allows us to consider the intersections of *samaaj* (community) and family with 'history' and how Dalit radicals brought about a profound individual and collective change in the Dalit *samaaj*.

Most importantly, Dalit women exercised historical agency, piecing together whatever was available to actively engage in the political practices of constructing themselves and their communities. They were thus not merely 'humble interpreters of a supernatural leader's vision',[52] as some historians (like Pandey) would like us to believe. Such approaches to studying the heretofore occluded history of women further diminish their creative roles and deny them even the small spaces available. Based on his reading of Babytai's translated autobiography, Pandey informs us that she was '*caught up* in the Ambedkarite movement from an early age'.[53] However, as this book will make clear, women were not 'caught up' or ensnared; they chose instead to engage critically with and contribute to the movement. Moreover, Babytai's original Marathi autobiography amply underscores how Dalits themselves articulated political concepts in their local, vernacular Marathi. She underscores that Ambedkar's movement led to the production of sphurti (enthusiasm and activity), courage and khambirpanaa (determinacy and positivity) in the Mahar community and details the processes through which '*ekaa ekaa vicharaalaa anek phaate phutu laagale*' (gradually one idea formed and sprouted forth many).[54]

The tension between Babytai's reminiscences and scholarly interpretations of them prises open a critical space to investigate gender history. What counts as absolutely critical to some may not affect or be perceived similarly by others. This once again brings to light the limitations in mainstream (male) scholarship: Pandey is reading one Dalit woman's autobiography and placing the agentive forces outside the Dalit self, allowing Dalit males to assimilate her into the movement – without her approval! He portrays Dalit females as entirely dependent upon and derived from male deeds and desires. He does not question why women were 'caught up' and consented with men. Moreover, what Pandey neglects is that although Dalit women's subjectivity was at times fragmentary and incoherent, they also forcefully exercised choices and made certain decisions: for example, choosing the leadership of Ambedkar and Phule over Gandhi. Many women like Babytai had ideas, engaged with local politics,[55] wrote about their sexual subordination, provided details of domestic violence and contested patriarchy, and were still firm about actively participating in the movement.

Significantly, Pandey falters again when he accuses 'Dalit memoirs, especially of women' and 'other writings of the same kind' of 'a persistent tendency to expel the political question from the domain of the family and locate it instead in the realm of the political party' or constitutional politics.[56] The problem with this argument is, first, that Pandey does not provide enough evidence to tell us who exactly the agents were. Are all autobiographies and women's accounts at fault for performing such erasures? Second, Pandey does not take into consideration the work of Dalit radicals, as I have revealed earlier, or recent feminist historiography, which, instead of 'shifting' the problem of the political to formal politics, has grounded it in the domain of the family, thus making the family a site of resistance and a political practice.

Historians thus need to ask adequate questions as well as provide some 'good' answers. For example, what was Bhimvaaraa? What did Ambedkar and *Bhimvaaraa* mean to Dalit women and men? Why was it so significant to them? How did women create the effect of a unified Dalit movement? Despite being 'brutally battered' and 'terribly thrashed', how did they articulate and write about the multiple struggles of the Dalit community in private and publicly? What was the movement's significance? How did women appropriate the agenda of the Dalit movement, the nationalist movement and their leaders for (un)intended purposes?

Most Dalits approached the concept of educational opportunity from a profound sense of shared responsibility. Few lost sight of how their achievements might affect Dalits still in villages, as well as women. To spread awareness among Dalit women, the *Bahishkrut Bharat* Bhagini Parishad was established and held conferences in different areas.[57] During one such women's conference, held in Naigao, Mumbai, to support Ambedkar's Dharmaantar (conversion to Buddhism) on December 31, 1935, its president Devikabai Damodar Kamble said,

> Our leader Babasaheb Ambedkar has started satyagrahas in Mahad and Nasik to provide us equal status. But hard-hearted Hindu sanatanists opposed these efforts. Hence Dr. Ambedkar has decided to convert and we have gathered here to express our full support to him.[58]

Seconding Kamble, the gathered Dalit women and men passed the resolution for *Dharmaantar*.

On June 3, 1953, in a public meeting under the auspices of the SC mahilaa mandal at Rawli Camp, Sion (Mumbai), Ambedkar addressed an audience of about 3,000 people. He advised women to carry on their programme of emancipation in spite of adverse criticism. The *mandal* contributed Rs.401 as its first instalment towards the SCF's Building Fund (Crime Investigation Department 1953).

Yet Dalit radicals' negotiations were contradictory, and the assertion and agenda of masculinity often encouraged patriarchal practices.[59] Control over women was also linked with more honour, dignity and respectability for them. Dalit radicals looked upon Dalit women as 'purifiers', responsible for the improvement of the community. Dalit women became saviours of Dalit men and the community. In making this political move, Dalit reformers could justify Dalit women's activity in the public sphere, which could lead (at least in some cases) to women's commitment and national activity. However, the roots of this outward-directed agenda were deeply embedded in women's place in the private sphere.

This was a double-bind: Dalit women's subjection was produced and restrained by the very structures of power through which they sought emancipation. Dalit women suffer(ed) from certain inherent contradictions in Dalit radicals' thinking, which raised as many questions about women and gender roles as it resolved. The management of female sexuality and the whole politics of honour and shame were a principal difficulty for most communities, including Dalits. Most of the time they were unattainable agendas. Another serious problem that reformers had to address was how to legitimate the need to educate women while simultaneously restricting them to the home as wives and mothers. Some emphasised conservative roles for Dalit women even as they incorporated their participation and thereby restricted their potential.

Dalit radicals did not consciously articulate gender equity as distinct from Dalit regeneration and the community's march towards modernity. Ideals of modernity centred on annihilating derogatory elements marking their caste and constructing a respectable replacement. The two aims of gender justice and community refashioning were part of the same project, so their gendered ideology and discourses did and did not change radically. Because of this they were to an extent unable to break free from gendered discourses, thus burdening women with private and public roles.

By emphasising the operations of interlocking technologies of education, caste, class, gender, sexuality, family and community, and persuading Dalit women to rethink their attitudes to womanhood, motherhood, public roles and employment, Ambedkar brought about a complete change in Dalit women's historical voice from the crucible of domestic and public politics. He wanted women to be independent-minded and daring; hence, he recognised their autonomous subjectivity, however conflicted and limited. Nevertheless, and most significantly, it is from the everyday ambiguity and negotiations of Dalit consciousness that actions, events and unintended results sprang forth actively. All the everyday contradictions and convergences of power and powerlessness, of vulnerabilities, of truth and illusions, of what women did and did not control, helped them to improve their knowledge of the means to transform their lives.

The post-1920 Ambedkar movement witnessed the increased prominence and self-assertion of Dalit women. They started attending schools and conferences, made public speeches (a truly revolutionary act for those who had been silenced and excluded), and became more confident. They recovered their self-respect, were actively involved in the movement, and agitated for their rights. They supported compulsory primary education, hostels and scholarships for Dalit girls and the appointment of untouchable women teachers.[60] With these vital actions, struggles and organisations, women gained a consciousness that penetrated their everyday lives and elevated them to new, hitherto unachievable heights. However, these tasks involved many and different difficulties.

Conclusion

Education technologies interacted with social and economic structures, moral reform and political power to work for Dalit emancipation. Hence, it is important to untangle these technologies' knotty relationships with different domains and with discursive and non-discursive practices in the Dalit march towards a certain modernity. Dalit women played a key role in this.

In the context of the Dalit movement, gender itself emerged as a very contested, unstable and fractured category. It became a generative process to imagine new kinds of emancipation and democratising techniques. Dalit radicals' critique of gender emerged from within the critique of caste and untouchability. Upper-caste men constructed hierarchies of gender, caste and sexuality in particular historical contexts. Phule and Ambedkar identified the cunning of upper-caste men and analysed the subordination of Dalit women, constructed Dalit women's subjectivities, and fashioned Dalit womanhood. The new Dalit woman was historically produced and her subjectivity shaped to enforce new forms of Dalit identity. She was an amalgamation of modernity and tradition for normativity, caste and sexuality as well as a rights-bearing subject of the state (unlike the upper-caste woman, who was always-already one). Dalit radicals, like Self-Respecters under Periyar in colonial South India, concentrated on female suffering and internal reform because the improved position of women was critical to them.

Moreover, Phule and Ambedkar were men who were deeply concerned about the feelings, emotions, desires, identity and dignity of women. Although they lived and struggled in different times, they shared a common approach to the nexus between knowledge, caste, sexual and gender discriminations. Yet there were differences: Phule, for example, was not concerned with any particular roles for women. Ambedkar, on the other hand, emphasised women's mothering roles and redrew the boundaries of the social reform of untouchability as an inherently political concern for Dalit women. There were contradictions in Ambedkar's approach to women. At one level, Ambedkar's disciplinary rectitude to an extent was similar to the bourgeois values of Victorian-brahmani notions of womanhood. Yet, on the other and deeper level, with his agenda of Modern Dalit women as agents 181 democratisation, he brought women into the modern public sphere to discover their new roles within the family, community and nation. In addition, Phule seemed more radical than Ambedkar; however, the impact of the latter's ideology, practices and the overall movement was and is deeper.

There was both continuity and discontinuity between the upper-caste and Dalit agendas of education and gender reform. In contrast to upper-caste agendas of education, which policed women and their sexuality, non-brahmin and Dalit interlocking technologies critiqued the compounded nature of caste, class, gender and education, and sought to bring Dalit women into the public sphere instead of fully entrenching domestic ideologies. Most importantly, unlike some upper-caste and Gandhian nationalists, Ambedkar did not create a dichotomy between the social and political, nor did he confine Dalit women to the social. Instead, in the case of Dalit women, the social deeply penetrated both formal and informal political struggles, and women bravely annexed new arenas of life. Moreover, Dalit women and men grasped and appropriated Dalit radicals' discourse and efforts for education and self-making, and forged strategies to trans-form their conditions. From these mutual processes emerged their political consciousness. In addition, by connecting the construction of caste to practices of endogamy (such as sati, enforced widowhood and child marriage), Ambedkar has taught us to see how the security of the home or the domestic space depends on a just social order.

The production of the Dalit woman was a contested process predicated on caste, class, gender and sexuality differentiations. This chapter has documented the complicated processes of shifting masculinities and femininities by which Dalit radicals departed from upper-caste femininity to forge new constructions of a masculine Dalit womanhood, vernacularising and claiming universal ideas of human rights, education, individualism, daring, resoluteness and emancipation. Moreover, unlike upper-caste males who 'controlled femininity to bolster the resilience and agency of native-caste masculinity',[61] Dalits instead incorporated the masculine attributes into the feminine and carved out a heroic agency. This production process, however, was also thwarted by the power of old patriarchies and differentiation from 'other' stigmatised women.

Dalit women's strategic subjectivity was born out of the social, political, emotional and intellectual agitations and turbulences of this expansion of the self and its experiential possibilities, which in turn fashioned the modern Dalit. Dalit women's participation in the movement also shaped the movement for their rights and for an organisation separate from the all-India women's movement. Women gained on both social and psychological grounds; some said the Dalit programme had transformed their lives from empty gossip and boredom to vital engagement and commitment. Ambedkar's political project emphasised the agency of Dalit women in building self-respect and confidence in the community. They were not simply latecomers to history or modernity; they adopted and critically transformed bourgeois ideals for their own benefits. Certainly, the fulfilment of these promises proved difficult.

Notes

1 This chapter has appeared as 'Modern Dalit Women as Agents', Chapter 4, in *Dalit Women's Education in Modern India: Double Discrimination*, New York: Routledge, 2014, pp. 146–86. Used with permission.
2 On such a retrieval and formulation of (upper-caste elite) women's subjectivity, see Antoinette Burton, *Burdens of History: British Feminists, Indian Women, and Imperial Culture, 1865–1915*, Chapel Hill: University of North Carolina Press, 1994; Mrinalini Sinha, *Specters of Mother India*, Durham, NC: Duke University Press, 2006.
3 Gyanendra Pandey, *A History of Prejudice: Race, Caste, and Difference in India and the United States*, New York: Cambridge University Press, 2013, p. 179.
4 Many scholars have focused on Dalit women's victimhood in terms of patriarchy, poverty and social injustice. See, e.g., Anupama Rao, *Gender and Caste*, New Delhi: Kali for Women, 2003, and more recently, Pandey, 2013. On the other hand, some scholars, such as Gail Omvedt in her *We Will Smash this Prison! Indian Women in Struggle*, and Maya Pandit, who translated Babytai Kamble's autobiography *The Prisons We Broke*, have focused on how women in peasant and Dalit communities have smashed the prisons.
5 Sharmila Rege, *Against the Madness of Manu: B.R. Ambedkar's Writings on Brahmanical Patriarchy*, New Delhi: Navayana, 2013.
6 I thank Shefali Chandra for these timely discussions.
7 Even a quick glance at the vast literature on 'Women in Modern India' will prove the scant attention paid to non-Brahmin and Dalit initiatives in education compared with Brahmin efforts mainly for upper-caste women.
8 Jotirao Phule, 'Trutiya Ratna', in *Collected Works of Mahatma Jotirao Phule*, Vol. I, translated by P.G. Patil, Bombay: Education Department, Government of Maharashtra, [1855] 1991.
9 Phule, [1855] 1991; also mentioned in Jotirao Phule, *Mahatma Phule Samagra Grantha*, Pune: Adhikari Prakashan, 1963, pp. 115–17.

10 Muktabai Salve, 'Mang Maharanchya Dukkhavishayi Nibandh' (An essay on the grief of Mang-Mahars), in S. Karve (ed.), *Streevikasachya Paulkhuna* (Important Achievements in the Development of Women), Dnyanodaya, February 15 and March 1, Pune: Pratima, [1855] 2003. (Marathi)
11 Svati Karve, *Streevikasachya Paulkhuna* (Important Achievements in the Development of Women), Pune: Pratima, 2003, p. 171. (Marathi)
12 Jotirao Phule, *Collected Works of Mahatma Jotirao Phule*, Vol. I, translated by P.G. Patil. Bombay: Education Department, Government of Maharashtra, 1991a, pp. 111–14.
13 I am referring here to the famous critical race theorists such as Kimberlé Crenshaw, 'Demarginalizing the Intersection of Race and Sex: A Black Feminist Critique of Antidiscrimination, Feminist Theory and Antiracist Politics', in Adrien Wing (ed.), *Critical Race Feminism*, 2nd ed., Albany: State University of New York Press, 2003 and Patricia Hill Collins, 1991, who have argued for 'intersectionality' as the primary analytical tool to analyse the multiple dimensions of marginalised subjects.
14 Phule, *Collected Works of Mahatma Jotirao Phule*, pp. 50, 111–14.
15 Phule, *Mahatma Phule Samagra Grantha*, p. 149.
16 Ibid., pp. 149–53, 154.
17 Jotirao Phule, *Samagra Vangmay*, Y.D. Phadke (ed.), Mumbai: Maharashtra State Literary and Cultural Committee, 1991c, p. 456.
18 Ibid., p. 447.
19 Ibid., p. 448.
20 Phule, *Mahatma Phule Samagra Grantha*, p. 156.
21 My argument is fortified by Inderpal Grewal, *Home and Harem: Nation, Gender, Empire, and the Cultures of Travel*, Durham, NC: Duke University Press, 1996, pp. 185, 208.
22 Phule continued to support Ramabai and to attack so-called modern reformers in his journal *Satsar* (Essence of Truth).
23 Jotirao Phule, *Collected Works of Mahatma Jotirao Phule*, Vol. II, translated by P.G. Patil, Bombay: Education Department, Government of Maharashtra, 1991b, pp. 8, 9, 152.
24 Phule, *Mahatma Phule Samagra Grantha*, pp. 229–32. In colonial South India, Periyar started *svaabhimaan vivaha* (self-respect marriages) as a part of his Self-Respect Movement.
25 Jotirao Phule, *Selected Writings of Mahatma Phule*, G.P. Deshpande (ed.), New Delhi: Left Word, 2002, pp. 191–97. See his letters to the Parsi reformer B.M. Malabari, who submitted to Viceroy Ripon two notes on child marriage and enforced widowhood for action by the British government.
26 Douglas Haynes, *Rhetoric and Ritual in Colonial India: The Shaping of Public Culture in Surat City, 1852–1918*, Berkeley: University of California Press, 1991, p. 14. I am borrowing the concept of 'negotiation' from Douglas Haynes, who discusses interactive patterns of colonial political encounter and the creative role played by local elites. I extend it for my purposes.
27 Quoted in Urmila Pawar and Meenakshi Moon, *Amhihi Itihas Ghadavala: Ambedkari Chalvalit Streeyancha Sahabhag* (We Also Made History: Women in the Ambedkar Movement), Pune: Sugava, [2000] 1989, p. 90. (Marathi); see also Rao, 2009, pp. 63–65.
28 *Mooknayak*, September 11, 1920.
29 Charu Gupta, 'Feminine, Criminal, or Manly? Imagining Dalit Masculinities in Colonial India', *Indian Economic and Social History Review*, Vol. 47 No. 3, 2010, pp. 309–42. Scholars have already studied masculinity in colonial India and illustrated how the British constructed Indian men as 'weak' and 'lacking in manliness'. See Ashis Nandy, *The Intimate Enemy: Loss and Recovery of Self Under Colonialism*, Delhi: Oxford University Press, 17 June 2009, pp. 1–63; Mrinalini Sinha, *Colonial Masculinity*, Manchester and New York: Manchester University Press, 1995; Indira Chowdhury, *The Frail Hero and Virile History: Gender and the Politics of Culture in Colonial Bengal*, Delhi: Oxford University Press, 1998, pp. 120–49; Bhikhu Parekh, *Colonialism, Tradition and Reform: An Analysis of Gandhi's Political Discourse*, New Delhi: Sage Publications, 1989, pp. 172–206.
30 Rubin, 1993, p. 15.

31 Various scholars have emphasised how women were used to counter their social marginalisation. See; and Sekhar Bandyopadhyay, *Caste, Culture and Hegemony: Social Dominance in Colonial Bengal*, New Delhi and London: Sage, 2004. For views on how women in turn asserted themselves, see Searle-Chatterjee and Sharma (eds.), *Contextualising Caste: Post-Dumontian Approaches (Sociological Review Monographs)*, Wiley-Blackwell, 1995; P. G. Jogdand, *Dalit Women in India: Issues and Perspectives*, New Delhi: Gyan Publishing House, 1995; Uma Chakravarti, *Gendering Caste: Through a Feminist Lens*, Calcutta: Stree, 2003; Anupama Rao (ed.), *Gender and Caste*, New Delhi: Kali for Women, 2003; and Sharmila Rege, *Writing Caste/ Writing Gender*, New Delhi: Zubaan, July 1, 2006.
32 Burton, *Burdens of History*, pp. 33–44.
33 Pawar and Moon, *Amhihi Itihas Ghadavala*, p. 209. (Marathi)
34 Ibid., p. 224.
35 Ibid., p. 228.
36 Pawar and Moon, *Amhihi Itihas Ghadavala*, p. 213, emphasis added.
37 Ibid., p. 95.
38 Ibid., p. 273.
39 Ibid., p. 275.
40 P. G. Jangalgop, 'Samataa Mahila Sainik Dal', *Janata*, April 13, 1940.
41 *Times of India*, March 3, 1930.
42 Pawar and Moon, *Amhihi Itihas Ghadavala*, pp. 266–67.
43 *Janata*, March 26, 1949.
44 Archana Hatekar, 'Dalit Movement and Dalit Woman's Question', in Vandana Kulkarni (ed.), *Dalit Stree Asmitecha Avishkara va Disha*, Pune: Alochana, 1999, p. 76.
45 Urmila Pawar and Meenakshi Moon, *We Also Made History: Women in Ambedkarite Movement*, introduced and translated from Marathi by Wandana Sonalkar, New Delhi: Zubaan Academic, 2014, first published as *Amhihi Itihas Ghadavala*, 1989. See p. 98 in original.
46 Chandrakanta Sonkamble, Interview with the author, Pune, 2002. Sonkamble is a female politician from Chinchwad, Pune.
47 Ambedkar, *Janata*, July 4, 1936.
48 *Bahishkrut Bharat*, November 4, 1927.
49 Baby Kamble, *The Prisons We Broke*, translated from the original Marathi by Maya Pandit, Hyderabad: Orient BlackSwan, July 9, 2018, first published in 1990 as *Jimha Amucha [Our Living]*. See pp. 64–65, 113 in original.
50 Pawar and Moon, *Amhihi Itihas Ghadavala*, p. 246.
51 Kamble 1990, pp. 121, 123.
52 Gyanendra Pandey, *A History of Prejudice: Race, Caste and Difference in India and United States*, New York: Cambridge University Press, 2013, p. 179.
53 Ibid., p. 180, emphasis added.
54 Kamble, 1990, pp. 108, 112, 113.
55 Ibid., pp. 112–15.
56 Pandey, *A History of Prejudice*, p. 190.
57 *Bahishkrut Bharat*, January 4, 1936.
58 *Nirbhid*, January 5, 1936.
59 For an insightful discussion of Dalit masculinity, see Gupta, 'Feminine, Criminal, or Manly'.
60 *Nirbhid*, March 8, 1936. Anusayabai Ingole presided over the Berar Untouchable Women's Conference in 1936, which passed important resolutions and marked the growing awareness of women in the social and political spheres.
61 Shefali Chandra, *The Sexual Life of English: Languages of Caste and Desire in Colonial India*, Durham, NC: Duke University Press, 2012, pp. 81, 223.

5

AMBEDKARITE WOMEN[1]

Wandana Sonalkar

Dalit women's politics

Since the 1990s we have seen Dalit women asserting themselves politically in a new surge of consciousness. They are trying to define themselves in relation to the Dalit movement in contemporary society, still largely dominated by men, and to a women's movement largely initiated and sustained by upper-caste women; and raising questions for both. Their critiques of what they refer to as the brahmanical ethos of the Indian women's movements leads them to form their own organisations, articulate their own positions on various issues. Comparisons have of course been made with feminists' critique of a largely white middle-class women's movement in the United States. The political configurations are, however, different as well as similar.

One context of Dalit feminists' new mobilisation is related to what is referred to as the 'Mandir-Mandal' politics of the 1990s; one can read it as a form of identity politics, an assertion of difference, in relation to an Indian women's movement whose protagonists have been, in the main, urban, middle-class and upper-caste. The arguments here are similar to some of the positions taken up by Black feminists in the United States: see, for example, writings of the Black feminist bell hooks: 'In hooks' analysis Black/poor women's oppression becomes more real, more relevant to political thinking ... hooks suggests that those at the very bottom of the social hierarchy see more broadly the condition of society since they are not blinded by the rewards of that society and are consequently less committed to it. They are more in contact with the truth of society'. hooks is also critical of white women who claim to speak for 'all women'; her strongest criticism is directed at liberal feminism and radical feminism; the former because it is blind to the race/class privilege enjoyed by white middle-class women, the latter because it is narcissistic.[2]

In India, the women's movement of the 1970s, while it involved mostly urban, upper-caste women from economically privileged backgrounds, had, from the beginning, strong links with communist and radical left politics. Many feminists of that period took up organisational work among rural and working-class women and among the adivasis– people belonging to forest-based communities and falling outside the Hindu caste hierarchy. One of the early national campaigns taken up by women's groups concerned the rape in a police station of an adivasi girl named Mathura;[3] this led to changes in the Indian law on rape. One of the major assertions of the new Dalit feminism, then, centres on the claim to self-representation: they are no longer content to have upper-caste feminists acting and speaking on their behalf.

We will see that this claim of the right to self-representation was also one of Ambedkar's concerns, when he pressed the demand for separate electorates for the untouchables. This claim has been the common ground for the formation of several organisations of Dalit women in recent times.

Identity politics is also a part of politics; the creation of new symbols, icons and celebrations lays claim to cultural space. Arguing that in India one cannot fight for women's liberation unless one challenges brahmanical domination and caste hierarchy, several Dalit women's organisations have, since 1996, celebrated December 25 as *Bharatiya Stree Mukti Diwas* or Indian Women's Libration Day. This marks the anniversary of the symbolic burning of the Sanskrit text of the *Manusmruti* by Ambedkar during a collective mass action in 1927. After some initial hesitations, their lead has been followed by other women's organisations within and outside Maharashtra as well.

The act of burning the *Manusmruti* was carried out by Ambedkar in 1927 at the time of the *satyagraha*, or peaceful agitation, at Mahaad near Mumbai, when untouchables under his leadership reclaimed the right to use the water of a public tank. The *Manusmruti* is the Sanskrit scriptural text, dated about the second century BCE, that lays down a code of behavior for Hindu men and women. Besides being extremely patriarchal, it outlines the norms of a strict caste hierarchy and relegates the lower castes, or shudras, to a position of subjugation. Historians of the colonial period have pointed out that the British, by taking the *Manusmruti* as their reference point for traditional Hindu law, made rigid the codification of patriarchal caste hierarchy in India. Since then the *Manusmruti* has become symbolic of the traditional brahmanical order, for its supporters as well as for those who challenge that order. When Dr Ambedkar, as Law Minister in the central government in newly independent India proposed the Hindu Code Bill encompassing several progressive, that is, anti-caste and woman-friendly changes in the personal laws, or laws governing marriage and inheritance for Hindus, right-wing upper-caste Hindu opponents asked, 'Does he think he is the new Manu?' while making disparaging references to his caste.

There has recently also been a resurgence of academic interest in Dalit issues, and even in Dalit women's identity, their experiences, their consciousness and their organisations: an area of study that had hitherto been of specialised interest, in which women scholars from outside India like Eleanor Zelliot and Gail Omvedt had done pioneering work. Gail Omvedt, of course, can no longer be referred to us as a foreign scholar, having spent most of her life in India, based in a small village of Kasegaon in Sangli district in Maharashtra, with a lifelong commitment to Dalits' and women's concerns. Dalit and bahujan scholars, like Gopal Guru, Sukhdeo Thorat, Kancha Ilaiah, have occasionally written about women's issues while Sharad Patil, a rebel from the Communist Party of India (Marxist), has placed caste and women's issues at the crux of his theoretical contributions. Scholars such as Ruth Manorama, V. Geetha, Anupama Rao, Susie Tharu and Sharmila Rege have tried to explore how the position of Dalit women in Indian society – 'triply oppressed' because of their class, caste and gender – is critical to the way power configurations work themselves out in India's society, economy, politics and culture. The work of Dalit-bahujan women mainly writing in Indian languages, is being translated into English so that it becomes available to a wider readership: Pratima Pardeshi, Saroj Kamble, Rekha Thakur, are a few examples from Maharashtra. Pawar and Moon's text, a substantial work in terms of its size and subject matter, should find its place among these initiatives and open up possibilities for further research and exploration of the past. I have tried to illustrate in this section how many of the issues that were central for the Dalit leadership of Ambedkar's time continue to be relevant today: the question of the right to speak, and the right of self-representation in political bodies; the question of educational opportunity and of education as a path to emancipation of the Dalits, the sexual exploitation of Dalit women. These issues take on a new significance in today's political conjecture, in which Dalit women's organisations are staking their claims and adding their own angels.

Women in the Ambedkar movement

One of the first issues taken up for the emancipation of Dalits by associations formed in the early 1900s was, of course, education. Meenakshi Moon and Urmila Pawar quote statistics of literacy among the untouchable castes taken from the 1921 All-India Census figures for the C. P. and Berar region. The Mahaars were the only caste among these to have any significant numbers of literate persons: the literacy percentage was 1.9% overall and 2.6% for men. Only 555 women were literate in a female Mahaar population of over 500,000. Of a female population of 450,000 in the Chambhar caste, 386 women were literate, and male literacy was 0.7%.

Although Jyotiba Phule had made efforts to set up schools for Dalits, including Dalit girls, in Pune in the mid-1800s, upper-caste social reformers in Maharashtra had not in general much favoured the education of untouchable girls and women. Schools founded by Christian missionaries did admit boys and girls of all castes, but even there the school managements often backtracked when they came up against strong reaction from the parents of students from the higher castes. D.D. Karve, who founded a school for girls in Pune, refused to admit untouchable girls because he felt it would harm his cause, which was the fight against the traditional ill-treatment of high-caste widows. The cause of education for untouchables was taken up by princes like Shaju Maharaj of Kolhapur in Western Maharashtra, Sayajirao Gaekwad in Baroda, as well as by social reformers of the non-brahmin movement such as V.R. Shinde.

In the Vidarbha region, as we have seen, there existed a class of successful traders and relatively wealthy persons from the untouchable castes around this time, and they took the initiative to set up schools for untouchable students early in the twentieth century. When Shahu Maharaj visited Nagpur in 1920, he too appealed to the untouchable community to pursue the cause of education. When Ambedkar took up leadership, he highlighted education as essential for the emancipation of the untouchables, and always emphasised the importance of educating women. He also became an ideal for the untouchables, a personification of what could be achieved by a Dalit once he was educated.

The education of women and girls was an integral part of Ambedkar's vision of social emancipation for the Dalits. Some of his speeches made on occasion of historical importance for the struggle are quoted extensively, notably the speech addressing women at the Mahaad satyagraha, and the 1942 speech at the All-India Dalit Mahila Parishad held on July 20, 1942, in Nagpur. When women began to take active part in mass actions under his leadership, they first of all appealed to women to educate themselves and their sons and daughters. Further, some of them trained to be teachers, started schools and managed hostels for Dalit girls and so on.

Ambedkar did, at least for some time, believe that untouchables had more hope of social justice in the cities, and he famously exhorted his followers to leave the oppressive social order of the village and seek their fortune in the cities. But the facts on entry of Dalit women into prostitution belie this hope of the modernising effect of rural-urban migration, at least for Dalit women. Early efforts by untouchable social reformers called on parents not to dedicate their daughter to the gods. The parents of daughters are being asked to exercise a choice. Ambedkar himself made moral appeals to the devadasis and muralis to give up prostitution, even though that would entail economic hardship. The practice is clearly seen, however, as one of the oppressive traditions of Hinduism and U. Pawar and M. Moon declare, rather bravely, that 'the custom of giving up girls to the god under the name of Devadasis, Muralis and Jogtinis came to an end by itself among neo-Buddhists after their conversion'.[4]

There are also accounts of youths in the Ambedkar movement coming forward in response to a call to marry devadasis and muralis. Ambedkar believed that the spread of inter-caste marriages (between Dalits and non-Dalits) would be a way to eliminate caste. In its earlier phase, Ambedkar defined tradition by proposing that marriages of untouchables be carried out according to Vedic rites, which were forbidden to them according the brahmanical tradition, though in a simplified form, eschewing an excess of ceremony and cutting out rituals that were demeaning to women. Ambedkar did not have worked-out programme of progressive 'self-respect' marriages as did E.V. Ramaswami 'Periyar' in Tamil Nadu in south India. Rather, Satyashodhak wedding ceremony proposed by Jyotiba Phule was adopted by his followers, and adapted to incorporate elements of Buddhist rites after the mass conversion to Buddhism.

There were Dalit women who performed in tamasha groups as dancers and singers. Ambedkar also took a moral stand against the sexual exploitation of these women. For example, when Patte Bapurao, the famous (brahmin) song writer and tamasha group master offered to donate to Ambedkar's cause, he declared, 'I don't want the money raised by making Pawalabai dance'. When the tamasha form was adapted by troupes of Ambedkar's in the Ambedkari jalsa, women were excluded, and the women's parts were played by men and boys.

In the Mahaad speech, Ambedkar calls on Dalit women to be neat and clean in appearance, and to give up the styles of dress and jewellery that mark them as being from the untouchable caste.[5] Some upper-caste women, usually wives of Ambedkar's close high-caste associates, even showed the Dalit women how to tie their saris after the fashion of brahmin women. Again, we should remember that this is an earlier stage of the movement, when Ambedkar still sought equality and justice for untouchables within the Hindu religious community. Also, we can note a difference here between racism, in which the person discriminated against is marked by the colour of her skin, and untouchability, which imposes markers on the *atishudra*, the one who is lower than all castes, so that others can recognise her. These markers vary in their details in various parts of India. Dalits have been forced to tie brooms around their waists to sweep away their polluting footprints as they walk, or to tie mud pots around their neck so that their spittle does not contaminate the ground. Dalit women have been forbidden to wear blouses with their saris, and in Maharashtra were marked out by their wearing of heavy jewellery make of base metals. Casting off these signifiers of the subjugation and humiliation is a first act of rebellion, an act of self-respect, to use a term associated with the anti-caste Tamil leader E.V. Ramaswamy 'Periyar'.

One may contrast the appeal made by Gandhi to women in the struggle for India's independence. It is said that when he called on women in the audience to donate their jewellery for the cause, thousands responded to his charismatic appeal. Gandhi's own practice of austerity inspired both men and women to follow his example, and he was responsible for bringing women out of their homes in large numbers as active participants in the independence movement. But Ambedkar, with his respect for liberal values, was skeptical about the use of charisma in politics, as he explains in his article, 'Ranade, Jinnah and Gandhi'.[6] His appeal to women in the Mahaad speech was essentially different: the call to give up modes of dress and ornament marked with a subordinate status was a programme for emancipation. It is not just a matter of emulating the upper castes – a process named 'sanskritisation' by the Indian sociologist M.N. Srinivas[7] – but of casting off the markers of inferiority. In fact it is clear that tying their nine-yard saris so that draped gracefully at their ankles would not have been very convenient for women who had to do physical labour!

What is more, Ambedkar's position changed over the long period of time from his renunciation of Hinduism until he converted to Buddhism in 1956. I think we have indications that not only did he passionately appeal to his women followers to have self-respect, and to gain the boldness to speak in public and articulate their views, but he also actually listened to what they had to say, and was open to their influence. For example, let us see what Meenambal Shivraj said at third conference of the All India Untouchable Women's Federation held in Bombay on May 6, 1945: 'Women of the untouchable community traditionally have the right to divorce and our widows can remarry; their situation is worsened by the fact that Hindu laws are imposed on them'.[8] Therefore, explained Meenambal Shivraj, Hindu customs and Hindu laws should not be applied to us.

In his journey from the claim to equality and justice for untouchables within Hinduism, to his renunciation of Hinduism in 1956, Ambedkar had an ear for the voice of the Dalit women who were at the bottom of the caste-patriarchal hierarchy under Hinduism. After his central role in framing of the constitution of the new Indian nation, when he was Law Minister in the Union Government in the late 1940s, he drew up the Hindu Code Bill, which aimed at reforming personal laws for Hindus. Ambedkar felt that it was as important to frame a code for laws of marriage, adoption, divorce and inheritance based on equality among castes and between men and women as it was to frame a constitution based on equality of citizenship. He studied existing traditional Hindu laws regarding marriage and inheritance and made women-friendly modification to ensure, for example, monogamy, the right of divorce for women and recognition of inter-caste Hindu marriages. He resigned as Law Minister when the Bill was defeated after vehement opposition from orthodox upper-caste Hindu men in Parliament, although he had the support of Prime Minister Jawaharlal Nehru and of women in the Congress Party. Later, some of the laws he proposed were passed separately.

Notes

1 This chapter is an excerpt from the 'Translator's Introduction' of Urmila Pawar and Meenakshi Moon (eds.), *We Also Made History: Women in the Ambedkarite Movement*, translated by and introduced by Wandana Sonalkar, New Delhi: Zubaan Academic, 2014, pp. 9–20, 26–33. Reproduced with permission.
2 bell hooks, *Feminism is for Everyone: Passionate Politics*, London: Pluto Press, 2000.
3 *Adivasis*: The word means 'original inhabitants'. It is used to denote forest people or members of what the Constitution refers to as Scheduled Tribes.
4 See U. Pawar and M. Moon, *We Also Made History: Women in the Ambedkarite Movement*, translated and introduced by Wandana Sonalkar, New Delhi: Zubaan Academic, 2014.
5 Dalit women typically wore jewellery made of base metals, and tied their nine-yard saris well above the knees. This form of dress enabled them to do physical labour, but also made possible a less restricted department in general.
6 B. R. Ambedkar, 'Rande, Jinnah and Gandhi', Ambedkar, B. R. *Collected Works*, published by Government of Maharashtra.
7 M. N. Srinivas, *Religion and Society Among the Coorge of South India*, New Delhi: Oxford University Press, 1952.
8 For details, see U. Pawar and M. Moon, *We Also Made History: Women in the Ambedkarite Movement*, translated and introduced by Wandana Sonalkar, New Delhi: Zubaan Academic, 2014.

6

RAMABAI AND AMBEDKAR[1]

Sharmila Rege

In the aftermath of Mandal, feminist scholars such as Uma Chakravarti and V. Geetha felt the imperative to engender histories of caste, and encaste gender; whereas Dalit feminist scholar Abihinaya Ramesh pointed to the limits of border crossing through a detailing of structures and processes of brahmanical surveillance.[2] What implications does this have for the dominant methodology and critiques of feminism? In other words, did these feminist interpretations of the caste question confront the accepted meanings of violence, sexuality or labour in women's studies? The answer is yes and no.

At the same time, invoking the intersection of caste, class and gender has become a mantra that is repeated as if it were a guide to method. The truth is we are still wanting in engaged debates on brahmanical patriarchy in its various historical and cultural manifestations. In seminar discussion, while some feminist scholars reject the concept as overarching, others misrecognise it as 'Brahmin patriarchy' and ask, 'then what about Dalit patriarchy? Within women's studies, pluralism has to mean a relative absence of debate and thus a 'peaceful co-existence' between those who 'do caste' and those who do not – as if caste were a matter of choice for those 'doing gender'.[3]

The interrogation of the obvious influence of canonical disciplinary perspectives on caste in feminist studies and the tokenism of the mantra of 'caste, class and gender' would call for a programmatic intervention in women's studies. I suggest that as part of such an intervention, we turn to new sources and methods of interpretation for understanding Ambedkar in his times and ours, and reclaim some of his writings on brahmanical patriarchy as feminist classics. Classics are fluid, not sacrosanct. They have a persuasive force that allows contemporary interpreters to debate conflicting and complementary opinions.[4] Recovering Ambedkar's writings as feminist classics draws both from their authorial brilliance and the possibilities opened up by contemporary interpretative appropriations. The politics of the 1990s, which spelt out why and how claiming caste is not casteism, deepened Indian democracy. The push towards a more inclusive democracy demands a move towards democratising knowledge, suggesting that women's studies needs to move beyond merely including the excluded. This calls for confronting confusing, diverse and heterogeneous sources of knowledge across different locations – social, institutional and epistemic.

Feminist denial of the 'political' on 'personal' grounds

Let me begin with an incident narrated by Urmila Pawar, a well-known Dalit feminist writer in her testimonio *Aydaan: The Wave of My Life*. Pawar recalls a seminar discussion on Dalit women's issues at a renowned institute in Mumbai. A woman professor claims that 'Dr. Ambedkar did nothing for women. Hindu Code Bill was a political stunt! He never brought his wife forward; unlike Phule, he did not educate her'.[5]

Pawar is struck by the lack of reaction by other feminist scholars. Only a friend bursts out laughing at Pawar's stunned face. Shocked by the trivialisation of a serious issue, Pawar observes that the gathering of scholars could not understand the difference that sociocultural milieu and economic strata can make to lives.

Pawar's narrative points to typical ways in which feminists deny the political contribution of feminism of Ambedkar. This is done most commonly by referring to the sphere of the personal or at other times labelling his contribution as being particularistic – limited to the social improvement of Dalit women.[6] It also draws attention to the importance of exploring the ways in which public and personal spheres are constituted differently in diverse social locations. Therefore, a discussion on the 'personal' and the 'political', albeit briefly, becomes crucial for at least two reasons. Firstly, it is necessary to understand the paradox of the feminist denial of Ambedkar's political contributions by referring selectively and erroneously to the personal sphere. Secondly, it is important to open up different meanings of the public and the private – spaces of household and community as they came to be fashioned by the Ambedkar movement – towards a more emancipator notion of the modern in India.

How may we explain the paradox of the feminist denial of the political contributions of Ambedkar by the selective and erroneous underscoring of the personal sphere? Historically, the colonial public sphere in India comprised different groups and communities forming publics and counterpublics, all of which were in friction with one another. The privileged castes, in constituting the middle class public sphere, used older resources of power and privilege and newer ideas of politics and society, stitching together Manu and Mill, thereby fashioning of fractured modernity.[7] This modernity, while disavowing caste in the public sphere, joined new principles of individualism with endogamy, and *varnashrama dharma* with notions of universal division of labour, and thus made claim to universal modernity. Feminist scholarship has convincingly demonstrated that the making of this middle class public sphere had significant effect on the restructuring of the 'personal', especially the invention of the model of companionate marriage.[8]

Marathi women's autobiographies written between 1910 and 1950 offer varying narratives of companionate marriage. Caste rarely figures here. And if it does, it appears as belonging to someone else – women in the mills or vegetable vendors or to women of a time gone past. Thus the dominant narrative of gender and modernity, that has concealed the complicity of brahmin women in class privilege and brahmanical patriarchy, highlights privileged caste women's struggle with tradition and their desire to be modern. Non-Dalit feminists have not been unaffected by the splintered modernity of their class. They perceive the absence of a dominant model of companionate marriage in Ambedkar's life as prioritising 'community' over 'wife', and by extension over women's issues, and for that reason not feminist enough.[9]

In contrast, Ambedkar fashioned a notion of the modern that combined new Western ideas and emancipator materialist traditions like Buddhism from Indian history. He did so by underlining the historical character of caste-based exploitation, rejecting the varna order and advocating the annihilation of caste as the only path to egalitarian society. In seeking a rational re-examination of the core values of Hindu metaphysics he heralded an Indian Enlightenment,[10] which imagined new caste and gender codes and radical meanings of modernity. A few scholars have charted the career of India's political modernity fashioned by Ambedkar's agitations against the language of obligations and negative rights embedded in caste hierarchy, and the new language of self-respect, equality and rights.[11] Urmila Pawar and Meenakshi Moon's studies of Ambedkarite women have reinstated the agency of Dalit women in the making of anti-caste modernity.[12] However, we are yet explore fully how gendered ideologies and practices of the public/private mediated the constitution of alternate modernities that sought to move beyond the binaries of political/social, colonial/national, Indian tradition/Western modernity and community/nation. For instance, how were conjugal relations and the household recast in the light of tensions between nation and caste amidst upheavals in the Ambedkarite counterpublics? How did challenges to the brahmanical caste order question principles of kinship – the conflicts between given and chosen relations? How did the articulation of collective interest produce 'new' households and sociality?

Ambedkar and Ramabai

We can turn to Ramabai, known as 'Ramaai' (the mother of the community), as also the suspicion and debate heaped on Sabitabai's role in Ambedkar's life, to argue that the representations of the personal/conjugal in the Ambedkarite booklets and musical compositions question the dominant ideal of companionate marriage that constituted brahmanical middle class modernity. In the musical compositions of the life of Ambedkar and Ramabai, companionship transcends the realm of the private. It suggests that community, the household and the political realms are inseparable.

The depiction of Ramabai's life in the booklets and songs does not suggest a model of an inherently sacrificing wife and mother. Rather, they highlight transformation – from 'Raami', the young orphaned girl who marries Ambedkar, to 'Ramaai', the political community's mother figure. Descriptions both in the songs and the booklets highlight her initial expectations that Ambedkar would become a householder on returning from the United States, that he would lead a normative life with his job as lecturer at Sydenham College in Bombay. She questions his aspiration for further studies, is angry and gives up on any conversation with him for days to end. But Ramaabai eventually recognises his aspirations and goes on to offer unconditional support, organising the household economy with 50rupees a month and even managing to save five rupees towards contingency expenses. Ramabia's dignified negotiation of poverty after Ambedkar leaves for London in 1916 has a special place in all the songs. Also foregrounded is her refusal of charity despite the daily struggle for food and the household subsisting on the four *bhakris* (jowar bread) a day.

Ramabai's growing interest in the political movement led by Ambedkar unfolds through her curiosity about the Mangaon Parishad of 1920 and Shahu Maharaj's work,[13] her keenness to contribute to the 1927 Mahad Satyagraha (not by leading the women's meeting as Ambedkar suggests, but as a cook), to addressing a gathering of woman at J.J. Hospital premises in Mumbai.[14]

Before leaving for London in 1920, Ambedkar organised a *shraddha* (annual offering for his deceased father) braking the conventional practices of the Hindu ritual by inviting 40students from the boarding house of the Depressed Class Mission for a meal. Ramabai had plans for the traditional sweetmeat offering but Ambedkar argued that the students be served meat and fish – what they missed the most in the hostel. Shocked, Ramabai initially questioned the appropriateness of serving meat as a ritual offering but went on to transgress the Brahamanical rules, serving meat to the students instead of *puranpoli* (sweet bread).[15] Whether it is this incident or other like Ramabai's desire to visit religious places to worship, and Ambedkar efforts to convince her with rational arguments against the same, the musical and printed accounts of the Ambedkarites do not present the relationship between Ambedkar and Ramabai as a given. Instead they detail the meaning and values as felt and lived – outlining ways in which particular incidents in their lives combine into ways of living and thinking. Compositions on Ramabai's refusal to educate herself despite Ambedkar's anger, her initial irritation with his expenditure on books but her sustained support later, even selling her gold bangles to make possible the 'Rajagriha', Ambedkar's library, underline the making of their relationship through argument and dialogue.

Radhabai Varale – who along with her husband, the well-known writer Balwant Varale, managed the hostel started by Ambedkar for Backward Caste student at Dharwad in 1929 – has noted in her memoirs how Ramabai went to become the chief guest at the first inter-dining event of its kind for women from different untouchable sub-castes. Young Ambedkarites in Dharwad, keen to bring untouchable caste women into public inter-dining meetings, were initially doubtful of Ramabai's participation. Ramabai hailed from the Konkan region known for its strict caste rules pertaining to exchange and consumption of food. Verale recalls that hearing Ramabai learning of this, Ambedkar exclaimed – 'How the *mahar bhatin*[brahmanical Mahar woman] has transformed!'[16]

Several compositions on Ramabai describe her efforts to extend the household to accommodate members of the kingship network. She had welcomed into her home an eight-year-old boy of the Mang caste and helped sustain a hostel for Backward Caste students by pawning her jewellery – suggesting that she allowed her household to encompass a political community. The compositions detail Ramabai's contributions as emerging from her love, dedication and admiration for her extraordinary husband. Yet she is not seen as a 'mindless follower', but as someone who developed political convictions of her own. Ambedkar's complete dependence on Ramabai is highlighted in all the compositions, which emphasise his grief over her death. His dedication to her in his book *Pakistan or Partition of India* reads:

> As a token of my appreciation of her goodness of heart, her nobility of mind and her purity of character and also for the cool fortitude and readiness to suffer along with me which she showed in those friendless days of want and worries which fell to our lot.[17]

Ramabai is thus credited with the making of a *yugpurush* ('Man of the Epoch') by drawing on a common social lineage with Yashodhara, Buddha's wife, and Savitribai, Jotiba Phule's wife. In contrast to this is the Ambedkarite community's suspicion and anger toward, or sometimes a studied silence on, Savitabai Ambedkar.[18] This is borne out of Savitabai's stated intent to write an autobiography three decades after Ambedkar's death. She claimed wanting to write it in order 'to put facts before the community' and to clear the clouds of suspicion caste on her role in the demise of Ambedkar.[19] Writing in a defensive mode, Savitabai stresses Ambedkar's feelings for her by including their private correspondence and recounting episodes from their years together in terms of an ideal companionate marriage. She concludes that vested political interests planted doubt and suspicion in Yashwant's mind and in the community. Some booklets published following Savitabai's death in 2003 seek to undertake a rational critique of the 'truth and falsehood' surrounding her role in Ambedkar's demise. One such booklet stresses the Individualised nature of her relationship with Ambedkar – a relationship that does not always see building bridges between the household and the political community as an integral part of the conjugal, thus bringing rejection from the community.[20]

In contrast to the non-Dalit feminist position (noted earlier in Wandana Sonalkar's account), the articulations of Ambedkarite community on conjugality suggest that studying the 'personal' and the 'political' in Ambedkar's life cannot be an exercise in stating 'self-evident' truths. Against the conflicting pressures on Dalits to claim selfhood and collectivity,[21] life histories of the Ambedkar household provide dynamic models to make and remake public and private selves.

Notes

1. This chapter is an excerpt from the 'Introduction' of B. R. Ambedkar, *Against the Madness of Manu*, Selected and Introduced by Sharmila Rege, New Delhi: Navayana, 2013, pp. 21–27, 36–40. Used with permission.
2. For an incisive theorisation of Brahmanical patriarchy and Brahmanical surveillance, see Uma Chakravarti, 'Conceptualising Brahmanical Patriarchy in Early India: Gender, Caste, Class and State', *Economic and Political Weekly*, April 3, 1993, pp. 579–85; Abhinya Ramesh, 'Brahmanical Surveillance and Possibilities of Border Crossing', paper presented at the National Seminar on Interrogating Discourses: Ambedkar and Discursivity, Dr Ambedkar Adhyasan and Thought Centre, University of Pune, March 14, 2011. For comprehensive feminist engagements with the caste question in India, see Uma Chakravarti, *Gendering Caste: Through a Feminist Lens*, Calcutta: Stree, 2003; V. Geetha, *Gender*, Calcutta: Stree, 2001.
3. I draw this inference from my experience at several seminars, workshops, refresher courses where, following presentation by/of Uma Chakravarti's conceptualisation of Brahmanical patriarchy, the discussion tends to take either of these two routes.
4. For competing definitions, criteria and utility of classics, see Peter Baehr and Mike O'Brien, 'Founders, Classics and the Concept of a Canon', *Current Sociology*, Vol. 42 No.1, 1994, pp. 53–72.
5. Urmila Pawar, *Aydaan: The Weave of My Life: A Dalit Women's Memoirs*, translated from the Marathi by Maya Pandit, Calcutta: Stree, 2008, pp. 260–61.
6. Most readings of Ambedkar by non-Dalit feminists tend to see the contribution of Ambedkar to the women's question only in terms of Dalit or Mahar women beginning to speak out. See for example Pratibha Ranade, *Stree Prashnanchi Charcha: Ekonishave Shatak* (Debate on the Woman Question: The Nineteenth Century), Mumbai: Popular Prakashan, 1991, p. 380. Ranade, in discussing the women's question in nineteenth-century Maharashtra, notes the contributions of Phule, and contrasts it with the privileged caste reformers' neglect of the issues concerning women of the subordinated castes. The author suggests that *savarna* women could progress because of the well educated, conscious *savarna* men and hopes that Dalit women would receive similar help and strength from their men.
7. I borrow the conception of 'fractured modernity' from Sanjay Joshi, *Fractured Modernity: Making of a Middle Class in Colonial North India*, New Delhi: Oxford University Press, 2002.
8. Feminist scholarship has detailed the ways in which a generation of Indian nationalists and reformers constituting the emergent middle class attempted to undercut the authority of family elders and create a new patriarchy of more nuclear and exclusive relations with their wives. Several scholars have analysed the discourse of social reform and nationalism, advice manuals and women's life stories from different regions of India to outline how women of the new middle class used competing patriarchies to launch their own explorations of agency and self-identity. See for instance Sudesh Vaid and Kumkum Sangari (eds.), *Recasting Women: Essays in Colonial History*, New Delhi: Kali for Women, 1989; Tanika Sarkar, 'The Hindu Wife and the Hindu Nation: Domesticity and Nationalism in Nineteenth-Century Bengal', *Studies in History*, Vol. 8 No.2, 1992, pp. 213–35; Janaki Nair, *Women and Law in Colonial India*, New Delhi: Kali for Women, 1996; Patricia Uberoi, *Social Reform, Sexuality and the State*, New Delhi: Sage, 1996; Anshu Malhotra, *Gender, Caste and Religious Identities: Restructuring Class in Colonial Punjab*, New Delhi: Oxford University Press, 2002; Judith E. Walsh, *Domesticity in Colonial India: What Women Learned When Men Gave Them Advice*, Lanham: Rowman and Littlefield, 2004.
9. For a detailed discussion, see Rege, introduction to *Writing Caste/Writing Gender*, pp. 27–64. Chapter 9 in this Reader.
10. See Gopal Guru, 'Dalits in Pursuit of Modernity', in Romila Thapar (ed.), *India: Another Millennium*, New Delhi: Penguin, 2000, pp. 123–37; Meera Nanda, *Breaking the Spell of Dharma and Other Essays*, New Delhi: Three Essays Press, 2002.

11 For details see Gail Omvedt, *Dalit and the Democratic Revolution: Dr Ambedkar and the Dalit Movement in Colonial India*, New Delhi: Sage, 1994; Anupama Rao, *The Caste Question: Dalits and the Politics of Modern India*, New Delhi: Permanent Black, 2009 for a theoretically rich reflection on the salience of Ambedkar and the Dalit movement for a re-evaluation of political modernity in India.
12 By far the best documentation of women's participation in the Ambedkar movement is to be found in Urmila Pawar and Minakshi Moon, *Aamhihi Itihas Ghadawla: Ambedkari Chalvalit Streeyancha Sahabhag*, Pune: Sugawa Prakashan, 1989, 2000. See the English translation by Wandana Sonalkar, *We Also Made History: Women in the Ambedkarite Movement*, New Delhi: Zubaan, 2008.
13 Shahu Chattrapati, the Maharaja of Kolhapur, was the patron of the non-Brahmin movement in Maharashtra in the early twentieth century. He inaugurated the system of reservations in 1902 when he issued an order for recruitment of only non-Brahmins in state service until they formed 50% of the post. This was followed by orders for Compulsory Primary Education (1917) and the Law for Registration of Inter-caste and Inter-religious Marriages and the Law Against Physical and Mental Cruelty to Women (1919). He sponsored hostels for untouchables and sponsored small businesses – even becoming a regular patron of teashops. Shahu met Ambedkar in 1920 and sponsored a two-day conference at Mangaon on March 19 and 20, 1920, to felicitate Ambedkar. For details, see Jaisinghrao Pawar, *Rajashri Shahu Smarak Granth* (Shahu Maharaj Memorial Volume), Kolhapur: Maharashtra Itihas Prabhodini, 2001.
14 This speech is mentioned in Acharya Suryakant Bhagat, *Matoshri Ramabai Ambedkar* (Mother Ramabai Ambedkar), Nagpur: Sugat Prakashan, 2006, p. 39. The author does not mention the exact date on which the speech was delivered.
15 Brahmanical rules were broken at least in three ways: disregarding the Hindu calendar; calling Dalit students for a meal instead of a ritual offering to Brahmins and blood relatives; and serving meat and fish since students would prefer this over customary ritual food.
16 Recalled in the memoirs of Radhabai Balwantrao Varale, *Matoshree Ramabai Ambedkaranchya Sahavasat* (In the Company of Respected Mother Ramabai Ambedkar), Aurangabad: Prabuddha Bharat Prakashan, 2004, pp. 49–50.
17 First published in December 1940, reprinted in *BAWS*, Vol. 8, Bombay: Education Department, 1990.
18 One may note that well-known Ambedkarite scholars like Raosaheb Kasbe had written against such cloud of suspicion cast on Savitabai. Savitabai was active with the Dalit Panthers in the agitation against the Shiv Shenas rioting against the Maharashatra state's ban on 'Riddles in Hinduism', and also participated in the 1980s effort to form a united opposition to the Congress party in the state.
19 See Savita Ambedkar, *Dr Ambedkaranchya Sahvasat* (In the Company of Dr Ambedkar), Mumbai: Dr Ambedkar Foundation, 1990, p. v.
20 Rajesh Kolombkar, *Maisaheb Ambedkar: Kaay Khare Kaay Khote?* (Maisaheb Ambedkar: What's True/What's False?), Mumbai: Udgar Prakashan, 2003, pp. 14–15.
21 See Ravikumar, 'Introduction – Private and Public Selves', *Ambedkar: Autobiographical Notes*, for a brief but incisive account of the binary of public and private as it confronts Dalit and the struggle in claiming selfhood and collective identity.

PART III
Lived experience as *'difference'*

Part III presents chapters on Dalit women's lived experiences, which constitute an important element in theorising and developing a fuller understanding of caste-inflected social realities. These chapters broadly depict three spheres of Dalit women's reality, which are specific to *their* everyday life, and rather distinct from caste-privileged Indian feminists. First, we focus on violence as a permanent threat, due to Dalit women's peculiarly vulnerable socio-political-economic status working in the public domain. Second, we turn to representations of Dalit women in religious texts and Hindu mythologies, which have always exhibited Dalit women as a threat to 'purity' and 'fortune'. Third, we turn attention toward Dalit women as new subjects of investigation and objects of research, as current academic and political discourses on gender manifest an anxious interest in their life narratives.

Sharmila Rege (Chapter 7) reviews various ways in which violence occurs against women and argues that the issue of violence 'must be located in the links between' caste and gender, failing which Indian feminism might itself end up contributing to inequalities. Vizia Bharati (Chapter 8) presents different, deeply degrading images of Dalit women as portrayed in Hindu writings, and offers evidence that ancient as well as modern literature does not depict Dalit women in a humane and dignified manner. Y. S. Alone (Chapter 8) identifies locations of resistance within current aesthetic practices that speak back to these degrading portrayals. Finally, Sharmila Rege (Chapter 9), in her book *Writing Caste/Writing Gender*, initiates a debate over the consumption of Dalit autobiographies by mainstream writers, and presents a comprehensive review of many Dalit thinkers and creative writers who have reflected on this issue. She concludes that these testimonies reveal that Dalit women have been strong agents and bearers of major social reforms through their valuable contribution in Phule-Ambedkarite politics, school education, literary and academic spheres of life.

Part III, then, gives us a glimpse of some realities that partially contribute to Dalit women's lived experiences as a ground for their 'difference' with respect to savarna women. This difference has been neglected by mainstream Indian feminist discourse, despite its abiding relevance to theorising the lives of everyday women and in fighting patriarchy in a concrete sense. This lacuna with respect to lived experience further establishes the necessity for founding an authentic and pragmatic feminist theory in India, toward which *Dalit Feminist Theory* aims to substantially contribute.

7
BRAHMANICAL NATURE OF VIOLENCE AGAINST WOMEN[1]

Sharmila Rege

Let us review the different ways in which the issue of violence against women has been addressed in the last 200 years in India. The basic questions that arise are those pertaining to the forms of violence, the location of individuals and groups addressing the issue and the specific contexts of their addressal. The missionaries, the orientalists, colonial administrators, social reformers and the post-independent Indian nation-state have all addressed the issue of violence against women as a part of either their 'civilising mission', 'revival or modernisation of Indian tradition' or 'women as weaker section' projects. The Edwardian and Victorian feminists addressed the issue as the white women's burden while the first wave Indian feminists lobbied for amendments in the Hindu law of property and marriage; for 'status' rather than 'revival'.

All these discourses, in universalising the category of Indian women, often encroached on the customary rights of the lower-caste women. Much of the American and British, second wave, white feminist discourse on Third World women carries the notion of Third World women as 'always and already victims'. The second wave feminists in India who formed autonomous women's groups in the 1970s, had broken away from the 'larger/mass' movements which overlooked gender for the fear of dividing the movement. The autonomous women's groups politicised the issue of violence against women and attempted to build a sisterhood in struggling against violence. The divisions by caste and religion that threaten this sisterhood have become apparent in recent times. Steven Lukes' 'Radical View of Power'[2] and Harding's 'Epistemology of Rainbow Coalition Politics'[3] provide relevant theoretical frameworks for the analysis of violence and the strife in sisterhood. The violent practices against women reveal definite variations by caste; while upper caste are subjected to controls and violence within the family, it is the absence of such controls that makes lower-caste women vulnerable to rape, sexual harassment and the threat of public violence. To varying degrees, these different practices are 'accepted' as given and some of them like 'sati' and 'devdasi' practice may even be glorified. Lukes has argued that the supreme exercise of power is through compliance, by control over the thoughts and desires of the other. The collusion and contestation between patriarchies and 'brahminism' (upper-caste practices and ideologies) reveals the exercise of such power through the differential definitions and management of gender by caste. Gender was and is crucial to the maintenance of reproduction of caste inequalities. Further, Lukes has argued that power presupposes human agency and that agents consist in a set of expanding and contracting opportunities. Together these constitute the structural possibilities which specify the power of agents varying between time and over agents.[4] Women's agency needs to be located in the context of the structural possibilities of class, race, caste and community. The state has in all its programmes assumed the women to be 'free agents'; outside the boundaries of caste, class and religion. The contradiction between the state's explicitly stated commitment to the annihilation of caste and upgradation of women and the increasing violence against women and the lower caste, is legitimised through the maintenance of caste and gender as separate issues on the political agenda, precisely because of the important links between the two. The 'real interests' of women must be conceptualised from the perspective of the marginalised; in this case the perspectives of the Dalit women. Centring from the perspective of the marginalised prevents the distortion of both; those at the centre and at the margins.[5] Further, such an analysis need not amount to speaking for the marginalised or speaking for the 'Dalit' women for the multiple and contradictory subject agent of feminism is also logically the subject of every other libratory project. In following Harding, we agree that this is not only an epistemological but also a moral and political issue.

The first major challenge to the women's movement in India has come from the state-sponsored programmes of modernisation. But in recent times, a major threat is being posed by the Hindu fundamentalists who spread insidious propaganda that not only 'others' the muslims but provides a utopia of 'Ramrajya' (rule of the divine). To the educated unemployed and the educated upper-caste women confined to the domestic sphere, the Hindu fundamentalists provide a public forum. Women's power as in the Hindu religious mythology is being posed as opposed to the 'western' concept of women's liberation. The IMF (International Monetary Fund) guided liberalisation of the economy and the near acceptance of the Dunkel draft by the Indian government as against alternative paths of development pose a major threat to the women workers and peasants. In such a context, the left, the anti-caste, ecology, tribal and women's movement in India are realising the need of interlinkages of 'rainbow' coalition politics. Social activist groups working in diverse areas in different parts of India are coming together, attempting to work out a political agenda. This chapter is part of such attempts; exploring the essential links between caste and violence against women. The first section attempts to give a brief summary of the issues that the contemporary women's movement in India has to confront. The second section traces the ways in which the debates and reform or legislation against violence has in fact realigned patriarchal interest with changing political formations. The third section presents cases of violence against upper-caste women; the continuum ranging from everyday practices of verbal abuse to the cases of widow burning, the cases of rape of lower-caste women which reveal the links between 'virtue' and the right to protest against rape and the recent cases of violence against lower-caste men; in which upper-caste women were reported to have not only incited their menfolk into violence but also participate publicly in the acts. In the last section, the impasse that the women's movement faces and the need to form coalitions, the important links between caste and gender that can help from such coalitions are outlined.

Vast differences distinguish the lives of women in different parts of India and within different caste, class, religious and ethnic groups. Eighty percent of India's population lives in the rural areas and more than 70% of India's female labour force falls in the category of landless agricultural labour. The struggle for these women revolves around procuring food, fuel and water for their families. The number of female-headed household have been on the increase and there has been a growing deterioration and privatisation of the country's common property resources on which the poor in general and women in particular depend.[6] Food allocation in the family is heavily biased in favour of men and even in the agriculturally prosperous state of Punjab, women's average consumption of calories is only two-thirds of that of men; despite the fact that women in this region perform at least 15hours of arduous labour. This contributes to a higher mortality rate among women. For the women of the rich peasant and upper castes, it is a struggle against seclusion and torture within the family.[7] In urban India, the female labour force is concentrated in the informal section; mainly as domestic servants, construction labour and casual labour. Only 10% of the female labour force is employed in industries. There has been a visible improvement in the lives of the middle-class, upper-caste, educated women, in terms of their participation on education and employment. Several studies have revealed that employment for women of these classes has not brought much change in the power axes of the family.[8] Women's labour in fact remains a flexible resource.[9] There is therefore, the paradoxical co-existence of constitutional guarantees of equality and brutal expression of violence and the relative powerlessness of women. The population of women in India has been declining and the sex ratio has declined from 972 females to 1,000 males in 1901 to 927 females to 1,000 males in 1991. Only 24.8% of the women are literate and only 5.7% can ever reach the university. More than 70% of the female labour force is in the unorganised section, which means long hours of work, wage differentials and no security. Birth of daughters is unwelcome and new forms of female foeticide are emerging. The birth of a daughter means the liability of guarding her virginity and debts in paying the dowry in marriage to the bridegroom's family. This payment, however, does not guarantee any security for the women as there is always a demand for more in the form of festive offerings and gifts. In the capital city of New Delhi, two women die of burns every day; the cases being either of 'suicide' or dowry murders. In 1991, the number of women who faced the torture of rape, were estimated at two million, and the majority of the victims were tribal, Dalit; the incidence of rape being higher in areas declared to be turbulent and where the army or the police have been stationed.[10]

The women's movement in India has been in a lull after the declaration of independence and the granting of constitutional guarantees of equality and freedom for all irrespective of caste, creed or sex. Disillusionment with the rhetoric of socialist democracy and planned development set in, during the mid-1960s and women began to participate in large number in the tribal, working class, Dalit and student's movements. The declaration of emergency and withdrawal of civil rights in 1975 had led to several atrocities. As the emergency war lifted, civil liberties groups brought to light several cases of gang rapes of lower-caste women in northern India. Against such a background the autonomous women's groups emerged as the political force on the issue of violence against women. Nationwide networking of women's groups emerged on the issue of rape and dowry murders and the state was pushed into legal amendments.[11] As feminist groups in urban India began to focus on the violence outside and within the home, the media projected them as 'western' and disrespectful of Indian tradition. The left and the anti-caste movements labelled the feminist focus on violence as 'middle class' and saw the women's centres as being 'welfaristic' and not 'revolutionary' enough. All political parties were quick to catch on and revitalised or created a women's wing, taking care to draw on symbols of female power from popular Hindu mythology.

The state-sponsored programmes of redistribution of land and modernisation had begun in the 1960s, and by the 1980s, it was apparent that these had led to increased inequalities in income and wealth. For the first 30years after Independence, women figured in the planned development as only 'mothers' in the 'mother and child welfare programmes'; despite the fact that more than 50% of the agricultural labour was provided by women.[12] The development projects such as the green revolution project and the large dam projects have marginalised the poor and especially women. In the so-called prosperous green revolution region, the inequalities in income have increased and the number of dowry deaths and malnutrition of women have shown a steady increase.[13] In the industrial sector, in the free trading zones, women have been exploited as cheap labour and have been made to work under conditions of strict supervision and physical abuse. Attempts at unionisation have been brutally squashed with police assistance.[14]

The family planning programmes and population policies under the cover of 'cafeteria' approach have made political grounds of women's wombs.[15] International organisations, such as IPPF (International Planned Parenthood Federation) and the Population Council, have promoted the use of hormonal implants and injectibles and the MNC's who produce them, invoke the demands of the women's movement (control over body and fertility) as they market these drugs. Women's groups and health activists have opposed these on three grounds; side-effects, inadequate public health services to meet the demands of such implants and the fact that these drugs have not been standardised for women in India and that biochemical and epidemiological studies are essential before their introduction in India. Women's right to choose and freedom are invoked while the politics of the private and health care is sidetracked.[16]

For the majority of women in India, the uppermost problem is of survival. Poverty, dowry murders, widow burning, female infanticide have assumed new forms with modernisation and technological advancement. These contexts of fatal aggression seem to normalise the everyday practices of violence by the family, community, state and global economy. This reality of oppression is being measured, codified, as struggles are reduced to manipulable data to be filled into neat theoretical frameworks. Baxi comments that women's studies seem to be harnessed to producing a third gender – men, women and PhDs in women studies.[17] Deprivatisation of the knowledge seems to be the first step in developing an approach towards violence against women and collective political violence in India.[18]

To call the questions that were raised at the onset in the last 200 years, what were the different forms of violence against women that have been addressed? Who were the individuals or groups engaged in the public debates on the issue? And most significantly, who is the 'Indian Woman' on whose behalf they plead? The status of Indian women occupied a prominent position in the nineteenth-century discourse. The need to reform Indian society was incorporated into the reform of Indian woman's position and Indian woman like Indian tradition was defined across a particular axis of religion, class and caste.[19] From the late eighteenth century, the missionaries had begun to attack a range of 'degenerate' Hindu practices, majority of which were directed expressly against women. The missionaries brought out a volley of tracts and pamphlets directed at the British government and public, giving dramatic and empirical details of practices like widow burning and proclaiming Indian men to be moral monsters. The aim was to contrast Hinduism to Christianity, the location of women's position at the centre of such a critique is seen as part of an ongoing process of creating and projecting a superior national identity of Britain – of which the English woman was a central motif, along with the English art, rural life, literature and character.[20]

The appeals made by the missionaries led the colonial administration to intervene through social legislation. This intervention was varied in the different regions of India and reveals a complex interrelationship of contest and collusion between indigenous patriarchal norms and those held by the British administration. This is largely, but rarely noted visibly in the colonial regulation on agrarian relations.[21] Several Western educated, Indian intellectuals, concerned, no doubt, with the plight of Hindu women entered the arena of reform. These social reformers fall into two categories: those who saw reform as a revival of the 'Golden' period of Hinduism and those that sought the modernisation of 'Indian' tradition. The debates were all based on the upper-caste religious texts and the forms of violence being addressed (widow burning, child marriage, seclusion, enforced widowhood) were all primarily upper-caste Hindu practices. The lower-caste women who were being marginalised by the new land legislation and exposed to the threat of sexual violence under the 'Zamindari' system of land legislation and the distress sale of women following the new land settlements in the eighteenth century are absent in these debates.[22] The

'Indian woman' in the reform debate was essentially Hindu, upper caste and symbolic of the emergent middle class; women being tied to the very process of cultural homogenisation of the middle class.[23] Such a reform movement had very little reach but served to provide a model of Indian womanhood. The position of the Indian woman had occupied much of the early and the mid-nineteenth-century debates; towards the close of the century this issue disappears from the arena of public debate. The overwhelming issues are directly political ones, concerning the politics of nationalism.[24] It has been argued that nationalism resolved the 'woman's question' in accordance with its preferred goals. This resolution was built around a separation of the domain of culture into two spheres, the material and the spiritual domain, the East was considered as superior and this was to be the spiritual essence of the national culture. This distinction of the material/spiritual was condensed into the ideologically superior dichotomy of inner/outer, home/world.[25] This spirituality of the inner sanctum, the home was to be maintained by the woman as the torch bearer of tradition (all violence within the family was thus rendered invisible), and by reverse logic all those women (lower-caste working class) who 'did not' were designated as 'impure'.

British feminism had matured during the age of the empire but as Burton has argued the British feminist participated in the assumptions of national and racial superiority. She argues that Josephine Butler's campaign on behalf of Indian women is an example of imperial feminism. Her review of the feminist periodical literature of the nineteenth century reveals that British feminism constructed the image of the helpless Indian womanhood, on which their own emancipation in the imperial nation state relied. Burton concludes that not only the Victorian and Edwardian feminists reproduce the moral discourse of imperialism but embedded Western feminism deeply within it.[26] Ramusack has referred to the British feminists as the 'maternal imperialists'[27] while Paxton argues that for the feminists the choice was limited, between being racist and loyal or being disloyal to the civilisation.[28] India remained an imaginative landscape of the British feminists who addressed the issue of violence against Indian women.

The first wave feminists in India (twentieth century) were women related to the reformers or the nationalists, mainly upper-caste women who lobbied tirelessly for the right to property and amendments in the Hindu law of marriage. These first wave feminists were preoccupied with issues of 'status' rather than 'survival'. It was therefore, the upper-caste, middle-class women who drew the benefits from the constitutional guarantees and legal measures.[29] The second wave feminists in India who formed autonomous groups politicised the issue of violence against women, both inside and outside the home. Free legal aid centres and counselling groups were set up and consciousness raising through street plays and posters on the issue of violence became a regular practice in urban areas. As a result of several such campaigns, the laws against Rape and Dowry Prohibition Act were amended. The issue on Uniform Civil Code was taken up on a nationwide scale; however, the ruling Congress Party fearing the loss of minority vote banks backtracked on the issue. Those second wave feminists who did not accept autonomy and separatism and had to remain in 'mass' movements argued that violence against women was no doubt an important issue but the campaigns for legal amendments and crisis centres were urban and middle class and that the economic issues were more urgent for the masses of woman. The recent upsurge in caste and communal violence and the participation of the women of the dominant groups in this violence points towards the impasse facing the woman's movement in India.[30] In the next section cases of violence are presented, before undertaking an analysis of the impasse.

For most of us the issue of widow burning or 'sati' was a historical issue, till we saw a revival of the practice in 1987. The women's movement later unearthed the fact that after independence, there had been 38 cases of widow burning in India. Historically, the custom has been prevalent only in certain regions of India and among the upper castes and the landed. In regions where the widow had a right in the deceased husband's property, the practice became prevalent in the twelfth and thirteenth centuries. The custom can be seen as the ultimate resolution of the management and control over the widow's sexuality. The anxiety over controlling the widow's sexuality was so high that in certain region the practice of 'cold sati' was devised for ensuring the commitment of 'sati' by the child widows. The child widow would be poisoned in course of a festive celebration of her declaration to become a 'sati' and then the cold body placed on a pyre of the husband. The lower castes did not practice this custom and the lower-caste widows could remarry freely, until the colonial intervention through the Widow Remarriage Act of 1856.[31]

The debate on widow burning began in the 1780s when the missionaries first took up the issue. The colonial administration first intervened in the civil society on the issue of 'sati'. A debate ensued between the colonial officials and the Western-educated Indian intellectuals on one hand and the conservatives on the other. The entire debate is preoccupied with preserving true tradition. The widow is either the victim or the heroine and both the parties intercede on her behalf to save her from 'true tradition'. The reformers claimed that the high tradition to be followed while the conservatives argued that true tradition demanded that for her own salvation and that of her family a widow must commit 'sati'. Mani had argued that in this debate women are neither the subjects nor the objects but become the grounds for debate.[32]

The revival of the practice in 1987 led to a nationwide controversy. There were mainly tow positions taken; the liberals saw the practice as barbaric and a failure of modernisation while the conservative pro-sati lobby defended the practice as 'Indian' tradition. What is important to note is that the region which saw the revival of the practice, has never had a history of widow burning. Since 1954, the region has seen the upper castes build 105 temples dedicated to the 'satis'. The custom had been systematically used to revive the identity of the upper castes (Rajputs) who had faced a downfall after the state-sponsored land reform programme in which some of the middle castes had benefitted and had consolidated their political position. The protesting feminists came to be portrayed as a threat to the Hindu identity and an all India association for the preservation of sati as a religious duty was formed. The state fumbled, there was no moment for 11 days, as pressure from a progressive coalition built up on Sati Prohibition Act of 1829 was amended. The new act is again an upholder of 'true tradition' as it declares that the custom is banned since no religion in India endorses it. Moreover, the new Act treats the women as a free agent, by making her act punishable,[33] the upholders of the practice brought forth the issue of the widow's will and voluntary 'sati'. Feminists argued that one can hardly conceive of the widow's will when widowhood imposes social death and its own regime of misery for women. By raising the issue of women's agency, in the Indian context, one walks on a tight rope. If widow burning is at the extreme end of the continuum of violent practices within upper-caste families, a critique of the day-to-day life practices in the upper-caste homes would reveal the different intermediate forms of control that operate. Firstly, there are linguistic clues; both verbal abuse and the reinforcing of stereotypes. There are also severe controls over women's labour in that under the ideology of 'grihalaxmi' (the woman as the goddess of the household) the burden of domestic work is glorified and often women begin to view this burden as their privilege. It must be noted here that the arduous tasks of domestic work are performed by the lower-caste women who constitute the majority of domestic labour. Attempts of unionisation by domestic workers have been viewed negatively by their upper-caste women employers; strikes have resulted in loss of jobs for most of these women.

In the upper-caste families, women are denied the right to work outside the home and it has been observed that elevation in caste status is preceded by the withdrawal of womenfolk from work outside the family. Among the urban middle classes (upper caste), more flexibility seems to be operating than implied by the categories of public and private. Women's labour is used to meet the increasing inflating but to ensure that this does not erode its own control, private patriarchal authority brings into use ideology which on one hand highlights women's total commitment to the needs of the household and on the other consistently reiterates taboos against sexuality or reproduction outside family and caste mores.[34] There are then the controls exercised through actual physical abuse; wife beating, enforced seclusion, denial of basic necessities are common methods of exercising control, the elder women of the family, generally the mother-in-law being the enforcing agent. The unmarried girls are closely guarded and any transgression of norms results in their being withdrawn from public life; they are brought up to believe that their husband's extended family is their final destination and that their parental home is only a transit lounge. That is, in all regional languages in India, unmarried girls are reflected as property that does not belong to the family. The post-independence Indian state has offered women equal facilities for education and training but in no way has it questioned or bypassed the household's authority to decide whether or not women can avail of any of these facilities.[35] The state in all its programmes has maintained a 'woman within the family approach'. The women in India perform within the family any of the functions that have long been, at least partially, the responsibility of the state; alternative ways of fulfilling these functions would be extremely costly for the state. More importantly under modern rationalisations of 'cultural legitimacy' women have been kept within the family, rights for women outside the family would pose a threat to the caste system and thereby to the hegemony of the upper castes. The very fundamental rights and freedom granted by the Indian Constitution to all citizens, the right against forced labour, the freedom of movement, freedom of speech and expression, have been denied to women by their families. Paradoxically, there is a strong tradition of according forms of responsibility and veneration to women as 'mothers'. Women can gain access to power in the family only as agents of domination and oppression of the younger women in the family.[36]

In case of lower-caste women the fact that their labour outside the family is crucial for the survival of the family, leads to the lack of stringent controls on their labour mobility and sexuality and this renders them 'impure' or 'lacking in virtue'. In several instances the rape of Dalit women may not be considered as rape at all because of the customary access that the upper-caste men have had to Dalit women's sexuality. In almost all regional languages in India the word for 'rape' is equivalent to the phrase 'stealing the honour of' and since lower-caste women by the virtue of their double oppression have no 'honour' to speak of the right to redressal is often denied. In a recent incident at Birati in West Bengal, the police argued that since the women 'crying rape' were prostitutes the matter could be overlooked.[37] The legal courts, too, operating along this ideology became apparent in the two cases of rape; one of the lower-caste beggar woman (Laxmi) and the other of a tribal landless labourer (Mathura). In both the cases, the courts acquitted the rapists who were policemen. Question about the 'virtue' of these women were raised and it had been argued that their character was questionable. These cases were taken up by the women's movement in India and the supreme court pushed into reopening the cases and finally into amending the law against rape, to recognise custodial rape and to put the onus of proof on the rapist and not the woman. Dalit women suffer rape as a part of the ongoing caste confrontations. In rural India, defiance of caste restrictions by the Dalits have most often resulted in arson and gang rapes of women of the lower caste. If rape is at one end of the continuum of violent practices against lower-caste women, there are the less obvious and also normalised practices such as the successive marginalisation of the lower-caste performers and the attempts to reform them and their creative expressions; thereby pushing the majority of these artistes into hidden forms of prostitution.[38] The percentage of female headed households among the lower castes is as high as 70% to 75%; since the incidence of desertion is very high and even in cases where the husband is present, (often just his presence is seen as necessary by the women to ward off the sexual threat of the men from their community), it is the women's income that goes towards the survival of the family since the husband's income is spend on arrack or bigamy being common; the income goes towards the maintenance of the 'preferred' wife. Lower-caste women in Andhra Pradesh have at the local level organised antiarrack movements, in a way that threatens the state; since most of the state revenue comes from arrack. In Maharashtra, the 'deserted' women went on a march through the state in an attempt to draw the state's attention to the gravity of the problems and the issue of maintenance.[39] The situation of the Dalit women who are at the receiving end of both the upper-caste and lower-caste patriarchies, has been portrayed by Tersamma, a lower-caste activist in a poem:

> We go to work for we are poor,
> But the same silken beds mock us,
> While we are ravished in broad daylight,
> Ill-starred our horoscopes are,
> Even our tottering husbands hiss and shout for revenge;
> If we cannot stand their touch.
> (Quoted by Dietrich, 1990)

In rural India, the participation of Dalit women in the different local struggles for water, land or forests, has been on the increase.[40] These struggles have to a large extent regained from taking up the issue of violence against women. The women's movement, which addresses the issues of sexuality and violence, has been limited to the urban centres. In recent times, there have been at least three widely reported cases of violence against the lower caste (Chunduru in Andhra Pradesh, Gothala and Pimpri Deshmukh in Maharashtra) in which the lower-caste men had been hacked to death, because of their alleged indecent behaviour towards upper-caste women. The upper-caste women in all the three cases had, it was reported, not only incited their menfolk into the violent acts but also participated in them. These cases present a problem for the feminist movement in that the alleged sexual harassment of the upper-caste women by the lower-caste males could be 'cover up' for caste confrontations;[41] in that the agency of upper-caste women had been invoked in caste confrontations (Professor Gopal Guru's field reports support such an argument).[42] Even if one grants that the upper-caste women were being sexually harassed by the lower-caste males, the issue has to be seen in the light of the years of sexual abuse of the Dalit women by the upper-caste males and the customary sanctions that legitimised such violence, the cases pointed to the urgent need of coalitions between the women's movement and the Dalit movement; such coalitions require a historical analysis of the links between caste and gender, the next section attempts to contribute to such analysis.

A caste-wise analysis of the violent practices against women would reveal that the incidence of dowry murders, controls on mobility and sexuality by the family, widow burning are more frequent among the upper castes while Dalit women are more likely to face the collective threat of rape, sexual harassment and physical violence.[43] This has implications for the sociological analysis of caste; volumes of which have overlooked the essential links between caste and gender, thereby rendering a partial understanding of the caste system. Castes and patriarchies have been maintained and reproduced through the 'textually mediated practices'[44] of sociology.

Sociologists, (under the influence of structure-functionalism), with varying emphasis, delineated the following characteristics of the caste system in India:

1   Each linguistic division in India shows a wide variation of caste, about 200 groups with distinct names, birth in one of which determines the status of an

individual in society. These groups are further divided into sub-castes, which fix the limits for marriage and effective social life. Each caste had its own governing body, the 'caste and panchayat'; to this day several of the interfamilial and intrafamilial grievances are referred to these bodies.[45]

2. The caste system operates on a principle of hierarchy and difference.[46] There is a scheme of social precedence amongst the castes, though this varies with the regions, in most cases it is the 'brahmins' who are at the top of the ritual scale and the 'untouchable' or the 'scavenger' castes at the bottom. Elevation in economic and political status for a caste can lead to a collective change in its position within the caste hierarchy. (Such changes, as mentioned earlier, have been accompanied by withdrawal of women from work outside the household.)

3. The caste system outlined the religious and civil disabilities and privileges of the different castes, these ranged from the denial of use of public resources like wells, roads, temples, the denial to use certain kinds of clothing, housing and differential punishments by caste and definite restrictions on feeding and social intercourse.[47] (Such privileges of the upper castes also included the sexual rights of upper-caste men over lower-caste men.) Though the Indian law marks discrimination by caste and practice of untouchability a crime, such practices continue, especially in rural India.

4. The caste system restricted the choice of occupation; in a land-based economy, the callings were based on heredity. This factor has undergone considerable change and there is no one-to-one correspondence between castes and occupations.

5. The essence of caste system according to most sociologists is the practice of endogamy or marriage within the sub-caste. Though there are exceptions to this rule in that some castes practiced hypergamy, wherein to give ones daughter in marriage to a man of higher caste was a preferred form of marriage; the reverse, the marriage of a lower-caste man with a woman of higher caste, was severely punished. (What sociologists have concealed under the rubrics of endogamy is the fact that women were and are the 'gateways' to the caste system.)[48]

The principles of caste and the rule of conduct for the different castes were codified in the 'shastras' or the instructional treatises of the Hindus which date back to the third century BCE. These were written by the 'Brahmins' or the priestly castes who legitimised the rule of the 'kshatriya' caste or the warrior castes. These rules were popularised through the 'Puranas' or mythological stories. In these treatises women have been equated to the lower castes and definite restrictions have been placed on both. Both have been defined as impure, of sinful birth and as having a polluting presence. Both the lower castes and women had to observe practices of verbal difference, temporal distance and dress codes as an index of their subordinate status.[49] Around 800 BC these treatises begin to make a definite division between the upper-caste women and those of the lower castes. In the 'Manusmriti', the most influential treatise, the realignment of castes and patriarchies is apparent in the 'ideology of the *pativrata* (one who worships the husband and his kin without any grievances)'. Becoming a 'pativrata' was posed as an alternative for upper-caste women to rise above their sinful birth and an access to salvation. It was posited that an upper-caste woman must always be under the control of her father, husband or son.[50] This ideology secured the compliance of the upper-caste women and rendered them 'pure' as against the lower-caste women. While strict control over the sexuality and labour of upper-caste women came to be legitimised; the social and sexual labour of the lower-caste women was made available to the patrilineal land economy. Paradoxically, the very 'failure' of the lower-caste men to control the sexuality of their women was projected as a major root of their impurity. In a patrilineal society, the caste determined not only the right to property but also the right to occupation. The upper two sections, the 'brahmins' and 'kshatriyas', were not related directly to the land, and monopoly was developed through clear cut ideas of purity and pollution. These ideas were linked to heredity and it became essential to prove that the women of the upper castes could not have sexual relations outside of their caste. However, there were no physical characteristic that could prove caste purity and the women of the upper castes in their daily routine did come in contact with the males of the potter, bangle seller and other artisan and lower castes. Hence severe restriction came to be placed on women and 'chastity' of women assumed unwarranted importance. This argument is further strengthened by the fact that the severe controls in the form of pre-puberty marriages and widow burning became most pronounced in those periods when 'brahminism' faced a threat whether from Buddhism or the 'Bhakti' and 'tantra' movements. Feminist writings on caste have argued that gender ideology that was constructed in these texts not only legitimised the structures of patriarchy but also the very organisation of caste.[51] Vaid and Sangari have argued that the lives of women exist at their interface of caste and class inequalities and that the description and management of female sexuality is crucial to the reproduction of these inequalities.[52] The counterfactual to this argument may be seen in the challenges posed by the 'tantric' and 'bhakti' movement. The 'tantric' movement is seen in the form of different cults based on the folkways and worship of the mother goddesses. These cults focused on the release and celebration of sexual energies as against controls over sexuality. The ritual practices of these cults involved the sexual intermingling of castes. These cults were brutally curbed or in some regions their revolutionary potential lost by their integration into mainstream Hinduism. The 'bhakti' movement on the other hand was a movement led by the poet saints who stressed the direct relationship of human beings, men and women alike, to god; thereby challenging the hegemony of the upper castes, mainly the 'brahmins' in their self-proclaimed role of mediators between the divine and the human. However, this movement did not directly address this issue of sexuality and therefore of the caste-based division of labour and this perhaps, partly explains, the relatively tolerant attitude of the 'brahmins' towards this movement. The medieval ages have been labelled as the 'dark ages' by the colonial historians and their 'brahmin' colluders; we suspect that the stories of the dark ages could well be the stories of rebellion.

To conclude, the issue of violence against women, cannot be seen as either a 'caste' issue or a 'gender' issue, but that it must be located in the links between the two. In a political system where dominant factions lobby, organise and mobilise along caste alliances of the rich and middle peasantry; effective action requires coalitions between the 'Dalit' and women's movements. In fact, delineating the 'real interest' of women requires the analysis of the complex interlinkages of gender and other structural inequalities or else the demands of the women's movement could well lead to the consolidation of some of these inequalities.

Notes

1 This chapter has appeared as 'Caste and Gender: The Violence against Women in India', Chapter 3, in P. G. Jogdand (ed.), *Dalit Women in India: Issues and Perspectives*, forwarded by U. B. Bhoite, New Delhi: Gyan Publishing House in collaboration with University of Poona, Pune, 2013, pp. 18–36. Used with permission.
2 S. Lukes, *Power: A Radical View*, London: MacMillan, 1974.
3 S. Harding, 'Subjectivity, Experience and Knowledge: An Epistemology from/for Rainbow Coalition Politics', *Development and Change*, Vol. 23, No. 3, Sage, 1992: 175–193.
4 Lukes, *Power*.
5 Harding, 'Subjectivity, Experience and Knowledge: An Epistemology from/for Rainbow Coalition Politics', 1992.
6 B. Agarwal (ed.), *Structures of Patriarchy: State, Community and Household in Modernising Asia*, New Delhi: Kali for Women, 1988.
7 M. Kishwar and R. Vanita, *In Search of Answers*, New Delhi: Horizon India Books, 1991.
8 Guy Standing, 'The Road to Workfare: Alternative to welfare or Threat to Occupation?', *International Labour Review*, Vol. 129, No. 6, 1990: 677–692.
9 N. Banerjee, *Patriarchy and Work*, Shimla: IIAS, 1992.
10 N. Gandhi and N. Shah, *Issues at Stake*, New Delhi: Kali for Women, 1992.
11 Ibid.
12 *Towards Equality*, Report of the Committee on Status of Women in India, Ministry of India Publication, New Delhi, 1975.
13 B. Agarwal, 'Women, Poverty and Agricultural Growth in India', *Journal of Peasant Studies*, Vol. 13 No. 4, July 1986.
14 S. Trikha, *A Study of Women's Employment in Kandla Free Trade Zone*, Mimeo, New Delhi: ICRIER, 1985.
15 Something Like a War, 1992.
16 S. Tharu and T. Niranjana, *Problems for a Contemporary Theory of Gender*, Investigating Hyderabad, 1992. Chapter 2 in this edition.
17 Upendra Baxi, 'From Human rights to the Right to Being Human', in Upendra Baxi, Geeti Sen and Jeanette Fernandes (eds.), *The Right to Be Human*, New Delhi: India International Centre, 1987.
18 Ibid.
19 E. Wolf, *Re-inventing Tradition*, Shimla: IIAS, 1992.
20 Ibid.
21 Sudesh Vaid and Kumkum Sangari, *Recasting Women: Essays in Colonial History*, New Delhi: Kali for Women, 1990.
22 Ibid.
23 S. Banerjee, 'Marginalisation of Women's Popular Cultural in Nineteen Century Bengal', in S. Vaid and K. Sangari (eds.), *Recasting Women*, New Delhi: Kali for Women, 1990.
24 P. Chatterjee, 'The Nationalist Resolution of the Woman's Question', in Vaid and Sangari (eds.), *Recasting Women*.
25 Ibid.

26. A. Burton, 'The White Woman's Burden', *Women's Studies International Forum*, Vol. 13 No. 4, 1990.
27. B. Ramusack, 'Cultural Missionaries, Maternal Imperialists, Feminist Allies', *Women's Studies International Forum*, Vol. 13 No. 4, 1990.
28. N. Parton, 'Feminism Under the Raj', *Women's Studies International Forum*, Vol. 13 No. 4, 1990.
29. G. Omvedt, *Theories of Violence*, New Delhi: Kali for Women, 1991, 1985.
30. Tharu and Niranjana, *Problems for a Contemporary Theory of Gender*. Chapter 2 in this edition.
31. P. Choudhary, 'Customs in a Peasant Society', in Vaid and Sangari (eds.), *Recasting Women*, 1990.
32. L. Mani, 'Multiple Meditations', *Inscriptions* No. 5, University of California, 1989.
33. Vasudha Dhagamwar, *Towards the Uniform Civil Code*. Bombay: N. M. Tripathi Private Ltd., under the auspices of the Indian Law Institute, New Delhi, 1988.
34. Banerjee, *Patriarchy and Work*.
35. Ibid.
36. Kishwar and Vanita, *In Search of Answers*, 1991.
37. T. Sarkar, 'Reflections on the Birati Rape Cases', *Economic and Political Weekly*, February 2, 1991.
38. S. Rege, *Sati: A Critical Analysis*, Monograph: WSC, Department of Sociology, University of Poona, 1989.
39. Samata Andolan, 1990. For details, see https://www.samtaandolan.co.in/.
40. G. Omvedt, *Theories of Violence*, New Delhi: Kali for Women, 1990.
41. V. Bhagwat and S. Rege, 'Towards a Gender-Sensitive Sociology', paper presented at the UGC National Seminar, March 1993.
42. G. Guru, 'Dalit Killings in Marathwada', *Economic and Political Weekly*, Vol. XXVI No. 51, December 21, 1991.
43. G. Dietrich, 'The Relationship Between Dalit Movements and Women's Movement: Cases and Conceptual Analysis', paper for the IAWS, Calcutta, 1990.
44. Dorothy E. Smith, *Texts, Facts and Femininity: Exploring the Relations of Ruling*, London: Routledge, 1990.
45. G. Ghurye, *Caste and Race in India*, Bombay: Allied, 1956.
46. D. Gupta, *Social Stratification*, New Delhi: Oxford University Press, 1992.
47. Ghurye, *Caste and Race in India*, 1956.
48. Ira Das, 'Sati: A Heinous System of Women Oppression', *Shodhak*, Vol. 17, Part A, Sr. No. 49, 1988.
49. R. Guha, *Elementary Forums of Peasant Insurgency in India*, New Delhi: Oxford University Press, 1983.
50. P.V. Kane, *History of Dharmashastra: Ancient and Medieval Religious and Civil law in India*, Vol. 1, Part. 2, Government Oriental Series, Pune: Bhandarkar Oriental Research Institute, 1930, reprinted in 1974.
51. Uma Chakravarti, 'Conceptualising Patriarchy in Early India: Gender Caste, Class and State', Economical and Political Weekly, Vol. 28, No. 14, Special Articles, April 3, 1993:579–585; J. Liddle and R. Joshi, *Daughters of Independence*, New Delhi: Kali for Women, 1986; Vasanth Kannibaran and Kalpana Kannibaran, 'Caste and Gender: Understanding Dynamics of Power and Violence', *Economic and Political Weekly*, Vol. 26, No. 37, September 14, 1991: 2130–2134.
52. Vaid and Sangari, *Recasting Women*.

8

VILIFYING DALIT WOMEN[1]

Epics and aesthetics

Excerpt from 'Hindu Epics: Portrayal of Dalit Women'[2]

Vizia Bharati

According to reports issued by the Ministry of Welfare, over half of the rape cases officially registered in India concern women belonging to the scheduled castes and tribes. On average more than 1,000 such cases of rape are reported each year, and they are often not investigated and difficult to prove. The use of torture and other forms of cruel behaviour towards poorer and oppressed sections is not new in Indian society. There are many examples in our literature to show that.

Dalit women were portrayed in distinct ways in both epics, '*Mahabharata*' and '*Ramayana*'. I will focus on five characters, though there are many others that could also be discussed: (1) Matanga Kanyas; (2) Tataka; (3) Shurpanakha; (4) Aayomukhi; and (5) Mandodari. There is much to say about the genealogy of these people, who each fall within the 'Shudra' category.

Our holy scriptures say 'Asura' means Rakshasa. They are opposed to the 'Sura' race. *Mahabharata* and *Ramayana* speak highly of the 'Deva' race and degrade the 'Asura' race. One can also notice Arya and Anarya differences in both the epics. On the whole, the Puranas say that the Asura, Rakshasa and Desyu races are opposed to Aryan culture. They are aboriginal and depicted as wicked people. In that sense one can conclude that these were oppressed races – the Dalits of that era. *Ramayana* tells us clearly how Rama killed Rakshasas to protect sages (priests) and Yajnas. But the main point I wish to make here is about how Rakshasa women were insulted by Rama, who belonged to a higher caste.

Matanga Kanya

Mahabharata speaks of pastoral communities as well as hunting tribes. The story of 'Satya Harishchandra' is a famous one, and Matanga Kanyas (girls from an untouchable family) play an important role. The story appears in almost all regional languages in India. It was propagated as Sravya Kavya and Drisya Kavya (i.e., drama), and has become popular as cinema also.

King Harishchandra was a famous king of Tretayuga. He is one among the six famous kings. He is praised for his Satyavach (truthfulness). Let us examine some facts of the story. Once King Harishchandra went to the forest for hunting. He was much tired. Two matanga girls approached him and entertained him with their dance and music. The king was sought to give them a token in praise of their talent. On his request, they asked for an 'umbrella'. An umbrella in those days was a symbol of royal honour, for which only higher caste people were eligible. The lower castes, howsoever talented, could not ask for such an honour; it was regarded as a sin. The king got angry and rejected their wish, but he gave them another chance to ask for a wish. The girls expressed their wish to marry the king. The king was stunned. He rejected their wish saying that the girls were untouchable – he could not marry them. In the beginning of the story the girls were described as very beautiful and well mannered. All the same, they suffer discrimination; as untouchables they were insulted and sent off. They were abused in the name of their caste.

Later, the sage Vishwamitra comes to the king and declares them as his pet daughters; thus, he asks the king to marry them. Though the sage assures the king that it was no sin, the King rejects the proposal saying that the girls were untouchables. King Harishchandra expresses his aversion towards the lower castes repeatedly. He says that he cannot disgrace his pious caste by marrying the Matanga girls.

The Puranas, propagating varnasrama dharma, depict Harishchandra as an ideal king. The story was given wide publicity: King Harishchandra stood adamant for caste and was ready to undergo anything instead of such a polluting marriage. He lost his kingdom, son, wife and everything for the sake of caste.

Tataka

Ramayana can be read as a tale of upper and lower class conflict; Aryan and non-Aryan conflicts for power. The killing of Tataka, as recounted in the epic, is the consequence of the domination of sages over Dandakaranya, Tataka's native place. Its express purpose was 'gobrahminhithardhaya', the welfare of cows and brahmins, and 'caturvarnahitardhaya', the welfare of the varna system.

Tataka is a dignified and powerful ruler of Malada and Karusha. Subsequent tradition regards her as a godling (Yakshini) who was transformed into a Rakshasi as punishment for having disturbed the Rishi Agastya. Manu asserts that births as dancers, arrogant men and rakshasas are the effects of the refined kind of Tamasaguna. Birth as shudras are the middle kind of Tamasaguna. However, births as gandharva, guhyaka, Yaksha, the attendants of Gods and Apsaras are the superior kind of Rajasaguna.[3] Thus, Manu is equating shudra and rakshasa births more or less with Tamasaguna.

Tataka being a Yakshini by birth is of Rajasaguna, superior to shudras. But she became a Rakshasi by the curse of Agastya, falling victim to the domination of higher castes. They killed her husband and cursed her son such that he also become a rakshasa. Oppressed and degraded, she can be equated to a Dalit woman.

Tataka by birth was a beautiful and strong woman, and a peace-loving ruler. She opposed yajnas (sacrifices), which involved killing, or himsa (violence). The sages were thus prohibited from performing yajnas in her territory and were thus greatly displeased by her attitude toward ahimsa. They went to the king Dasharatha and brought his sons Rama and Lakshmana along with them for help and attacked Tataka. She was killed and they occupied her territory.

The realities of the story were not focused properly in *Ramayana*. Tataka was neither cruel nor of an aggressive nature. Vishwamitra brought Rama to her land ('Tatakayaamvanam') purposefully and caught her unaware. Tataka was neither given the chance to fight nor to protect herself. They attacked her mercilessly, defamed her by cutting off her nose and ears and killed her most cruelly. In contemporary incidents of sexual exploitation, especially when a girl refuses to submit to the desire of a higher-caste man or landlord, the girl's nose and ears are cut off, and in some cases she is stripped naked and paraded. It is interesting to note that the same punishments were in vogue in the great Hindu epics *Ramayana* and *Mahabharata*. In the latter, Draupadi was insulted in a full court, and they tried to strip her naked. The reasons as well as her caste status were of course different, but the punishment indicative of a similar logic of misogyny.

Shurpanakha

Shurpanakha is Ravana's sister; thus, a rakshasi. When she encounters Rama, Lakshmana and Sita in Dandakaaranya forest, she asks Rama why he has come there to her land, with his wife and brother. She is said to inquire in a friendly manner, being sincerely curious. Rama replies, and in turn asks about her, but does not let her answer, interjecting – 'because you are not having nice features I think you are a Rakshasi'. Rama's pride and his denigrating attitude are both apparent. It is the paradigmatic attitude of upper-caste people towards lower-caste women.

Ramayana indicates that Shurpanakha wanted to marry Rama, and that Rama did not agree to the proposal, recommending Lakshmana for the marriage instead. Both brothers made a fool of Shurpanakha, and when she discovered it she took her revenge by trying to hurt Sita. The two brothers then caught hold of her and exacted the cruel punishment of cutting off her nose and ears.

Aayomukhi

Another woman in *Ramayana* whom we should attend to is Aayomukhi. According to the story in the epic, she comes to Lakshmana and asks him to marry her. She too is of Rakshasa background. She too gets the same punishment as Shurpanakha, but even more cruelly: Rama and Lakshmana cut off her nose, ears and her breasts.

Mandodari

The final character from *Ramayana* whom we will mention is Mandodari. She is the wife of Ravana, and daughter of Maya (the architect of the Asuras). She used to play chess with Ravana and is represented as the founder of the game. Valmiki portrayed her character with much care. In Yuddha Kanda – when the war between Rama and Ravana was going on – Ravana started a puja to gain more strength. At that time the *vanaras* (Rama's army) wanted to divert Ravana's attention. They brought Ravana's queen Mandodari to the place of puja, dragged her by her hair and ill-treated her, insulting her in front of her husband. After much humiliation she requested Ravana to save her and his concentration was thus disturbed. *Ramayana* describes this incident in detail.

Though Sita was kidnapped and kept in Lanka in Ravana's Ashoka garden for such a long time, there was no ill-treatment towards her. It is presented in the epic that she was looked after with great respect. But Mandodari was ill-treated by Rama's soldiers, and Surpanakha and Aayomukhi were ill-treated by Rama and Lakshmana. All of these stories combine to show the provenance in Indian history of its outlook towards Dalit women.

§

Contesting image representation

Y. S. Alone

Representation is no more understood in the context of imitation and a mere figure representation. Image representation is equally embedded in social facts. Often the image is read as symbolic representation, but their understanding is related with the nature of consciousness. Sigmund Freud, the acclaimed figure of psychoanalysis, had early on converted the functions of the human mind into Id, Ego and Superego; in the later revisions and reworking of the discipline, Jacques Lacan chose the terms imaginary, symbolic and real. Both Freud and Lacan have put forth the functioning of unconsciousness in reference to manifestations of symbolic activities, and many psychoanalysts would like to probe the issues of gender-violence from this perspective.

Though patriarchy is often considered as the sole umbrella under which inflicting violence and legitimating this violence systemically gets subsumed, the embedded power of a sort of right to violence is never dissected, though it may derive its legitimacy from the conceptual formulations of human consciousness, and indeed, from religious sanctions. Concepts from outside the umbrella of patriarchy may have great purchase within the economy of violence. Religion-sanctioned caste stratification could be understood in this respect.

Griselda Pollock's work has systematically dismantled the idea of male-gaze and female-gaze. Nevertheless, it is worthwhile observing caste-gender image representation to see what it reveals in this regard. In this chapter, we will examine the works of some of the painters who come from Dalit communities. How have caste-perversions been converted into the pictorial image representation, and what questions and challenges get revealed thereby?

Here we bring in the appropriate ideas which help us to identify the fragments and dismantle the innumerable presuppositions. A Dalit feminist theorist such as Urmila Pawar would argue in terms of the equality of gender; on the need for the realisation of that equality by all possible means. In these terms, it becomes a righteous move to dismantle the presuppositions of patriarchy. Pawar's objective and its formulations stem from Dr Ambedkar and his writings; likewise, many have been advocating practical measures to ward off ignorance, which originates in many presuppositions, including patriarchy.

Presuppositions have created many meta-narratives over time, and though there have been claims of dismantling these presuppositions, in reality, many presuppositions are re-legitimised in the very process. The fact that painters make an attempt to come out of certain presuppositions by way of image representation makes the latter an interesting act to consider. Such a painting forms a casestudy waiting to be analysed. Female artists in India from privileged social locations have positioned themselves from their own vantage point and engagement with feminism; however, they fail to question the religious and cultural presuppositions that exist in day-to-day life. Symbolic means of oppression are understood as normal and hence there is a lack of focus on understanding or exposing these presuppositions. Such binaries are not addressed by those artists, or even those feminists, who have emerged from the privileges of the hierarchical arrangement which caste creates. Middle- and upper-class women artists locate their problems in patriarchy, but balk at seeing how patriarchy is legitimised through religious practices, or for that matter, the ways that patriarchy gets idealised through religious injunctions – for example, through the idealisations of Rama and Sita in the caste-Hindu household.

How many persons, whether artists or feminists, could break out from the entanglement of such ideals is a question that needs detailed analysis. The forms and means of understanding of many cultural symbols, as also their utility, need to be determined in order to unfold the status of normative, especially the normative as a given ideal without any criticality. Sudhir Kakar pitches this idealisation in the upbringing of the Hindu family. But how do they mediate between the ideologies and the consequences? How can one understand those mediating tools through the works of painters and photographers?

A pertinent question at this point would be, why do such idealisations, religious normative orders, not exclude the practice of *Devdasi*? Savi Sawarkar is the first male painter who dared to paint the plight of *Devadasi* (Figure 8.1). For Savi, image representation becomes an interesting body of expression that has both the dimension of the internal and external observer. No female feminist painter has yet dared to paint the images of *Devadasi* the way Savi has painted them. Complicating the question of perception of the male and female gaze, through his position as outsider, Savi questions the very ethicality of the Indian society that still nurtures the practice of the *Devadasi* tradition. While living in Saundatti – famed for its temples – in disguise, Savi became the inside observer and made a very meticulous reflection.

Devadasi are untouchable women. Savi found the very act of creating *Devadasi* a heinous 'psychotic perversion', where the temple authority, in this case a brahmin priest, and a fellow caste-Hindu are hand-in-glove, and are the principle agents who could both be seen as 'sexual perverts'. Perversion in this case is an act of consciousness, rituals that both the priest and the patron perform in order to legitimise control over the body of the young Dalit girl under sacredness and divine sanction.

In this religiously sanctioned norm, the role of the girl is reduced to subservience; she is a mere 'object of desire', despite the articulated claim that she is married to god. Needless to add, this marriage does not entitle her to claim any of the wealth or privileges that accrue to the god. Interestingly, neither the caste-Hindus nor the brahmins find this 'a problem' in society. Savi thus positions himself outside, presenting a critique of the tradition; therefore, he differs from many feminist artists who have used the female body as a subject of representation more in terms of their liberty to express oneself as well as rightfully exposing the patriarchal perception of the males who are governed by the same norms and presuppositions of their own societal environment.

The image of the *Devadasi*, an untouchable woman, is used by Savi juxtaposed alongside a male untouchable, both shown with a sputum pot hanging around their necks. It's a life of dejection, both sharing a pain and inflicted violence, but the image of *Devadasi* has the sense of 'double' disgust, as she is untouchable and a woman. Her body is that of a woman who becomes more vulnerable for being used for the pleasure of a male with whom she is always forced to conjugate.

But how does Savi handle the composition of multiple women images? (See Figure 8.2.) It is interesting to observe that the corporeality of women's body image, though appearing voluptuous, nevertheless shows the bodily contours as distorted – they are made into multiple curves. Those multiple curves are directed to show how these bodies are used as caste-regulated bodies, where the *Devadasis* have no right over their own physicality. They become the tormented body. What made them different in terms of body representation is the forehead having the patch of vermilion. It's a very typified patch that gets associated with the tradition of *Devadasi*. The image lying on the ground, whose face alone is visible, depicts the death of a *Devadasi*, and the other three surrounding figures are mourning the death of their colleagues who die from STDs. It's a gloomy reality, which they will also have to face.

Their vulnerability is a result of a power relationship, and the so-called order. Order in this situation is ordained by the religious injunction of the brahmin priest. Therefore, vulnerability gets deeply associated with the normative practices of the behaviour of the caste-Hindus and a brahmin priest, which translates into the practice of sexual bodily pleasure where the ordering of the ordained is a conscious practice of a 'right to have' and 'right to pleasure'. In a figure representation, such vulnerability of the body is difficult to read; Savi resolves it by simply visualising a mere body part (Figure 8.3).

Devdasi with Crow is a graphic depiction of the darker side of their lives. The owner of the *Devadasis* refuses to grant any claims made on behalf of the child she

FIGURE 8.1 Savi Sawarkar, *Untouchable and Devdasi*, mixed media, 29 × 23 cm.

Source: Artist's collection. Used with permission.

FIGURE 8.2 Savi Sawarkar, *Two Untouchable Women and Yellow Cloud*, mixed media, 321 × 45 cm.

Source: Artist's collection. Used with permission.

would bear. Here the so-called order does not empower one to claim anything, which the reproduced life would like to make. Therefore *Devdasis* go under scissor-operation to remove the unwanted foetus. It becomes a traumatic series of forced abortions that are flushed out on a regular basis. Savi captures those body cuts on the stomach of the *Devadasi* whose body has been used for constant sexual pleasure. The body cuts are shown wide open with thick stitch-marks. It's a sign that one can read as to how a particular female has gone through a tormented process. It's a representation of a body that has become older with age and is now a discarded body.

Another fact of their life is equally degrading. The imposed condition of sex slavery that violates their dignity and liberty and makes for a beleaguered life. Sexual slavery gets imposed by the conscious acts of caste-Hindus. This is symbolised in Savi's work by the temple flag, or the vermilion on the forehead, or the holding of a small temple in the hand. *Devadasis* are sold for a few thousand rupees in the red-light areas of Mumbai. The only investment that she has is her body. By observing the state of affairs of such lives with which Savi had interaction, Savi chooses to conceal the identity of that person and brings in his power to handle the images in a more nuanced way by choosing visible elements that would disturb the viewers and above all those whose ideal of Rama-Sita dwells in their Hindu houses.

Through such a tormented life, a ray of hope is found in the changing nature of consciousness, which is also a social fact in contemporary times. The element of

FIGURE 8.3 Savi Sawarkar, *Devdasi with Crow*, etching, 40 × 28 cm.

Source: Artist's collection. Used with permission.

FIGURE 8.4 Savi Sawarkar, *Untitled*.

Source: Artist's collection. Used with permission.

informed introspection has made the *Devadasi* to rethink about her situation, and she has desired to come out of the clutches of the religious oppression of Hinduism. There is a work showing this introspection in the life of the *Devadasi* as a visual response which acts as an archiving of the ongoing changes. The *Devadasi* is shown clinging to a brahmin priest whose psychotic perversion is grounded in the religious sanction which allows him to hold her tightly where she has no escape; nonetheless, her hands emerge, they are shown breaking free from the body of the brahmin priest. The *dhammachakra* is visible, showing that the woman is coming into the Buddhist fold, discarding ages-old Hindu practices.

A Dalit woman's giving birth to a child is an anxious state of her being. Being vulnerable has also embedded reproductive life that produces another body. The reproduced becomes helpless when it comes to claim dignity. In this *Untitled* representation (Figure 8.4), there is a Dalit woman whose legs are visible and a newborn baby is emerging. On the right corner, a face is shown. Savi Sawarkar appeals them to assert their power of conscience through this art, against of an abject surrender to the circumstances. The face looking at the emerging baby depicts the same woman who is giving birth. Each and every Dalit woman is encouraged to deliberate over her act of childbearing and to take steps ensuring a humanly dignified life to her newborn.

Now let me draw your attention to the photographs that have been made by Sudharak Owle. The medium of photography captures the natural make-believe images that are observed by the naked eye. Sudharak captures the life of the prostitute by becoming an insider: one who does not make her a sex symbol and yet another victim of the male gaze. For Sudharak, it is a quest to capture the representation of the prostitute's body, which experiences a tormented life. Society turns a blind eye to their existence since they come from the lower ebb of society, predominantly scheduled caste communities.

Mumbai's red-light area of Kamathipura is one such telling example that exists in Sudharak's repertoire. The flesh trade which happens in dingy places and in such abject living conditions is a telling truth of the conscious perversion which surrounds them (Figure 8.5). A bathroom, toilet, bed, kitchen, everything is clubbed in

FIGURE 8.5 Sudharak Owle, photograph from the Kamathipura series.

Source: Artist's collection. Used with permission.

one space where the fulfilment of hunger is the only criteria. The community has evolved to live and share together without any haste, but there is always a hidden anger. They carry forward their ritual practices of earlier *Devadasi* life, making their caste an open secret.

Sexual psychotic perversions can be reconstructed through series of Tantrik texts in Sanskritic tradition. Text such as *Rudrayamaltantra* advocates choice of a female partner in the ritual of sexual copulation on the basis of *varna* hierarchy. There is also the tradition of *nagnapuja* being practiced in the state of Karnataka, Andhra Pradesh and in Odisha secretly. Uttam Kamble records the vivid account of the *randpurnima* and the *nagnapuja* and the problems faced by those seeking to forbid such practices. The ritual involves going unclothed to the temple of Devi and offering a *puja*. It also echoes the tradition of *randpurnima* being observed in Saundati in Karnataka. Women and usually lower-caste girls bathe in the river and then run naked to the temple, while others, mainly caste-Hindus, happily watch them. Despite the fact that the image of the goddess has been bestowed with all kinds of power and blood, there is no similar sanction to her female followers.

But these social realities of Dalit women acquire a different dimension when it comes to the so-called liberated and civilised spaces reserved for image representation. When J. Nandakumar painted *Blind Faith*, which was based on *nagnapuja*, and exhibited the work in Mumbai, it created havoc. People found the work offensive, as it went against their ethos of morality and the ethics of religious practices. It suddenly drew the wrath of caste-Hindu groups for the fact that the very image generated tremendous anxiety, which made them boil and left them agitated. Such people made all possible efforts to impose a withdrawal of this work along with another painting of Gandhi entitled 'Pune-Karar'.

Why the volatile reaction? The painting(s) served to shatter their consciousness of the sacred and their belief in the sanctity of tradition. It may be observed that the painting, although it lacked a sensual-sexual depiction of the goddesses, has nevertheless also evoked a backlash by many liberals. Does their Rama-Sita ideal get questioned?

The images of the goddess, presumably goddess Durga, are widely believed to not have sexual bodily representation in the canon of paintings. The dominant Durga images are conceptualised off of the images of Durga that have been carved in many of the brahmanical Ellora caves. Today, many would love to call theses 'Hindu' caves, reflective of the changed nomenclature enacted during colonial rule. J. Nandakumar's visual sources have themselves come from Durga images in the Ellora caves themselves that are highly sensuous.

In the painting *Blind Faith* (Figure 8.6), the Durga image has no facial features. It is a simple face. Her body is crafted like a generic nude study with angular planes. She is sitting on an animal that is difficult to identify, but a viewer is forced to read it as a tiger. It is a very symbolic representation of an animal whose identity is very difficult to establish by any creative standards, as the legs of the image are too tall and body of the animal is very roundish. Interestingly, Nandakumar has painted two main hands, the right hand in *varadamudra* and the left hand is placed

FIGURE 8.6 Nandakumar, *Blind Faith*.

Source: Artist's collection. Used with permission.

opposite to the abdomen. The sitting posture is like a posed picture. There are six additional hands shown in white at the back of the image, making those hands reflective of traditional images which denote the divinity of the image. The right hands are shown holding a lotus, trident and a raised index figure whereas the left ones are shown holding a lance and dagger. The image of the *devi* occupies the central block. On the right side of the *devi*, a figure of a man holding a begging bowl is shown. What is noteworthy is the head of the man and its erected phallus coming out of his clothes. The elongated head of the male image is that of a ram. The ram is a symbol used to denote the nature of a male who is a blind believer and has no righteous consciousness. The erected phallus of the devotee becomes the 'bone' of contention.

What J. Nandakumar is doing here is attempting to go into the psyche of the devotee, for whom the goddess, in spite of being a divine female body, is actually the desired body. Although Lacan identifies desire as a crucial component of perversion, Buddhist psychology locates desire as part of the manifestation of conscious mind. But the desirous mind is that which has no control over its thinking or over the consequent action that manifests from such thinking. The latter is essential to the character of the human mind that gives rise to desires. Wantonness evolves through sense perception and gives a guiding direction to the senses.

What we learn, then, is that the desired body is an 'imagined body' where a male seeks to relate with his sexual fantasies within the sphere of religious devotion. Thus, for a devotee, the body of the female is conceived as the sensual desired body and the consciousness attached to it is that of a dialogue where consciousness is not a mere subject, but an inner urge waiting to be manifested through the discursive realms of divinity and sacredness. Nandakumar, therefore, questions the very presuppositions of such practices by applying a very direct confrontation through the visual metaphors. Thus, it becomes appropriate to raise the very logic of discursive space, which is based on the terrain of presuppositions. Fragments, in this case, are just fillers to redefine the conduct of a caste-Hindu towards its own cultural practices or to be more precise, to re-legitimise the hierarchical subjugation.

Notes

1 Excerpted from 'Hindu Epics: Portrayal of Dalit Women', chapter 6, in P. G. Jogdand (ed.), *Dalit Women in India: Issues and Perspectives*, New Delhi: Gyan Publishing House in collaboration with University of Poona, Pune, 2013, pp. 93–104. Used with permission.
2 Excerpted from 'Hindu Epics: Portrayal of Dalit Women', chapter 6, in P. G. Jogdand (ed.), *Dalit Women in India: Issues and Perspectives*, New Delhi: Gyan Publishing House in collaboration with University of Poona, Pune, 2013, pp. 93–104. Used with permission.
3 Manu, *Manumriti*, 12–46.

9

DALIT WOMEN'S AUTOBIOGRAPHIES[1]

Sharmila Rege

In the last couple of years, there has been a spurt of interest in mainstream English publishing in Dalit life narratives.[2] S. Anand argues that though the creativity of Dalits has been thriving in various Indian languages, the effort to render these writings into English has been lacking.[3] While it is a positive development that this has now started to happen, several questions about the politics of translation and publication, which have been raised, cannot be bypassed. S. Anand's invitation to publishers, writers, translators, scholars and teachers of Dalit studies to reflect on the politics of consumption of Dalit literature provides important insights into the issue.[4]

Most of the recently published Dalit writings are autobiographical in nature, a circumstance that has led some scholars to question the radical potential of the increased accessibility of Dalit writings. Can reading and teaching of Dalit autobiographies radicalise the perception of readers? Do readers conveniently consume these narratives as narratives of pain and suffering refusing to engage with the politics and theory of Ambedkarism?

Since the 1960s, there has been considerable debate on issues related to the politically appropriate nomenclature for the literature of protest and revolt and the significance of Dalit life narratives. It is important to recall here that Babasaheb Ambedkar had coined the word 'Dalit' in 1928 in his writings in *Bahishkrut Bharat* (India of the Ex-communicated) and the concept of Dalit literature came to be accepted by the 1950s. However, at the second Dalit literary meet organised in Pune in 1961, the term 'Dalit' came to be contested and a resolution was passed to rename the literature 'Buddhist'. Since then, there have been several debates on whether the literature that emerges from perspectives challenging the given social structure and cultural practices can be called Dalit, Phule-Ambedkarite, Ambedkarism-inspired, Buddhist, rebellious or non-brahmanical.[5]

The entire debate on whether the hateful past should be written and brought into the present suggests the complex relationship between official forgetting, memory and identity. Dalit life narratives cannot be accused of bringing an undesired past into the present, for they are one of the most direct and accessible ways in which the silence and misrepresentation of Dalits has been countered. My argument here is that Dalit life narratives are in fact *testimomios*,[6] which forge a right to speak both for and beyond the individual and contest explicitly or implicitly the 'official forgetting' of histories of caste oppression, struggles and resistance.

Dalit life narratives are testimonies; acts testifying or bearing witness legally or religiously. In a testimony, the intention is not one of literariness but of communicating the situation of a group's oppression, imprisonment and struggle. The narrator claims some agency in the act of narrating and calls upon the readers to respond actively in judging the situation. In doing so they create new generic possibilities and invite different ways of being read. Dalit life narratives thus historically created the genre of testimonies in which the individual self seeks affirmation in a collective mode. Yet, we need to remember that by bringing into the public domain details of life, they also challenge the communitarian control on self.[7] This dialectics of self and community assumes further significance in Dalit women's testimonios for, situated as women in the community, they articulate concerns of gender, challenging the singular communitarian notion of the Dalit community.

The introduction of Dalit testimonios as historical narratives of experience is a way of introducing the counter views on the caste system. As Gopal Guru puts it succinctly, testimonios have the ability to convert 'what is considered pathological into subversive chemicals'. These writings perform a double function; they inflict an inferiority complex in the minds of adversaries by resurrecting Dalit triumphalism and bring out guilt in the minds of 'upper castes' by recoding social wrongs done by ancestors.[8] The role of critical translation for foregrounding the social and political content of the testimonios cannot be undermined. Reading Dalit 'autobiographies' minus the political ideology and practices of the Dalit movement does stand the risk of making a spectacle of Dalit suffering and pain for non-Dalit readers. However read as testimonios of caste based exploitation, everyday resistance and organised anti-caste struggles, they bring new insights and theories into elite brahmanical institutions of academia. The ways in which we construct curricula, pedagogies and position the narratives, that is, how we learn, are at least as important as what we learn. We cannot ghettoize the testimonios in separate optional courses on Dalit writings and expect to radicalise our understanding of caste. When the purpose of reading is one of democratisation of knowledge rather than colonisation, locating the narratives historically and relationally becomes crucial. In bringing Dalit women's testimonios into the curricula there has to be a deliberate exercise in thinking out issues. Some of the questions that have arisen are: Why Dalit women's testimonios? Do Dalit women 'remember and write differently? How may this 'difference' be historically located in the articulations of caste and the women's question?

'Translating' testimonios/'Translating' standpoints

Constructing oppositional Dalit feminist pedagogies, a complex and difficult process, is distinct from efforts to 'caste-sensitise' women's studies curricula or curricula in any discipline or academic field. Two models of 'including' Dalit women in the curricula that are commonly practiced can be best described by what Mohanty has referred to as the feminist-as-tourist and feminist-as-explorer models.[9] While the first model prescribes, 'add Dalit women and stir' the other suggests 'add Dalit women as separate and equal'. The feminist-as-tourist model operates a paradigm that assumes unmarked feminism as 'original' ad makes brief forays into the 'problems' of Dalit women through a single module or example. The picture then is one of monolithic images of Dalits who have the problems, and unmarked feminism, which has the theory and historical agency. The feminist-as-explorer model operates though pedagogical strategies that may be misconstrued as sensitive because entire courses seem to be dedicated to Dalit women. The explorer model constructs separate courses on Dalit women's writings by largely falling into a framework of cultural relativism. Therefore, in such courses it appears as if women from different cultures write differently, so we are treating them separately but equally. All questions of power, agency and common criteria for evaluation are thus silenced in such curricular models. Oppositional Dalit feminist pedagogies, by contrast, are built on a complex relational understanding of social location, experience and history. An uncritical classical anthropological gaze at Dalit women is clearly rejected and their analytical gaze thrown back at theories and praxis that do not state caste on its own terms. In such curricular models, narratives of Dalit women's historical experience become crucial to thinking and theorising not because they present an unmediated version of 'truth' but because they destabilise received truths and locate debate in the complexities and contradictions of historical life.[10] Located in the general text of struggles, engaging with translations of Dalit women's testimonios is a way of pushing towards greater objectivity in theory and practice – an engagement with a Dalit feminist standpoint.

A Dalit feminist standpoint acknowledges the significance of the experience of oppression and resistance among Dalit women acquiring a perspective against an unjust order but it does not celebrate oppressive traditions merely because they are practised by the oppressed. By directing attentions to the cultural and material dimension of the interface between gender and caste, the focus of a Dalit feminist standpoint is squarely placed on social relations, which convert difference into oppression. Such a view points to the failure of upper-caste women to critically and systematically interrogate their situation of advantage. The structural and individual dimensions of caste are often 'invisible' from privileged positions and require a 'conscious' effort to problematise the complexly constituted social locations that women occupy. An easy way out has been an additive approach, prescribed in varying ways by the two curricular models discussed earlier. Just adding to an axis of patriarchy an axis of caste oppression, assumes that gender can be isolated from caste and that in the last instance there is something (some form of oppression) that is 'common' to all women. Again, in the name of a commonality of interest, women who occupy social locations that are advantaged in caste and class terms and are subjected to only gender-based oppression are considered normative. This often means non-Dalit women talking ad nauseam about the difference of Dalit women in terms of their being 'thrice/twice oppressed' but their oppression *as* women continues to be seen as shared in common. It is as if the 'difference' of Dalit women exists in some separable 'non-woman' (caste) part of them: 'translating' Dalit women's historical experience, in writing caste/writing gender, underscores the inseparability of caste and gender identities and the material and symbolic gains of complicity for upper-caste women and undifferentiated community for Dalit men.

In the 1980s, Dalit women's testimonios agitated their way into a public sphere is which the narratives of the Dalit movement and the women's movement were already in circulation. Lokhande has observed that in Dalit men's testimonios Dalit women were only selectively remembered as sacrificing wives and mothers, or victims of caste-based practices. Further, she argues, the reproduction of patriarchal practices within the community and those idealised by brahmanical patriarchy were only inadequately remembered.[11] At best, Dalit women were written into these testimonies of Dalit struggles as supporters of a 'larger cause', which is men assumed to be a male cause. The narratives of the second wave of the women's movement in redefining feminist identity through a retrieval of forgotten women as well as women's remembrances of the past, 'officially' forgot caste. As a modern form of inequality reproduced in modern ideologies and practices like those of feminism, caste was 'forgotten'. In the common sense of the movement, caste belonged only to Dalit women, who then were addressed only as victims and never as active historical agents of feminism. Dalit women's testimonios offered counter narratives that challenged the selective memory and univocal history both of the Dalit and the women's movements. Following Nora, it may be argued, that at the current conjuncture, the passage of these testimonios from acts of memory to history is happening at a movement when Dalit feminism is being redefined through a revitalisation of history.[12] Testimonios engage us in processes of 'rememory'[13] or the reconstructing of histories of institutions and practices in a nation actively invested in forgetting them. Dalit testimonios underscore caste as an oppressive tradition and modernity as both weakening some and reproducing other aspects of caste inequality and thus contest an affirmation of the nation-state that forgets the presence of community. Dalit women's testimonios, in addition to agitating into the public the presence of communities, also problematise the denial of the community to affirm their difference. Their public articulation of relational identities of caste and gender, thus inscribes into history not only what dominant groups would like to forget or think of as belonging to another time but also the selective memory of the community. Alternative accounts that write gender/write caste into histories of the nation-state and communities are generated through the oppositional struggles of Dalit women. Objective knowledge of phenomena like caste and gender, whose distorted representation benefits the dominant, is dependent on the theoretical knowledge that activism creates.[14] Since an attempt at an objective explanation is continuous with oppositional political struggles, Dalit women's historical narratives provide 'objective' ways of looking at the world. Readers are invited to engage with the 'translations' of testimonios and see how they read when looked at from this perspective.

Notes

1 This chapter is an excerpt from 'Debating the Consumption of Dalit 'Autobiographies': The Significance of Dalit *'Testimonios"* of Sharmila Rege (ed.), *Writing Caste/Writing Gender*, Zubaan, July 1, 2013, pp. 10–19, 84–103. Reproduced with permission.
2 For a list of published titles on English translations of Dalit literature, see S. Anand, *Untouchable Tales: Publishing and Reading Dalit Literature*, Chennai: Navayana, 2003. Translations of Dalit narrative and literary writings from Maharashtra include Mulk Raj Anand and Eleanor Zelliot, *An Anthology of Dalit Literature*, New Delhi: Gyan Publishing, 1992; Arjun Dangle (ed.), *Poisoned Bread: Translation from Modern Marathi Dalit Literature*, Hyderabad: Orient Longman Limited, 1992; Laxman Gaikwad, *Uchalya: The Branded*, New Delhi: Sahitya Akademi, 1998; Laxman Mane, *Upara: The Outsider*, New Delhi: Sahitya Akademi, 1997; Kishore Shantabai Kale, *Against All Odds*, New Delhi: Penguin, 2000; Vasant Moon, *Growing Up Untouchable in India*, translated from the Marathi by Gail Omvedt, introduced by Eleanor Zelliot, New York: Rowman & Littlefield Publishers, 2001, first published as *Vasti*, Mumbai: Granthali, 1995; Narendra Jadhav, *Outcaste*, New Delhi: Penguin, 2003; Sharankumar Limbale, *Akkarmashi: The Outcaste*, New Delhi: Oxford University Press, 2003.
3 Anand, *Untouchable Tales*, 2003.
4 Ibid.
5 Dhammapal Ratnakar (ed.), *Dalit Sahitya Namaantaracha Vaad* (debate about changing names in Dalit literature), Pune: Sugava, 1997.
6 'Testimonio' is a Spanish term, which literally means 'testimony'. A testimonio is a narrative in book or pamphlet form, told in the first person by a narrator who is also the real protagonist or witness of the events he or she recounts and whose unit of narration is usually a 'life' or significant life experience. See (John Beverley, 'The Margin at the Center: On "Testimonio" (Testimonial Narrative)', in S. Smith and J. Watson (ed.), *De/Colonizing the Subject: The Politics of Gender in Women's Autobiography*, Minneapolis: University of Minnesota Press, 1992, pp. 92–93.
7 Gopal Guru, 'Dalit Women Talk Differently', in Anupama Rao (ed.), *Gender and Caste*, New Delhi: Kali for Women, 2003.
8 Ibid., p. 71.
9 C.T. Mohanty, 'Under Western Eyes' Revisited: Feminist Solidarity through Anticapitalist Struggles, *Signs: Journal of Women in Culture and Society*, Vol. 28 No. 2, 2003.
10 Ibid., p. 244.
11 Pradnya Lokhande, *Women's Buddhism, Buddhism's Women: Tradition, Revision, Renewal*, Pune: Mansanman Prakashan, 1996, p. 96.
12 Pierre Nora, 'Between History and Memory: Les Lieux de Memoire', *Representations*, 26, Spring, 1989, p. 15.
13 Toni Morrison, *Beloved*, New York: Knopf, 1987.
14 Satya Mohanty, *Literary Theory and the Claims of History: Postmoderism, Objectivity, Multicultural Politics*, Ithaca: Cornell University Press, 1993, p. 213.

PART IV
What difference does 'difference' make?

Part IV presents foundational works toward theorising feminism of the marginalised across the world. The articulation of any inquiry is not free from the influence of the socio-economic-political status of the articulator. Since academic writings on feminism have historically preponderantly originated from white, First World feminists – largely on account of their privileged institutional locations – the mainstream articulation of gender-based issues tended to neglect the deeper afflictions of Black women. Black women's struggle of day-to-day resistance against race and gender discrimination gradually helped them to enter into the field of articulation. During this long process, Black women realised that their social reality was not captured or reflected in mainstream feminism, from which they were marginalised – mainstream feminism thus took on the character of a 'white' feminism from the point of view of the racially marginalised. For mainstream feminists, patriarchy, not race, was *their* problem. Consequently, Black feminists forwarded strong critiques of mainstream feminism for its failure to address the issues of *all* women.

Thanks to writings such as appear here in Part IV, Black feminist thought has emerged as an established discipline in contemporary academia. Kimberlé Crenshaw (Chapter 10) originated the concept of intersectionality based on Black women's 'difference' from race-privileged women, filling the lacuna of First World feminist discourse which had failed to address the issues of *all* (First World) women.

Indian feminism, similarly, has evolved from caste-privileged women who failed to capture the experiences of, and consequently marginalised, the issues related to Dalit women. Gopal Guru (Chapter 11) argues that there is a difference in Dalit women's way of talking and living due to a long history of their deprived socio-economic-political status. Sharmila Rege (Chapter 12) poses a disciplinary challenge to Indian feminism by asserting that the addition of Dalit difference is a precondition for constructing a 'real feminism'. It is important to observe the various ways in which the category 'woman' is constituted differently in different social contexts. In this respect, the difference which emerges from a Dalit perspective offers an epistemic contribution to feminist theory toward its goal of achieving a gender-just society for *all* women, irrespective of their caste, class, race, religion, region and other determinative variants.

10

'DIFFERENCE' THROUGH INTERSECTIONALITY[1]

Kimberlé Crenshaw

One of the very few Black women's studies books is entitled *All the Women Are White; All the Blacks Are Men, But Some of Us Are Brave*.[2] I have chosen this title as a point of departure in my efforts to develop a Black feminist criticism because it sets forth a problematic consequence of the tendency to treat race and gender as mutually exclusive categories of experience and analysis. In this chapter, I want to examine how this tendency is perpetuated by a single-axis framework that is dominant in antidiscrimination law and that is also reflected in feminist theory and antiracist politics.

I will centre Black women in this analysis in order to contrast the multidimensionality of Black women's experience with the single-axis analysis that distorts these experiences. Not only will this juxtaposition reveal how Black women are theoretically erased, it will also illustrate how this framework imports its own theoretical limitations that undermine efforts to broaden feminist and antiracist analyses. With Black women as the starting point, it becomes more apparent how dominant conceptions of discrimination condition us to think about subordination as disadvantage occurring along a single categorical axis. I want to suggest further that this single-axis framework erases Black women in the conceptualisation, identification and remediation of race and sex discrimination by limiting inquiry to the experiences of otherwise-privileged members of the group. In other words, in race discrimination cases, discrimination tends to be viewed in terms of sex- or class-privileged Blacks; in sex discrimination cases, the focus is on race- and class-privileged women.

This focus on the most privileged group members marginalises those who are multiply burdened and obscures claims that cannot be understood as resulting from discrete sources of discrimination. I suggest further that this focus on otherwise-privileged group members creates a distorted analysis of racism and sexism because the operative conceptions of race and sex become grounded in experiences that actually represent only a subset of a much more complex phenomenon.

After examining the doctrinal manifestations of this single-axis framework, I will discuss how it contributes to the marginalisation of Black women in feminist theory and in antiracist politics. I argue that Black women are sometimes excluded from feminist theory and antiracist policy discourse because both are predicated on a discrete set of experiences that often does not accurately reflect the interaction of race and gender. These problems of exclusion cannot be solved simply by including Black women within an already established analytical structure. Because the intersectional experience is greater than the sum of racism and sexism, any analysis that does not take intersectionality into account cannot sufficiently address the particular manner in which Black women are subordinated. Thus, for feminist theory and antiracist policy discourse to embrace the experiences and concerns of Black women, the entire framework that has been used as a basis for translating 'women's experience' or 'the Black experience' into concrete policy demands must be rethought and recast.

As examples of theoretical and political developments that miss the mark with respect to Black women because of their failure to consider intersectionality, I will briefly discuss the feminist critique of rape and separate spheres ideology, and the public policy debates concerning female-headed households within the Black community.

The antidiscrimination framework

One way to approach the problem of intersectionality is to examine how courts frame and interpret the stories of Black women plaintiffs. While I cannot claim to know the circumstances underlying the cases that I will discuss, I nevertheless believe that the way courts interpret claims made by Black women is itself part of Black women's experience and, consequently, a cursory review of cases involving Black female plaintiffs is quite revealing. To illustrate the difficulties inherent in judicial treatment of intersectionality, I will briefly consider the case *DeGraffenreid v GeneralMotors*.[3]

In *DeGraffenreid*, five Black women brought suit against General Motors, alleging that the employer's seniority system perpetuated the effects of past discrimination against Black women. Evidence adduced at trial revealed that General Motors simply did not hire Black women prior to 1964 and that all of the Black women hired after 1970 lost their jobs in a seniority-based layoff during a subsequent recession. The district court granted summary judgement for the defendant, rejecting the plaintiffs' attempt to bring a suit not on behalf of Blacks or women, but specifically on behalf of Black women. The court stated:

> [P]laintiffs have failed to cite any decisions which have stated that Black women are a special class to be protected from discrimination. The Court's own research has failed to disclose such a decision. The plaintiffs are clearly

entitled to a remedy if they have been discriminated against. However, they should not be allowed to combine statutory remedies to create a new 'super-remedy' which would give them relief beyond what the drafters of the relevant statutes intended. Thus, this lawsuit must be examined to see if it states a cause of action for race discrimination, sex discrimination, or alternatively either, but not a combination of both.[4]

Although General Motors did not hire Black women prior to 1964, the court noted that 'General Motors has hired . . . female employees for a number of years prior to the enactment of the Civil Rights Act of 1964'.[5] Because General Motors did hire women – albeit *white* women – during the period that no Black women were hired, there was, in the court's view, no sex discrimination that the seniority system could conceivably have perpetuated.

After refusing to consider the plaintiffs' sex discrimination claim, the court dismissed the race discrimination complaint and recommended its consolidation with another case alleging race discrimination against the same employer.[6] The plaintiffs responded that such consolidation would defeat the purpose of their suit since theirs was not purely a race claim, but an action brought specifically on behalf of Black women alleging race *and* sex discrimination. The court, however, reasoned:

> The legislative history surrounding Title VII does not indicate that the goal of the statute was to create a new classification of 'black women' who would have greater standing than, for example, a black male. The prospect of the creation of new classes of protected minorities, governed only by the mathematical principles of permutation and combination, clearly raises the prospect of opening the hackneyed Pandora's box.[7]

Thus, the court apparently concluded that Congress either did not contemplate that Black women could be discriminated against as 'black women' or did not intend to protect them when such discrimination occurred. The court's refusal in *DeGraffenreid* to acknowledge that Black women encounter combined race and sex discrimination implies that the boundaries of sex and race discrimination doctrine are defined respectively by white women's and Black men's experiences. Under this view, Black women are protected only to the extent that their experiences coincide with those of either of the two groups.[8] Where their experiences are distinct, Black women can expect little protection as long as approaches, such as that in *DeGraffenreid*, which completely obscure problems of intersectionality prevail.

Judicial decisions which premise intersectional relief on a showing that Black women are specifically recognised as a class are analogous to a doctor's decision at the scene of an accident to treat an accident victim only if the injury is recognised by medical insurance.

Similarly, providing legal relief only when Black women show that their claims are based on race or on sex is analogous to calling an ambulance for the victim only after the driver responsible for the injuries is identified. But it is not always easy to reconstruct an accident: Sometimes the skid marks and the injuries simply indicate that they occurred simultaneously, frustrating efforts to determine which driver caused the harm. In these cases the tendency seems to be that no driver is held responsible, no treatment is administered, and the involved parties simply get back in their cars and zoom away.

To bring this back to a non-metaphorical level, I am suggesting that Black women can experience discrimination in ways that are both similar to and different from those experienced by white women and Black men. Black women sometimes experience discrimination in ways similar to white women's experiences; sometimes they share very similar experiences with Black men. Yet often they experience double-discrimination – the combined effects of practices which discriminate on the basis of race, and on the basis of sex. And sometimes, they experience discrimination as Black women-not the sum of race and sex discrimination, but as Black women.

Black women's experiences are much broader than the general categories that discrimination discourse provides. Yet the continued insistence that Black women's demands and needs be filtered through categorical analyses that completely obscure their experiences guarantees that their needs will seldom be addressed.

DeGraffenreid is a doctrinal manifestation of a common political and theoretical approach to discrimination which operates to marginalise Black women. Unable to grasp the importance of Black women's intersectional experiences, not only courts, but feminist and civil rights thinkers as well have treated Black women in ways that deny both the unique compoundedness of their situation and the centrality of their experiences to the larger classes of women and Blacks. Black women are regarded either as too much like women or Blacks and the compounded nature of their experience is absorbed into the collective experiences of either group or as too different, in which case Black women's blackness or femaleness sometimes has placed their needs and perspectives at the margin of the feminist and Black liberationist agendas.

While it could be argued that this failure represents an absence of political will to include Black women, I believe that it reflects an uncritical and disturbing acceptance of dominant ways of thinking about discrimination. Consider first the definition of discrimination that seems to be operative in antidiscrimination law: Discrimination which is wrongful proceeds from the identification of a specific class or category; either a discriminator intentionally identifies this category, or a process is adopted which somehow disadvantages all members of this category. According to the dominant view, a discriminator treats all people within a race or sex category similarly. Any significant experiential or statistical variation within this group suggests either that the group is not being discriminated against or that conflicting interests exist which defeat any attempts to bring a common claim.[9] Consequently, one generally cannot combine these categories. Race and sex, moreover, become significant only when they operate to explicitly *disadvantage* the victims; because the *privileging* of whiteness or maleness is implicit, it is generally not perceived at all.

Underlying this conception of discrimination is a view that the wrong which antidiscrimination law addresses is the use of race or gender factors to interfere with decisions that would otherwise be fair or neutral. This process-based definition is not grounded in a bottom-up commitment to improve the substantive conditions for those who are victimised by the interplay of numerous factors. Instead, the dominant message of antidiscrimination law is that it will regulate only the limited extent to which race or sex interferes with the process of determining outcomes. This narrow objective is facilitated by the top-down strategy of using a singular 'but for' analysis to ascertain the effects of race or sex. Because the scope of antidiscrimination law is so limited, sex and race discrimination have come to be defined in terms of the experiences of those who are privileged *but for* their racial or sexual characteristics. Put differently, the paradigm of sex discrimination tends to be based on the experiences of white women; the model of race discrimination tends to be based on the experiences of the most privileged Blacks. Notions of what constitutes race and sex discrimination are, as a result, narrowly tailored to embrace only a small set of circumstances, none of which include discrimination against Black women.

To the extent that this general description is accurate, the following analogy can be useful in describing how Black women are marginalised in the interface between antidiscrimination law and race and gender hierarchies: Imagine a basement which contains all people who are disadvantaged on the basis of race, sex, class, sexual preference, age and/or physical ability. These people are stacked – feet standing on shoulders – with those on the bottom being disadvantaged by the full array of factors, up to the very top, where the heads of all those disadvantaged by a singular factor brush up against the ceiling. Their ceiling is actually the floor above which only those who are *not* disadvantaged in any way reside.

In efforts to correct some aspects of domination, those above the ceiling admit from the basement only those who can say that 'but for' the ceiling, they too would be in the upper room. A hatch is developed through which those placed immediately below can crawl. Yet this hatch is generally available only to those who – due to the singularity of their burden and their otherwise privileged position relative to those below – are in the position to crawl through. Those who are multiply burdened are generally left below unless they can somehow pull themselves into the groups that are permitted to squeeze through the hatch.

As this analogy translates for Black women, the problem is that they can receive protection only to the extent that their experiences are recognisably similar to those whose experiences tend to be reflected in antidiscrimination doctrine. If Black women cannot conclusively say that 'but for' their race or 'but for' their gender they would be treated differently, they are not invited to climb through the hatch but told to wait in the unprotected margin until they can be absorbed into the broader, protected categories of race and sex.

Despite the narrow scope of this dominant conception of discrimination and its tendency to marginalise those whose experiences cannot be described within its tightly drawn parameters, this approach has been regarded as the appropriate framework for addressing a range of problems. In much of feminist theory and, to some extent, in antiracist politics, this framework is reflected in the belief that sexism or racism can be meaningfully discussed without paying attention to the lives of those other than the race-, gender- or class-privileged. As a result, both feminist theory and antiracist politics have been organised, in part, around the equation of racism with what happens to the Black middle-class or to Black men, and the equation of sexism with what happens to white women.

Looking at historical and contemporary issues in both the feminist and the civil rights communities, one can find ample evidence of how both communities' acceptance of the dominant framework of discrimination has hindered the development of an adequate theory and praxis to address problems of intersectionality. This adoption of a single-issue framework for discrimination not only marginalises Black women within the very movements that claim them as part of their constituency but it also makes the elusive goal of ending racism and patriarchy even more difficult to attain.

Feminism and Black women: 'Ain't we women?'

Oddly, despite the relative inability of feminist politics and theory to address Black women substantively, feminist theory and tradition borrow considerably from Black women's history. For example, 'Ain't I a Woman?' has come to represent a standard refrain in feminist discourse.[10] Yet the lesson of this powerful oratory is not fully appreciated because the context of the delivery is seldom examined. I would like to tell part of the story because it establishes some themes that have characterised feminist treatment of race and illustrates the importance of including Black women's experiences as a rich source for the critique of patriarchy.

In 1851, Sojourner Truth declared 'Ain't I a Woman?' and challenged the sexist imagery used by male critics, to justify the disenfranchisement of women.[11] The scene was a Women's Rights Conference in Akron, Ohio; white male hecklers, invoking stereotypical images of 'womanhood', argued that women were too frail and delicate to take on the responsibilities of political activity. When Sojourner Truth rose to speak, many white women urged that she be silenced, fearing that she would divert attention from women's suffrage to emancipation. Truth, once permitted to speak, recounted the horrors of slavery, and its particular impact on Black women:

> Look at my arm! I have ploughed and planted and gathered into barns, and no man could head me – and ain't I a woman? I could work as much and eat as much as a man – when I could get it – and bear the lash as well! And ain't I a woman? I have born thirteen children, and seen most of 'em sold into slavery, and when I cried out with my mother's grief, none but Jesus heard me – and ain't I a woman?[12]

By using her own life to reveal the contradiction between the ideological myths of womanhood and the reality of Black women's experience, Truth's oratory provided a powerful rebuttal to the claim that women were categorically weaker than men. Yet Truth's personal challenge to the coherence of the cult of true womanhood was useful only to the extent that white women were willing to reject the racist attempts to rationalise the contradiction – that because Black women were something less than real women, their experiences had no bearing on true womanhood. Thus, this nineteenth-century Black feminist challenged not only patriarchy, but she also challenged white feminists wishing to embrace Black women's history to relinquish their vestedness in whiteness.

Contemporary white feminists inherit not the legacy of Truth's challenge to patriarchy but, instead, Truth's challenge to their forbearers. Even today, the difficulty that white women have traditionally experienced in sacrificing racial privilege to strengthen feminism renders them susceptible to Truth's critical question. When feminist theory and politics that claim to reflect *women's* experience and *women's* aspirations do not include or speak to Black women, Black women must ask: 'Ain't *We* Women?' If this is so, how can the claims that 'women are', 'women believe' and 'women need' be made when such claims are inapplicable or unresponsive to the needs, interests and experiences of Black women?

The value of feminist theory to Black women is diminished because it evolves from a white racial context that is seldom acknowledged. Not only are women of colour in fact overlooked, but their exclusion is reinforced when *white* women speak for and as *women*. The authoritative universal voice–usually white male subjectivity masquerading as non-racial, non-gendered objectivity[13] – is merely transferred to those who, but for gender, share many of the same cultural, economic and social characteristics. When feminist theory attempts to describe women's experiences through analysing patriarchy, sexuality, or separate spheres ideology, it often overlooks the role of race. Feminists thus ignore how their own race functions to mitigate some aspects of sexism and, moreover, how it often privileges them over and contributes to the domination of other women. Consequently, feminist theory remains *white*, and its potential to broaden and deepen its analysis by addressing non-privileged women remains unrealised.

An example of how some feminist theories are narrowly constructed around white women's experiences is found in the separate sphere's literature. The critique of how separate spheres ideology shapes and limits women's roles in the home and in public life is a central theme in feminist legal thought. Feminists have attempted to expose and dismantle separate spheres ideology by identifying and criticising the stereotypes that traditionally have justified the disparate societal roles assigned to men and women. Yet this attempt to debunk ideological justifications for *women's* subordination offers little insight into the domination of *Black* women. Because the experiential base upon which many feminist insights are grounded is white, theoretical statements drawn from them are overgeneralised at best, and often wrong. Statements such as 'men and women are taught to see men as independent, capable, powerful; men and women are taught to see women as dependent, limited in abilities, and passive',[14] are common within this literature. But this 'observation' overlooks the anomalies created by crosscurrents of racism and sexism. Black men and women live in a society that creates sex-based norms and expectations which racism operates simultaneously to deny; Black men are not viewed as powerful, nor are Black women seen as passive. An effort to develop an ideological explanation of gender domination in the Black community should proceed from an understanding of how crosscutting forces establish gender norms and how the conditions of Black subordination wholly frustrate access to these norms. Given this understanding, perhaps we can begin to see why Black women have been dogged by the stereotype of the pathological matriarch or why there have been those in the Black liberation movement who aspire to create institutions and to build traditions that are intentionally patriarchal.[15]

Because ideological and descriptive definitions of patriarchy are usually premised upon white female experiences, feminists and others informed by feminist literature may make the mistake of assuming that since the role of Black women in the family and in other Black institutions does not always resemble the familiar manifestations of patriarchy in the white community, Black women are somehow exempt from patriarchal norms. For example, Black women have traditionally worked outside the home in numbers far exceeding the labour participation rate of white women.[16] An analysis of patriarchy that highlights the history of white women's exclusion from the workplace might permit the inference that Black women have not been burdened by this particular gender-based expectation. Yet the very fact that Black women must work conflicts with norms that women should not, often creating personal, emotional and relationship problems in Black women's lives. Thus, Black women are burdened not only because they often have to take on responsibilities that are not traditionally feminine but, moreover, their assumption of these roles is sometimes interpreted within the Black community as either Black women's failure to live up to such norms or as another manifestation of racism's scourge upon the Black community. This is one of the many aspects of intersectionality that cannot be understood through an analysis of patriarchy rooted in white experience.

Another example of how theory emanating from a white context obscures the multidimensionality of Black women's lives is found in feminist discourse on rape. A central political issue on the feminist agenda has been the pervasive problem of rape. Part of the intellectual and political effort to mobilise around this issue has involved the development of a historical critique of the role that law has played in establishing the bounds of normative sexuality and in regulating female sexual behaviour.[17] Early carnal knowledge statutes and rape laws are understood within this discourse to illustrate that the objective of rape statutes traditionally has not been to protect women from coercive intimacy but to protect and maintain a property-like interest in female chastity.[18] Although feminists quite rightly criticise these objectives, to characterise rape law as reflecting male control over female sexuality is for Black women an oversimplified account and an ultimately inadequate account.

Rape statutes generally do not reflect *male* control over *female* sexuality, but *white* male regulation of *white* female sexuality. Historically, there has been absolutely no institutional effort to regulate Black female chastity. Courts in some states had gone so far as to instruct juries that, unlike white women, Black women were not presumed to be chaste. Also, while it was true that the attempt to regulate the sexuality of white women placed unchaste women outside the law's protection, racism restored a fallen white woman's chastity where the alleged assailant was a Black man.[19] No such restoration was available to Black women.

The singular focus on rape as a manifestation of male power over female sexuality tends to eclipse the use of rape as a weapon of racial terror. When Black women were raped by white males, they were being raped not as women generally, but as Black women specifically: Their femaleness made them sexually vulnerable to racist domination, while their Blackness effectively denied them any protection.[20] This white male power was reinforced by a judicial system in which the successful conviction of a white man for raping a Black woman was virtually unthinkable.[21]

In sum, sexist expectations of chastity and racist assumptions of sexual promiscuity combined to create a distinct set of issues confronting Black women. These issues have seldom been explored in feminist literature nor are they prominent in antiracist politics. The lynching of Black males, the institutional practice that was legitimised by the regulation of white women's sexuality, has historically and contemporaneously occupied the Black agenda on sexuality and violence. Consequently, Black women are caught between a Black community that, perhaps understandably, views with suspicion attempts to litigate questions of sexual violence, and a feminist community that reinforces those suspicions by focusing on white female sexuality. The suspicion is compounded by the historical fact that the protection of white female sexuality was often the pretext for terrorising the Black community. Even today some fear that antirape agendas may undermine antiracist objectives. This is the paradigmatic political and theoretical dilemma created by the intersection of race and gender: Black women are caught between ideological and political currents that combine first to create and then to bury Black women's experiences.

Expanding feminist theory and antiracist politics by embracing the intersection

If any real efforts are to be made to free Black people of the constraints and conditions that characterise racial subordination, then theories and strategies purporting to reflect the Black community's needs must include an analysis of sexism and patriarchy. Similarly, feminism must include an analysis of race if it hopes to express the aspirations of non-white women. Neither Black liberationist politics nor feminist theory can ignore the intersectional experiences of those whom the movements claim as their respective constituents. In order to include Black women, both movements must distance themselves from earlier approaches in which experiences are relevant only when they are related to certain clearly identifiable causes (for example, the oppression of Blacks is significant when based on race, of women when based on gender). The praxis of both should be centred on the life chances and life situations of people who should be cared about without regard to the source of their difficulties.

I have stated earlier that the failure to embrace the complexities of compoundedness is not simply a matter of political will, but is also due to the influence of a way of thinking about discrimination which structures politics so that struggles are categorised as singular issues. Moreover, this structure imports a descriptive and normative view of society that reinforces the status quo.

It is somewhat ironic that those concerned with alleviating the ills of racism and sexism should adopt such a top-down approach to discrimination. If their efforts instead began with addressing the needs and problems of those who are most disadvantaged and with restructuring and remaking the world where necessary, then others who are singularly disadvantaged would also benefit. In addition, it seems that placing those who currently are marginalised in the centre is the most effective way to resist efforts to compartmentalise experiences and undermine potential collective action.

It is not necessary to believe that a political consensus to focus on the lives of the most disadvantaged will happen tomorrow in order to recentre discrimination discourse at the intersection. It is enough, for now, that such an effort would encourage us to look beneath the prevailing conceptions of discrimination and to challenge the complacency that accompanies belief in the effectiveness of this framework. By so doing, we may develop language which is critical of the dominant view and which provides some basis for unifying activity. The goal of this activity should be to facilitate the inclusion of marginalised groups for whom it can be said: 'When they enter, we all enter'.

Notes

1 This chapter (here abridged) originally appeared as 'Demarginalizing the Intersection of Race and Sex: A Black Feminist Critique of Antidiscrimination Doctrine, Feminist Theory and Antiracist Politics', *University of Chicago Legal Forum*, Vol. 1989 No. I, Article 8, pp. 140–67. Reprinted with permission from the *University of Chicago Legal Forum* and the University of Chicago Law School.
2 Gloria T. Hull et al. (eds.), *All the Women Are White, All the Blacks Are Men, but Some of Us Are Brave*, Old Westbury, New York: The Feminist Press, 1982.
3 413 F Supp 142 (E D Mo 1976).
4 *DeGraffenreid*, 413 F Supp at 143.
5 Ibid., p. 144.
6 Ibid., p. 145. In *Mosley v General Motors*, 497 F Supp 583 (E D Mo 1980), plaintiffs, alleging broad-based racial discrimination at General Motors' St. Louis facility, prevailed in a portion of their Title VII claim. The seniority system challenged in *DeGraffenreid*, however, was not considered in *Mosley*.
7 Ibid., p. 145.
8 I do not mean to imply that all courts that have grappled with this problem have adopted the *DeGraffenreid* approach. Indeed, other courts have concluded that Black women are protected by Title VII. See, for example, *Jefferies v Harris Community Action Ass'n.*, 615 F. 2d 1025 (5th Cir.1980). I do mean to suggest that the very fact that the Black women's claims are seen as aberrant suggests that sex discrimination doctrine is centered in the experiences of white women. Even those courts that have held that Black women are protected seem to accept that Black women's claims raise issues that the 'standard' sex discrimination claims do not. See Elaine W. Shoben, 'Compound Discrimination: The

Interaction of Race and Sex in Employment Discrimination', Vol. 55 no. *NYU L Rev*793, 1980, pp. 803–4 (criticising the *Jefferies* use of a sex-plus analysis to create a subclass of Black women).
9   See, for example, *Moore,* 708 F. 2d, p. 479.
10 See Phyliss Palmer, 'The Racial Feminization of Poverty: Women of Color as Portents of the Future for All Women', *Women's Studies Quarterly*, Vol. 11, Fall 1983, pp. 3–4 (posing the question of why 'white women in the women's movement had not created more effective and continuous alliances with Black women' when 'simultaneously . . . Black women [have] become heroines for the women's movement, a position symbolized by the consistent use of Sojourner Truth and her famous words, 'Ain't I a Woman?').
11 See Paula Giddings, *When and Where I Enter: The Impact of Black Women on Race and Sex in America*, 1st ed., New York: William Morrow and Co, Inc, 1984, p. 54.
12 Eleanor Flexner, *Century of Struggle: The Women's Rights Movement in the United States*, Cambridge, MA: Belknap Press of Harvard University Press, 1975, p. 91. See also bell hooks, *Ain't I a Woman*, Boston: South End Press, 1981, pp. 159–60.
13 'Objectivity is itself an example of the reification of white male thought'. Hull et al. (eds.), *But Some of Us Are Brave*, p. XXV (cited in note 2).
14 Richard A. Wasserstrom, Racism, Sexism and Preferential Treatment: An Approach to the Topics, *UCLA L Rev*, Vol. 24(1977), pp. 581, 588. I chose this phrase not because it is typical of most feminist statements of separate spheres; indeed, most discussions are not as simplistic as the bold statement presented here. See, for example, Taub and Schneider, *Perspectives on Women's Subordination and the Role of Law*, pp. 117–39 (cited in note 36).
15 See hooks, *Ain't I a Woman*, pp. 94–99 (cited in note 34) (discussing the elevation of sexist imagery in the Black liberation movement during the 1960s).
16 See generally Jacqueline Jones, *Labor of Love, Labor of Sorrow: Black Women, Work, and the Family from Slavery to the Present*, New York: Basic Books, 1985; Angela Davis, *Women, Race and Class*, New York: Random House, 1981.
17 See generally Susan Brownmiller, *Against Our Will*, New York: Simon and Schuster, 1975; Susan Estrich, *Real Rape*, Cambridge, MA: Harvard University Press, 1987.
18 See Brownmiller, *Against Our Will*, p. 17; see generally Estrich, *Real Rape*.
19 Because of the way the legal system viewed chastity, Black women could not be victims of forcible rape. One commentator has noted that '[a]ccording to governing sterotypes [sic], chastity could not be possessed by Black women. Thus, Black women's rape charges were automatically discounted, and the issue of chastity was contested only in cases where the rape complainant was a white woman'. Note, 6 *Harv Women's L J*, p. 126 (cited in note 48). Black women's claims of rape were not taken seriously regardless of the offender's race. A judge in 1912 said: 'This court will never take the word of a nigger against the word of a white man [concerning rape]'. Ibid., p. 120. On the other hand, lynching was considered an effective remedy for a Black man's rape of a white woman. Since rape of a white woman by a Black man was 'a crime more horrible than death', the only way to assuage society's rage and to make the woman whole again was to brutally murder the Black man. Ibid., p. 125.
20 Gerda Lerner, *Black Women in White America: A Documentary History*, New York: Random House, 1973, p. 173.
21 See generally, Note, 6 *Harv Women's L J*, p. 103 (cited in note 47).

11

DALIT WOMEN TALK DIFFERENTLY[1]

Gopal Guru

Over the last several decades women's issues have become a part of global public agenda. While it is due to their ceaseless struggles that women have acquired visibility at the global level, women's assertion assumes particular expression by operating on a particular terrain shaped by forces of a particular country. The scenario of the women's movement in India, particularly in the context of Beijing conference, is characterised by groups affiliated to formal political formations. In a situation, where the organisation of politics around difference has become a major focus of feminist politics, the organisation of Dalit women around the notion of difference is bound to be a logical outcome. An independent and autonomous assertion of Dalit women's identity found its first expression in the formation of National Federation of Dalit Women (NFDW) at Delhi on August 11 1995.

In order to understand the Dalit women's need to talk differently it is necessary to delineate both the external and external factors that have bearing on this phenomenon. Some women activists apprehend that contingent factors like the upcoming Beijing conference were responsible for the national level meet at Delhi. It may be true that the all India mobilisation of Dalit women, which is a culmination of such conferences previously held in Bangalore, Delhi and Pune during the last couple of years, was visualised by the Dalit women activists keeping in view the representation of Dalit women to Beijing conference. However, the issue of representing Dalit women, both at the level of theory and politics, ha erupted time and again in the discourse on Dalit women. Dalit women justify the case for talking differently on the basis of external factors (non-Dalit forces homogenising the issue of Dalit women) and internal factors (the patriarchal domination within the Dalits).

Social location which determines the perception of reality is a major factor (as we shall see in the context of argument made by Dalit women) makes the representation of Dalit women's issues by non-Dalit women less valid and less authentic. But this claim of Dalit women activist does not mean a celebration of plural practices of feminism. However, there are feminists who seek to understand the need to talk differently, keeping in mind certain external factors. For example, Gail Omvedt would link the Dalit need to talk differently *vis-a-vis* the left forces to the betrayal of the promises given to the Dalits by latter. Rajni Kothari shares the same opinion but rather differently. He says,

> [w]ith the erosion of institutions, the unsettled controversies over public policies, and the growing uncertainty over ideological issues, as well as the decline of democratic functioning of the political process, faith in the capacity of the modern nation-state to provide framework of both order and equity has declined, and so, too, the reliance on mainstream governmental and party political process. The result has been the rise of a series of movements as distinct from the earlier gainer of more specific economic movements such as trade union or co-operative movements'.

Kothari calls this phenomenon of 'talking differently' a 'discourse of dissent'.

But focusing on certain external factors does not provide access to the complex reality of Dalit women. For example, the question of rape cannot be grasped merely in terms of class, criminality, or as a psychological aberration or an illustration of male violence. The caste factor also has to be taken into account which makes sexual violence against Dalit or tribal women much more severe in terms of intensity and magnitude. This differential experience was expressed by Dalit women activists at the Delhi meet and also previously at a conclave organised by Satyashodhak Mahila Aghadi in Maharashtra. However, these activists lament that the caste factor does not get adequate recognition in the analysis done by non-Dalit, middle-class, urbanised women activists.

Dalit women did appreciate feminist radicalism in the early phase of new peasant movements in Maharashtra. Yet, they did not approve of the ultimate subordination of the Dalit voice of the Shetkari Sanghatana in Maharashtra and the Rayat Sangha in Karnataka. They questioned the populism of these peasant movements, who, representing the interests of rich farmers, entered into direct contradiction with the interests of Dalit agricultural labourers over the issue of minimum wages.

Secondly, Dalit women would not make common cause with the 'moral economy' advocated by the Shetkari Sanghatana and its feminist supporters. They are of the opinion that the moral economy of the Sanghatana offered no solution to their poverty, instead it sought to naturalise their poor living conditions. Dalit women are also not well disposed to the eco-feminist call for development of environment consciousness. In fact, Dalit men and women from Kannad taluka of Aurangabad district uprooted saplings planted by the social forestry department. Now, some environmentalists might remark that these Dalit women lack ecological understanding. But the fact of the matter is that these Dalits have been denied legitimate piece of land from the ceiling land which the village landlords still control. Further, the Dalits do not have equal access to common property resources of the village. In fact, the experience of gram panchayats in Uttar Pradesh shows that an egalitarian distribution of landholding is a precondition for tension-free management of forest resources.

Thirdly, the claim for women's solidarity at both national and global levels subsumes contradictions that exist between high caste and Dalit women. The latent manifestations of these contradictions involve subtle forms of caste discrimination as practised by upper-caste and upper-class women against Dalit women in the rural areas. The contradictions also take a violent as when the Shiv Sena women attacked Dalit women in Sawali village of Chandrapur district in 1988. Thus, beneath the call for women's solidarity the identity of the Dalit women as 'Dalit' gets whitewashed and allows a 'non-Dalit' women to speak on her behalf. It is against this background that Dalit women have of late protested against their 'guest appearances' in a text or a speech of a non-Dalit woman and instead organised on their own terms. They consider the feminist theory developed by non-Dalit women as unauthentic since it does not capture their reality. This comprehension gets clearly reflected in the 12-point agenda adopted by the NFDW and in several papers presented by the Dalit women at the Maharashtra Dalit Women's Conference held in Pune in May 1995. Dalit women activists quote Phule and Ambedkar to invalidate the attempt of a non-Dalit woman to don Dalit identity.

Dalit women's claim to 'talk differently' assumes certain positions. It assumes that the social location of the speaker will be more or less stable; therefore, 'talking differently' can be treated as genuinely representative. This makes the claim of Dalit women automatically valid. In doing so, the phenomenon of 'talking differently' foregrounds the identity of Dalit women.

Though it is difficult at this stage to make any definitive comments on the Dalit women's movement, one can question the validity of the preceding assumptions. There is a notable shift taking place in the location of Dalit women. Dalit women from Maharashtra are better educated and employed than their counterparts from Karnataka. And it would be the former who would represent Dalit women at Beijing. Thus, here too, a certain section of Dalit women will be rendered anonymous. That is why the second point in the agenda of NFDW mentions the need to associate with grass roots Dalit women. Further, for challenging male dominance in politics, Dalit women are dependent on the state to create a space for them. This exposes them to the danger of co-option as was the case with their male counterparts. Nevertheless, the process of empowerment of Dalit women makes the terrain of nation-state more contested.

Also, the Indian state is keen on projecting itself as well-intentioned on gender issues and has sponsored the delegation of Indian women to Beijing. The state by incorporating women's movement within the jurisdiction of its apparatus intends to 'domesticate' the movement. Hence, the crucial question which arises with regard to the NFDW is whether it will succeed in evading this trap of domestication. On the basis of available evidence, it is possible to argue that Dalit women can challenge the state and state-mediated patriarchy. This was proved when Dalit women of Bodh Gaya in Bihar who opposed the state's decision to hand over land in the names of Dalit men since it would further marginalise them. Dalit women under the Bahujan Mahila Aghadi and Shetmajur Shetkari Shramik Aghadi in Maharashtra oppose the process of globalisation. Incidentally, the newly formed NFDW also has made clear its intention to fight the Indian state's new economic policy of privatisation and globalisation.

Dalit women, particularly at the grass roots level in Maharashtra, are exhibiting a spontaneous and strong solidarity across caste and region against the violence let loose by the Hindutva forces. Dalit women are participating in the ongoing struggle regarding pasture land. In this context, the anti-Hindutva campaign organised by Women's Voice of Bangalore, which is a major component of NFDW, deserves mention. Thus, Dalit women's perception while critical of the homogenisation of a dominant discourse, does not make a fetish of its own reality, and therefore, prevents the ghettoisation of Dalithood.

Note

1 This chapter is a slightly abridged version of the article 'Dalit Women Talk Differently', published in *Economic and Political Weekly*, Vol. 30 No. 41/42, October 14–21, 1995, pp. 2548–50. Used with permission.

12

DEBATING DALIT DIFFERENCE[1]

Sharmila Rege

A significant shift in the feminist thought of the 1980s and 1990s was the increasing visibility of Black and Third World feminist work. Yet there has been a reluctance on part of white feminists to confront the challenges posed to them by Black and Third World feminism. Often, this reluctance has been justified in terms of white feminists refraining from an appropriation of the voices of Black and Third World women.[2] This reluctance and relative silence on part of the white feminists amounts to an assumption that confronting racism is the sole responsibility of Black feminists or to a reassertion of the old assumption that the political process of becoming anti-sexist includes by definition the process of becoming anti-racist. Much of this state of stasis in Western feminism may be explained in terms of the alliance between feminism and post-structuralism/postmodernism; more specifically in terms of the category of 'difference' coming to the centre of feminist theorisation. A commitment to feminist politics demands that the limited political and analytical use of this category of 'difference' be underlined.

In the Indian context, the political pitfalls of the ever increasing impact of post-modernist and post-structural approaches in terms of the rise of 'culturological' and communitarian approaches;[3] the rise of the 'later subaltern subject'[4] and the post-colonial subject have been noted.[5] In the framework of post-orientalism studies, the focus remains on colonial domination alone, thereby the pre-colonial roots of caste, gender and class domination come to be ignored. The application of Saidian framework, therefore presents a problem, especially when applied to the non-brahmin movements and movements by or on behalf of women; for both these had utilised the colonial law, justice and administration as major resources.[6] Recent feminist scholarship in adopting the Saidian framework not only falls into the aforementioned traps, but ends up with a frame that completely overlooks the contributions and interventions of women in the non-brahmin movement. The invisibility of this lineage has led scholars to conceive the recent autonomous assertion by Dalit women – as 'a different voice'.

The 1980s were marked by the newly exploding caste identity and consciousness and theoretical and political issues involved the debate on caste and its role in social transformation came to be debated.[7] The early 1990s saw the assertion of autonomous Dalit women's organisations at both regional and national levels. Such an assertion had thrown up several crucial theoretical and political challenges, besides underlining the brahminism of the feminist movement and the patriarchal practices of Dalit politics. The formation of autonomous Dalit women's organisations initially propelled a serious debate, drawing responses from both left party-based as well as autonomous women's organisations. However, the debates seemed to have come to rest and the relative silence, and the apparent absence of a revisioning of feminist politics thereafter only suggests an ideological position of multiple plural feminist standpoints. That to say, the separate assertion by Dalit women's organisations comes to be accepted as one more standpoint and within such a framework of 'difference'; issues of caste become the sole responsibility of the Dalit women's organisations. An absence of an exploration of each other's positions – hinders the dialectics; both of a revisioning of contemporary feminist politics and a sharpening of the positions put forth by autonomous Dalit women's organisations. This chapter seeks to open some of these issues for debate.

The chapter is organised into four sections: Section I seeks to review the changing categories of feminist analysis. It traces the processes by which 'difference' as a category came to occupy a central place in feminist analyses. This, it is argued, has meant a backtracking from some of the core categories in feminism. It is imperative for feminist politics that 'difference' be historically located in the real struggles of marginalised women. Section II undertakes in such an exercise of historically locating the 'different voice' of Dalit women in their struggles, tracing the lineage through the Satyashodhak and Ambedkarite movements. It is further argued that the reinscription of these struggles in our historical mappings poses a challenge to Chatterjee's analysis of the 'Nationalist Resolution of the Women's Question'; an analysis that has come to inform much of the theorisation on gender and nation.[8] Section III seeks to trace the exclusion of Dalit women's voices in the two important new social movements of the 1970s: the Dalit movement and in more detail the women's movement. Tracing the issues at stake in the post Mandal-Masjid phase of the women's movement, it is argued that the assertion of Dalit women's voices in the 1990s brings up significant issues for the revisioning of feminist politics. Finally, Section IV argues that the assertion of Dalit women's voices is not just an issue of naming their 'difference'. 'Naming of difference' leads to a narrow identitarian politics – rather this assertion is read as a centring of the discourse on caste and gender and is viewed as suggesting a Dalit feminist standpoint. A large part of the chapter draws upon our understanding of and engagement in the contemporary women's movement in Maharashtra.

Feminist theorisation: from 'Difference' to more 'Difference'

Feminism of the 1970s had developed difference from the Left. Crucial to this difference, were three categories viz – woman, experience and personal politics, which were central to feminist theorisation.[9] Though these categories were powerful as political rhetoric – they posed theoretical problems. The category 'woman' was conceived as collectively, their being oppressed by the fact of their womanhood. The three categories deployed in combination and this often led to exclusions around race, class ethnicity. Since most of the vocal feminists of the 1970s were white, middle class and university educated – it was their experience which came to be universalised as 'women's experience'. Thus, sweeping statements such as 'All Women are Niggers' were made.[10] The ambivalence of the left towards the notion of women's issues was thus countered by an assertion that women were essentially connected with other women and 'subjective experiences of knowledge' became the base of the universal experience of womanhood. Thus 'experience' became base for personal politics as well as only reliable mythological tool for defining oppression.[11] At least three major postulates emerged from such an epistemological position, one that there is system of male domination, that this system is political and that politics included are power relationships regardless of whether or not that power operated in the public sphere (i.e., to say the 'personal' was declared to political and as focus came to be on power in intimate relationships, critiques of state or capitalism took a back seat. In such a theoretical position, Black women come to be excluded as a structural consequence of the deployment of the categories of 'woman' and 'subjective experience'.

Theoretical debates came to centre around the theme of patriarchy, its material base, its persistence across modes of production and different levels within modes of production. Socialist feminists and radical feminists posed the issues in terms of capital needs vs male control. The crux of the differences between them rested on their differential conceptualisation of the causes of women's oppression. Yet there was a consensus between them, in that they believed in the search for fundamentals of social causation, i.e., both the camps asked the question 'what is the original or founding cause of women's oppression?' But by the 1980sthis consensus had broken up and 'difference' came to the centre of feminist analysis.[12]

Several factors have played a constitutive role in the processes that brought the category of 'difference' to the centre of feminist analyses. This has meant a focus on language, culture and discourse to the exclusion of political economy; a rejection of universalism in favour of difference; an insistence on fluid and fragmented human subject rather than collectivities; a celebration of the marginal and denial of their all causal analysis.[13] This shift in perspective has been aided in different ways by the following key factors.

The collapse of actually existing socialisms and the loss of prestige that this brought about for Marxism in the Anglo-American academies. The enormous and continued political interrogation of white, middle-class feminism by Black and

Third World feminists. This was welcome and had a tone level led to micro-level analyses of the complex interplay of different axes of inequality. For example, Black feminists questioned the sex/class debate of the 1970s arguing that the complex interplay between sex, class, race needed to be underlined. But at another level these interrogations took a more cultural path, i.e., the 'different the voices' of Black, Afro-American, Chicana, Asian women, etc., came to be celebrated.

The growing interest in psychoanalytic analyses which led to 'sexual differences' is being viewed as intransigent and positive. Therefore, for instance, feminist writings began to celebrate 'motherhood' as a positive different experience of being female. We must underline here that this suited the agenda of the New Right who had sought to combine in its ideology – values of free market, neo-nationalism and conservatism. The rise of post-structuralism and postmodernism and the increasing alliance of feminism with the same. This has meant broadly taking one of the following two positions.

1. Position of cultural feminism – which sees feminists as having the exclusive right describe and evaluate women. Therefore, 'passivity' comes to mean peaceful, sentimentality means nurture, etc., i.e., to say the very 'defining of woman' is not challenged only the dominant male definitions of the same come to be challenged.
2. Position of nominalism – It is argued that a category called 'woman' cannot exist – it is fictitious because there are several differences (race, class, etc.) that construct women differently. They replace a politics of agenda with plurality of difference.[14] Therefore, feminist politics is completely lost as the key activity becomes one of dismantling and deconstructing the differences among women. Thus using the category of 'difference' – feminists came to celebrate the aspects of femininity that were previously looked down upon or the 'different voices' of women of different nationalities, races, classes, etc. come to be celebrated – i.e., their plurality is underlined without an analysis of the structures of racism, patriarchies, international division of labour and capitalism. Therefore all analyses come to focus on identities, subjectivities and representations.

At this point, it is important to take note of the fact that there has been a resurgence of identities and the importance of naming the differences that emerge out of race, sex and so on cannot be denied. But it is important to underline the fact that we don't have to accept postmodernist notions of 'plurality' or 'difference' in order to take note of these differences, i.e., to say that 'no doubt, the notion of difference did play a significant role in Black and Third World women naming their oppression. But as an analytical and political tool its value is limited. A shift of focus from 'naming difference' or 'different voice' to social relations that convert difference into oppression is imperative for feminist politics. We may recall here the impasse that Black feminist politics has landed in even as Black feminist literature finds an ever expanding market. In such a situation, many of the very vocal Black feminists

(P. H. Collins for instance) have in their recent writings made a shift to relativism. Consider, e.g., the following statement 'Black feminist thought represents only a partial perspective . . . by understanding the perspectives of many groups, knowledge of social reality can become more complete'.[15] That is, there is an unwillingness to privilege any one viewpoint and Collins seems to make a shift/a confusion between generating knowledge from the experience of the oppressed as opposed to generating knowledge from the subjectivities of the oppressed.[16]

We shall argue that what we need instead is a shift of focus from 'difference' and multiple voices to the social relations which convert difference into oppression. This requires the working out of the cultural and material dimensions of the interactions and interphases between the different hierarchies of class, gender, race and so on. In other words this means transforming 'difference' into a standpoint. This is something we shall turn to in the last section of the chapter. With these 'lessons to be learnt' from the contemporary political impasse of Black feminism, we shall in the next section seek to historically locate the 'difference' of Dalit women's voices in their real struggles. A historical reinscription of Dalit women's struggles into the historiography of modern India poses major challenges for our established understanding of nationalism and the women's question in nineteenth-century India.

Historicising difference: women in non-brahmin movement

History of late colonial India has always prioritised Indian nationalism, such that it comes to be assumed that the world of political action and discourse can be comprehended only through the categories of nationalism, imperialism and communalism. The radical historiographies of colonial India, though they emphasised the autonomous role of peasant, labour and other subaltern groups, equated the historiography of colonial India with that of Indian nationalism.[17] The non-brahmanical reconstructions of historiography of modern India in the works of Omvedt, Patil and Alyosius have underlined the histories of anti-hierarchical, pro-democratising collective aspirations of the lower-caste masses which are not easily encapsulated within the histories of anti-colonial nationalism.[18] In fact these histories have often faced the penalty of being labeled as collaborative and have therefore being ignored in a historiography which is dominated by narratives of nationalism.

Feminist historiography made radical breakthroughs in teasing out the redefinitions of gender and patriarchies, i.e., to say in 'pulling out the hidden history swept under the liberal carpet of reforms'.[19] Feminist renderings of history have been ever since concerned with comprehending the linkages between reforms and the realignments of patriarchies with hierarchies of caste, class, ethnicity and so on. Vaid and Sangari make a significant distinction between the 'modernising of patriarchal modes of regulating women' and the 'democratizing of gender relations' both at home and the workplace.[20] They underline both the revolutionary potential and inherent contradictions that the democratising movements constituted for peasant

Debating Dalit difference

and working class women. While these democratising movements are seen as heralding 'class rights for women' as 'against and over' simply familial or caste-related identities; the histories of the non-brahmin democratic movements, ever so crucial to the emancipatory discourse on caste and gender come to be overlooked. This is true of most of the renderings of feminist history of modern India; though there are notable exceptions.[21]

More recent feminist studies have adopted poststructuralist and postmodern perspectives and this has resulted in studies dwelling 'obsessively on the limitations of west inspired reform initiatives'.[22] Most of the feminist studies of the late colonial period have come to be predetermined by Partha Chatterjee's frame of 'char/bahar' and the nationalist resolution of the women's question.[23] In Chatterjee's theoretical framework of the self/other, he introduces a new binary opposition – between home/world, public and private domains and argues that the nationalist counter-ideology separated the domain of culture into the material and spiritual. The colonised had to learn the techniques of the Western civilisation in the material sphere while retaining the distinctive spiritual essence of the material. These new dichotomies, it is argued matched with the identity of social roles by gender; and during this period the 'new woman' came to be defined within this frame and therefore as distinct from the common lower class female, further he argues that in the nineteenth century, the woman's question had been a central issue but by the early twentieth century this question disappeared from the public domain. This is not because political issues take over but because nationalism refused to make women's question an issue of political negotiation with the colonial state. Chatterjee argues that the changes in middle class women's lives were outside the arena of political agitation and the home became the principal site of struggle through which nationalist patriarchy came to be normalised. Thus Chatterjee concludes that the nationalists had in the early decades of the century 'resolved' the woman's question, all subsequent reworkings of the women's question by Dalit and working class women, thus come to be precluded. The period marked by Chatterjee as the period of the 'resolution of women's question'; as we shall note later – is the very period in which women's participation in the Ambedkarite movement was at its peak. But in Chatterjee's framework, such movements would be dismissed as Western-inspired, orientalist, for they utilised aspects of colonial policies and Western ideologies as resources.[24] If 'difference' of Dalit women's protest is to be historicised then these protests and struggles must be reinscribed; what has been excluded must be remapped and renamed.

One of the most significant counter narratives was Jotiba Phule's project for the liberation of the shudras, ati-shudras and women from the slavery of brahminism. He conceptualised a Bali Rajya of equality of all men in opposition to Ram Rajya based on Varna Ashrama Dharma, thus reversing the Aryan theory and giving a liberatory vision of history. His contestation of brahmanical patriarchy stands in contestation with the recasting of patriarchies by upper-caste brahmanical male reformers. His recognition of the material and sexual consequences of enforced widowhood is apparent in the reformist work done by him.

Muktabai (a student in Phule's school), in an essay entitled 'About the Girls of Mangs and Mahars' draws attention to the deprivation of lower castes from their lands, the prohibition of knowledge imposed on them and the complex hierarchies wherein even the lower castes were stratified into more or less polluting. She then compares the experiences of birthing for lower-caste and brahmin women, underlining the specificities of experiences of lower-caste women.[25] Savitribai Phule's letters reveal an acute consciousness of the relationship between knowledge and power and crucial need for democratic access to knowledge for the shudras and women.

Tarabai Shinde's 'Stree Purush Tulana', a text against women's subordination was written from within the Satyashodhak tradition.[26] This text launched an attack not only on brahmanical patriarchy but also the patriarchies among the 'kunbi' and other non-brahmin castes. Going beyond a mere comparison between men and women, Tarabai draws linkages between issues of de-industrialisation, colonialism and the commodification of women's bodies.[27]

The early decades of the twentieth century saw protests by 'muralis' against caste-based prostitution in the campaigns launched by Shivram Janoba Kamble. The 1930s saw the organisation of independent meetings and conferences by Dalit women in the Ambedkarite movement. This was an obvious consequence of Ambedkar's practice of organising a women's conference along with every general meeting and Sabha that he called. In these 'parishads' of the 1930s, Dalit women delegates passed resolutions against child marriage, enforced widowhood and dowry; critiquing these practices as brahmanical. Women's participation in the Mahad Satyagraha, their support to the Independent Labour Party and the Schedule Caste Federation have been well documented.[28] Women in large numbers supported Dharmantaar as a need to a religion that would recognise their equal status. Women's participation in the Ambedkarite movement must be read in the context of the fact that in Ambedkar's theory of caste there is also a theory of the origins of sub-ordination of women and that he saw the two issues as intrinsically linked.[29]

In a review of the different definitions of caste put forth by Nesfield, Risley, Ketkar and others, Ambedkar points to the inadequacy of understanding caste in terms of 'idea of pollution'. He argues that 'the absence of intermarriage or endogamy is the one characteristic that can be called the essence of castes'.[30] Thus it is the superimposition of endogamy on exogamy and the means used for the same that hold the key to the understanding of the caste system. Ambedkar then draws up a detailed analysis of how numerical equality between the marriageable units of the two sexes within the group is maintained. Thus he argues that practices of sati, enforced widowhood and child marriage come to be prescribed by brahminism in order to regulate and control any transgression of boundaries, i.e., he underlines the fact that the caste system can be maintained only through the controls on women's sexuality and in this sense women are the gateways to the caste system.[31] In his speech at the gathering of women at the Mahad satyagraha, he draws linkages between caste exploitation and women's subordination by underlining this; calls upon women to contest the claims of upper-caste women's progeny to purity and the damnation of that of the lower caste to impurity. He locates the specificities and varying intensities of women's subordination by caste and thereby draws their attention to the specificities of their subordination, both as 'Dalit' and as 'women'.[32]

These contentious non-brahmin images of identities for women however come to be silenced by the Fundamental Rights Resolution of the Indian National Congress in 1931. This Resolution postulated freedom, justice, dignity and equality for all women as essential for nation-building. The political contestations between competing political visions of how various national subjects would be related to each other were thus leveled out. In the post-Ambedkarite phase of the movement, women's participation marked a decline excepting the major upsurge during the Dadasaheb Gaikwad led struggle for land rights and the Namaantar movement. However, it must be noted that there are regional variations in these patterns of participation in struggles. A recent study by Guru has drawn attention to the sustained organisation of Dalit women through the mahila mandals in Akola region.[33] These mandals though primarily organised around Trisaran and Panchshil, sensitise their members to the Ambedkarite ideology. The Dalit women of these region have been vocal on the cultural landscape in the post-Ambedkerite phase. Their compositions ('ovi' and 'palana') are rich in political content, for instance one of the ovis reads

> Maya dari Nib! Nibale Phullera Babasahebanchy kotale Sonaychi Zalai (This ovi suggests that the golden border on Ambedkar's suit is more precious than the rose on the suit of Nehru).[34] This juxtaposing of Ambedkar against Nehru is a statement on the political contradictions between dalit politics and the politics of the Congress.

A review of all these counternarratives underlines the fact that the 'difference' or 'different voice' of the Dalit women is not an issue of identitarian politics; some 'authentic direct experience' but from a long lived history of lived struggles. Dalit women play a crucial role in transferring across generations, the oral repertoire of personalised yet very collective accounts of their family's interaction with Babasaheb or other leaders of the Dalit movement. The question that emerges then is 'Why is this different voice of the Dalit women' inaudible in the two major new social movements of the 1970s, namely the Dalit movement and the women's? The next section traces the issue through the latter while making brief references to the former.

Masculinisation of Dalithood and savarnisation of womanhood

The new social movements of the 1970s and the early 1980s saw the emergence of several organisations and fronts such as the Shramik Mukti Sanghatana, Satyashodhak Communist Party, Shramik Mukti Dal, Yuvak Kranti Dal none of whom limited the Dalit women to a token inclusion; their revolutionary agenda, in different ways accorded them a central place. This is however not the case with the two other movements of the period – the Dalit Panther and the women's movement; as constituted mainly by the left party-based women's fronts and the then emergent autonomous women's groups. The Dalit Panthers made a significant contribution to the cultural revolt of the 1970s – but in both their writings and their programme – the Dalit women remained encapsulated firmly in the roles of the 'mother' and the 'victimised sexual being'.

The Left party based women's organisations made significant contribution towards economic and work-related issues as the autonomous women's groups politicised and made public the issue of violence against women. Serious debates on class vs patriarchies emerged, both parties however did not address the issues of brahminism. While for the former 'caste' was contained in class, for the latter the notion of sisterhood was pivotal. All women came to be conceived as 'victims' and therefore 'Dalit'; so that what results is a classical exclusion. All 'Dalits' are assumed to be males and all women 'savanna'. It may be argued that the categories of experience and personal politics were at the core of the epistemology and politics of the Dalit Panther movement and the women's movement. Such a position resulted into a universalisation of what was in reality the middle class, upper-caste women's experience or the Dalit male experience.

The autonomous women's groups of the early 1980s had remained largely dependent on the left frame even as they emerged as a challenge to it.[35] With the women's movement gathering momentum – sharp critiques of mainstream conceptualisations of work, development, legal process and the state emerged and this led to several theoretical and praxiological reformulations. Debates on class vs patriarchy, were politically enriching for both the parties to the debate. It must be underlined here that most of the feminist groups broadly agreed that in the Indian context, a materialistic framework was imperative to the analysis of women's oppression. However in keeping with their roots in the 'class' framework, there were efforts to draw commonalities across class and to a lesser extent castes or communities.[36] This is apparent in the major campaigns launched by the women's movement during this period. The absence of an analytical frame that in the tradition of Phule and Ambedkar would view caste hierarchies and patriarchies as intrinsically linked is apparent in the in the anti-dowry, anti-rape and anti-violence struggles of the women's movement.

An analysis of the practices of violence against women by caste would reveal that while the incidence of dowry deaths and violent controls and regulations on the mobility and sexuality by the family are frequent among the dominant upper castes – Dalit women are more likely to face the collective and public threat of rape, sexual assault and physical violence at the work place and in public.[37] Consider e.g., the statements issued by women's organisations during the Mathura rape case. While the NFIW looked at rape in 'class' terms the socialist women in terms of 'glass vessel cracking' and therefore in terms of less of honour; the AIWC sought psychological explanations of the autonomous women's groups highlighted the use of patriarchial power.[38] Looking back at the agitation, it is apparent that the sexual assaults on Dalit women in Marathwada during the 'Namaantar' agitation do not become a nodal point for such an agitation, in fact they come to be excluded. The campaign therefore becomes more of a single issue campaign. Consider also the campaign against dowry, while the left based women's organisations viewed dowry in terms of the ways in which capitalism was developing in India; the autonomous women's groups focused on the patriarchial power/violence within families.[39] The present practices of dowry cannot be outside the processes of brahminisation and their impact on marriage practices. That brahmanic ideals led to a preference for dowry marriage is well documented. In fact it is the colonial establishment of the legality of the Brahma form of marriage that institutionalises and expands the dowry system. The brahminising castes adopted the Brahma form of marriage over the other forms and thereby establishing 'dowry' as an essential ritual.[40] Moreover the principle of endogamy and its coercive and violent perpetuation through collective violence against inter-caste alliances are all crucial to the analysis of the dowry question.

The relative absence of caste as a category in the feminist discourse on violence has also led to the encapsulation of the Muslim and Christian women within the questions of 'Talaq' and 'Divorce'. Recent studies by Razia Patel for the Times Foundation and Vilas Sonawane for the Muslim OBC Sanghatana have revealed that encroachment on caste-based occupational practices and issues of education and employment are listed as crucial issues by a majority of the Muslim women.

Thus in retrospect, it is clear that while the left party-based women's organisations collapsed caste into class, the autonomous women's groups collapsed caste into sisterhood – both leaving brahminism unchallenged. The movement has addressed issues concerning women of the Dalit, tribal and minority communities and substantial gains have been achieved but a feminist politics centring around the women of the most marginalised communities could not emerge. The history of agitations and struggles of the second wave of the women's movement articulated strong anti-patriarchal positions on different issues. Issues of sexuality and sexual politics – which are crucial for a feminist politics remained largely within an individualistic and lifestyle frame. Issues of sexuality are intrinsically linked to caste and addressal of sexual politics without a challenge to brahminism results in lifestyle feminisms.

In the post Mandal agitations and caste violence at Chunduru and Pimpri Deshmukh for instance women of the upper castes were involved as feminist subjects assertive non-submissive and protesting against injustice done to them as women (at Chunduru or Pimpri Deshmukh) and as citizens (anti-Mandal). In the anti-Mandal protests young middle class women declared that they were against all kinds of reservations (including those for women) and they mourned the death of merit and explicated that they were out to save the nation. Their placards said 'we want employed husbands – sexuality and caste became hidden issues as they protested as 'citizens'.[41] At Pimpri-Deshmukh in Maharashtra, following the hacking to death of the Dalit kotwal (active mobiliser for the local Buddha Vihar) by upper-caste men, the upper-caste women came out in public complaining that the Dalit man had harassed them and was sexually perverted. They claimed that they had incited their men to protect their honour, thus the agency of upper-caste women was invoked. The issue was not an issue of molestation alone or one of violence against Dalits alone, but one that underlines the complex reformulations that brahmanical patriarchies undergo in order to counter collective Dalit resistance.

The increasing visibility of Dalit women in power structures as 'sarpanch' or member of the panchayat and in the new knowledge making processes (such as Bhanwari Devi's intervention through the Saathin programme) has led to increased backlash against Dalit women. The backlash is expressed through a range of humiliating practices and often culminates in rape – or hacking to death of their kinsmen. Such incidents underline the need for a dialogue between Dalit and feminist activists, since inter-caste relations at the local level may be mediated through a redefinition of gendered spaces. Kannabiran and Kannabiran have pointed to how the deadlock between kshatriya and Dalit men caused by Dalit agricultural labourer women 'dressing well' could be solved only by a decision taken by men of both the communities.[42] It was decided that women of either community would not be allowed to step into each other's locations. The sexual assault on Dalit women has been used as a common practice for undermining the manhood of the caste. Some Dalit male activists did argue that in passing derogatory remarks about upper-caste girls (in incidents such as Chanduru) Dalit men were only getting their own back. The emancipatory agenda of the Dalit and women's movements will have to be sensitive to these issues and underline the complex interphase between caste and gender as structuring hierarchies in society.

The demolition of the Babri masjid and the series of incidents that followed and women's active participation in the Hindu Right has led the women's movement to backtrack on the demand of the Uniform Civil Code. The Right Wing government in Maharashtra has appropriated the crucial issue of indecent representation of women too. The formation of the Agnishikha Maanch with its agenda of regulation of morality and 'working mothers' is a case in point. In the name of saving from the negative impact of the West the Right Wing government has launched public campaigns against glossies and advertisements and has sought to clean Mumbai by launching a campaign of rounding up prostitutes and segregating those found to be HIV positive. Gender issues are appropriated as cultural issues and become grounds for moral regulation. All this calls for reformulation of our feminist agenda, to reclaim our issues and re-conceptualising them such that feminist politics poses a challenge to their very cross-caste/class conceptualisation of brahmanical Hindutva.

Such a re-conceptualisation calls for a critique of brahmanical hierarchies from a gender perspective. Such critiques have the potential of translating the discourse of sexual politics from individual narratives to collective contestations of hierarchies. In the brahmanical social order, caste-based division of labour and sexual divisions of labour are intermeshed such that elevation in caste status is preceded by the withdrawal of women of that caste from productive processes outside the private sphere. Such a linkage derives from presumptions about the accessibility of sexuality of lower-caste women because of their participation in social labour. Brahminism in turn locates this as the failure of lower-caste men to control the sexuality of their women and underlines this as a justification of their impurity. Thus gender ideology legitimises not only structures of patriarchy but also the very organisation of caste.[43] Similarly, drawing upon Ambedkar's analysis of caste, caste ideology (endogamy) is also the very basis of regulation and organisation of women's sexuality. Hence caste determines the division of labour, sexual division of labour and division of sexual labour.[44] Hence there exist multiple patriarchies and many of their overlaps and differences are structured.[45] Brahmanisation has been a two way process of acculturation and assimilation and through history there has been a brahmanical refusal to universalise a single patriarchal mode. Thus the existence of multiple patriarchies is a result of both brahmanical conspiracy and of the relation of the caste group to the means for production. There are, therefore, according to Sangari, discrete (specific to caste), as well as overlapping patriarchal arrangements.[46] Hence, she argues that women who are sought to be united on the basis of systematic overlapping patriarchies are nevertheless divided on caste, class lines and by their consent to patriarchies and their compensatory structures. If feminists are to challenge these divisions then mode of organisation and struggles 'should emcompass all of the social inequalities that patriarchies are related to, embedded in and structured by'. Does the different voice of Dalit women challenge these divisions? In the next section we seek to outline the non-brahmanical renderings of women's liberation in Maharashtra.

Non-brahmanical rendering of women's liberation

In the 1990s, there were several independent and autonomous assertions of Dalit women's identity; a case in point is the formation of the National Federation of Dalit Women and the All India Dalit Women's Forum. At the state level, the Maharashtra Dalit Mahila Sanghatana was formed in 1995, a year earlier, the women's wing of the Bhartiya Republican Party and the Bahujan Mahila Sangh had organised the Bahujan Mahila Parishad. In an historical happening, in December 1996, at Chandrapur a 'Vikas Vanchit Dalit Mahila Parishad' was organised and a proposal for commemorating December 25 (the day Ambedkar set the *Manusmriti* on fames) as Bharatiya Streemukti Divas was put forth. In 1997 the Christi Mahila Sangharsh Sanghatana, an organisation of Dalit Christian women was founded. These different organisations have put forth varying non-brahmanical ideological positions and yet have come together on several issues such as the issue of Bharatiya Shreemukti Divas and the issue of reservations for OBC women in parlimentary bodies.

The emergence of autonomous Dalit women's organisation led to a major debate; set rolling by the essay 'Dalit Women Talk Differently'.[47] A series of discussions around the paper were organised in Pune by different feminist groups. A two-day seminar on the same was organised by Alochana – Centre for research and Documentation on Women in June 1996. Subsequently there were two significant responses to the emergence of autonomous Dalit women's organisations; one by

Kiran Moghe of the Janwadi Mahila Sanghatana and the other by Vidyut Bhagwat argued out the different issues at stake.

Guru had argued that to understand the Dalit women's need to talk differently, it was necessary to delineate both internal and external factors that have a bearing on this phenomenon.[48] He locates their need to talk differently in a discourse of dissent against the middle class women's movement by the Dalit men and the moral economy of the peasant movements. It is a note of dissent, he argues, against their exclusion from both the political and cultural arena. It is further underlined that social location determines the perception of reality and therefore representation of Dalit women's issues by non-Dalit women was less valid and less authentic.[49] Though Guru's argument is well taken and we agree that Dalit women must name the difference, to privilege knowledge claims on the basis of direct experience on claims of authenticity may lead to a narrow identity politics. Such a narrow frame may in fact limit the emancipatory potential of the Dalit women's organisations and also their epistemological standpoints.

The left party-based women's organisations have viewed the emergence of autonomous women's organisations as 'setting up separate health'.[50] Moghe argues that despite the earlier critiques of the left party-based women's groups made by the autonomous women's groups, the context of Hindutva and the New Economic Policy has brought both parties together and the autonomous women's groups had once again come to share a common platform with the left. The subtext of Moghe's arguments is that autonomy is limiting, and that the Dalit women's autonomous organisations faced the threat of being 'autonomous from the masses', in case they did not keep the umbilical relation with the Republican Party. In such a context the efforts, she argued, would be limited by the focus on the experiences and the intricacies of funding. In a critique of Moghe's position,[51] Bhagwat argued that the position was lacking in self reflexivity and that the enriching dialectics between the left parties and the autonomous women's groups had been overlooked in highlighting only one side of the story.[52] To label any new autonomous assertion from the marginalised as identitarian and limited to experience, she argues, was to overlook the history of struggles by groups to name themselves and their politics.

Several apprehensions were raised about the Dalit Mahila Sanghatans' likelihood of being a predominantly neo-Buddhist women's organisation. Pardeshi rightly argues that such apprehensions are historically insensitive and overlook the historical trajectories of the growth of the Dalit movement in Maharashtra.[53] Yet she also cautions that a predominantly neo-Buddhist middle class leadership could have politically limiting consequences – for instance, at many of the proceedings of the Parishad; brahmanisation came to be understood within a narrow frame of non-practice of Trisaran and Panchasheel. Such a frame could limit the participation by women of middle castes.

There are as of today, at least three major contesting and overlapping positions that have emerged from the struggles and politics of Dalit women. One of the earliest and well defined position is the Marxist/ Phule-Ambedkarite position of the Satyashodak Mahila Sabha.[54] A position emerging out of the Dalit-bahujan alliance is that of the Bahujan Mahila Mahasangh (BMM) which critiques the vedic, brahmanical tradition and seeks to revive the Bahujan tradtion of the 'Adi-maya'. The secular position is critiqued as brahmanical and individualistic and the Ambedkarite conceptualisation of Dhamma in community life is underlined. The Common civil codes is opposed and customary law and community based justice is upheld. Significantly the BMM seeks to combine both the struggles for political power and a cultural revolution in order to revive and extend the culture of Bahujans.[55] Such a position is crucial in order to problematise the dominant brahmanical culture and thereby underline the materiality of culture. Yet it faces the danger of glorifying Bahujan familial and community practices, any traces of patriarchal power therein are acquitted at once by viewing them as a resultant of the processes of brahmanisation.

The Dalit Mahila Sanghatana has critiqued the persistence of the 'Manuvadi Sanskriti' among the Dalit male who otherwise traces his lineage to a Phule Ambedkarite ideology. The Sanghatana proposes to put forth its manifesto – at the centre of which would be the most Dalit of Dalit women.[56] The Christi Mahila Sangharsh Sanghatana is a Dalit Christian women's organisation. In the initial meetings the loss of traditional occupations of the converts, their transfer to the service sector, the hierarchies among the Christians by caste and religion and the countering of oppositional forces led by the church and state level Christian organisations come to be debated.[57]

These non-brahmanial renderings of feminist politics have led to some self reflexivity among the autonomous women's groups and their responses could be broadly categorised as (1) a non-dialectical position of those who grant that historically it is now important that Dalit women take the leadership but they do not revision a non-brahmanical feminist politics for themselves, (2) the left position that collapses caste into class and continues to question the distinct materiality of caste and who have registered a note of dissent on the declaration of December 25 as Bharatiya Streemukti Divas, (3) a self-reflexive position of those autonomous women's groups who recognise the need to reformulate and revision feminist politics for the non-biahmanical renderings are viewed as more emancipatory.

To go back to where we began this chapter, namely, the issue of difference. It is apparent that the issues underlined by the new Dalit women's movement go beyond naming of the 'difference' of Dalit women and calls for a revolutionary epistemological shift to a Dalit feminist standpoint.[58]

The intellectual history of feminist standpoint theory may be traced to Marx Enge1sandLukacsinsightsinto the standpoint of the proletariat. A social history of standpoint theory focuses on what happens when marginalised peoples begin to gain public voice. The failure of dominant groups to critically and systematically interrogate their advantaged situation leaves their social situation scientifically and epistemologically a disadvantaged one for generating knowledge.[59] Such accounts may end up legitimating exploitative 'practical politics' even though they may have good intention. A Dalit feminist standpoint is seen as emancipatory since the subject of its knowledge is embodied and visible (i.e., the thought begins from the lives of Dalit women and these lives are present and visible in the results of the thought). This position argues that it is more emancipatory than other existing positions and counters pluralism and relativism by which all knowledge based and political claims are thought to be valid in their own way. It places emphasis on individual experiences within socially constructed groups and focuses on the hierarchical, multiple, changing structural power relations of caste, class, ethnic, which construct such a group. It is obvious that the subject/agent of Dalit women's standpoint is multiple, heterogeneous even contradictory, i.e., the category 'Dalit woman' is not homogemous – such a recognition underlines the fact that the subject of Dalit feminist liberatory knowledge must also be the subject of every other liberatory project and this requires a sharp focus on the processes by which gender, race, class, caste, sexuality – all construct each other. Thus we agree that the Dalit feminist standpoint itself is open to liberatory interrogations and revisions.

The Dalit feminist standpoint which emerges from the practices and struggles of Dalit woman, we recognise, may originate in the works of Dalit feminist intellectuals but it cannot flourish if isolated from the experiences and ideas of other groups who must educate themselves about the histories, the preferred social relations and utopias and the struggles of the marginalised. A transformation from 'their cause' to 'our cause' is possible for subjectivities can be transformed. By this we do not argue that non-Dalit feminists can 'speak as' or 'for the' Dalit women but they can 'reinvent themselves as Dalit feminists'. Such a position, therefore avoids the narrow alley of direct experience based 'authenticity' and narrow 'identity politics'. For many of us non-Dalit feminists, such a standpoint is more emancipatory in that it rejects more completely the relations of rule in which we participated (i.e., the brahmanical, middle-class biases of earlier feminist standpoints are interrogated). Thus adopting a Dalit feminist standpoint position means sometimes losing, sometimes revisioning the 'voice' that we as feminists had gained in the 1980s. This process, we believe is one of transforming individual feminists into oppositional and collective subjects.

Notes

1 This is an abridged version of the article 'Dalit Women Talk Differently: A Critique of "Difference" and Towards a Dalit Feminist Standpoint Position', *Economic and Political Weekly*, Vol. 33 No. 4, October 31–November 6, 1998, pp. WS39–WS46.
2 I. Whelehan, *Modern Feminist Thought*, Edinburgh: Edinburgh University Press, 1995.
3 S. Joseph, 'Cultural and Political Analysis in India', *Social Scientist*, Vol. 19 Nos. 9–10, October–November 1991, 1997.
4 S. Sarkar, 'Indian Nationalism and Politics of Hindutva', in D. Ludden (ed.), *Making India Hindu*, New Delhi: Oxford University Press, 1997.
5 A. Ahmad, 'The Politics of Literary Postcoloniality', in P. Mongia (ed.), *Contemporary Postcolonial Theory*, New Delhi: Oxford University Press, 1996.
6 S. Sarkar, *Writing Social History*, New Delhi: Oxford University Press, 1997.
7 Rajni Kothari, 'Rise of Dalits and the Renewed Debate on Caste', *Economic and Political Weekly*, June 25, 1994, pp. 1589–94.
8 Partha Chatterjee, 'Nationalist Resolution of the Women's Question', in S. Vaid and K. Sangari (eds.), *Recasting Women: Essays in Colonial History*, New Delhi: Kali for Women, 1989.

9 Judith Grant, *Fundamental Feminism: Contesting the Core Concepts of Feminist Theory*, New York: Routledge, December 1, 1993.
10 G. Rubin, 'Woman as Nigger', in B. Rosazk and T. Rosazk (eds.), *Masculine/Feminine: Readings in Sexual Mythology and the Liberation of Women*, New York: Harper and Row, 1969.
11 Grant, *Fundamental Feminism*.
12 M. Barrett and A. Phillips (eds.), *Destabilishing Theory*, Cambridge: Polity Press, 1992.
13 E. M. Wood, 'Modernity, Postmodernity or Capitalism', *Monthly Review*, Vol. 48 No.3, July–August 1996.
14 L. Alcoff, 'Cultural Feminism Versus Post-Structuralism: The Identity Crisis in Feminist Theory', *Signs: Journal of Women in Culture and Society*, Vol. 13 No. 3, 1988.
15 P. H. Collins, *Black Feminist Thought: Knowledge Consciousness and the Politics of Empowerment*, Boston: Urwin, 1990, p. 234.
16 S. Mann and L. Kelly, 'Staining at the Crossroads of Modernist Thought', *Gender and Society*, Vol. II No. 4, August 1997, pp. 391–409.
17 Sarkar, *Writing Social History*.
18 G. Omvedt, 'Cultural Revolt in Colonial Society: The Non-Brahman Movement in Western India 1873–1930', in *Indian Social Science Society*, Mumbai: Scientific Socialist Education Trust, 1976; G. Omvedt, *Reinventing Revolution: India's New Social Movements*, New York: Sharpe, 1993; G. Omvedt, *Dalits and Democratic Revolution: Dr. Ambedkar and the Dalit Movement in Colonial India*, New Delhi: Oxford University Press, 1994; G. Aloysius, *Nationalism without a Nation In India*, New Delhi: Oxford University Press, 1997.
19 S. Vaid and K. Sangari (eds.), *Recasting Women*, New Delhi: Kali for Women, 1989.
20 Ibid.
21 Omvedt, 'Cultural Revolt in Colonial Society'; S. Patil, *Dasa-Sudra Slavery*, Mumbai: Allied Publishers, 1982; R. O'Hanlon, *A Comparision Between Women and Men: Tarabai Shinde and the Critique of Gender Relations in Colonial India*, Madras: Oxford University Press, 1994; Vidyut Bhagwat, *Kanishtha Jathinchi Calval aani Jyotirao Phule*, Pune: Women's Studies Centre, University of Pune, June, 1990, pp. 80–86; V. Geetha, 'Gender and Logic of Brahmanism: E V Ramaswamy Periyar and the Politics of the Female Body', paper presented at the Seminar on Women's Studies, IIAS, Shimla, 1992; U. Chakravarti, *Rewriting History: The Life and Times of Pandita Ramabai*, New Delhi: Kali for Women, 1998.
22 Sarkar, 'Indian Nationalism and Politics of Hindutva', in Ludden (ed.), *Making India Hindu*.
23 P. Chatterjee, *The Nation and Its Fragments: Colonial and Postcolonial Histories*, Bombay: Oxford University Press, 1989.
24 Sarkar, *Writing Social History*, 1997.
25 Chakravarti, *Rewriting History*.
26 Tarabai Shinde, 'Stree Purush Tulana', 1882.
27 Vidyut Bhagwat, *Maharashtrachya Samajik Itihasachya Dishene* (Towards a Social History of Maharashtra), Pune: Krantijyoti Savitribai Phule Women's Studies Centre, University of Pune, June, 1997.
28 Pawar, Urmila, and Moon, Meenakshi. *We Also Made History: Women in the Ambedkarite Movement*, translated and introduced from Marathi by Wandana Sonalkar, New Delhi: Zubaan Academic, 2014, first published as *Amhihi Itihas Ghadavala*, 1989.
29 P. Pardeshi, *Dr Ambedkar Aani Streemukti Vaad*, Pune: Krantisinh Nana Patil Academy, 1997.
30 B. R. Ambedkar, 'Castes in India', in *Speechs and Writings of Dr Babasaheb Ambedkar*, Vol. I, Bombay: Government of Maharashtra, 1982–90, 1992.
31 Ibid., p. 90.
32 Pardeshi, *Dr Ambedkar Aani Streemukti Vaad*.
33 G. Guru, *Dalit Cultural Movement and Dialectics of Dalit Politics in Maharashtra*, Mumbai: Vikas Adhyayan Kendra, 1998.

34 Ibid., p. 25.
35 Omvedt, *Reinventing Revolution*.
36 Ibid.
37 S. Rege, 'Caste and Gender: The Violence Against Women in India', in P. Jogdand (ed.), *Dalit Women*, New Delhi: Gyan, 1994.
38 S. Akerkar, 'Theory and Practice of Women's Movement in India', *Economic and Political Weekly*, Vol. XXX No.17, 1995, pp. WS-2–WS-24; R. Kumar, *History of Doing*, New Delhi: Kali for Women, 1993.
39 Radha Kumar, *The History of Doing: An Illustrated Account of Movements for Women's Rights and feminism in India, 1800–1990*, New Delhi: Zubaan, January 1, 2011.
40 Ranjana Sheel, 'Institutionalisation and Expansion of Dowry System in Colonial North India', *Economic and Political Weekly*, Vol. 32, No. 28, July 12–18, 1997: 1709–1718.
41 Susie Tharu and Tejaswini Niranjana, 'Problems for a Contemporary Theory of Gender in India', *Social Scientist*, Vol. 22, March–April 1994. Chapter 2 of this Reader.
42 Kalpana Kannabiran and Vasanth Kannabiran, 'Caste and Gender: Understanding Dynamics of Power and Violence', *Economic and Political Weekly*, Vol. XXVI No.37, September 14, 1991.
43 J. Liddle and R. Joshi, *Daughters of Independence Gender, Caste and Class in India*, New Delhi: Kali for Women, 1986.
44 Sharmila Rege, 'Hegemonic Appropriation of Sexuality: The Case of the Erotic Lavani of Maharashtra', *Contributions to Indian Sociology*, Vol. 29 Nos. 1 and 2, 1995.
45 Kumkum Sangari, 'Politics of Diversity: Religious Communities and Multiple Patriarchies', *Economic and Political Weekly*, Vol. 30, No. 51, December 23, 1995: 3287–3310.
46 Ibid.
47 Gopal Guru, 'Dalit Women Talk Differently', *Economic and Political Weekly*, Vol. 30 No. 41/42, 1995.
48 Ibid.
49 Ibid., p. 2549.
50 K. Moghe, 'Dalit Streeanche Vegale Chool', *Maharashtra Times*, September 7, Mumbai, 1996. (Marathi)
51 Ibid.
52 Vidyut Bhagwat, 'Marathi Literature as a Source of Contemporary Feminism', *Economic and Political Weekly*, April 29, 1995: WS24–WS29. Also see Vidyut Bhagwat, 'Dalit Women: Issues and Perspectives' in P. G. Jogdand (ed.), *Dalit Women: Issues and Perspectives*, forward by U. B. Bhoite, New Delhi: Gyan Publishing House, 1995, pp. 1–7.
53 Pratima Pardeshi, *Samaj Prabodhan Patrika*, Vol. 931–32, April–May, 1995: 119–21. (Marathi)
54 For more details see Patil, 1994 and the manifesto of the Satyashodhak Communist Party.
55 R. Thakur, *Adimayache Mukti*, Mumbai: Prabhuda Bharat, 1996. (Marathi)
56 K. Pawade, 'Pitrupradhanta aani Dalit Streeyancha Sangharsha', paper presented at the conference organised by Alochana, Centre for Documentation and Research on Women, Pune, 1996. (Marathi)
57 Nirmala Bhakre, 'Punyatil Christi Samajik Sanghatana anni church hyanche Lingabhav Vishayak Drishtikon', (mimeo), Pune: Women Studies Centre, Pune University, 1997. (Marathi)
58 See S. Harding, 'Subjectively Experience and Knowledge: An Epistemology from/for Rainbow Coalition Politics', in J. Peterse (ed.), *Emancipations: Modern and Postmodern*, London: Sage, 1991.
59 Judith Grant, *Fundamental Feminism*.

PART V
Intersectionality in India

Part V presents articles offering an application of intersectionality to the Indian context, and highlighting many of the reasons for its necessity. Although the concept of intersectionality originated in Black feminist history and theory, it certainly bears universal applicability for its deep philosophical relevance and insight. Intersection denotes a junctional point where two or more elements meet. In the context of the First World, race, gender and class constitute the crucial intersection for Black feminism; in the Indian context, caste, gender and class would seem to constitute the crucial intersection for Dalit feminism. In both contexts, intersectionality operates as a tool to observe and address the patriarchal injustices faced by the most marginalised and vulnerable women of the world.

Aloysius *et al.* (Chapter 13) argue that Dalit women are most prone to violence from the caste-class-gender axis through untouchability, labour control, gender control and control on Dalit women's sexuality, which defines their everyday hierarchical relationships with dominant caste men and women, as well as with Dalit men. Susie Tharu (Chapter 14) presents a close study on how caste-class-gender factors shape Dalit women's lives in India, exposing the brahmanical nature of Indian feminists, which leads them seamlessly to relegate caste to the margins, and which forces 'Dalit women – scholars and intellectuals included – [to] fade and die unappreciated'. Mary E. John (Chapter 15) criticises mainstream feminist Nivedita Menon's blunt rejection of the application of intersectionality in India, demanding engagement with the concept, since it is 'an excellent candidate' to help us to achieve our feminist ends. Meena Gopal (Chapter 15) too offers a critique of Menon's rejection of intersectionality and clarifies that salient issues of gender injustice that preoccupy Menon (e.g., bar dancing) are indecipherable merely via class analysis alone.

These discussions highlight the important role of intersectionality for an adequate conception of the nature of gender-based inequalities in India, and for any viable hopes for attending to it systematically, to the mutual benefit of all women. From this vantage point, it seems as though the refusal of mainstream Indian feminists to take intersectionality seriously hints at a resistance to abjure the many discrete privileges of caste dominance.

13

WHY INTERSECTIONALITY IS NECESSARY[1]

S. J. Aloysius, J. P. Mangubhai and J. G. Lee

Empirical research strongly argues for the egalitarian character of the Dalit community and for the view that brahmanical class-caste-based patriarchy, alien to Dalits and their culture, has had an overpowering impact on them in history.[2] Evidence of this includes Dalit women's experience of equality and freedom with men in such areas as speech, physical movement, establishing contracts and relationships, choice of work and employer, earning and spending on household goods. As daily wage labour is the mainstay of family income, supplemented in some cases by animal rearing, in a majority of cases all the members – women, men and children – have to contribute their share of labour towards earning the family's livelihood. In fact, in a number of instances, it is the woman who is the principal breadwinner in the family. Sharing this common livelihood venture, irrespective of gender and age difference, brings a measure of equality of Dalit women in their relationship with men.

Likewise, evidence of Dalit women's experience of equality in combination with freedom of speech is to be found in their freely spoken exchanges with their husbands and other family members on such vital issues as economic resources, labour, wages, household expenditure and family welfare. Moreover, many instances point to the women's assertiveness vis-à-vis their dominant caste empowers or contractors, often with even greater vehemence than their male counterparts, on such matter as wages or assaults on them.

Assimilation into the patriarchal caste system

Although the preceding argues in favour of Dalit women enjoying a sense of equality and freedom in their families and communities, nevertheless the powerful control of brahmanical patriarchy substantially erodes their egalitarian mooring. In the process, three sets of actors continually exert influence and pressure on Dalit women. One is dominant caste men under whom Dalit women work as labourers and with whom they interact on a daily basis, who force the women into submission and subservience to dominant caste male authority. On the one hand, the weak bargaining position of Dalit women as regards labour and livelihood, and on the other the dominant social, economic and political status of dominant caste men, grant the latter leverage to exert a dominating influence on the former. Secondly, dominant caste women, who are already conditioned by patriarchal ideology, rely on the strength of their male counterparts' economic, social and political positioning to influence or pressurise Dalit women into patriarchal ways of thinking and acting. Thirdly, Dalit men, specifically Dalit women's husbands and male relatives, are subjected to patriarchal influences and pressures in similar ways. They, in turn, exert male control over their women.

The end-product of this assimilation of patriarchal caste ideology by Dalit, and women in particular, is a situation in which Dalit subgroups are considered 'jatis' falling within the overall framework of the hierarchical caste order. A specific feature of this assimilation process lies in the acceptance and adoption of patriarchal endogamy with its attendant six consequences: (1) the adherence to the practice of maintaining caste and sub-caste identity and purity in the Dalit community; (2) the acceptance of Dalit male superiority and authority in the family; (3) the legitimisation of the principle of patrilineal succession in terms of familial authority and control over resources; (4) the exercise of dominant caste male/female and Dalit male control in particular over Dalit women's identity and dignity, subjectivity, and personhood, body and sexuality, resources and labour; (5) the practice of gender-based discrimination against Dalit women with implications for their personal rights; and (6) the perpetration of gender-based violence as a matter of male right when Dalit women assert their rights.

Reflecting further, one can say that Dalit women, a fortiori Dalit men and their community as whole, are placed in a situation of bipolar tension: on the one hand, at the horizontal level in relation to their families and community, the women experience relative equality of relationships and freedom of movement; on the other hand, due to their free movement and interactions in the larger society, the woman face the impact of patriarchy flowing from the vertically structured class-caste society. Their problem becomes more complex and exacerbated for three important reasons. The first is the Dalit community's relatively weak position in term of economic, political and knowledge resources, which hinders it from waging a frontal assault on patriarchal ideology and supportive formal and informal structures such as caste codes and traditions, religious beliefs, marital alliances and practices, dominant caste, male-dominated traditional and electoral panchayats, and the like. Secondly, the current increase in sub-caste identity assertions among Dalits appears to make endogamy imperative as a biological and social mechanism to protect and sustain sub-caste purity. As a consequence, this augments Dalit male control over their women's bodies and sexuality in terms of choice in marital alliances, etc. one the basis of 'Dalit sub-caste honour' and 'Dalit male honour', value very similar to the 'caste honour' and 'male honour' of patriarchal dominant caste culture. Thirdly, dominant caste men and women perceive higher stakes, in comparison to Dalit men, in perpetuating patriarchy in the Dalit community in terms of legitimating their discrimination and violence against Dalit women. This last point requires further elucidation in order to understand discrimination and violence against Dalit women in the class–caste–gender framework.

Gender-class axis: discrimination and violence through labour control

Although Dalit men's practice of endogamy and their control over their women's sexuality brings them benefits, the advantages accruing to them are proportionately less than those that accrue to dominant caste men and women. For Dalit men, pecuniary benefits from Dalit women's labour and property ownership obtained from the women's natal families largely in the form of dowry are the immediate gains. Notwithstanding the men's control over their women's bodies and sexuality, and their authority exercised in relation to various family matters, these benefits can be explained largely, though not solely, in terms of their poverty or meagre access to resources.

On the other hand, dominant caste men and women enjoy dual benefits from Dalit men upholding endogamy and controlling Dalit women's bodies and sexuality. The short-term gain lie, first, in the realm of appropriation of their labour, using livelihood concerns as bait and Dalit men's patriarchal control over their women as leverage. Secondly, in order to determine the price of labour as well as property ownership on grounds of gender discrimination, 'male honour' becomes a useful tool for the dominant castes to exploit Dalit men in order to control the cost-value of Dalit women's labour. In both ways, the supply of labour and enhancement of resources are assured for the dominant castes.

As regards the long-term economic and political interests of dominant castes, Dalit men's practice of endogamy ensures continuing reproduction and supply of steady labour through the sexual reproduction of Dalit women. This aspect highlights how the gender–class axis of the caste system can provide scope for dominant castes and classes to purchase labour not only directly from Dalit women, but also reproduced labour indirectly from Dalit women through Dalit men. At the same time, this axis enables dominant castes to control Dalit women's sexuality through the latter's male counterparts.

To sustain the economy of Dalit women's labour, and in effect reproduced the unequal class division in the caste system, the control devices employed by the dominant castes include, first, the imposition of a subsistence economy on Dalit women and their families. This forces Dalit to be bonded to, and therefore dependent upon, the landowning castes for their livelihood. Secondly, closely linked to and reinforcing this subsistence economy, is the denial to the women of their right to access economic resources, including landownership, gender parity in wages, and operation of commercial enterprises. Thirdly, denial of rights prevent the women from availing their steady and cheap labour, the use of violence by the dominant castes to degrade dalit women's honour, harm their self-respect and control their bodies and sexuality, enforces them to supply labour. This is particularly the case when the women assert their rights to wages, access to land and water, sale of products, etc. A point to be highlighted here is that such violence is also intended to keep Dalit women and their families, and the Dalit community as a whole, dependent on the dominant castes for their livelihood, and to prevent them from approaching any redressal mechanism – traditional panchayats at the village level, or formal state enforcement agencies at the local, state or national levels – when their rights are violated.

Gender-caste axis: discrimination and violence through untouchability

Another important device of control used by the dominant caste, with implications for their economic and political interests, is untouchability. To ensure the permanent availability of Dalit women's menial labour for the dominant castes, such labour, considered polluted, abhorrent and repulsive to the latter, has been marked as dominant caste-mandated low caste-performed. That manual scavenging is still predominantly the task of Dalit women in certain rural and urban areas, despite it having been banned by law, attests to the benefits dominant castes enjoy from Dalits performing this work. Similarly, the ritual-based devadasi occupation among Dalit women is also an offshoot of untouchability that is beneficial to dominant caste. The low social status attached to Dalit women by untouchability to functions as an opportune rationale for dominant castes to discriminate against women and accordingly devalue their capabilities. This has negative implications for women's opportunities of access to and control of economic resources, acquisition of education and skills, and obtaining knowledge and information. In other words, denial of these opportunities prevents any change in the balance of development and power between Dalit women and dominant castes.

Untouchability, moreover, serves as a means of legitimising dominant caste appropriation of whatever little natural or financial resources Dalit women and their families possess, and to deny them any political status, as in the case of panchayat governance. These denials are based on the argument that women's impure status do not warrant any property ownership precluding their any capacity to govern. That Dalit women do not merit the status of property ownership provides the rationale for dominant castes to appropriate their labour. Again, by associating women with criminality, untouchability is also used by dominant castes to view Dalit women with suspicion, and even to make criminal allegations against them; for example, the allegation of criminal trespass by Dalit women who use dominant castes' agricultural fields as pathways for collecting firewood in or close to their fields.

Discrimination and violence based on the dominant caste's practice of untouchability is more palpable is in the area of 'touching' Dalit women in social relationships. Physical contact with Dalit women, such as sitting with dominant castes in public transport, standing with or close to them at polling booths and public distribution (ration shops) queues, eating with them, cooking food for them at school midday meals centres, drinking coffee/tea using the same glasses in public restaurants, drawing water from the same common village water sources, and other similar activities are prohibited to Dalit women due to the stigma of impurity attached to them. However, the contradiction in practices of untouchability is no more apparent than in dominant caste's physical or sexual violence against Dalit women, where an undisputed claim is assumed their bodies. Moreover, the touch of the women's agricultural labour in the dominant caste's fields and their domestic work in the dominant caste's houses are interpreted as essential services that preclude the strict practice of untouchability.

Untouchability also has an important bearing on Dalit women in relation to the high value attached to the dominant caste's purity and identity, with implications for property relationships between Dalit women and dominant castes. The latter's interests in protecting caste purity and having permanent control over economic and political assets preclude any marital alliances with Dalits. Therefore, a dominant caste male partner's fear of caste pollution-allegedly occasioned by blood impurity from a Dalit woman in an inter-caste relationship or marriage-results in the denial to her and their children of any right to a share in his property. He may or may not face ostracism from his family or community, but she is never assured of her property rights, or of his fidelity to her. In either case, her situation can become worse if she is from a poor family, or if either or both her natal and marital families disown her. By contrast, failure to observe caste codes of endogamy invites severe and public penalties in the case of a Dalit man's sexual relationship with a dominant caste woman. Whatever the consequences that Dalit women or men have to face in the event of inter-caste marriages or cohabitation, what is noteworthy is that while untouchability is a threat to dominant caste patriarchy, this patriarchy in turn serves as a shield for them to protect their women, and through them to safeguard their community identity and property. The instances of atrocities against Dalit women and men over the issue of inter-caste marriages or cohabitation illustrate the degree to which dominant castes can go to uphold patriarchy. To be noted here is the contradiction of untouchability becoming a taboo for dominant castes who, claiming to be 'pure' and therefore not wishing to associate with 'impure' Dalits, find no difficulty in having sexual relationships with Dalit women.

Gender axis: discrimination and violence through gender control

Discussion on untouchability as a control device for discrimination and violence against Dalit women leads to further reflections on how patriarchal ideology exploits this device to discriminate between Dalit women and those of the dominant caste; and at the same time, why dominant caste women, under the influence of the same ideology, discriminate against and perpetrate violence against Dalit women.

While it is true that dominant caste women, like Dalit women, are subjected to discrimination and violence by dominant caste men, there is some specificity to Dalit women's experiences. This has important implications for an understanding of the position of Dalit women vis-à-vis dominant caste women in the ritual-based ordering of the caste system. As women, both are subjected to gender discrimination and violence. In the case of Dalit women, however, the devaluation of her personality takes on a double dimension: she is devalued *not only as woman, but also as Dalit*. Patriarchy submits her to male control of her body and sexuality. The ritual-based caste structure allocates demeaning labour to her and denotes her low social standing as being due to her impure caste, distinguishing it from that of the dominant caste women's higher status. Thus, the systemic discrimination and violence that Dalit women face is uniquely different from women of the dominant caste: that is, at the gender level both dominant caste and Dalit women suffer discrimination and violence from dominant caste men, whereas at the class and caste levels Dalit women are under the control of both dominant caste women and men. This is not to argue for a wedge to be driven between Dalit women and those of the dominant caste as a gender-oppressed collective. Rather, it is to emphasise how caste-class-patriarchy itself is responsible for producing this division. This underlines the necessity for dominant caste women to recognise this reality, and accordingly give greater and specific weight to Dalit women in every aspect of struggles for women's emancipation.

A point to be noted here is dominant caste women's experience of double patriarchal conditioning, which is manifested in their relationships with Dalit women or men. One aspect of this conditioning is related to their relationship with their dominant caste male counterparts, where the caste code of 'male superiority-respect' requiring 'female inferiority-deference' seeks to define their self-identity and self-respect. The second aspect concerns dominant caste women's relationship with Dalit women and men, in which it is their 'caste superiority-honour' that is seen in relation to their self-identity and self-respect. In both cases, to the degree that it is conditioned by brahmanical patriarchy, dominant caste women's self-identity and self-respect is *derivative*, for it is dependent on their male partners' male superiority-respect and male caste status-honour. There is, therefore, a systemic nexus between dominant caste men and women in any relationship with, and for that matter in any violence committed against, Dalit women. Therefore, when discussing caste-class-gender intersectional violence against Dalit women, it is important to equally review discrimination, control and violence against Dalit women by both dominant caste men and women in relation to that of their male counterparts. Recognition of this reality is important for the joint struggles of Dalit and dominant caste women against patriarchy, while at the same time underlining the necessity to focus Dalit women's concerns in the overall efforts towards gender emancipation.

Discrimination and violence through control over Dalit women's sexuality

Against the backdrop of discrimination and violence experienced by Dalit women at different levels of their existence, it is necessary to discuss how caste patriarchy has controlled their bodies and sexuality.

Three principles of brahmanical patriarchy

Regarding human sexuality, three inter-connected principles are at work in the brahmanical patriarchal worldview. First, with regard to social status, the male is superior to the female. Therefore, in terms of reproductive sexuality, the male is the 'giver' while the female is only the 'receiver' and 'caretaker' of the offspring which is considered to be in the likeness of the male as far as caste purity and identity is concerned. The implication underlying this principle is that the man, due to his superior status, can reserve to himself the right to give or refuse, and the woman has the duty to receive when given, or philosophically accept his refusal. Refusal on her part, however, invites force, or even violence, from him. Thus, his freedom becomes her obligation and his dominance her submission.

Secondly, as the male is considered to be both superior to the female and the repository of caste purity, the male offspring born of a dominant caste man from a woman of low caste status is still considered to be superior in caste status. The low-caste woman must therefore understand her relationship with him as a privilege granted by him. If, however, a man of low-caste status has a male offspring from a dominant-caste woman, that offspring is considered to be of mixed caste and is said to lose thereby any right and privileges of superior dominant castes. What is implied in this understanding is that the caste-wise superior man enjoys prerogative rights over the body and sexuality of a low caste woman, and for her it is a 'privilege granted freely' by him. A low caste women's refusal of such privilege justifies force and violence from the dominant caste man. This situation may appear to have changed in urban India. However, the crude manifestations of dominant caste male control over Dalit women's body and sexuality through various forms of physical and sexual violence against women in rural areas and against those women working as sweepers and scavengers in municipal towns and city corporations still continue to this day. Therefore, the dynamics of power relations in the hierarchically structured social system are such that whatever comes from those positioned on top is good, valuable, and beneficial to those located below, but that the converse is not the case.

Thirdly, in the brahmanical ritual-based order, the discriminatory caste rule of law occupies a pre-eminent position in maintaining cohesiveness among the dominant castes by placing a premium on caste identity and purity. Accordingly, there is a stringent penalty of excommunication or banishment administered to those male offspring born of dominant caste men and low caste women. Such severe penalties act as deterrent against 'hybridisation of caste', as well as a measure to cleanse caste impurity in society. To achieve these aims, caste law plays a crucial role principally against low caste men in order to keep them in their fixed social position in the caste order. What is striking here is that the discriminatory laws of the caste system, while regulating the behaviour of men and women in all matters, including human sexuality, give latitude to dominant caste men in their relationships with low caste men and women, especially with the latter in the area of sexuality. The implication is that this discriminatory caste rule of law gives dominant caste men great latitude in relation to their appropriation of the body and sexuality of low caste women.

Caste-class-gender axis

The three aforementioned principles have serious implications for an understanding of the dignity and rights of Dalit women. Given their untouchability status and characterisation as women of 'loose morals', irrespective of age and marital status, they are perceived as available for male exploitation and control. For example, the imposed low caste status, legitimised by religion, denies marital rights to *jogini* women and makes them available to satisfy any man's sexual needs. Similarly, Dalit women's impure caste status serves as evidence for dominant castes' allegations of witchcraft and, accordingly, justifies assaults on these women's bodies as punishment for the alleged crimes of causing illness and death to humans and animals in the village.

As dominant caste honour and property ownership are considered non-negotiable principles in caste ideology, Dalit women face the risk of being deserted by their dominant caste partners after having had sexual relationship through legal marriage or cohabitation. At the same time, the patriarchal association of shame and dishonour with women losing their virginity outside of marriage, and the consequent perception of such women as being of immoral or loose character, provides privileged scope for male exploitation of women's bodies and sexuality. Dalit women's bodies and sexuality are also used as means to secure labour, dispense punitive measures for assertion of labour rights, appropriate their family's land, and wreak vengeance on the Dalit community for supporting their women in instances of violence against them. Thus, absence of caste laws with stringent sanctions to control male sexuality vis-à-vis Dalit women-in contrast to the case of dominant caste women who enjoy protection from Dalit males through caste codes and penalties, and power, in practice of these traditional caste laws which supersede or trump modern secular laws of the Indian state-exacerbate the threat of violence against Dalit women.

Patriarchal implications of caste patriarchy for Dalit women

From the preceding analysis, it is obvious that under the patriarchal caste system Dalit women are subjected to interlinking caste, class and gender discrimination and violence. Dominant caste-class men, dominant caste-class women conditioned by patriarchal ideology, and Dalit men who have assimilated the values of this ideological system all subject Dalit women to discrimination and violence.

Moreover, with the informality and the authority of common sense, the patriarchal caste system in everyday practice defines Dalit women's relationship with dominant caste men/women and Dalit men in all areas of life.

Notes

1 This chapter is an excerpt from 'Conceptual Framework', Chapter 1, of S. J. Aloysius, Jayashree P. Mangubhai, and Joel G. Lee (eds.), *Dalit Women Speak Out: Violence Against Dalit Women in India*, Zubaan, New Delhi, 2006, pp. 47–57. Reproduced with permission.
2 See F. Franco, J. Macwan, and S. Ramanathan (eds.), *The Silken Swing: The Cultural Universe of Dalit Women*, Calcutta: Stree, 2000.

14

THE DALIT WOMAN QUESTION[1]

Susie Tharu

I

Two events that took place in the early years of the contemporary upsurge of Dalit politics sometimes spoken of as the 'second wave', give us a sense of the complexities of the question of women in these movements. They also help us appreciate the originality and depth of the new propositions in writing by Dalit women.

In 1985 and again in 1986, activists of the Dalit Sangharsh Samithi (DSS) along with other groups, notably the women's collective, Manavi, tried to stop the yearly *bettaleseve* (nude worship) in the Chandragutti temple. Generally undertaken in fulfilment of a vow or a request for a boon, the *seve* involved bathing in the Varada river and then running up – a distance of about five kilometers – to the temple naked. Those taking part in the ritual were mainly Dalit and backward class women. The reformists were mostly Dalit and progressive/rationalist men and upper-caste women who felt that the practice was humiliating to Dalits – upper-caste women were never involved in such rituals, they pointed out – and that the state had a responsibility to stop it. The humiliation was aggravated, they said, in the changed circumstances, in which the press and a large numbers of voyeuristic outsiders, armed with cameras, arrived to gape at the show. Their opponents, of course, argued that this was a matter of faith and tradition and was undertaken freely. No one was coercing the women.

What took place in 1986 turned out to be something of a fiasco for the Dalits, rationalists and feminists. A major intervention had been planned to dissuade the women, and if necessary to use the force of the state to stop the ritual. But it was the worshippers, no doubt also encouraged by the temple authorities, who forced the reformers to retreat. They turned violent, 'beat up some of the social workers; cameras were broken and policewomen were stripped'.[2] The event was debated for months and has been extensively written about. We only want to point here to a situation, typical of the early years of the Dalit and feminist movements, in which Dalit women, claiming a right to tradition or identity, appear pitted against well-intentioned activists who are Dalit men and non-Dalit women.

Again, in 1995, this time in Andhra Pradesh, we encounter a stalemate of a similar kind. Following the publication of a startling and generally well-received collection of Dalit poems, *Nishani* (Thumbprint), the feminist writer – intellectuals and activists Volga, Vasanth Kannabiran and Kalpana Kannabiran made an intervention in the debate on Dalit literature. Clearly stating that they considered the Dalit movement and Dalit poetry progressive, they argued for the need to strengthen Dalit and feminist connections. They objected to the language used in the poems, which they described as the language of the ruling patriarchal classes and insulting to women. It was regrettable that abusive terms referring to women's body parts were being claimed as Dalit culture. True, it was an upper-caste culture that had stigmatised these terms, but was it not possible to develop a new language, one that does not humiliate women, to express anger and hatred? Dalit poetry, they said, needed to invent a new and more egalitarian language.[3]

The poets (all men) did not respond positively to the critique. They did not think of themselves as disrespectful of women and felt misunderstood. Readers joined the fray. Some quickly criticised the response as an upper-caste attack on a new movement and its poetry, and described the feminist movement as brahmanical and 'Hindu'. Others argued that it was the upper castes who consider the everyday behaviour and ordinary language of Dalits as violent or vulgar. It was this politics of language and culture that should be the focus of discussion, not vulgarity. This time it was a face-off between Dalits and feminists. The silence of Dalit women, and their absence from the world of Dalit literature, was palpable.

II

Women writers, intellectuals and activists feature prominently in the Tamil and Malayalam collections as well in the texts from Kannada and Telugu compiled in the dossier.[4] The names of Bama, Sivakami and Sukirtharani are often among the very first to be mentioned by anyone asked to list significant contemporary Dalit writing in Tamil. In Telugu, Gogu Shyamala and Joopaka Subhadra enjoy growing respect as activists and as writers, as do Challapalli Swaroopa Rani, Jajula Gowri and Vinodini. The adivasi leader, C.K. Janu, is rarely spoken of as a *woman* activist, but as the interview with her so clearly indicates, being a woman is a significant part of her experience. Her interviewer, Rekharaj, is among a small but effective group of Dalit women who have made their mark as public intellectuals. In Kannada, the status of Du Saraswathi and B.T. Jahnavi, both of whom began writing in the late 1980s and are widely recognised, also directs our attention to the sad fact that few women writers or thinkers emerge from the earlier, otherwise awe-inspiring Dalit Sangharsh Samiti or the Dalit – bandaya contexts of the 1970s and 80s.

Without exception, these writers are critical of existing feminism, which they describe as upper caste in its assumptions about women, its understanding of women's lives and women's issues, its concept of India, and not least, in its personnel and leadership. Vinodini, who cut her teeth as a critic and writer on the Telugu feminist poetry of the 1980s, observes that it was only after she became involved in the Dalit movement in the 1990s that she realised that feminism had dulled her consciousness of being a Dalit woman. 'Feminism made me overlook the fact that there was a problem worse than patriarchy: caste'. Questions that were asked by feminists, Vinodini points out, take on a radically different form in the Dalit context:

> The issues here are not of attraction, desire and so on, but of hate, of being detested, spat upon. Remember what happened to Bhanwari Devi in Rajasthan? What does it mean, when a person is raped by a man, his son, his son-in-law at the same time? Is the object of this violence simply a *woman*? What is she? Chalam's Rajeswari is a brahmin girl. [Rajeswari is the protagonist of the novel *Maidanam* by the well-known Telugu writer, Chalam (1894–1979), a crusader for women's emancipation.] I feel I don't really know her. [People like me] do not experience her rage and lust. In the context of our lives, the cold war between husband and wife that feminism talks about seems so thin, so empty.[5]

Also palpable is Joopaka Subhadra's anger about the assumptions made, even in people's movements, that upper-caste women merit more attention and require different living conditions. She complains that only upper-caste women and their issues receive recognition by the media, by the leaders of people's movements as well as by 'mainstream' feminists, who simply assume they can speak for Dalit women. The wild flowers that bloom and die in Challapali Swaroopa Rani's poem are Dalit women — scholars and intellectuals included — who fade and die unappreciated.

Despite this critique, however, the mark of feminism is evident both in the grain of the voice and the ideas of these writers and intellectuals. Bama's feisty village women are feminist (without using or knowing the term) in their rebellions and their support for each other. Both Du Saraswathi and Vinodini lay out engrossing questions of body image, 'pure and impure' sexualities and explore the traumas of growing up as Dalit women. Sukirtarani's finely crafted poems are a brave and moving engagement with sexuality that draws on the feminist reclamation of desire and sexual pleasure. B.T. Jahnavi's 'Vyabhichara' (Adultery) was regarded outrageous when it first appeared, more so since it came from a woman writer. One might say that the critique in these works is not so much of feminism, but of a caste-blind elite feminism and its authority. Dalit feminists claim feminism and look to African American feminists, Latino and African feminists for inspiration. Rekharaj calls herself an 'unavoidable companion of the feminist movement in Kerala'. She points out, however, that she feels more at home in the Dalit movement than among feminists, although she is also unhappy with it.

This conceptual and political connection between feminism and the Dalit movement is evident also in the fact that among the many new ideas that the legendary Pondicherry-based little magazine *Nirapirikkai* introduced to its eager and predominantly male readership were those of feminists from across the world. Lovely Stephen's account of the Dalit Women's Society (DWS) in Kurichi near Kottayam records the lectures and discussions that it enabled and the springboard it provided to the group of Dalit students who went on to become leading intellectuals and artists of the 1990s and after. New research being done on important early Dalit women leaders, such as Velayudhan Sadalakshmi (a political worker and Andhra Pradesh's minister for endowments in the 1970s) suggests that they trod an imaginative and deeply political path in elaborating and consolidating Dalit politics.

In her analysis of the suicide of Rajani – a college student who had secured a 'merit list' admission to a computer science course – Rekharaj points out that banks require surety for loans, and since in Kerala, the ownership of property is caste-based, Dalits students do not get loans. Without the loan, Rajani was unable to pay the professional college's fees. Her experience points to the predicament of Dalit students who are 'forced to study outdated courses in government institutions at a time when self-financing colleges are offering course geared towards . . . job opportunities'. Rajani, she observes, 'committed suicide because of her inability to continue in the professional course, given the inadequacy of the government stipend and the refusal by banks to provide a loan . . . . In this context there is absolutely no reason for Rajani's sexual life becoming a topic of discussion. However, the equation that a Dalit woman is a bad woman/an immoral woman persists on the strength of social prejudice'. Such events, she concludes, require 'closer scrutiny and greater alertness' than existing liberal, Marxist or feminist analyses provide.

The potential of such scrutiny and alertness is evident in Gogu Shyamala's 'Radam' (A Festering Sore), in which she takes up an 'evil' that social reformists have engaged with for over a century – that of women who are 'dedicated' to the temple as devadasi, jogini or basavi, and are then considered sexually available to the upper-caste men of the village. Shyamala tells the story from the point of view of a young Dalit girl who discovers, only when her father hurries her out in the middle of the night to catch a bus on which she must escape, that she has been 'selected' to perform this task in the village. They quickly bundle up a few belongings and steal out of the village before the patel get wind of their plans. She is uprooted and lonely in the social welfare hostel to which he takes her, worried about what will happen to her father in the village, but temporarily safe. He returns to face the landlord's wrath. There is a murderous attack on him and, fearing for his life, he leaves the village. The family loses the small piece of land they owned. Her mother struggles to raise the other children after the father leaves. Shyamala poses the jogini question as one that must be understood in a political geography of caste as described from the madiga quarter. It is a question in which sexuality, land, childhood, schooling, caste violence and family life all come into play. So does the desire for education and escape from a power that is upper caste and patriarchal. The father, who in another story returns from his wanderings, weary and anxious, and suddenly turns violent, accusing his wife of having cheated on him, is her ally here, and the child's too; they pull together in the story of her escape.

Reformist talk (of abolition or eradication of a social evil) rings hollow in this setting. So does its elite moralism. The utopian urge here is for self-determination, for freedom, for the right to refuse and escape, not the need to cleanse or upgrade from tradition into modernity and the monogamous family. Epochal promises – of eradication, legal protection, progress, equality for women – fade in the complex formation and uneasy temporality of this festering sore, but the critical energy and the utopian aspirations of the narrator-protagonist open onto a future that may be without these guarantees, but is worth fighting for – personally.

Similar reformulations that have transformative potential for the feminist understanding of violence within the family, and perhaps to begin a new discussion on the theory of violence itself, may be found in Shyamala's story 'Mother may only be a small basket and Father an elephant, but a small basket . . .',[6] as well as in Anu Ramdas's article 'My Man'.[7] Using the example of the family of migrant Dalit construction workers who acquire the coveted (because it comes with the right to put up a residential shelter at the site) position of 'watchman', she writes: 'Only a seasonal migrant labourer knows how precious this offer is, and uncannily so does the contractor. It took me some time before I fully realised this move up almost always involved the sexual exploitation of the watchman's wife and his female relatives by the contractors and their contacts'.

There were frequent family feuds, and both husband and wife carried scars of those encounters. Ramdas comments, 'she'd cry when people enquired about her scars, receiving sympathy and advice; he remained coldly silent to similar queries, never letting anyone know his feelings about subjecting his wife to verbal and physical violence and being the recipient of counter violence'. The point here is not that both parties are equally guilty of violence. The questions she asks are altogether different:

> This was violence between two individuals – man and woman, husband and wife. Or was it? How much of this domestic violence is linked to the violence that society bequeaths this couple? How much chance do they have of avoiding the many forms of violence including domestic violence, as migrant dalit labourers? . . . [Between these two], domestic violence was basically about betrayal. Whose betrayal? Hers. She was supposed to mythically avoid sexual exploitation while still ensuring a roof over the family. He was supposed to mythically protect his wife from sexual exploitation while still ensuring a home. Society's. Society was expected to mythically not take advantage of chronically disempowered persons, whose labour, bodies and minds it could manipulate at ease.[8]

The analysis, alert as it is to the dense layering of the issue, ends with: 'I knew them as wonderful parents to three children with mutual dreams of a different world for them. Tenderness between this married couple and the children bring back fond and nourishing memories'.

Analysts often write about Dalit women's issues as those in which questions of caste and gender 'intersect'. What we find here, however, is not an intersection of issues (caste, gender) that have separate real lives elsewhere (in the Dalit movement; in feminism). As these writers wrestle with questions that touch their lives and lay claim to a political subjectivity, issues of land, water, housing, bank loans, education, political leadership, family, domestic violence, sexuality, history, literature, food, play, friendship, laughter, anxiety, fear and a hundred other things come into sometimes uneasy confluence. There is a critical engagement with the Left and even the primarily reformist, Ambedkarite understanding of these questions, as well as with that of feminism in its early days. The frames that these writers propose – say for an understanding of domestic violence, suicide, or sexuality – are more comprehensive than those of what now appears more and more clearly as an upper-caste feminism. We like to think that in the idea that patriarchy is better described and analysed as a *caste* patriarchy, as well as in the actual issues these writers and thinkers raise, there is promise for a renewal of the woman's question as well as the Dalit question.

Notes

1 This chapter originally appeared as 'The Dalit Woman Question', in *Indialogs*, Vol. 1, 2014, pp. 152–59. Used with permission.
2 P. Radhika, 'Nude Worship in Karnataka', *Economic and Political Weekly*, Vol. XLVII No. 44, November 3, 2012, pp. 30–34, 310.
3 Volga Vasanta Kannabiran and Kalpana Kannabiran, 'Yajmani Ayudhaloto Yajmani Soudanni Koolagottaganama', in S.V. Satyanarayana (ed.), *Dalita Vadivivadalu*, Hyderabad: Vishalandra Publishing House, 2000, pp. 115–20.
4 See K. Satyanarayana and Susie Tharu (eds.), *No Alphabet in Sight, New Dalit Writing from South India, Dossier 1: Tamil and Malayalam*, New Delhi: Penguin, 2011, Dossier 1.
5 Vinodini, in Satyanarayana and Tharu (eds.), *No Alphabet in Sight, New Dalit Writing from South India, Dossier 1*, Dossier 2, p. 742.
6 This is the title story of a collection; Gogu Shyamala, *Father May Be an Elephant and Mother Only a Small Basket, But . . .*, translated from Telugu, Hyderabad: Navayana,. January 6, 2012.
7 Anu Ramdas, 'My Man', *Round Table India: For an Informed Ambedkar Age*, published on July 4, 2012. Retrieved from http://roundtableindia.co.in/index.php?option=com_content&view=article&id=5364:my-man&catid=119:feature&Itemid=132, accessed on 27/7/12; some changes have been made in the text's layout.
8 Ibid.

15
RESPONSES TO INDIAN FEMINISTS' OBJECTIONS

Menon on intersectionality: rejection or critical dialogue?[1]

Mary E. John

In her article 'Is Feminism about "Women"? A Critical View on Intersectionality from India' (i.e., Chapter 1 in this Reader), Nivedita Menon offers a series of arguments that, taken together, amount to a rejection of the concept of intersectionality, at least for feminism in India. Given that this concept has been infrequently discussed in our context, Menon's piece offers a welcome opportunity to examine it afresh. In this response I suggest that, instead of dismissing intersectionality, we might be better off engaging with it. This requires us to critically examine whether it offers any insights into our questions, dilemmas and challenges. Such an examination is rendered difficult by the fact that intersectionality has often been enmeshed in confusion and seems to invite misinterpretation. A second difficulty, emphasised by Menon herself, is that intersectionality has turned into a buzzword in recent years. The reasons for its newfound popularity remain unexplained, though it does seem to carry a degree of institutional power today, and is being promoted by UN agencies and international funders. Surely there is something quite paradoxical about an idea from a marginal location like Black feminism in the US, designed to tackle the challenges of theorising and advancing the political struggles of Black women, turning into a tool of power.

Let me begin by trying to summarise Menon's arguments: (1) Intersectionality is the latest example of the imperialism of categories, whereby only Western/northern concepts have the power of being universal and even replacing non-Western/southern understandings. (2) By virtue of being pushed by international funding, it strongly risks depoliticisation. As an aspect of 'gender mainstreaming' it is part of global agendas of governmentality. (3) The idea of intersectionality is not new in the United States itself. (4) In India, the term not only adds nothing to our understanding of the problem it addresses, namely interlocking structures of oppression, but obscures our history. 'Woman' was never a pre-existing category nor did the women's movement in India simply adopt a single axis framework. Rather 'the presumed subject of feminist politics has been destabilised in India most notably by the politics of caste, religious community identity and sexuality'.[2] (5) The concept of intersectionality was developed by Kimberlé Crenshaw in the context of the law, which makes it a project doomed to failure, since the law is unable to heed our complex ethical positions. (6) Amplifying the argument in (4), Crenshaw's image of being at the intersection of multiple axes (roads), does not allow for the provisional nature of each of these roads in the first place. (7) No scholarship outside the West/North is ever alluded to in debates on intersectionality. (8) Intersectionality presumes that the interlocking structures of oppression are only reinforcing; however, none of the structures of patriarchy, capitalism or caste are closed – 'their borders are porous, the social order fragile and every structure is constantly destabilised by another outside of it'.[3] Based on all these arguments, Menon concludes that what is needed is diversity and a greater awareness of the inadequacy of universal paradigms.

This is quite a daunting list of objections. I cannot hope to answer them all, nor is that the purpose of this note, which is intended to encourage (rather than discourage) further debate on intersectionality. My response is composed of four main points: Firstly, I believe that much more needs to be said regarding what intersectionality may be about and what gave it some purchase in the first place. Secondly, I do not think that the prominent examples Menon offers (on the Women's Reservation Bill and the Uniform Civil Code) demonstrate the absence of single axis thinking in our context or the redundancy of intersectionality as an idea. Thirdly, the arguments regarding the problems of universality and governmentality are too simply posed. Finally, destabilisation alone is no guarantor of a more genuinely inclusive politics.

Brief thoughts on intersectionality

It is quite striking that Kimberlé Crenshaw introduced the concept of intersectionality in 1989 by openly acknowledging that it is a term that names an older problem, one that is more or less co-terminous with the entangled history of Black women with feminism in the United States (see Chapter 10 of this Reader for Crenshaw's writing). Crenshaw's 1989 article begins by citing the title of the first volume on Black women's studies, 'All the women are white, all the blacks are men, but some of us are brave' as a pithy way of illustrating the problem.[4] Among other writings of the 1980s that Crenshaw alludes to is bell hooks 'Ain't I a Woman?'[5] which is the refrain borrowed from the famous speech attributed to Sojourner Truth. Speaking at a women's rights convention as far back as 1851, Sojourner Truth spoke of things 'being out of kilter for the white man between the negroes of the south and the women of the north'. She said that she was never helped over ditches, had arms as strong as any man, and lived to see her children sold into slavery, but her cries were heard by no one but Jesus. 'Ain't I a woman?', she repeatedly asked. There are other antecedents Crenshaw neglects to mention such as the programmatic statement of Black lesbian members of the feminist Combahee River Collective who in 1977 argued that women like themselves needed an identity politics precisely because they were getting lost within the simultaneous workings of race, patriarchy and heterosexuality within systems of imperialism and capitalism.[6]

So it is important to begin by noting that intersectionality references a prior legacy with roots going all the way back to the nineteenth century – it is not trying to be 'new'. Some accounts of this pre-history do not even mention Crenshaw and include feminist scholars of colonialism such as Lata Mani and Anne McClintock.[7] This kind of approach, where a term is strongly associated with particular histories of collective struggle rather than with the person(s) who actually coined it, is extremely uncommon. In intellectual history, it is far more usual for the reverse to happen; that is, for terms born out of larger processes to become associated with particular individuals who may be prominent interpreters. By way of comparison, consider a concept like gender which first emerged as an idea in sex-change medicine and psychology in the 1950s (in the work of pre-feminists like John Money); but these origins were, till quite recently, forgotten and its insights mostly ascribed to various feminist theorists from Joan Scott to Judith Butler. I am not so much arguing that prior legacies must always be acknowledged, but simply want to point out that, regardless of how later users perceive it, in the eyes of its own 'inventors', intersectionality is quite self-consciously not-new.

The next question would be – has the term intersectionality proved useful in any context? Has it provided anything different by way of fresh insight into an old problem? To begin with, it certainly represents an advance over the more generic use of multiple axes of oppression, double and treble burdens and so on, and is a corrective to the commonly deployed notion of multiple identities. This way of alluding to the effects of 'race, class, gender' (or, in our context, 'class, caste, community, gender') is quite widespread, as I am sure readers are aware. The idea of being 'multiple' misleadingly suggests that identities are formed by adding together the various structures or axes that constitute them. In such a view, Black women's identities become a combination of being Black and being women. Instead, as Crenshaw discusses in the many examples she takes from Black women's experiences of discrimination at the workplace and in women of colour's encounters with institutions created to address domestic violence, the simultaneous operation of structures of oppression makes these experiences *qualitatively different*.[8] More often than not, Black women *disappear* at the intersections of racism and sexism because their experiences prove to be more than, or other than, the sum of the various 'parts' that are thought to constitute it. In other words, Black women's experiences cannot be addressed by adding together general discussions of racism (where Black men are the implicit norm) and sexism (where white women are the implicit norm). To put it differently, the additive equation Black woman = Black + woman actually translates as Black woman = Black man + white woman.

This is why I see intersectionality as providing insight into the problem itself, by pointing to a place where identities fail to appear or be recognised as we might have expected them to. The failure to 'see' the intersectional subject is compounded at the political and discursive levels, when it comes to analysing and opposing such structures or social divisions. In the US context, the history of the struggle against race in the name of all Black people has primarily served the interests of Black men. Similarly, feminism in the United States, though speaking for all women, has been a discourse and practice that most advanced the cause of white women. In this sense, therefore, intersectionality is not a solution but the statement of a problem – that additive frameworks don't work for Black women, because their experiences cannot be grasped as a combination of those of white women and Black men.

But if intersectionality has done this much to name a problem, and that too an old problem, it runs into difficulties of its own. Some of these are discussed by Menon. Others wonder what kind of methodology an intersectional analysis entails, whether it be the complex effects of multiple structures on one particular group, or on any person or group.[9]

At this point in time, intersectionality is being used in many different ways. For some it continues to bear a special relationship to questions of race and gender. For others it has become another name for undertaking multivariate analyses of all possible axes of discrimination in a society on people – race, caste, class, gender, disability, sexuality, age, nationality and so on. So not only can the number of 'roads' or axes multiply, so too can the number of persons or groups under consideration. It is therefore a matter of debate whether the considerable expansion in the use of intersectionality takes it in the direction of a more inclusive mode of thinking, or whether it runs the danger of losing focus or getting flattened in the very effort to become more comprehensive.

This brings me to my next issue, namely, Menon's claim that, unlike in the West, feminists in India have not rested content with thinking along a single axis or structure, and therefore have no need of intersectionality in whatever form.

The Indian context

There can be little doubt about the unique historical trajectory of the women's question and feminism in a context like ours, given the profound role that colonialism, and later nationalism, came to play in that history. I have also tried to offer some thoughts on how this affected the frameworks within which women's issues came to be addressed from the nineteenth century onwards.[10] But I remain unsure whether the particular trajectories taken by Indian feminism have translated into a more successful engagement with the problem that intersectionality identifies, namely, the working out of the simultaneity of structures of oppression, especially for those occupying locations of marginality.

Certainly, if we examine the history of feminism in India we will run up against issues of caste and communalism going back to the very beginning of the women's movement in the first decades of the twentieth century. But unfortunately the fact that problems were recognised does not imply that they were addressed or engaged with – it is a matter of historical record that women's organisations were unable to sustain their early efforts towards a more inclusive politics. Soon after their successful support for the passing of the Child Marriage Restraint Act in 1927 (which cut across all castes and communities to raise the age of marriage from 12 to 14 years, and represents a unique moment of liberal universalism in India), the same leaders came to subscribe to a politics that was effectively elite, Hindu and upper caste.[11] Menon offers the example, from many decades later, of opposition to the Women's Reservation Bill, which took the form of raising the issue of sub-quotas for OBC and Muslim women within the proposal for one-third reservations for women. Here was a case where questions of caste and community intervened within those of gender, thus challenging the idea that 'women' in general were being effectively excluded from electoral politics. And yet, when we consider the stand-off for almost 20 years that has blocked a legislation first announced in 1996, what is striking is the unyielding position taken by women's organisations and supporters in favour of the Bill *without* sub-quotas. Even those who proposed alternatives to the Bill saw no need to address this issue. While OBC (male) leaders who had proposed the sub-quota were only intent on preserving their caste numbers in Parliament, those pushing for the legislation saw no reason to grant special consideration to OBC women – that is to say, both sides were engaging in single axis thinking. How often has it been said by feminists that if OBC men have made their way into politics (without benefit of reservations) then so too can their women, once the legislation is passed? (Only in the case of Muslim women has there been some belated recognition that their very low numbers might, at a later stage, need redressal.) What this implies, then, is that existing modes of thinking appear to be shaped by the political fortunes of men of different communities and castes rather than an appreciation of the effects of unequal patriarchies. As a result, OBC women disappear. In other words, we in India are up against the surprising tenacity of 'single axis' agendas within the women's movement, and need to come up with adequate explanations for this.

The trajectory of the Uniform Civil Code, also brought up by Menon, is clearly different. As is well known, the Shah Bano case in 1985 represented a crisis point of enormous proportions, so much so, that a decade later – in the face of the rise of the Hindu Right – the subject of the UCC was at the heart of one of the most heavily fought debates within the women's movement. While some shifted their stance from the need for national uniformity to a new frame of 'gender just laws', others advanced ideas of reform that worked with diverse communities from within. In a recent article, Flavia Agnes has revisited her long time involvement with the changing figurations of the 'Muslim woman', from the Shah Bano case of 1985 to the communal carnage and sexual violence unleashed in Gujarat 2002.[12] She deploys the idea of intersectionality in relation to gender and minority/communal identity by questioning the tendency to consider the Shah Bano case and the UCC mainly through the lens of gender justice, and the Gujarat violence and attacks on women through the rubric of communal conflict. She then interrogates the widespread practice of making Muslim women visible in public discourse only as victims. I do not think this is simply an instance of the retrospective use of a universal Western concept obscuring (rather than opening up) the cracks at the intersections of gender/community. In fact, I would argue that the intersectionality frame enables Flavia Agnes to highlight a hitherto little noticed *positive* fallout of the Shah Bano judgement with the controversial Muslim Women's Right to Maintenance Act 1986 becoming independent India's first codification of Muslim personal law, bringing it within the purview of justiciable fundamental rights.

Universality and governmentality

This brings me to the third issue for further discussion – the dominance of Western concepts, and the role of international agencies. No one can dispute the huge power differentials between the West and rest, including in intellectual matters. In fact, recent decades have witnessed the strengthening of US hegemony especially in the academic sphere, so much so that even Europe feels left behind. (For example, Nira Yuval-Davis' criticisms about the entry of intersectionality into the UN Declaration against Racism in Durban in 2001, where Crenshaw was invited to speak, is centrally about how almost identical work like hers located in the UK did not find mention, even though it had a lot to offer.) US hegemony has clearly produced the kind of effects that Menon has described – so one finds, for instance, references to 'India's affirmative action policy' even though the much longer history of reservations in our context is not equivalent to US style affirmative action. At the same time, however, we also have more complex instances of the arrival of Western concepts on our shores: consider the emergence of sex-work as a category in India and its role as the rallying identity for a new movement, which grew out of heavily funded international HIV AIDS campaigns that targeted prostitution as the source of the spread of the disease. Or again, take the example of disability in India whose emergence as a new paradigm for activism and scholarship (compared to the prior frame of the handicapped) cannot be disentangled from the agendas of international agencies whether it be the UN Year of Disabled Persons in 1981 or the pressure to sign the 2006 Convention on the Rights of Persons with Disabilities.

It is true that, given our colonial and postcolonial histories, our intellectual spaces are cluttered with false universalisms. But it is equally true that we have been trapped by false particularisms, and even false rejections of the universal. There is no better instance of this than the term feminism itself, which has been repeatedly rejected for being Western and against 'Indian culture'. Indeed, the history of the ideas and frames of the women's movement in India offers extraordinarily complex instances of how feminists have charted a nuanced politics between false universals and equally false rejections of them. Even the Dalit movement sought to overcome perceptions of being exceptional and purely local by seeking inclusion within the UN Declaration against Racism in 2001. I therefore believe that – at least in the twenty-first century – we will need a much more multilayered notion than a simple imperialism of categories to be able to capture the ways in which subordinated peoples have been able not just to make sense of their worlds but also to fight back.

This also means that even the portals of governmentality are not closed to feminist intervention. For instance, 'gender mainstreaming' is not only or simply a tool of power in the hands of corporate globalisation as Menon seems to suggest. Once again we need much more nuanced accounts, in this instance of the history of state policy in a country like India. Here it might be worth mentioning as an aside that compared to the extensive attention paid to the law (which currently seems to be saturating our public feminist spaces for reasons that have nothing to do with intersectionality) we are much more poorly served when it comes to debating state policy. From the *Towards Equality* Report of 1974, to the creation of a special chapter on women in the Sixth Five Year Plan, efforts at 'engendering' the Eleventh and Twelfth Plans, down to the current dismantling of even the pretence of an interactive policy interface, there is a lot that awaits excavation and critique. 'Gender mainstreaming' in policy regimes is about demanding accountability from the state and all its ministries and departments – finance especially; it could be likened to efforts within academia to ensure that feminist perspectives are not confined to women's studies programmes but enter all disciplines. I have not encountered intersectionality in even its most diluted common sense form in Indian policy documents. In fact, during discussions on engendering the most recent Plans, it was a few feminists who demanded that gender and poverty ought to be considered in their intersections with other axes of inequality and discrimination, so that issues of disability, caste, minority status and so on would not get left to the Ministries of Social Justice or Minority Affairs alone, but also achieve some recognition as worthy of being 'mainstreamed'. This seemed to us to be a step forward from the hodge podge of 'weaker sections' and 'marginalised groups' that usually grace policy documents.

Far be it for me to suggest that engagements with policy carry any guarantees of positive change – only that, like the law, it is a regime that we cannot refuse to engage with. Nor is it always true (or the biggest problem) that our categories and identities are frozen into rigidity when they enter the world of governmentality. The state can at times appear quite flexible, as when it refuses to count caste because this would 'fix' categories that are fluid and multiple.

The strategy of destabilisation

To come to my last point, it is not enough to rely on strategies of destabilisation when it comes to our politics. The problem identified by intersectionality is the difficulty of working at the intersections because these are spaces that obscure rather than illuminate. The axes or roads under consideration could well be unstable depending on the approach being taken – in other words, a single axis, whether of capitalism, gender, caste, sexuality and so on, tells us nothing about how a particular axis is being conceptualised. Any particular 'axis' is itself the product of different levels of analysis involving structures, subjects produced by these structures and the discourses that advance them, which, depending on the moment and the context, may yield categories that are both fixed and fluid. It is also quite possible that an elite upper-caste subject be 'destabilised' in the sense of experiencing positive transformation in her world without necessarily changing the larger social order. B.R. Ambedkar said as much in his criticisms of the social reform agendas of leaders like Ranade in his essay on the Annihilation of Caste. Certainly, from that time forward, Dalit women have repeatedly interrogated their upper-caste counterparts for their exclusions and demonstrated the uniqueness of their social and political struggles.[13] Has there therefore been a genuine decentring of the upper-caste subject of feminist politics or the dominance of single axis thinking? I believe that we are still at the early stages of this particular journey, in spite of significant advances such as the concept of brahmanical patriarchy,[14] and critiques of the subject of feminist politics.[15] Dalit feminists have also frequently found inspiration in the history of Black women, which makes me wonder whether some dimension of the intersectionality problem might speak to them. It would surely be odd to reject this out of hand.

If intersectionality is to have any genuinely liberatory potential it must be that it contributes to building solidarity across subjects that are recognised as otherwise getting lost between movements and agendas. A major (if less noted) aspect of the success of US hegemony in the intellectual field is its heterogeneity, its capacity to house positions of opposition and to find space for immigrant differences. Voices that come from elsewhere are therefore too rarely of major consequence and the direction of traffic continues to be largely one way. This makes it conceivable that the trajectories of intersectionality could mark yet another instance of global unidirectionality, since even the struggles of Black feminism are not immune to their geo-political location in the world's only super power. Above all else, then, there is a profound need for more critical dialogue across global feminist margins and centres. I, for one, think that intersectionality would make for an excellent candidate in such an endeavour.

§

Appropriating intersectionality for our own purposes[16]

Meena Gopal

This is a brief critique of some of the positions put forth in Nivedita Menon's article 'Is Feminism about "Women"? A Critical View on Intersectionality from India'. The paper covered diverse and complex grounds, delving into each through layers of connections. In the first part of the essay, Menon goes over the terrain she has made us all familiar with – the instability of the category 'woman'. She explores the terrain in the context of discussions around the contradiction between the rights of the individual and the religious community. She also tries to understand the category 'woman' in the context of tension between individual political representation and group identity.

The question of relevance of universality of concepts and, their hegemony, has been addressed through a series of engagements by feminists across the globe. Such interventions have broadened the scope of postcolonial feminism, especially when 'significant women's movements and gender issues in many postcolonial nations ... are linked with feminist studies in the academy there, as well as works originating in the First World ... relate to women and women's movements in the Third World'.[17] Such interventions have also broadened the scope of postcolonial feminism within cultural studies or transnational feminism. This would be an interesting path to pursue the relevance of conceptual categories.

While questioning the universal relevance of intersectionality, Menon flags several points as problematic, but does not clarify them adequately. I will choose to offer a few here for the uninitiated. It was urged that 'the subject of feminist politics has to be brought into being by political practice'.[18] But this has been integral to feminist scholarship in India that has addressed intersections. These include interventions as varied as those on brahmanical patriarchy[19] and ones that discuss the disappearance of women at the margins of multiple oppressions, especially in the context of domestic and public labour.[20]

Voices from within

Although its arguments draw from diverse politics, the article offers a not-so-nuanced representation of the women's movement. It is nobody's case that the women's movement is not a contested terrain. This, however, has been an indicator of its organic resilience. Even when voices have challenged dominant conceptualisations, they have been mostly from within.[21] But in Menon's accounts such voices from within feminism are made to appear extraneous – especially with constant pointers such as, 'Thus, feminist politics must always be sensitive to the significance of different locations, different in terms of both time period and geographical location'.[22] They make one wonder whose feminist politics is being referred to.

Further Menon's account suggests there is a binary opposition between caste politics and feminist politics. An instance of this presupposition is the statement: 'The challenges to feminist politics from caste politics erupt also in other contexts. A revealing moment of tension was manifested at the National Conference of Autonomous Women's Groups in Kolkata (2006), between the newly politicised bar dancers of Mumbai and Dalit feminist groups'.[23] Some of Menon's assertions as 'the opposition between them is not easily amenable to an elite/subaltern division since often both identities, as in this case (Dalit/bar dancer), are equally subaltern'[24] misrepresent an issue that was much debated in Western India and makes it appear like an elites-versus-subalterns issue.

Similarly, the 'homogeneity' versus 'heterogeneity' dichotomy simplifies the complex debates around the need for a civil code or the continuing pleas for gender-just laws that encompass not just relational arrangements and entitlements, but social security as well. Such simplification dehistoricises the trajectory of the women's movement and the sociopolitical context that shaped it and continues to do so.

Slippages

There are also some slippages, especially in the discussion of queer politics and its terminology, and in complex existential matters such as identity and body. For example, Menon notes, 'Queer politics has produced a public discourse that insists on the potential fluidity of sexual identifications'.[25] Sexual identification here actually refer to gender identity and expression, in spite of the fact that gender and sexuality have been now analysed to be distinct.[26]

Menon also exhibits a lack of clarity in speaking of the relationship between body and gender expression, and her piece has some confusing allusions to queer politics: 'Queer politics in India engages with the question of biology critically, treating sexuality as fluid, not a biological or genetic given. . . . [I]t does not attempt to produce a new universal, within which all sexual identities will be submerged'.[27] When Menon says 'the politics of sexuality throws into disarray the certainty of recognisably gender coded bodies',[28] perhaps she meant struggles around gender identity that destabilise the binaries of male and female – challenges from the experiences of those who defy the gender norm.

Offering clarifications to the preceding would mean an entirely new essay. In all of the preceding discussions, class is totally absent. Despite the opening call to locate theory, there seems an urgency to theorise in response to global debates. This leaves us, even after going through the latter half of the essay, asking for more. The essay has opened up the possibilities of claiming intersectionality for our own purposes. The sphere of anti-discrimination, for instance, in law would seem an area to explore.

Notes

1 This is excerpted from 'Intersectionality: Rejection or Critical Dialogue', *Economic and Political Weekly*, Vol. L No. 33, August 15, 2015, pp. 72–76. Used with permission.
2 Nivedita Menon, 'Is Feminism About "Women"? A Critical View on Intersectionality from India', *Economic and Political Weekly*, Vol. L No. 17, April 25, 2015, pp. 37–44, 38.
3 Ibid., p. 44.
4 Gloria T. Hull et al., *All the Women Are White, All the Blacks Are Men, but Some of Us Are Brave*, Old Westbury, NY: Feminist Press, 1982.
5 bell hooks, *Ain't I a Woman: Black Women and Feminism*, Boston: Beacon Press, 1981.
6 See Elizabeth L. Eisenstein, *The Printing Press as an Agent of Change: Communications and cultural transformations in early-modern Europe*, Vols. I and II, New York: Cambridge University Press, 1979.
7 For example, Aftar Brar and Ann Phoenix, 'Ain't I a Woman: Revisiting Intersectionality', *Journal of International Women's Studies*, Vol. 5 No. 3, 2004, pp. 75–86.
8 Kimberlé Crenshaw, 'Demarginalising the Intersection of Race and Sex: A Black Feminist Critique of Antidiscrimination Doctrine, Feminist Theory and Antiracist Politics', *University of Chicago Legal Forum*, Vol. 140, 1989, pp. 139–67. Chapter 10 of this Reader. Crenshaw, Kimberlé, 'Mapping the Margins: Intersectionality, Identity Politics and Violence against Women of Color', *Stanford Law Review*, Vol. 43 No. 6, 1991, pp. 1241–99.
9 Leslie McCall, 'The Complexity of Intersectionality', *Signs*, Vol. 30 No. 3, 2005, pp. 1771–800.

10 Mary E. John, 'Feminist Trajectories in Time and Space: Perspectives from India', *Economic and Political Weekly*, Vol. 49 No. 22, 2014, pp. 121–31.
11 Mrinalini Sinha, *Spectres of Mother India*, Durham: Duke University Press and New Delhi: Zubaan, 2007.
12 Flavia Agnes, 'From Shah Bano to Kausar Bano: Contextualising the 'Muslim Woman' in a Communalized Polity', in Ania Loomba and Ritty A. Lukose (eds.), *South Asian Feminisms*, Durham: Duke University Press and New Delhi: Zubaan, 2012.
13 Meenakshi Moon and Urmila Pawar, *We Also Made History: Women in the Ambedkarite Movement*, translated by Wandana Sonalkar, New Delhi: Zubaan, 2008; Ruth Manorama, 'Dalit Women: The Downtrodden Among the Downtrodden', in James Massey and Bhagwan Das (eds.), *Dalit Solidarity*, New Delhi: SPG Publications, 1992, pp. 165–76; Sharmila Rege, *Writing Caste, Writing Gender: Dalit Women's Testimonios*, New Delhi: Zubaan, 2006.
14 Uma Chakravarti, 'Conceptualising Brahminical Patriarchy in Early India: Gender, Caste, Class and State', *Economic and Political Weekly*, April 3, 1993, pp. 579–85.
15 S. Tharu and T. Niranjana, 'Problems for a Contemporary Theory of Gender', in Shahid Amin and Dipesh Chakravarty (eds.), *Subaltern Studies, IX*, New Delhi: Oxford University Press, 1996. Chapter 2 of this Reader.
16 This originally appeared as 'Struggles Around Gender: Some Clarifications', *Economic and Political Weekly*, Vol. L No. 33, August 15, 2015, pp. 76–78. Used with permission.
17 Rajeswari Sunder Rajan and You-me Park, 'Postcolonial Feminism/Postcolonialism and Feminism', in H. Schwarz and S. Ray (eds.), *A Companion to Postcolonial Studies*, Oxford: Blackwell Publishing, 2005, p. 53.
18 Menon, 'Is Feminism About "Women"?', pp. 37–44, 43.
19 Chakravarti, 'Conceptualising Brahminical Patriarchy in Early India', pp. 579–85.
20 Mary E. John, 'The Problem of Women's Labour: Some Autobiographical Perspectives', *Indian Journal of Gender Studies*, Vol. 20 No 2, 2013, pp. 177–212.
21 Ruth Manorama, 'Dalit Women: The Downtrodden among the Downtrodden', in Mary E. John (ed.), *Women's Studies in India: A Reader*, New Delhi: Penguin, 2008, pp. 445–52; Moon and Pawar, *We Also Made History*.
22 Menon, 'Is Feminism About "Women"?', p. 39.
23 Ibid.
24 Ibid.
25 Ibid.
26 LABIA, 'Breaking the Binary: Understanding Concerns and Realities of Queer Persons Assigned Gender Female at Birth across a Spectrum of Lived Gender Identities', a Study by LABIA: A Queer Feminist LBT Collective, 2013, https://sites.google.com/site/labiacollective/we-do/research/report-btb (accessed on 6 June, 2015); Sunil Mohan and Sumathi Murthy, *Towards Gender Inclusivity: A Study on Contemporary Concerns around Gender*, Bangalore: Alternative Law Forum, 2013.
27 Menon, 'Is Feminism About "Women"?' p. 40. Chapter 1 of this Reader.
28 Ibid., p. 38.

PART VI
Toward a Dalit feminist theory

Part VI presents contemporary perspectives useful toward the construction of a viable Dalit feminist theory. The wide-ranging chapters include discussions on the politics of 'international sisterhood', and an important scrutiny of various modes of 'experience' for different women: 'suffering' or 'struggle' as experience for the objects under feminist analysis; 'positive' or 'revelatory' experience for the subjects doing feminist inquiry; 'identification' as experience for the hypothesised woman reader; and, on how and why this category of 'experience' is not questioned by mainstream approaches in Third World feminism. The chapters also detail different standpoints on 'experience' and its contested relation(s) with respect to theorisation.

Julie Stephens (Chapter 16) offers a critique of contemporary feminist writings in India, arguing that the category 'non-Western women' is a fiction insofar as it avoids sincere engagement with its own 'history' under cover of doing battle with Western hegemony. Further, Stephens highlights mainstream feminists' manipulation of the category 'experience' in Third World feminism. Smita M. Patil (Chapter 17) employs categories borrowed from Marx, Mignolo and Oyewumi to argue that Dalit feminist thought presents a challenge to the authenticity of knowledge and offers an epistemic turn for feminist thinking that must be recognised and implemented to advance the efficacy of Indian feminist discourse. Kanchana Mahadevan (Chapter 18) comprehensively discusses debates concerning the category 'experience' in feminist research, criticising the experience-theory dichotomy, and offers an insightful alternative arguing for theorising by the collective shared experience of those who live, share, as well as articulate experience in a scholarly form. That is, an authentic theorisation is possible *only* when the subjects and the objects of feminist research coincide.

Thus, the final part of the Reader presents significant contemporary perspectives on theorising Third World feminism, which indicates a revisiting and interrogation of the ground realities and their potencies. Theorising feminism from the

Indian context requires centralising caste in our feminist endeavour as it plays a central role in marginalising the most marginalised women of India. *Dalit Feminist Theory* undertakes this task thereby helping to correct Indian feminist thought in particular, and hopefully also contributing to the progress of feminist theory more generally.

16

FEMINIST FICTIONS

A critique of Indian feminism[1]

Julie Stephens

> *a feminism that cannot criticize itself cannot,*
> *in the last analysis,*
> *serve as the bearer of emancipatory possibilities*[2]

A distinguishing feature of contemporary feminist discourse is that it purports to speak about 'real' women. This emphasis on realness, this faith that the descriptions of Indian women it offers are unproblematic representations of the objective, separates feminism from other discourses dealing with the same subject. Feminist studies aim to supplant the mythic and idealise 'Indian womanhood' of the nationalists or the objectified 'woman' of orthodox anthropology. Yet, in a discourse so concerned with challenging the very process by which traditional 'images' of women are produced, it is surprising to find feminist texts blind to their own image-making and laying claim to accurately portray 'real' Third World women.[3]

The following is an exploration of a textual body of knowledge on Indian women with particular reference to the problem of the unmediated association between representation and reality that surfaces when non-Western women are the object of feminism's gaze.[4] What is addressed is the overlap between Indian and Western feminist portraits of Indian women. Whilst this overlap is a textual one – thus excluding important instances of women's protests informed often by more heterodox ideologies – and covers only a section of the literature, it is large and significant enough to warrant discussion.[5] The discussion therefore concerns a strain of feminism operating at the intersection of East and West, the Third and First Worlds. The purpose is to examine this juncture as the point at which feminism collides and colludes with the discourse of Orientalism.

The institutional site from which feminism speaks of Indian women is 'the field'. It shares this site with anthropology but adopts a particular style and approach to it. 'The field' in feminist studies of Third World women is more than simply an area for specialist academic research; it is stressed as the place where 'everyday' experiences occur. A deliberate attempt is made to bypass theoretical frameworks in favour of the 'direct experience'.[6] Value-free commentary, academic prose and the idea of objective scholarship, all common features of the orthodox anthropological study, are rejected. They prefer 'the conversational mode to the structural interview technique',[7] using no formal questionnaire. The aim is to fill the gap between an 'unashamedly critical' approach to the study of Indian women and 'dispassionate documentation'[8] and to separate 'what people really do from what they say they do'.[9] 'These are not academic studies carried out in social and political isolation', claims a review of three texts from this strain of feminism, but an 'attempt to transmit the immediacy of experience and knowledge gained in struggle, in order to overcome the split between theory and activism'.[10]

There are countless ways of marking a text as 'information', and this deliberately non-theoretical approach is one of them. Verisimilitude is established by stressing 'the field' as the site of the discourse. While fieldwork is not a device in itself which necessarily legitimates a narrative, the way it is invoked, in this type of feminist research, assumes that it does. The discourse places great emphasis on the 'immediacy' and the 'directness' of the investigator's experience. Often the lengthy descriptions of atmosphere and surroundings are written in the present tense, restructuring time to reinforce place; the picture is of the investigating subject really being there'. This endorses the text as credible, legitimate information. It also makes the image of Indian women conveyed appear more like a photograph than a portrait. Predicating 'the field' and the indisputability of the eyewitness report operate as a very persuasive truth tactic.

The effectiveness of the 'I was there so it must be true' position rests on an assumed unfiltered identity between fieldwork (as presented in feminist texts) and reality. This identity appears as taken for granted. The narrative techniques borrowed from realist fiction which crate this identity are hidden. The fieldwork experience not only legitimates feminist texts on Third World women, but it also structures all description and analysis.[11] In these texts the link between fieldwork and reality is forged by a category granted a peculiar objectivity in the discourse: the 'direct experience'. Feminism paradoxically insists that the 'direct experience' textually conveyed is somehow more real than the indirect textual experience, thus denying that its own textual productions are implicated in another kind of image-making.

Alongside the positivist empiricism of the 'I was there so it must be true' position is the position 'I am a woman, so it must be true'. What Elshtain describes as the 'mask of unquestioned, inner authenticity based upon claims of the ontological superiority of female being-in-itself' can be recognised again and again in the texts under scrutiny.[12] For example, 'women as *women*' are seen to have a special drive for liberation';[13] what are considered 'questionable' research methods are replaced by the unchallengeable 'we were simply women talking together'.[14] However, the most frequently used claim to truth is the inclusion of and emphasis on the 'voice' of non-Western women. The discourse prides itself on being unique in providing the opportunity for Third World women to 'speak for themselves'. But what does 'speaking for themselves' mean in this context? Firstly, it certainly does not mean that these women actually do speak. Feminism laments the silencing of 'our Third World sisters',[15] chides itself for ever trying to speak for them and then 'grants' them a voice in much the same way as women are 'given' equal rights. It 'allows', 'encourages', or 'lets' them speak; it claims not to speak for them. The problems inherent in such premises need further examination.

In 'Sexual Class in India', Mody and Mhatre simultaneously assert that Indian women are capable and incapable of 'speaking'.[16] They argue that 'the public voice [of the Indian woman] has long been stifled' by a 'male-dominated society' and see 'her present silence on the problems she faces' as connected to 'a self-image [which] is severely distorted and repressed'.[17] Their interview and subsequent article provide the forum or the 'little encouragement' needed for the Indian woman, 'to shake off this imposed reticence and speak on her own behalf of her problems and their solutions'.[18] Yet whose voice is it that we hear in what follows?

After a brief description of 'the field', in this case the slums of Bombay, we are introduced to three women who live there. The first interview begins: 'Janabai gives her age as forty-five. Though she appears much older, her tiny frame is erect and strong'.[19] What follows are details of Janabai's life, her attitude to Congress and her views on the problems of Bombay. They are listed in simple, unadorned prose giving the appearance that Janabai's words are being read directly, and not those of the writers. However, to return to these opening lines, it is not Janabai saying she is 45 that we hear. It is Mody and Mhatre who intervene with 'she *gives* her age as forty-five although she *appears* much older'. The italicised words place the reader alongside the investigator, observing Janabai. We are invited *not* to believe Janabai's knowledge of her own age but rather the initial impressions the interviewers have of it. Why not begin (if indeed the aim is to present genuine interviews) with, 'Janabai is forty-five'? Clearly the answer is that would both convey too little and that the discourse wants to make the investigating subject *appear* invisible, not actually *be* invisible.[20] As it stands, the opening lines economically build a picture of 'the Other', the tiny but strong, overworked ('she appears much older') peasant woman trapped in an urban slum. These lines tap into a familiar and clichéd picture which hardly requires the 'two dozen green bangles' and 'decorative tattoos' as elaboration.

Janabai, Lucy and Shevanti's words are stifled by those so desperate to hear them. Instead of interviews with questions and answers and direct speech, we are given summaries, edited into a neat and tidy package written from the point of view of the investigator. Nevertheless, the appearance that Third World women are 'speaking for themselves' is maintained despite the constant interruptions and corrections made to their so-called speech.

The semblance of coherence is sustained by the argument that a woman such as Janabai, for example, has no voice because she speaks in the mode 'of the social mechanism which represses women'.[21] According to Mody and Mhatre, 'she has not the ability to think or act otherwise'.[22] What then constitutes a voice in the feminist discourse if it is not women actually speaking? How do these researchers, who choose 'the field' as the site legitimating their own speech, identify amongst the babble of tape recordings and sheets of notes, what is and is not a voice?

Voice and consciousness are linked in confusing and inconsistent ways. Some texts see 'the women's lack of consciousness of rights which should be hers' as preventing her 'from acting on her own behalf'.[23] Consciousness therefore comes outside, when women 'are encouraged to voice their resentment, to identify their oppressors and to struggle to improve their condition'.[24] The unresolved paradox here is that consciousness relies on voice to be recognised and generated yet there can be no voice without consciousness.

*

What is 'not said' in the feminist discussion of Third World women ensures that contingent utterance has the status of unconditional truth. The 'never said' enables certain categories to be produced which appear self-evident and beyond question. Feminism, to convincingly portray itself as universal, relies on promises which are taken as given, above challenge. It is validated as much by what it does not say as by what it actually says. The notion of an 'international sisterhood' is founded on the proposition that a woman's experience is true – 'experience' being treated as an objective category in the discourse – and that women can learn from the experience of women in other cultures because in some ways, 'they' are better/stronger/more militant than 'us'. However, the questions not asked are: what constitutes 'experience' in the discourse and how do some subjects of feminist research come to be unqualifiedly valorised?

Contemporary feminist studies of Third World women emphasise the directions or the 'day to dayness' of the experiences of the women they represent. The discourse attempts of offer 'glimpses of the vast, complex and unplumbed reality of the day to day struggles of millions of ordinary women in India'.[25] In ascribing value to the ordinary, feminism is inverting the traditional patriarchal view that the day to day activities of women are trivial. It is a reaction against discourses which concentrate on 'image of women' over what women actually do.[26] This rebellious inversion is crystallised in the feminist motto of the 1970s, 'the personal is political'. While this position has become increasingly sophisticated as second wave feminism has developed,[27] it is automatically given the status of 'objective' scientific truth. This is particularly evident in feminist studies of Third World women where the category of 'experience' has not been challenged. Even when the discourse reproaches itself for its own imperialism, the prestige of 'experience' remains unquestioned. Experience is seen to be something concrete, quantifiable ('women have had half of the world's collective experience'[28]) and objective; a pure state, on which the validity of a feminist analysis rests. What then constitutes 'experience' in the discourse?

Despite its apparent simplicity, 'experience' in studies of Third World women is not a simple construct. Three different types of experience interlock to form what is designated as 'the experience of being a woman'. Firstly, there is the experience of the subjects under investigation. Secondly, there is the experience of the investigating subject, the woman conducting the research, the narrator of the texts. Thirdly, there is the experience of the hypothesised women reader, an integral part of the textual construction.

Feminism considers all aspects of a women's experience to be important. Nevertheless, what is identified as an 'experience' conforms to a particular pattern. It is not just any event or happening in a woman's life that earns the status of an experience in feminist utterance. A process of selection occurs (certain types of events are included and other excluded) despite the discourse's claim to simply record the direct experiences of women. This pattern of inclusion and exclusion in feminism is not created by 'the experience itself', but by what a particular experience represents. Take the subject under investigation, a woman going to fetch water at the well, for example. Such an event is deemed 'an experience' only because of what it signifies. If it can be made to demonstrate the hardship of a woman's lot, the extent to which she is oppressed or her strength in adversity, then it is included. An event not fulfilling these criteria simply would not be recorded, or if mentioned would be passed off as a false experience. Note the analysis that follows Janabai 'speaking for herself' in Sexual Class in India'.

> She relies on myth and religious doctrine to explain the events of her life. It was to her undeniably, the snake who evicted them from the village rather than the probable poverty of a small peasant. And her concept of her son as the reincarnation of the paternal head of the feudal family, clearly indicates the extent to which she depends on that framework for her own behavior. . . . Thus Janabai unselfconsciously acts out a definite role in the social mechanism which represses women. Thoroughly repressed herself, she has not the ability to think or act otherwise.[29]

In this case, the discourse contradicts its position on the importance of all aspects of a woman's experience; some obviously are more important than others. Why, when Janabai says her family left the village because of the retribution of an angry snake, is the experience *not* ranked as being *as true as* Shevanti's comments that 'a woman must work outside the home, not only because it is necessary to provide extra income, but also to avoid being dependent on anyone else'?[30] Clearly there is no such thing as the 'experience-in-itself' or the pure, direct experience without a subject defining it as such. Moreover, the experiencing subject, as depicted in these texts, often involves the investigating subject as well.

For 'experience' is a contingent category, formed and reconstituted by a continuous process of exclusion. It is not a given, something that is 'out there' for people to 'have'; it is created and has a history.

Clearly, it would appear that what comes to be designated as 'experience' (and what is identified as a 'voice') is often that which most closely resembles the thought-world of the investigating subject. S/he is the lynch-pin, holding together two levels of the category. The person conducting the research (in these cases a woman) usually identities strongly with the subjects under investigation even to the extent of dressing like them, and living as they do. The investigating subject goes to great lengths in the text to establish her credentials, or 'right', to conduct the research. She has access to the culture most others would lack, therefore, the record of her experiences must be true and reliable. This credibility is often demonstrated by the hardship and sacrifice involved in conducting the research.

Substantiating the reliability of the first person narrator is a literary convention usually confined to realist fiction. In feminist studies of Third World women, the narrator appeals to the 'authority of experience' to establish her qualifications. While that experience may involve identifying with her subject, Indian women, what constitutes 'experience' for her is very different from what she sees 'experience' as being for them.

Without wishing to over-schematise the way the category of experience functions in the discourse, it is possible to simplify it in point form.

1. Experience of the subject under investigation = an event which illustrates feminist concerns (i.e. 'suffering', 'struggle').
2. Experience of the investigating subject = positive and revelatory.
3. Experience of the hypothesised woman reader = identification.

It is interesting that the woman reader is urged *not* to identify with the investigating subject – with whom it could be assumed that she shared the same language and culture if not similar 'experience' – but instead is directed to the subject under investigation, with whom she shares only her womanness. The woman reader is positioned alongside the investigator, but is asked to identify with those being investigated. The discourse creates the illusion that (1) and (3) are in a direct relationship and that if (2) is there at all, it is simply to reveal, like a window, the direct experiences of (1). This impression is maintained despite the language of feminist individualism used to describe the investigator's 'extraordinary experiences', where the 'I' of the texts is simultaneously emphasised and de-emphasised. What the manifest discourse does not disclose is that in many respects the 'I' is the central subject of the texts. What sustains the impression that the 'I' is invisible is a range of textual conventions already mentioned: the notion of women speaking for themselves; journalistic techniques designed to make the reader feel she is really there; hiding the retrospectivity of the narrative; the idea that the investigator was invited to the research ('this is a book forced on me by the women themselves'[31]) and the unquestioned status of 'experience' in the discourse. If the 'not said' – that experience is a contingent, subjective, textually woven fiction – is said, then the belief that feminist concerns are international contradicts the very standards the discourse itself sets. Only if 'experience' as a 'never said' is taken to be a series of actual observations and facts beyond question can feminism claim to be universal.

Adulatory terms are often used to describe particular groups feminist research investigates. Tribal or peasant women are hailed for their strength, resistance or militancy and the cultures these groups inhibit are portrayed as unusual and exotic. In the manifest discourse, the West (or the West within) is described as commonplace, somehow less than the culture being represented. This is a deliberate inversion of the Orientalist perspective on the inferiority of the East; an attempt to dissociate feminism from such discourses. India, the Third World, or tribal women on the other hand, are seen as important because they offer vital insights of answers not be found in the West or the Westernised modernist. However, this valorisation rarely includes all women or all Indian women, nor does it romanticise everything about 'the Other'. What is 'not-said' is that behind the unqualified commendation of any particular group lies a whole system of values which, in the final analysis, serves to divide women, thereby undercutting the discourse's claim for a universal sisterhood.

Mody and Mhatre, however, use a liberal framework (in spite of the radical feminist sounding title of the article) as the basis for their valorisation of the 'modern'. Take Janabai again as an example. She has all the right credentials, crushing poverty, infant deaths, beatings by her husband, yet she is dismissed as superstitious, feudal and contributing to the oppression of women. Shevanti, on the other hand, who is much better-off economically and socially, is praised in glowing terms. 'If Janabai is part of the problem', they write, 'Shevanti is part of the solution'.

> She is a remarkably independent and outspoken young woman and has waged a consistent struggle in her own life against the forces oppressing her.... Shevanti sees education and knowledge of vocational skills for woman not just as an economic necessity but as a prerequisite to an independent life. She seems to be able to do without marriage as necessary for establishing her identity as an individual.[32]

She is made positive in the discourse because she has embraced bourgeois, liberal values: education and individualism. The extract even goes on to mention her desire for greater privacy in the Bombay slum where she lives. What is important in determining whether something is given the status of being 'unquestionably good' in the discourse is whether what the subject signifies corresponds to the semiotic system of the interviewer.

The constant then in the discursive pattern of organisation has little to do with Indian women or other such subjects under investigation. Once again, what is valued as real is that which most closely reflects the thought-world of the researcher. The arbitrary nature of the sign makes it possible for tribal women, for example, to stand for anything: utopian natural democracy, sexual freedom or devastating oppression.

However, it is not what women do that is important, or who they happen to be, but what their actions *mean* in a particular context. The constructed meanings vary. Indian women, at the moment, stand for something positive in the contemporary feminist discourse, the Third World Women being a particularly 'hallowed signified'.[33] In Katherine Mayo's day Indian women were viewed as a scale by which Indian civilisation was measured. Yet these two perspectives are generated from the same discourse; the discourse of Orientalism. Despite reversing the Orientalist problematic the terms of inferiority and superiority are still meted out by those observing the culture; in defining what is good and bad in Indian society it is their cultural hegemony that is maintained. Valorisation as a strategy aimed at dissociating feminism from the imperialist West does not work. Once the language of 'more than', 'less than', 'better than', 'worse than' comes into play, with only one side making the rules, the relationship between knowledge and power becomes more explicit. This can and has been interpreted as yet another form of racism.

At the heart of all the studies discussed in this critique is a belief that they serve the purpose of fostering mutual understanding between women of the world. This is expressed as shedding new light on the question of the position of women in India,[34] of showing 'women from many countries stitching together a truly international feminist consensus based on their experiences in many different cultures',[35] or as building 'a genuine international sisterhood, on the basis of mutual understanding'.[36] But while this international sisterhood needs to be created by connecting through discourse the 'diversity of women's experience', it is also viewed as something that already exists in the similarities between women's experience, and which is simply waiting to be revealed.

Despite the acknowledgement of minor variations, such as the way women dress, cook their food, etc., the essence of the 'experience of being a woman' is changeless. The process of communicating these experiences, then, becomes one of endless repetition. There can be no 'new light' shed on the question of women in India. If it is accepted that the currency of experience retains its value because it circulates the same experience, the question of whose experience it is and who gains from learning about it must be asked.

In challenging the hierarchy of categories that is recycled in feminist texts on Third World women, particularly the unquestioned status of 'experience', I have touched on a problem which is at the heart of the feminist debate. This is the problem of the uneasy relationship between feminism and history. While Marxism historicises even the origins of oppression, feminism is as yet undecided on whether women's oppression can be seen to have an historical origin. Because of this indecision, the 'universals' in feminism have an uncertain epistemological status. One project of this chapter has been to highlight the inconsistencies in the feminist discourse that arise from this uncertainty.

I am not arguing that these inconsistencies can be ironed out by an act of will. Feminism without a universal concept of itself and its adversary would lack the premise on which a feminist politics is based. Such a premise prevents women's protests from dissolving into individual, fragmented and empirical acts. I therefore recognise the immediate 'political' need for universals. Yet, a 'universal' that has not been sufficiently thought out creates problems for the development of feminist theory. As Alice Jardine has said, capturing the feminist dilemma on this point, to universalise 'woman' as beyond culture is to return to anatomical definitions of sexual identity, but to see woman solely as a cultural construction, as a metaphor 'means risking once again the absence of women as subjects'.[37]

A theoretical orthodoxy which could, in the short run, inform and support a feminist politics is no resolution to the problem that Jardine mentions. It may well be a political choice for us to accept at a theoretical level the 'undecidable' nature of the relationship between women's oppression and history. Yet, as I have argued here, the risk in such a choice is that we are then unable to purge our language of axioms of imperialism. Another theoretical choice available is to force the tension between feminist thought and 'history' in search of an approach that can critically engage within itself all tendencies to create closures at the same time as it fights orthodoxies outside.

Notes

1. This is an abridged version of 'Feminist Fictions: A Critique of the Category "Non-Western Woman" in Feminist Writings on India', in Ranajit Guha (ed.), *Subaltern Studies VI: Writings on South Asian History and Society*, New Delhi: Oxford University Press, February 1, 1994, pp. 92–125.
2. Jean Bethke Elshtain, 'Feminist Discourse and Its Discontents: Language, Power and Meaning', *Signs*, Vol. 7 No. 3, 1982, p. 612.
3. For a more detailed analysis of the texts under scrutiny, see my MA thesis 'Feminist Fictions', University of Melbourne, 1985.
4. The point is not to prove that these portraits are unreal or less real than they claim to be. Such an exercise would involve the contraposition of evidence and counter-evidence.
5. This overlap can also be observed in common institutional and cultural practices Women in Asia conferences or titles of feminist texts advertised in *Manushi* for example.
6. See Helen Roberts (ed.), *Doing Feminist Research*, London: Routledge, 1981, p. 98.
7. Perdita Huston, *Third World Women Speak Out*, New York: Praeger Publishers, 1979, p. 12.
8. Patricia Jeffery, *Frogs in a Well: Indian Women in Purdah*, London: Zed Press, 1979, p. 1.
9. E. S. Kessler, *Women: An Anthropological View*, New York: Holt, Rinehart and Winston, 1976, p. 8.
10. N. Murray, 'Book Review', *Race and Class*, Vol. xxv No. 3, Winter 1984, p. 91.
11. A similar trend in experimental anthropology has been discussed by G. E. Marcus and D. Cushman, 'Ethnographies as Texts', *Annual Review of Anthropology*, Vol. 11, 1982: 25–69, p. 29.
12. Elshtain, 'Feminist Discourse and Its Discontents', p. 605.
13. Eleanor Leacock, 'Women, Development and Anthropological Facts & Fictions', in G. Huizer (ed.), *The Politics of Anthropology*, The Hague, 1979, p. 132.
14. Huston, *Third World Women Speak Out*, p. 12.
15. Editorial statement, 'Third World: The Politics of Being Other', *Heresies*, Vol. 2 No.4, 1979.
16. S. Mody and S. Mhatre, 'Sexual Class in India', *B.C.A.S.*, Vol. 7, No. 1, 1975.
17. Ibid., p. 50.
18. Ibid.
19. Ibid.
20. This is Gayatri Chakravorty Spivak's phrase.
21. Mody and Mhatre, 'Sexual Class in India', p. 54.
22. Ibid.
23. Ibid., p. 56.
24. Ibid.
25. Kishwar, p. i.
26. See Dorothy Hammond and Alta Jablow, *Women in Cultures of the World*, California and Sydney: Cummings, 1976, p. i.
27. See L. Edwards and A. Diamond (eds.), *The Authenticity of Experience: Essays in Feminist Criticism*, Amherst: The University of Massachusetts Press, 1977.
28. M. McIntosh, 'Comments on Tinker's "A Feminist View of Copenhagen"', *Signs*, Vol. 6 No. 4, 1981, p. 774.

29 S. Mody and S. Mhatre, 'Sexual Class in India', *B. C. A. S.*, Vol. 7, No. 1, p. 54.
30 Ibid., p. 52.
31 Jeffery, *Frogs in a Well*, p. 14.
32 Mody and Mhatre, 'Sexual Class in India', p. 54.
33 Gayatri Chakravorty Spivak, 'The Rani of Sirmur: An Essay in Reading the Archives', *History and Theory*, Vol. xxiv, No. 3, 1985, p. 247.
34 Jeffery, *Frogs in a Well*, p. 13.
35 Margaret McIntosh, Aline K. Wong, Nilüfer Çağatay, Ursula Funk, Helen I. Safa, Leila Ahmed, Dafna N. Izraeli, Krishna Ahooja-Patel and Charlotte Bunch, 'Comments on Tinker's "A Feminist View of Copenhagen"', *Signs*, Vol. 6, No. 4, Summer, 1981: 771–790, p. 774.
36 See J. Everett, 'The Upsurge of Women's Activism in India', *Frontiers*, Vol. vii No. 2, p. 18.
37 A. Jardine, *Genesis: Configurations of Women and Modernity*, New York: Cornell University Press, September 1, 1986, p. 37.

17
REVITALISING DALIT FEMINISM[1]

Smita M. Patil

Current debates on Dalit feminism in Maharashtra articulate the epistemic departure of Dalit women's predicaments from mainstream brahmanic feminist investigations. It is positioned as a standpoint which is alert to the critiques as well as the differences that structure the diverse, unequal, social locations of Dalit women.[2] This chapter attempts to explore the Dalit feminism that addresses the caste question among Dalit women in Maharashtra through the seminal political understanding that formulates Mang and Mahar women in the state.[3]

Thus, it widens the conceptual scope of Dalit feminism to challenge the criticisms of the left as well as the feminist assertions that reduce Dalit feminism to identity politics. Drawing on a theoretical possibility based on Marx, Mignolo and Oyewumi and the epistemic nature of the politics that signifies aforementioned sections of Dalit women, I argue that Dalit feminism can deepen its ideological rigour by retracing the impact of the brahmanic nature of the left and of feminist critiques on the appropriation of knowledge that is generated by the Dalit critique in general and the Dalit feminist critique in particular.

Geopolitics of brahmanic sisterarchy

The pertinent questions that are being raised by Dalits in general and Dalit women in particular are suspected to be a form of political culture that disrupts political understanding on the basis of class and women's issues. There is a resurgence of the celebration of voices against the oppression of women in India. This is an appropriate moment to revisit the possibilities of Dalit feminism to deepen its critique against the conceptual homogenising of feminism in India. The ideological pursuit of Dalit feminism has to be explored in the context of the burgeoning critical appraisal of Dalit politics.

Does the critique that indicts Dalit politics as identity politics incline towards the negation of Dalit assertion and can that sort of critique wind up in a brahmanical intellectual tradition? For Rajan, identity politics includes communities or groups rather than individuals. Dalits and women are read against this backdrop as groups confined within the politics of difference or of divisive nature instead of as a 'whole' category that provides a critique to a secular universalising modernity. A critique of the modernity of Dalit bahujans is judged as extreme for its engagement with fragmented identities and for its failure to contextualise their positions based on socio-economic determinants. In turn, the claims regarding the embodied experiences that have an impact on Dalit politics are construed as ineffectual in nature.[4] What are the ways in which this quintessential critique of Dalit politics finds its political proximity which reduces the historicity of the Dalit assertion to that of identity politics?

Dalits, feminists and Gandhi

In a similar vein, the Dalit and feminist critiques of Gandhi, according to Gudavarthy, reproduce similar epistemological grounds of the Gandhian approach which is based on 'lived experience'. They circumvent the results of the politics that centres on essence and generates unproductive, 'inter-subjective communication' which is founded on defined terms rather than political categories. This premise is posited against the 'strong dimension of internal insularity that incapacitates dialogue between the various fragments of the lived experience, for instance, between Dalit women and their more dominant Dalit male counterparts'.[5] Such critique, deemed to be affiliated to post-structuralism, tends to subvert possibilities of multiple alliances. Gudavarthy contends that the politics of Dalits and women are fixated within the experiential realms of the social predicaments of these two groups.[6] Clubbing together Dalits, feminists and Gandhi to debunk identity politics is to negate the historical trajectories of the Dalit critique to Gandhian identity politics. It also challenges the left's detachment from the questions associated with the intersections of caste-cum-class-based oppression. The Dalit feminist project largely imbibes the anti-Dalit/non-Dalit/brahmanical-patriarchy agenda, and thus challenges the Gandhian, brahmanic left-cum-feminist agenda. In other words, the most oppressed section of Dalit women's assertions can question the limited reading of the materialist determinants of brahmanic knowledge producers/systems that cut across the spectrum of political ideologies.

How does Gudavarthy's critique of essentialism of identity politics and Rajan's position on Dalit politics differ from feminist proclivities such as the 'undiscriminating form of anti-essentialism which treats all identities and differences as repressive fictions' and the 'mirror-opposite tendency to adopt an undiscriminating version of multiculturalism, which celebrates all identities and differences as worthy of recognition'?[7] What happens to concerns over justice and equality? For Fraser, the aforementioned approach could not 'link with the cultural politics of identity' with the 'social politics of justice and equality'?[8] Therefore, Fraser demands the construction of a new equality/differences debate based on multiple intersecting differences.[9] Finally, Fraser argues for an anti-essentialist multiculturalism that coexists with the struggle for social equality and democracy.[10]

The confusing similarity of Indian and American ideas on identities, similarities and so on tempts us to ask whether dominant intelligentsia can move beyond the rhetoric of the charges of anti-essentialism and the imposition of the category of divisiveness on Dalits? Attributing the rubric of identity politics to the political perspectives of Dalits in general and Dalit women in particular symbolises totalitarian intellectual ways which arrest their innovative conceptual and political vibrancy. In addition to the conjectures discussed earlier, is there any accommodative project within feminism that addresses the knowledge that probes caste and gender? Does it circumvent the big questions of oppression based on caste, gender and patriarchy?

The dilemmas of identity politics that are demonstrated by Gudavarthy and Rajan attempt to broaden the leftist project in India without proper attention to Dalit analysis of the left in India.[11] Dalit politics, for Nigam, challenges the 'common sense of the secular-modern' and the categories of universal man/abstract working class.[12] Further, Pandian defends Dalits' 'step outside modernity' as a move beyond modernity. In a Paul Gilroyian sense, he termed it 'antagonistic indebtedness'.[13] Nevertheless, Nigam raises questions related to the inertia of secular, radical, communist intelligentsia in addressing anti-communism among Dalits and which has transformed into 'uninterrogated commonsense' that returns to essentialism.[14] Apathy exhibited towards the left coexisted with the unexplored potential within Dalit politics. Ambedkar's project of Buddhism resulted in a modernist, rational-historical narrative that recognised the 'denial of past to the Dalit'.[15] The Ambedkarian 'multilayered, counter-hegemonic reading of caste' itself 'was lost on three generation(s) of sociologists' in India and is judged as the responsible factor for the conservative drift within the discipline.[16] The erasure of the Dalit question from left politics constitutes a major challenge. Dalits were ruled out from the history of left politics and developmentalism, according to Devika, in the political aims that were beneficial to the upper or middle-caste elite.[17] Besides the ambiguous attitude of the left towards the Dalit assertions, it is important to unveil the manner in which the Dalit feminist question is being invoked within the mainstream feminist voices.

Drawing on Nkiru Nzegwu's category of 'Sisterarchy',[18] Oyeronke Oyewumi focuses on the contestation by African, Asian and Latin American feminists that the Western feminist legitimises Western women at the highest echelons of the 'sisterhood', which has global implications and emerges as a form of 'sisterarchy'. This sisterarchy is being activated through the 'western feminist social constructionism' that is embedded within the conceptual terrain of biology which perceives the 'natural' in social hierarchies. For Oyewumi, scholars who engage in the field of 'cross-cultural gender studies' attribute the so-called natural Western analytical tools on non-Western cultures. This results in the obfuscation of non-Western investigations and problematises the social constructionist nature of gender.[19] South Asian feminisms can be read as an extended version of Oyewumi's theoretical momentum due to its uncritical stance towards the unequal structures of caste and gender that divide women. The inclusive agenda of south Asian feminism has to be understood in order to unravel the complexities that underlie its problematique. For Ania Loomba and Ritty A Lukose,

> South Asian feminism ... engages complex new challenges to feminist theory and activism that have emerged in recent years. Our contention is that such feminist engagements in this region (with its long-standing and cross-cutting histories of colonialism, nationalism and women's movements as well as contemporary struggles around sexuality, religion, human rights, war, peace, globalisation and contemporary iterations of empire and labour) can productively enrich the larger horizon of feminist theorising.[20]

Does south Asian feminism offer any historiographic milieu to supplement its postulates? In a riveting preface to their edited book, Loomba and Lukose state:

> 'South Asian Feminism' is situated at the intersection of two histories: first, an academic-political configuration in the West where 'South Asia' and feminism have particular valence and second, a more contemporary resurgence and revitalisation of feminist thinking and organising in the region.[21]

How do feminist thinkers who propose south Asian feminism confront the appropriation that is determined by the debates on the universal category of gender?

Deploying Strasser and Tinsman's position on the engendering of world history via their critique of the construction of dominant-gender history's Eurocentric interpretative tools, Sinha shares her scepticism of the construction of gender as a universal category and its subsequent fall into Eurocentric contextualisation.[22] Though the south Asian feminist denial of Eurocentric power and knowledge is valid, it is insufficient to derive a critique on the brahmanic-gendered feminist intelligentsia in particular and dominant intelligentsia in general. Debates that are generated through dialogue among Dalit women in India find home within a Dalit feminist space which exists outside the citadels of south Asian feminism and other forms of feminist thinking in India. What is the future of the epistemological content which is reflected in the interventions of the Mang and Mahar women? The following section attempts to address the material and ideological grounds that mark their lives.

Being a Dalit woman: beyond social spaces of sub-caste?

Dalits have been victimised through the structural hierarchy of caste that perpetuates the ethos of inequality and maintains the segregation of power. Dalits are oppressed, exploited and discriminated against, and are being methodically erased through graded inequality at every level. So, there is hardly any space for Dalit women in either the public or the private sphere. Subjugation of Dalit women persists through the obnoxious linkages of caste, gender and class.

Dumont and Moffat argue that the caste system is a set of values acknowledged by both the dominant and the subjugated.[23] Ambedkar's analysis of caste as 'a division of labourers that is different from division of labour, a hierarchy in which the division of labourers are graded one above the other' establishes caste as political and suggests that it should be further examined within the realm of political discourse. It explains to us how castes systematically obfuscate 'graded inequality as an ascending scale of reverence and descending scale of contempt'.[24] This assumes further significance in light of the relationship between the structures of gender and caste that Ambedkar outlined succinctly, stating that women are the gateways to the caste system.[25] If we emphasise Ambedkar's model in the present context, the prevailing models of caste appear as viewing the system in a top-down manner, and it may be argued here that a gendered understanding of the graded system of hierarchy requires us to rethink on the grounds of Dalit women's interpretation of their realities. Further, the graded hierarchy of the caste system operates among Dalits too; community members exercise their power/autonomy over others (within and without) instead of building their collective consciousness for the common cause of fighting against the situated hierarchies. This can be seen in Maharashtra (among Mahars and Mangs), Andhra Pradesh (among Malas and Madigas) and elsewhere in India. This is explained by Srinivas as the adoptability of similar values and cultures borrowed from the immediate higher caste groups.[26] However, such explanations which portray the Dalits as capable of only emulating the upper castes further deny Dalits their intellectual and political histories.

Mainstream feminist responses to assertions by Dalit feminists often result in the displacement of one difference by another, thus highlighting the dominance of neo-Buddhist women over Mang and Chambhar women. As has been argued by Rege, displacing one difference with another can only lead to a proliferation of differences; it leaves the assumptions of dominant frameworks unquestioned.[27] Ambedkar foregrounded alternatives for the entire Dalit community by embracing Buddhism in 1956. This provided Dalits with a new identity and meaning since historically it was the only religion which provided space to women based upon the values of equality, liberty and fraternity. Hence, Dalit feminists of Maharashtra, who imbibed the ideology of Buddhism, and who in the 1990s talked of the 'internal' and 'external' patriarchy of Dalit women, now claim to be Buddhist women.[28] This act of naming unleashes a certain category of Dalit feminist knowledge which forces these women to claim a unique territory of their thinking.

These Buddhist women belong to the Mahar caste. The relationship Mahar women have with Buddhism persuades us to reflect on whether any other sections of Dalit caste women recognise themselves as daughters of Ambedkar, as Buddhist women? The recent conversion of the Mang community to Buddhism is also making a historical difference and may transform the collective consciousness of the Dalits in the future. Nevertheless, certain sections of Dalit women who belong to the Mangs, Dhor and Chambhar, and some Mahar women in certain areas of Maharashtra, do follow Hinduism and Christianity.

The dialogue and difference that characterise the shifting meanings of practices and thinking of Mang and Mahar women reflect the need to untangle the power of caste and gender that undo their alliances. How do these women unsettle their existential predicaments that are decided by external non-Dalit patriarchy and internal Dalit patriarchy? This section presents the experiences of Mang and Mahar women to do justice to the commonalities that prevent them from forging solidarity and fight against their oppression. In a way, it departs from the reductionist mainstream notions that arrest the comparative approach between Mang and Mahar women and tries to ponder on the recursive facets of their life.

Under the Balutedari system, the occupational mobility of Mang and Mahar and other Dalits was structured through the caste hierarchy of the Hindu social order. Broadly, the Mahars discarded their traditional occupations based on caste after converting to Buddhism. The decision to leave stigmatised labour was founded in the anti-caste ideas of Ambedkar. Consequentially, this void of such caste-bound, denigrated occupations was chosen by Mang males and females. The questions related to the rapprochement and adoption of those forms of work were ingrained in Mahars' engagement with Buddhism and Mangs' affinity towards the Hindu religion.

New forms of stigmatising jobs

Mangs in general and Mang women in particular are caught in the ideology of caste, which prevents them from selecting occupations that do not possess the stereotypes of caste-based labour. For instance, Mang women still continue to make broom, basket and rope which have caste implications in both urban and rural areas. They also work as ragpickers and daily wage workers on construction sites. Mang and Mahar women who are agricultural labourers face major challenges due to the changing agrarian conditions of Maharashtra. The seasonal nature of their agrarian work forces them to migrate to cities in search of new occupations. Thus, they are drawn to new forms of stigmatising jobs, as domestic help/servants and sex-workers, for example. However, rural Mang women are not properly represented in government-related jobs and the social mobility of Mahar women is slightly higher. In the context of Mahar and Mang women, their shift to, say, a sweeper's job forces them to remain in the symbolic domain of caste-based labour and patriarchy. It is this division of labour, exploited by the upper castes, that has also created a social space of patronage and dependency. For instance, the labour of sweepers and scavengers is perceived as a form of pollution and despised by caste Hindus. Hence, the upper castes do not get involved in such professions or occupations. The Mahar and Mang women are compelled to such forms of work that are abhorred by non-Dalit men and women. In what ways do these categories of Dalit women confront the ideological grounds that contain them through stigmatised social locations?

Mahar women consider education as a tool to challenge caste-based stereotypes about Dalits and meritocracy. Mang women are highly educated and are conscious of the threats to their right to education. A Mahar girl said that Mahar men and women are patriarchal when it comes to the education of girls. According to her, Mahar women do share the patriarchal values that challenge the aspirations of Mahar girls and educated families discourage girls' education. A Mahar woman who works on a sugar cane farm said that she endures some kind of bonded labour in that farm to support her children's education. The representations of Mahar women in different stages of education are higher than Mang women. An educated Mang girl said that patriarchal familial values limit their choices vis-à-vis education and should be challenged by women from the respective communities.

However, it is observed that in urban spaces the interactions between these women are leading to a kind of alliance that transcends sub caste-based schisms. Mahar and Mang women jointly fight against domestic violence in their families. Mahar women create legal and educational awareness among Mang women and conscientise them to eradicate internal patriarchy. It can be argued that a particular political consciousness brings them together instead of their ascribed social markers.

Thus, the unequal dimensions that connect the aforementioned sections of Dalit women necessitate the theoretical possibilities of Dalit feminism. The following section discusses some of these.

Dalit feminist move to 'We Are All Where We Think'

This section derives its energy from Marx and Mignolo's positions, reflected in the title of this section. It emphasises the emergence of a solidarity that emanates from particular Mang and Mahar women's approach towards Buddhism. Mang women who have converted to Buddhism renew the possibilities of Buddhism to challenge the absolutist, patriarchal, neo-liberal brahmanic culture of Maharashtra. Thus, it registers a new ideological milieu which can resurrect the anti-caste brahmanic political culture in a rigorous way. This specific section of Mang and Mahar women who are aware of their roots of oppression within the community and outside it reinvigorates the spirit of Dalit feminism.

I argue that Dalit feminism thus offers a radical critique to the geopolitics of knowledge in a path charted by Marx and Engels and Walter Mignolo that has been unanswered by the left and the feminist groups in India.[29] These forms of thoughts are necessary for the demonstration of a caste, class and homogeneous conception of gender that oppresses the political understanding from below. Ruling ideas, for Marx, are the ideas of the ruling class. This class acts as the 'ruling material force of the society' and 'ruling intellectual force'. It also controls 'means of mental production' through its 'means of material production'. In other words, 'dominant material relations' get implicated in the ruling ideas. Those who do not possess 'means of mental production' become the objects of the dominant ideas of the ruling class. It structures their location as the producers as the 'natural centre of the world'. It initiated the foundation of a 'new nomos of the earth with a new observer and epistemic foundation'. Mignolo calls this 'second consequence', which happened when the world was divided and international law originated, and depends on the Columbian philosopher Santiago Castro-Gomez's conception of the 'hubris of zero point' to dwell on the aforementioned second consequence. Ironically, zero point epistemology is authentic and absent in 'geohistorical location' and 'biographical configuration of bodies of ideas.'[30] It also emboldens us to reflect on whether the specificity of Dalit women's assertions is being contained by the homogenising nature of hegemonising feminist theory-praxis.

At a conceptual level, Mignolo promises certain insights which can be pushed to recover the repression of Dalit feminist thought. A synoptic review of some of the foundational ideas of Mignolo may lead us to grapple with the crux of his main assertion. Mignolo links 'decolonial thinking' as an 'unintended consequence of the Carl Schmittian conceptualisation of global linear thinking' that exposed 'the history of the imperial partition of the world since the sixteenth century'.[31] For Mignolo, the notion of Schmitt's global linear thinking ended in the 'modern-colonial world order' and 'the imperial foundations of knowledge' and also shows the 'epistemic sovereignty' through the interventions of the pope to separate the planet to accommodate the interests of the Spanish and the Portuguese monarchs. The pope's gesture is theorised as epistemic-cum-political in nature. The 'epistemic sovereign' was scaled through the search for the dividing line of the Atlantic. The power of god over 'legality of decision' and regulating authority of 'rules and acts of knowing' shifted to the pope and monarchs. According to Schmitt, legal theologians in Salamanca during the mid-sixteenth century started debating the power of the pope and the drawbacks of 'divine and natural law' and favoured 'human law' which resulted in the secular nature of the debates during the eighteenth century. Mignolo reads Schmitt's global linear thinking as a coexisting element which resulted in the formation of international law and highlights that root of the modern-colonial world in international law. Thus, Schmitt mapped the 'new *nomos* of the earth' as derived from the 'historical foundation based on papal partition of the earth' and 'consequential international law'. Mignolo is aware of the reactionary strands that underlie Schmitt's perspectives.[32]

Geopolitics and epistemology

Abraham Ortelius' *Orbis Terrarum*, for Mignolo, represented planet earth on the world map as an entity which is seen from 'above' and it configured an observer who is above the Atlantic. Thus, the Atlantic was legitimised as the 'natural centre of the world'. It initiated the foundation of a 'new nomos of the earth with a new observer and epistemic foundation'. Mignolo calls this 'second consequence', which happened when the world was divided and international law originated, and depends on the Columbian philosopher Santiago Castro-Gomez's conception of the 'hubris of zero point' to dwell on the aforementioned second consequence. Ironically, zero point epistemology is authentic and absent in 'geohistorical location' and 'biographical configuration of bodies'. Geohistorical and biographical knowledge locations are concealed in the 'transparency' and 'universality' that are attached to the notion of zero point and positioned as 'grounding without ground in the mind and not in the brain and heart'. Forms of knowing and sensing that do not fall under the rubric of zero point are relegated to the position of myth, local knowledge, legend and folklore. Castro-Gomez considers the strategy of concealing the appropriation of local knowledge that is very much part of the universal expansion.[33] Mignolo regards 'zero point' as the scale with which to grade 'epistemic colonial difference' and 'epistemic imperial difference'. In this context, Mignolo proposes that the location of those whose position is low in the 'global epistemic order' can be captured through the premise 'I am where I think'.

The Mignolian position also reminds us that you are also dispossessed of your location associated with your thoughts. It transforms into 'we are all where we think'. It departs from the basic idea of the European system of knowledge: 'I think therefore I am'. Mignolo affirms that 'I am where I think' is fundamental in that it 'legitimises' all forms of thinking and 'delegitimises pretence that a singular and particular epistemology, geo-historically and biographically located is universal'. Mignolo exhorts us to interlinkages that exist between geopolitics and epistemology and biography and epistemology and describes the relocation from 'I think therefore I am' to 'I am where I think' as 'decolonising epistemology' that may lead to 'epistemic democratisation'.[34]

Mang and Mahar women from Maharashtra, who are caught in the recognition that their thinking is trapped between communitarian and brahmanic patriarchal forms, anticipate a particular genre of politics that unshackles Dalit women from feminist and other critical intellectual traditions that are not sensitive to proliferating tangible and intangible forms of violence in the arena of their rights. The question arises whether Dalit feminists can reach a point of epistemic democratisation in the Mignolian sense and challenge ruling class ideas in a Marxian sense?

Is 'reflexive solidarity' (in the Jody Deanian sense) in south Asian feminism sufficient to flagellate brahmanical, gendered patriarchal accumulation of knowledge? Reflective solidarity, for Dean, orients feminists to move away from 'mechanical solidarity' and reflects upon 'them'; this type of solidarity is not reduced to the 'masculine universe'. Deploying the notion of 'we feminists' that derives from the 'communicative' and 'performative' sense of 'we', reflective solidarity acquires an 'achieved' relation rather than an ascribed one. It leads to the feminist 'we' through open engagements that can transcend the ascribed, hierarchical power relations that stratify feminists. It is built on their interactions.[35] It questions the 'them' of that which is attributed by the male universe to that of the 'we feminists' open space. Is this form of reflexive solidarity that is latent in south Asian feminism possible where caste acquires monopoly over knowledge production?

Dalit feminist tradition has to rekindle some of the crucial ruptures in Dalit studies on the structures of knowledge formation and intellectuals in India. Social science discourse in India, for Guru, is stratified along the constructions of the privileged 'theoretical Brahmins' who have monopoly over the theoretical manoeuvres and 'empirical shudras', and whose questions are sidelined as empirical questions that include the diverse aspects of Dalits' lives. Therefore, Dalit theoretical feats are required to overthrow brahmanic hegemony over theory.[36] At an institutional level, women's studies was streamlined according to the state institutions to concentrate on the 'practical approach to improve the status of women in the country'. Such an approach culminated in the undermining of theoretical and academic priorities.[37] Dalit feminists must also meaningfully address the waning of the theoretical tradition, noted by feminist scholarship, to face their conceptual and ideological opposites.

Conclusions

Dalit feminist thought has the epistemic vantage location to challenge the authenticity of knowledge that is generated for the emancipation of the oppressed through pointing out the caste-cum-class privilege of the dominant intelligentsia and brahmanical institutional histories. What will be the academic status of Dalit feminism within the academic cultures that legitimise the culture of meritocracy? In other words, how does Dalit communities' thinking, which is oppressed through the ideologues of brahmanic academic tradition, fight with the prevalent exclusionary intellectual spaces? Does the Dalit feminist project have to establish a feminist philosophy of its own? Judith Butler, in one of her persuasive critiques of philosophy, argues that the nature of the 'philosophical' is judged by the authoritarian voices which exist within the institutionalised philosophical spaces and current social assertions and which move away from the ambit of existing hegemonic philosophy to that of cultural dialogues which unmask the othering of the philosophy. Butler cites the remarkable works by West and Gilroy to illustrate her debunking of the limits of dominant philosophy.[38] Dalit feminism can render the gendered-sociological critique of philosophy as well as the larger intellectual productions to generate particular Dalit feminist philosophy. At the same time, it can subvert the ideological moves of dominant feminist and other forms of thought that undervalue the epistemological contours of Dalit feminism. Such an intellectual act should not convert into the political patronage of Dalit women and Dalits by such hegemonic intellectuals. It must discard the Indian versions of de-classing which appropriates epistemological priorities of Dalit women and Dalits.

Dalit feminist knowledge can creatively engage with certain anti-brahmanic intellectual trends within sexual minorities' assertions. Sexual minorities in India generate a valid unravelling of the homophobic Indian polity. However, activism among them, which resulted in the repeal of Section 377, has failed to foster solidarity amongst Dalits, adivasis and religious minorities.[39] Is it possible for the diverse streams within the progressive left and feminist organisation to declare its brahmanic nature of leadership, theory and practice? The form of political economy operationalised through caste-cum-class and gender in India is challenged by Dalit feminism thus providing the possibility of recovering Dalit studies from its depoliticised institutionalisation.

Notes

1 This chapter has appeared as an article entitled 'Revitalising Dalit Feminism: Towards Reflexive Anti-Caste Agency of Mang and Mahar Women in Maharashtra', Review of Women's Studies, *Economic and Political Weekly*, Vol. XLVIII No. 18, May 4, 2013, pp. 37–43. Used with permission.

2 Gopal Guru, 'Dalit Women Talk Differently', *Economic and Political Weekly*, Vol. 30 No. 41/42, 1995, pp. 2548–50, 2548. Chapter 11 of this Reader; Sharmila Rege, 'Dalit Women Talk Differently: A Critique of "Difference" and Towards a Dalit Feminist Standpoint Position', *Journal of Vikas Adhyayan Kendra*, Vol. VI No. 2, 1988, pp. 5–23, 14. Chapter 12 of this Reader.
3 This study was conducted in Western Maharashtra, particularly Ahmadnagar and Sangli districts and Miraj and Atpadi tehsils to map the condition of rural and urban women from the Dalit community there. It is based on the ethnographic study of the lives and the vision of the aforementioned sections of women.
4 Nalini Rajan, 'Left-liberalism and Caste Politics', *Economic and Political Weekly*, Vol. 38 No. 24, 2003, pp. 2346–49, 2346–49.
5 Ajay Gudavarthy, 'Gandhi, Dalits and Feminists: Recovering the Convergence', *Economic and Political Weekly*, Vol. 43 No. 22, 2008: 83–89, pp. 85–86.
6 Ibid.
7 Nancy Fraser, 'Equality, Difference and Democracy: Recent Feminist Debates in the United States', in Jodi Dean(ed.), *Feminism and the New Democracy; Re-siting the Political*, New Delhi: Sage Publications, 1997, pp. 98–109, p. 99.
8 Ibid, p. 99.
9 Ibid, p. 108.
10 Ibid.
11 Gudavarthy, 'Gandhi, Dalits and Feminists', pp. 83–90; Rajan, 'Left-liberalism and Caste Politics'.
12 Aditya Nigam, 'Secularism, Modernity and Nation: Epistemology of the Dalit Critique', *Economic and Political Weekly*, Vol. 35 No. 48, 2000, pp. 4256–68, 4256.
13 M. S. S. Pandian, 'One Step Outside Modernity: Caste, Identity Politics and Public Sphere', *Economic and Political Weekly*, Vol. 37 No. 18, 2002, pp. 1735–41, 1735–41.
14 Nigam, 'Secularism, Modernity and Nation', p. 4262.
15 Ibid.
16 Kalpana Kannabiran, 'Sociology of Caste and the Crooked Mirror: Recovering B R Ambedkar's Legacy', *Economic and Political Weekly*, Vol. 44 No. 4, 2009, pp. 35–39.
17 J. Devika, 'Egalitarian Developmentalism, Communist Mobilisation and the Question of Caste in Kerala State, India', *The Journal of Asian Studies*, Vol. 69 No. 3, 2010, pp. 799–820.
18 This concept is first used by Nkiru Nzegwu in her essay 'O Africa: Gender Imperialism in Academia', 2004.
19 Oyeronke Oyewumi, 'Visualising the Body: Western Theories and African Subjects', in Oyeronke Oyewumi(ed.), *African Gender Studies: A Reader*, New York: Palgrave McMillan, 2005, pp. 3–21.
20 Ania Loomba and Ritty A. Lukose, 'South Asian Feminisms: Contemporary Interventions', in Ania Loomba and Ritty A. Lukose (ed.), *South Asian Feminisms*, Durham and London: Duke University Press, 2012, pp. 1–29, 1.
21 Ibid, p. 25.
22 Ulrike Strasser and Heidi Tinsman, 'Engendering World History', *Radical History Review*, Vol. 91, 2005, pp. 151–64, cited in Mrinalini Sinha, 'A Global Perspective on Gender: What's South Asia Got to Do With It?' in Ania Loomba and Ritty A. Lokose (eds.), *South Asian Feminism*, Durham and London: Duke University Press, 2012, pp. 356–73, 357.
23 Uma Chakravarti, *Gendering Caste: Through a Feminist Lens*, Calcutta: Stree, 2003, pp. 6, 7.
24 Vasant Moon (ed.), *Dr Babasaheb Ambedkar, Writings and Speeches*, Vol. 7, Bombay: Education Department, Government of Maharashtra, 1990, p. 26.
25 Babasaheb Ambedkar, 'Rise and Fall of Hindu Women', in *The Journal of Mahabodhi Society*, Nagpur: Sugat Prakashan, Calcutta, Reprint, 1950, pp. 6–48.
26 M. N. Srinivas, *Caste: Its 21st Century Avatar*, New Delhi: Penguin, 1996, pp. 1–21.
27 Sharmila Rege, *Writing Caste/Writing Gender: Narrating Dalit Women's Testimonies*, New Delhi: Zubaan, 2006, p. 4. See Chapter 5 of this Reader for its Introduction.
28 *Mukanayika Bolu Lagalya*, 2005. It is an annual magazine which brought out a special issue on Dhammakranti Suvarna Jayanti Mahila Sammelan, 2005. On October 10, 2005,

Dhamma Diksha Suvarna Jayati Buddha Mahila Sammelan was organised at Nagpur in which this discourse was debated.

29 Karl Marx and Friedrich Engels, *The German Ideology*, New Delhi: People's Publishing House, Reprint, 2010; Walter Mignolo, 'I Am Where I Think: Re-mapping the Order of Knowing', in Francoise Lionnet and Shu-mei Shi (ed.), *The Creolisation of Theory*, Durham and London: Duke University Press, 2011, pp. 159–92.
30 Marx and Engels, *The German Ideology*, p. 67.
31 Karl Schmitt, *The Nomos of the Earth in the International Law of Jus Publicum Europaeum*, New York: Telos, 2003, cited in Mignolo, 'I Am Where I Think', p. 159.
32 Ibid., pp. 161–63.
33 Castro-Gomez, Santiago Castro-Gomez, 'The Missing Chapter of Empire: Postmodern Reorganisation of Coloniality and Post-Fordist Capitalism', *Cultural Studies (Globalisation and the Decolonial Option, Special Issue)*, Vol. 21 No. 2–3, Santiago, 2007, pp. 428–48, cited in Mignolo, 'I Am Where I Think', p. 161.
34 Mignolo, 'I Am Where I Think', pp. 161–69.
35 Jodi Dean, 'The Reflective Solidarity of Democratic Feminism', in Jodi Dean (ed.), *Feminism and the New Democracy; Re-siting the Political*, New Delhi: Sage Publications, 1997, pp. 244–61, 260.
36 Gopal Guru, 'How Egalitarian Are the Social Sciences in India', *Economic and Political Weekly*, Vol. 37 No. 50, 2002, pp. 5003–9.
37 Mary E. John (ed.), *Women's Studies in India: A Reader*, New Delhi: Penguin Books, 2008, p. 16.
38 Judith Butler, 'Can the "Other" of Philosophy Speak?' in Cressida J. Heyes (ed.), *Philosophy and Gender: Critical Concepts in Philosophy*, Vol. 1, London and New York: Routledge, 2012, pp. 91–104.
39 Asley Tellis, 'Why I Can't Join the Party ...', *The Hindu*, July 12, 2009.

18

DALIT WOMEN'S EXPERIENCE

Toward a Dalit feminist theory[1]

Kanchana Mahadevan

> In order to explain the relationship between the discursive materiality of women's lives and feminism as a counterhegemonic discourse, we need to understand more specifically how articulation occurs.[2]

> There were doubts in our minds; what will we get out of interviews with these women? Still (we thought) why not note down the experiences of those women who had ventured out of their homes for a specific purpose?[3]

Experience has been the driving force of feminist thought from its early period to the contemporary. However, as critiques by Scott and Butler reveal that first-person experience cannot be accorded a foundational role in an unproblematic way.[4] It tends to deviate from the gendered narrative of feminism by evoking an ahistorical and disembodied concept of experience. Moreover, the authority of individual experience cannot be the basis of gendered solidarity, as experiences between women vary, often due to the intersections of community, race and class. These intersections also reveal hierarchies between women, whereby privileged women have exploitative stakes in the subordination of other underprivileged women.

Differences amongst women constitute a challenge to feminist solidarity (de Beauvoir) grounded in experience, as women do not form a homogeneous group. Heterogeneity of experience apart, the relationship between first-person experience and its articulation in discourse is tenuous. For as a social movement, feminism depends upon representing women's experience; yet it is the women who occupy a hegemonic position on the mainstream of sociopolitical axes often articulate experience. Those with power – of race, class and caste – tend to represent their own position and that of the socially vulnerable. As Guru argues in context of caste in India such hierarchy is grounded on exploitation: Women from privileged castes often make professional use of the first-hand experiences of those from underprivileged castes in the name of representing them to which they have easy access and who they claim to represent.[5] Thus, it is not simply a question of diversity of experiences among women. The lack of a natural bond of community between women and the complexity of women's experiences (given intersectionality) raise crucial questions for representation that include: Can those who are privileged represent the experiences of those who are not? What are some of the arguments against this? If the privilege can represent the underprivileged, what are the grounds for doing so? To what degree is such representation valid? How does it disempower those who 'own' their experience represent them?

This chapter attempts to reclaim the notion of experience from an intersectional point of view, taking differences and exploitation between women into account. It situates itself in the context of the feminist debate on experience to respond to the criticism that mainstream Indian feminism has overlooked the life-worlds of socially vulnerable women, especially those disenfranchised by caste. It argues that discourses about the life-worlds of underprivileged women – fractured by caste and class – would have to reinterpret the notion of experience from historical, embodied and intersectional dimensions. It explores the possibility of remedying what Hennessy has termed as the gap between women's experiences and feminist theorising through practices of experience and representation.[6]

Experience in feminist research

Following de Beauvoir, it takes a woman to philosophise as a feminist, wherein first-hand experience of patriarchal oppression motivates and lends credibility to feminist theorising oriented to social change.[7] Experience gives women the agency to theorise themselves and the worlds in which they live. Foregrounding experiences from the standpoint of women became necessary because as de Beauvoir argues, women experience the world from their specific inhabited habitat of femininity – a situation in which they are often made aware of their gendered subjectivity. In contrast, a man does not experience the world from the specific location of masculine gender, but rather assumes that the singularity of his situation is universal; hence, a man does not theorise his condition as singular.[8] The appeal to experience, thus, becomes a key aspect of feminist thought. It has been crucial to feminist writings across a wide spectrum of theoretical positions as Harding and Hintikka, de Lauretis, Harding and Hartsock and others reveal.[9]

The gendering of disciplines such as philosophy, science, literature and the like is based on introducing the neglected dimension of women's experiences.[10] As a foil against the history of erasure, every woman is viewed as an authority of her own life, with a sense of self-worth. Consequently, feminist research believes in allowing equal significance to all experiences. Feminist research takes women's lives, specifically their authority over their own experiences, as an empirical point of reference; but, it nevertheless distances itself from such experiences to interpret, theorise and critique at the discursive level.[11] Experience captures the practices in which women are involved, so that its theorisation is rooted in women's *praxis*. Feminist thought does not fetishise women's experience as an abstract essential concept; it rather historicises, pluralises and contextualises experience within the theoretical framework of being committed to women's equality in the enterprise of institutional research and knowledge.[12]

Moreover, for feminist researchers experience is not a taken for granted given that is available with ease.[13] It arises through reflection and consciousness when women participate in movements for social change.[14] Conversely, feminist movements also gather and coalesce women's experiences through their interpretations and narrations. The latter could take the form of first person narratives or dialogues. One could term these as 'experiential expertise'.[15] Following Hennessy, standpoint theorists such as Harding who endeavour to include women's lives in scientific research have upheld the authority of such expertise. Although they do not use the term 'experience' (since standpoint theory is also a critique of feminist empiricism), they do consider women's lives as authorising their theories.[16] Moreover, for standpoint theory, women's lives are not merely descriptions, but also have normative undertones. Thus, there is an 'objective positionality'[17] that distinguishes them from the ambivalence of 'discursive positionality'.[18]

Yet, 'experiential expertise' is not the raw sense data of empiricism, as it is committed to the position of feminist politics and requires contextual conceptualisation. Moreover, since feminism is critical of the solipsistic subject, experience is not for the feminist a unique individual private property that is immediately given. Rather, it is in principle capable of being shared, since women's collective experiences are at stake in transforming an androcentric academic world. In the academic context, well-entrenched knowledge systems cannot be sufficiently challenged by expressing personal testimonies or aspirations. Since such self-expressions attempt to introduce women as producers and creators of knowledge, their role has to be interpreted to speak to institutionalised systems of knowledge. This in turn requires a professional researcher who can dwell on the experiences expressed in testimonies to mediate and filter them in the course of articulating them in more general modes. Hence, what Hennessy terms as 'discursive positionality' introduces another kind of expertise in feminist research, namely the 'presentational',[19] in which the researcher engages with the experiences of others and represents them – albeit from a third-person point of view.

The ability to present and represent is valuable because the researcher brings the experience of women to wider audiences in institutional and non-institutional contexts. The researcher is formally oriented with critical and organisational skills to select, focus and discursively bring out the experience in question. The researcher also has the ability to place the experience in wider contexts with access to publication and funds.[20] Besides such formal skills the researcher also needs to cultivate the informal art of listening to the participant with 'a capacity for insight, empathy, and attentive caring'.[21] While listening, the researcher allows his or her participant to speak – without intervening in the process with judgements and personal bias.[22] By speaking, participants are able to think over and convey what they have experienced to the researcher who in turn theorises it. The speaker too has a reflexive-reflective relationship with her experiences, where she or he can connect, refine and reorganise the experience while narrating it. Thus, while talking about his or her experience, the speaker simultaneously shapes it. The researcher – ideally at least – suspends his or her own subjective experiences to listen, interpret and cohesively articulate the experiential data of the participant in research. 'There is no "authentic" unpolluted female experience for these thinkers'.[23] Research is, thus, a process of collaboration between the participant speaker and the researcher who listens, a process in which both learn from each other.

Thus, feminist research on experience does not merely view it as data to be stored. Rather there is a conscious focus on testimonies so that they can travel across from non-institutional contexts to institutional ones to correct the gender bias in research.[24] Feminist research improves women's lives as its participants reflect on the quality of their lives, to interpret them and examine the choices that are opened. Thus, for instance, Gilligan's 29 research participants arrived at their own meaning giving roles in the course of discussing their pregnancies with her.[25] Rather than just express themselves or state so-called facts, the participants developed a critical consciousness towards themselves in the course of narrating their predicaments.

As the preceding discussion shows, the divide between experience and presentation/representation is not necessarily wide. Personal experience needs presentational ability, which is constituted by language and interpretation to reach out to those who are not its subjects. Moreover, presentational expertise is one of continuous discussion, as well as, 'negotiation and critical reflection' between researchers and their participants.[26] However, the ideal conscious relationship between the experiential and presentational poles of feminist research does not always prevail. Presentational ability has to face several challenges when it is employed to represent the experiences of other women besides the researcher. These challenges arise from gender's historical and contextual intersection with other social matrices such as caste, class and race. These intersections introduce hierarchies and relations of power – often at an unconscious level – into the course of research. Feminist researchers in academic contexts are often privileged women who voluntarily undertake the task of representing experiences of those who are not. This is the outcome of the movement(s) itself that has had a largely homogeneous base of privileged bourgeois women in leadership positions, until recently. In the context of Western feminism, the fact that researchers in institutions are for a large part white, heterosexual women has been visibilised by 'unorthodox'[27] feminists since the past two decades or so.[28] In a parallel Indian context, the hidden bias in the mainstream feminist researcher's privileged caste background in the course of representing experiences of women from socially impoverished ones has been exposed by interventions that take differences between women into account.[29]

What Hennessy has termed as the gap between women's lived experiences and their theoretical articulations is one of the socially privileged feminist researcher who patronises her participant/speaker while representing her and professionalises research in doing so. This gap has to be addressed because feminist research is deeply committed to transforming women's lives by rooting itself in them.

In order to remedy this gap, the late 1980s witnessed the Indian women's movement making space (though deeply inadequate) for women's narratives from underprivileged backgrounds. Dalit[30] feminist testimonies, often in the form of first person narratives,[31] challenged the homogeneous idea of 'woman' shared by all women.[32] Their testimonies revealed how their everyday lives differed from those of non-Dalit women due to their being forced to labour for their community rather than their own family. Moreover, their labour is not just monotonous, but also stigmatised. They are compelled to work in the public sphere – albeit in ways that are frowned upon by society – in caste-based occupations. Thus, they did not confront the question of choosing to enter the public realm in search of work, unlike non-Dalit women.[33] First person narratives clearly play a role in expanding the canvas of feminist thought – particularly demonstrating how the challenges posed by caste identity reveal the absence of homogeneity among women – that women are different.

The feminist debate in the Indian context has to an extent acknowledged the intersectionality of gender and caste by foregrounding the notion of lived experience. The latter has been authenticated for example in several important texts of women's autobiographies.[34] However, these works do not derive their wider relevance only by being rooted in the foundation in first-person experience. As Geetha[35] and Guru[36] note, experience cannot have the last word, but is on the contrary a starting point for reflexivity and reflection. Moreover, one cannot side-step the uncomfortable problem of the implicit hierarchy of representing experience from a third-person point of view. Instead, the possibility of an egalitarian relationship between the first-person and third-person perspectives on experience needs exploration. For the experiences of Dalit women has meaning both for non-Dalit women as well in the search for transformatory practices leading to an egalitarian social world. As Paik notes, Dalit women's perspectives open up the possibility for more democratic and inclusive approaches to politics and society.[37] In this endeavour, the feminist philosophical debate on experience in the West can perhaps be brought into contact with difference feminism in the Indian context. Moreover, the very idea of experience has to be interrogated further.

Critique of experience-theory dichotomy

In the Indian feminist context, there has been a shift to the authenticity of first-person experience to remedy the neglect of women from underprivileged caste groups. This assumes a one to one fit between women's lives/experiences and their narrations.[38] In reading the subject position of women exclusively and genuinely through their first hand experience – without putting the latter in larger contexts – one subscribes to a residual empiricist notion of experience as a bare sensation that is not mediated through culture or language – given its stress on the authenticity of women's experience. Such a gesture towards the 'exceptional nature of Dalit experience'[39] is troubling because it does not situate experience in the larger context of structural violence; consequently shirking from the responsibility of dismantling the entangled hierarchy of caste and gender. Moreover, such an exclusive focus on first-hand experience can lead to a split between an authentic victimhood of the speaker and insensitivity of the listener as responses.[40] This becomes a matter of simple difference, which does not take the hierarchy of intersection into consideration. It does not for instance, engage with the specific manner in which mainstream feminism, consciously or unconciously, neglects the caste question because of its dependence on Dalit women's labour. Privileged women often enter the public sphere to become feminists by employing socially vulnerable women as domestic help.[41] Following Geetha, personal testimonies by Dalit women are a resource for seeing how their subjectivity constituted in contexts of humiliation— which one might add are normalised— is also one of survival and resistance through 'alliances' that they work out with women and men from privileged castes.[42] To add to this point, Dalit women's testimonies also open up the opportunity for women from privileged castes to engage in self-criticism and question the ground of their own privilege. One needs to examine the extent to which Dalit women's labour has been reinforced by the interests of privileged non-Dalit women so that there is a self-examination by the latter provoking a rethinking of 'women's work' a central part of feminism. One needs to analyse the relationship of exploitation between women who experience the world in diverse ways – a relationship that could be inconvenient – since it questions the privileged ground of mainstream feminism – but would have to be nevertheless taken into account in the resistance to patriarchy. As Geetha maintains, 'Instead, what is continuously voiced is a register of angry lament and defiance, a voicing of experience, the rawness of which is called upon to attest to its truth'.[43] Additionally, as Paik notes, Dalit women's testimonies can be understood as non-linear struggles to acquire agency against the victimhood of caste and gender.[44] She rightly argues that Dalit women's personal narratives reveal that is not possible to assimilate their lives under a simplistic rubric of 'Indian feminism'[45] for they have a common cause with Dalit men against casteism that reinforces gendered oppression.

It is because of the difficulties of such authenticity that the appeal to personal experience has been called into question in feminist debates by thinkers as diverse as Scott, Hennessy and Butler.[46] Their prime contention is that it does not take the heterogeneity of women into consideration,[47] for 'woman' becomes a universal objective category accessible through experience. Consequently, the dualism between male and female is foregrounded and other social categories that constitute female subjectivity – such as race, caste and class – are obliterated to overlook differences between women. Dalit women experience both caste and gender oppression – their caste location makes them more vulnerable to gendered violence.[48] Further, as argued earlier the problems of Dalit women from the point of view of gender are not the same as those of women from privileged castes. Resisting dowry or asserting the right to reproduction were not obstacles for many of them, as much as the lack of access to government resources[49] or the resistance to closing country liquour (arrack) store, which was not taken too seriously by the mainstream women's movement.[50] The differences between women was not even acknowledged by organisations such as the National Women's Conference formed in 1982, which undertook an investigation of Dalit women only in 1994.[51] All of which makes suspect the simplistic homogeneous sisterhood among women founded on a common set of experiences.

But then as critics of personal experience have argued these differences, which are deeply entrenched in a hierarchical order, cannot automatically create a critical consciousness of resistance through autobiographical repetition. By merely affirming the subject position of an oppressed woman in an objective way or expressing her agony, one does not question the specific social structures that reinforce such experience of oppression. On the contrary, the status quo can be reiterated through such a first-person mode. These difficulties notwithstanding, one cannot allow the notion of experience to be brushed aside. Against this one could maintain (with Foss and Foss) that the utilisation of personal experience has subversive potential in opening up new ways of theorising women's lives. It overcomes the absolutism and hierarchy of the expert knower position, since experience is open to all. It reposes a sense of confidence in women that their point of view has a place in research. But these assumptions imply that the exceptionalism of the first person account be overcome by acknowledging the aspect of 'presentational expertise'. Since experience is never bare, its capacity to be presented and represented – either in the first person or the third (through the researcher)–is inextricably woven with the very possibility of experience. It can only be communicated on such a ground. Since presentation and representation are closely linked to experience, the researcher and participant subject (who narrates personal experience) are not necessarily stuck in an unequal relation. Rather they can participate in the research process as equals.[52] The researcher may have skills that give the participant new insight on her narratives so that she arrives at a critical consciousness through new interpretations.

Yet the Socratic researcher has a vantage point in the relationship with the participant who supplies the content of experience. However, the problem is that it is tilted towards the researcher who plays the Socratean role of illuminating the experience of the participant. Further, the participant's experiential expertise and the researcher's presentational expertise are qualitatively different from each other. Since experience is not constituted by language, thought or culture, the problem of relating the two sets of expertise becomes acute. This is also because experience itself is a singular event on this view to which the one who experiences has first-person access. Indeed, as Guru has observed this hierarchy is central to the inegalitarianism of social science practice in India.[53] As he argues, the gulf between theory and experience in the Indian academy points towards an intellectual inegalitarianism. He diagnoses the persistence of caste privilege in this dichotomy between social scientists who do theory and others who labour for the collection of empirical data. Guru argues that the prestige attached to theory in India emerges from privileged castes dominating theoretical work, while lived experience is confined to those who lack privilege. He argues that elite theoreticians in India were able to consolidate their position due to historical privilege, access to institutions and fellowships and the tyranny of language. Consequently, the experiences of their underprivileged colleagues became mere illustrative examples. Members of the oppressed castes, Guru maintains, got stuck with empiricism partly out of force and partly out of choice. The absence of historical privilege confined them to mechanical, unpleasant and often brutal labour on a routine basis. This did not, according to Guru, give them time to reflect on their condition. They choose practical routes like poetry, formal politics and activist work (to collect facts and figures to prove atrocities) that were based on the framework of empiricism and 'professionalised' their interests.[54] Guru notes that they also made a conscious intellectual choice towards poetry and empiricism for various reasons including (1) unique experiences do not require theoretical intervention; (2) privileged access to first-person experience need not be theoretically spelled out; and (3) abstract thinking is socially irrelevant and alienating. Each of these assumptions compartmentalise Dalit lived experiences, which can be shared through theoretical intervention. Guru aptly calls for a Dalit theory that overturns the caste hierarchy between theory and experience/practice by combining scholarship with social commitment.

Experiential agency mandates social vulnerable groups to move beyond the immediacy of unique experience to theoretically represent themselves. It is because they have not theorised their own experiences, that Dalit agency gets undermined with the patronising tone of brahmanical scholars who speak on their behalf, underplay their discursive capacity by limiting them to examples used in their theories and remained outside the ambit of the lived experience of oppression. Mainstream Marxist and liberal categories did not theorise the specificity of Dalit experience.[55] Feminist theory also took advantage of caste vulnerability of underprivileged women. According to Guru, women from privileged castes research and write theory by culling experiences of underprivileged women who narrate their autobiographies. However, going beyond Guru, there is the problem of privileged women also exploiting the labour of Dalit women for leading feminist lives by entering the public domain. Feminist theory in India has tended to overlook such exploitation, despite its emphasis on being different from Western feminism.[56] Feminist theory is, thus, an expression of privileged and reification which is predicated on the divide between presentational expertise and experiential expertise. The challenge posed by Guru is as follows: What authorises the researcher to communicate the oppression of her participant? Similarly, how does a Dalit woman represent her oppression? The two questions have to be addressed as related so that the reified relation between them changes to one of equality. These allied questions are urgent for contemporary feminism where privilege amongst women allows some women to do theory and others to experience oppression. These questions require a reinterpretation of the notion of experience itself, where the notions of authority and ownership (which Guru assumes is necessary) associated with them are challenged.

Living experience, sharing experience

Proponents of women's experiences as the starting point of research, have not theorised the term experience adequately. Scott has gestured towards its alternative theorisation of experience, by suggesting that experience has to be examined through the matrices of discourse and history.[57] Thus, the notion of experience itself and the manner in which structures of power leave their traces on them have to be held together in any analysis. But then this account of experience veers in the direction of extreme constructivism, repeating the errors of the foundational approach in taking discourse and history as givens.[58] It also evokes an ahistorical subject of experience. One might add to Kruks' criticism that the democratic gains of first-person narratives are sidestepped in the direction of a high theoretical account, which leaves no room for non-elite women – such as Dalit women in the Indian context. Consequently, the possibility of the researcher and participant having an egalitarian relation is also left unexplored.

Scott's critique of taking raw experience as the foundation of theory has however, demonstrated that one cannot attach notions of ownership, authenticity and authority to experience without qualification. Yet going beyond the feminist critiques of personal experience, without losing its democratic intent, requires that experience be reclaimed. Although feminist scholarship has drawn attention to the significance of experience, it has not quite paused to spell out the very notion of experience. A turn to Dewey, which in the context of Dalit feminism's critique of Indian feminism is motivated by the need to comprehend Ambedkar's legacy,[59] is instructive.

Dewey observes that the exclusive association of experience with cognition emerged with modern empiricism.[60] As a result it came to signify a subject's first-hand privileged unique access to a state of mind/feeling that could not really be shared with all. This is an objective passive model of experience, which Dewey terms as 'sensationalistic empiricism'[61] in which the acquisition of experience was a passive process of responding to the world as it impinged on the sense organs. It did not add anything to the world that it describes. A bare sensation cannot really provide justification for complex descriptions about the social world. Dewey makes the active practically engaged notion of experience the condition for passive experience and propositional knowledge, thus, relating the subjective and the objective. Yet if one wants to describe the world actively as Dalit women's testimonies do, one should have propositional knowledge about people's lives. This needs discourse, history and also embodiment.

In contrast, the ancient approach to experience was laden with the subjective and the practical 'ways of doing and being done to'.[62] Experience was understood in the context of culture and tradition as an active-passive phenomenon. An experienced person was someone who had the know-how or skilled knowledge in doing an activity in the world for a period of time. Such an experience, which is conservative, subjective, practical may not generate theory – for those who are engaged in it may not be able to verbalise it. Yet, it has the potential to do so, when one reflects on it – either from a first person or second person point of view. For Dewey then, 'The measure and value of an experience lies in the perception of relationships or the continuities to which it leads up'.[63]

Returning to the feminist contribution, Dewey's active experience is voiced by de Beauvoir in her notion of lived experience, which is influenced by Husserl and

Merleau Ponty.[64] Although she takes the concrete lived/ experiential dimension of people's lives as her point of departure, de Beauvoir does not treat the experiential dimension as that which is owned and authored by a single individual. For her empiricism divides consciousness from its object/world.[65] de Beauvoir's own relationship to her participants in research was not merely one of presenting their experiences faithfully. As several passages in the *Second Sex* reveal, de Beauvoir's account of women's lived experience – from formative years (of childhood, adolescence), to adulthood (marriage, motherhood or sex-workers) – is based on her relating her own personal experiences with the data she acquired as a researcher from other participants.[66] Hence, for de Beauvoir 'the meaning of an object is not a concept graspable by pure understanding. Its meaning is the object as it is disclosed to us in the overall relation we sustain with it, and which is action, emotion, and feeling'.[67]

Taking de Beauvoir's insight to the research situation, the researcher has to engage with the data of the participant in research through the so-called subjective lens of empathy, care and feeling. Collaboration between the researcher and the participant becomes possible because they inhabit common spaces through embodiment. Experiences of the world become possible by 'frequenting' it.[68] By residing in locations and situations or environments, one's body thrown in with other bodies (of other people and other things) to be touched by them. Thus, by living (not objectifying) and experiencing one's body in intersubjective (and not isolated) contexts the gap between subjects and objects is minimised. Rather than a subject-object distance, experience is an empathetic bond. It is, thus, an expression of care that has the potential to challenge a hierarchical order. Thus, while listening to the narration of the lived oppression of a Dalit woman, the privileged feminist woman would lose her separate isolated subjectivity. She will be able to recognise agency in the voice of someone who does not have the access to categories of high theory. In doing so, the privileged feminist would also be critically interrogating her own relationship of power to the Dalit woman-in terms of the opportunities and access to institutions that are available to her due to caste/class privilege. In the course of recognising her own implication in undemocratic social structures, the privileged feminist researcher would also learn to question and resist institutions that enable her by disabling her Dalit participant.[69]

A woman who articulates her trauma in public overcomes her own alienation from social structures to spell out a critique of institutions and her own aspirations. The critical relation between researcher and participant would then be acknowledged as one of conflict of interests, negotiation and collaboration. This is because experience is never an incorrigible starting point – but is rather a dialectical process of collective articulation by persons who have conflicting social locations. Experience as a lived phenomenon is never solely owned or authored by an individual. Hence, since the egocentric subject is abandoned in seriously listening to another's suffering or narrating one's own in public, one can speak about the pain of the other. For such an experience is never fully given nor is it authentic or complete. On the contrary, personal experience opens up other experiences. Hence, experience is a communication between the subject and the object – where the two are engaged. Embodied experience is also a reminder that there is a politics of experience – where the latter can never be an authentic given.

Lived experience as Dewey and de Beauvoir note, reveals that experience is both, objective and subjective, personal and collaborative, immediate and mediated, as well as, singular and universal. It is also a process of sensitisation towards one's own self and towards the other. For de Beauvoir the methodology of the researcher has to be heterogeneous in order to integrate the contradictions of the subjective and objective aspects of being in the world.[70] She brings her own personal experience into contact with those of her participants to illuminate the condition of women. Thus, there is no 'objective data' of experience, on the contrary, de Beauvoir connects the objective 'presentational expertise' and the subjective 'experiential expertise' through discourse. The fissure between experience and discourse that perplexes Hennessy can be dissolved if experience is acknowledged as neither authentic nor pure in the spirit of Dewey and de Beauvoir.

Lived experience is a web of the specific and the abstract in which both reason and affect play a role with 'ethical, political as well as philosophical implications'.[71] Besides opening up the collaborative space for women's discourse through the self or the researcher and the other or the participant it explored the ambiguities of consciousness raising in the world at large, the possibility of violence in transforming society and responsibility among several other themes.

Extending Dewey's and de Beauvoir's perspective on experience to 'presentational expertise', the researcher and the participant are entwined in a world that is made common through their embodiment. Their experience is not a ready-made given but an active process of collective agency which is embodied and temporal. Such a heterogeneous notion of experience allows for an egalitarian relationship between the researcher and the participant, who are not foreign to each other when they communicate, empathise and commune. Thus, the shared nature of experience allows for the researcher to take the point of view of the participant and vice versa. It is precisely such sharing – which presupposes embodiment – that allows feminists to undertake the emancipatory task of resisting caste privilege – which hinders feminist emancipation. Further, such sharing also makes it possible for men to be feminists. Speaking for the other, as much as, speaking for oneself are interrelated processes that combine experience and presentation in order to represent.

Notes

1 This chapter is a slightly modified form of an article entitled 'Experience and Representation: Beyond Hierarchy' that was published in *Labrys, etudes feminists/ estudos feministas* No. 27, January–June 2015, pp. 1–20. Retrieved from http: www.labrys.net.br. Used with permission. The revised version has benefitted from comments from Tom Bailey and Brunella Antomarini.
2 R. Hennessy, *Materialist Feminism and the Politics of Discourse*, New York and London: Routledge, 1993, p. 77.
3 U. Pawar and M. Moon, *We Also Made History: Women in the Ambedkarite Movement*, New Delhi: Zubaan, [2006] 2014, p. 38.

4 J. Scott, 'Experience', in Judith Butler and Joan W. Scott (eds.), *Feminists Theorize the Political*, London and New York: Routledge, 1992; J. Butler, *Bodies that Matter: On the Discursive Limits of Sex*, London: Routledge, 1993.
5 G. Guru, 'Egalitarianism and the Social Sciences in India', his Gopal Guru and Sudar Sarukkai (eds.), *The Cracked Mirror*, New Delhi: Oxford University Press, 2012.
6 Hennessy, *Materialist Feminism and the Politics of Discourse*, p. 74.
7 S. de Beauvoir, *The Second Sex*, translated by Constance Borde and Sheila Malovany-Chevallier, London:Vintage, 2010, pp. 3–5.
8 de Beauvoir was writing in the context of 1940s in Europe before the advent of masculinities studies, which emerged as a response to feminism.
9 S. Harding and M. Hintikka, 'Introduction', in Sandra Harding and Hintika Merryl (eds.), *Discovering Reality: Feminist Perspectives on Epistemology, Metaphysics, Methodology and Philosophy of Science*, Dordrecht: D. Reidel, 1983; de Lauretis, 'Feminist Studies/Critical Studies: Issues, Terms and Contents', in Theresa de Lauretis (ed.), *Feminist Studies/Critical Studies*, Basingstoke: Macmillan, 1988; S. Harding, *Whose Science? Whose Knowledge? Thinking from Women's Lives*, Ithaca: Cornell University Press, 1991; N. Hartsock, 'Experience, Embodiment, and Epistemologies', *Hypatia*, Vol. 21 No. 2, 2006, pp. 178–83.
10 K.A. Foss and S. Foss, 'Personal Experience as Evidence in Feminist Scholarship', *Western Journal of Communication*, Vol. 58, Winter, p. 39.
11 Hennessy, *Materialist Feminism and the Politics of Discourse*, p. 67.
12 Ibid.
13 Foss and Foss, 'Personal Experience as Evidence in Feminist Scholarship', pp. 39–40; Diana Mulinari, and Kerstin Sandell. 1999. 'Exploring the Notion of Experience in Feminist Thought', *Acta Sociologica*, Vol. 42 No. 4, 1999: 287–97, pp. 288–89.
14 See Molinari and Sandell, 1999, for an account of consciousness raising movements in creating a feminist consciousness about experience and a survey of the feminist debate on experience.
15 Foss and Foss, 'Personal Experience as Evidence in Feminist Scholarship'.
16 Hennessy, *Materialist Feminism and the Politics of Discourse*, p. 68.
17 Ibid.
18 Ibid.
19 The expressions "experiential expertise" and "presentational expertise" are derived from Foss and Foss, 'Personal Experience as Evidence in Feminist Scholarship', p. 40.
20 Foss and Foss, 'Personal Experience as Evidence in Feminist Scholarship', p. 40.
21 Ibid., p. 41.
22 Ibid., pp. 40–41.
23 Molinari and Sandell, 1999, p. 289.
24 Foss and Foss, 'Personal Experience as Evidence in Feminist Scholarship', p. 42.
25 C. Gilligan, *In a Different Voice: Psychological Theory and Women's Development*, Cambridge, MA: Harvard University Press, 1982.
26 Foss and Foss, 'Personal Experience as Evidence in Feminist Scholarship', p. 41.
27 This term counters the "feminist orthodoxies" of mainstream privileged women. See G. Lewis and M. Storr, 'Contesting Feminist Orthodoxies', *Feminist Review*, Vol. 54, 2005, pp. 1–2.
28 For overviews, see for instance, M. C. Lugones and E. Spelman, 'Have We Got a Theory for You! Feminist Theory, Cultural Imperialism and the Demand for "the Woman's Voice"', *Women's Studies International Forum*, Vol. 6, 1983, pp. 573–81; Hennessy, *Materialist Feminism and the Politics of Discourse*, pp. 100–38; Chandra Talpade Mohanty, 'Feminist Encounters: Locating the Politics of Experience', in Michele Barrett and Anne Phillips (eds.), *Destabilizing Theory: Contemporary Feminist Debates*, Cambridge: Polity Press, 1992, pp. 74–92.
29 For a detailed account, see Turner, 2014; U. Pawar and M. Moon (eds.), *We Also Made History: Women in the Ambedkarite Movement*, translated and introduced. by Wandana Sonalkar, New Delhi: Zubaan Academic, 2014; G. Guru, 'Dalit Women Talk Differently', in Anupama Rao (ed.), *Gender and Caste*, New Delhi: Women Unlimited, 2005; S. Paik, 'The Rise of *New* Dalit Women in Indian Historiography', *History Compass* e12491,

2018. Retrieved fromhttps://doi.org/10.1111/hic3.12491 accessed on 20/3/2019; S. Rege, 'A Dalit Feminist Standpoint', in Anupama Rao (ed.), *Gender and Caste*, New Delhi: Women Unlimited, 2005; S. Rege, 'Writing Caste, Writing Gender: Dalit Women's Testimonies', in Mary E. John (ed.), *Women's Studies in India: A Reader*, New Delhi: Oxford University Press, 2008; S. Rege, 'Introduction: Towards a Feminist Reclamation of Dr. Bhimrao Ramji Ambedkar', in Sharmila Rege (ed.), *Against the Madness of Manu: B.R. Ambedkar's Writings on Brahminical Patriarchy*, New Delhi: Navayana, 2013. However, this question has not been adequately explored in feminist contexts in India, despite the critique of white women's feminism in the Western context. Paik's writings pioneer an analogous critique of Indian feminism in recent contexts (see Paik, 'The Rise of *New* Dalit Women in Indian Historiography').
30 This term is currently used to signify groups and individuals who were formally branded as 'untouchables' in the Hindu social order. See Pawar and Moon, *We Also Made History*; A. Rao, 'Introduction: Caste, Gender and Indian Feminism', in Anupama Rao (ed.), *Gender and Caste*, New Delhi: Women Unlimited, 2005, for an account.
31 Rege, 'Writing Caste, Writing Gender'.
32 This chapter by no means assumes that Dalit women's feminist agency is confined to autobiography or first hand testimonies. On the contrary, it assumes that autobiographies – especially in the Dalit feminist context-have a distinct role in ushering in an awareness of neglected cultural and historical memory. Autobiographies such as those of Baby Kamble's, *The Prison We Broke*, Hyderabad: Orient Blackswan, 2008; Urmila Pawar's, *The Weaver of My Life: A Dalit Woman's Memoir* Kolkata: Stree, 2008, which differ in many ways, question both Brahminism and patriarchy. Indeed, Kamble's was a pioneering attempt to name the specificity of patriarchal oppression faced by Dalit women. There is a rich substantive range of Dalit women's interventions in mainstream and feminist politics, society and culture. Further, the new generation of Dalit women writers such as Pradnya Pawar, Chaya Koregaonkar and Shilpa Kamble define themselves as Ambedkarite, rather than "Dalit" to get past the constraints of identity politics (M. Pandit, 'How Three Generations of Dalit Women Writers Saw Their Identities and Struggle?' 2017. Retrieved from https://indianexpress.com/article/gender/how-three-generations-of-dalit-women-writers-saw-their-identities-and-struggle-4984202/ accessed on 25/4/2019; S. Paik, '*Amchya Jalmachi Chittarkartha* (The Bio-scope of our lives): Who Is My Ally?' *Economic and Political Weekly*, Vol. XLIV No. 40, 2009, pp. 39–47). See Paik, 2018 for a detailed account of Dalit women's struggles to become agents against the double-exploitation of caste and gender.
33 V. Geetha, 'Dalit Feminism: Where Life-worlds and Histories Meet', in Kavita Panjabi and Paromita Chakravarti (eds.), *Women-Contesting Culture, Changing Frames of Gender Politics in India*, Kolkata: Stree and Women's Studies, Jadavpur University, 2012.
34 See for example, Kamble, *The Prison We Broke*; Pawar, *The Weaver of My Life*.
35 Geetha, 'Dalit Feminism', p. 247.
36 Against Rege's claim 'A Dalit Feminist Standpoint', Guru does not privilege experience over theory. See Guru, 'Egalitarianism and the Social Sciences in India'.
37 Paik, Shailaja. 2018. 'The Rise of *New* Dalit Women in Indian Historiography', *History Compass* e12491. Retrieved from https://doi.org/10.1111/hic3.12491 accessed on 20/3/2019, p. 1
38 Hennessy, *Materialist Feminism and the Politics of Discourse*, p. 69.
39 Ibid., p. 247.
40 See Rege, 'Writing Caste, Writing Gender'.
41 See J. Tronto, 'The "Nanny" Question in Feminism', *Hypatia*, Vol. 17 No. 2, 2002, pp. 34–51; Ehrenreich and Hochschild 2004 for detailed accounts of this complex relationship. Such accounts have been neglected in the Indian feminist context, where maids from underprivileged castes routinely work in privileged women's houses. Further, such work has been legitimised by the caste system.
42 Geetha, 'Dalit Feminism', p. 246.
43 Ibid.

44 Shailaja Paik 'The Rise of *New* Dalit Women in Indian Historiography', *Wiley*, September 26, 2018, pp. 1–14. Retrieved from https://onlinelibrary.wiley.com/doi/epdf/10.1111/hic3.12491
45 Paik, '*Amchya Jalmachi Chittarkartha* (The Bio-scope of our lives)', p. 45.
46 Scott, 'Experience'; Hennessy, *Materialist Feminism and the Politics of Discourse*; Butler, *Bodies that Matter*.
47 Scott, 'Experience', p. 68.
48 Rege, 'Writing Caste, Writing Gender'.
49 A. Namala, 'Dalit Women: The Conflict and the Dilemma', in Mary E. John (ed.), *Women's Studies in India: A Reader*, New Delhi: Penguin, 2008, p. 463.
50 Ibid., p. 465.
51 Ibid.
52 Foss and Foss, 'Personal Experience as Evidence in Feminist Scholarship', p. 42.
53 Guru, 'Egalitarianism and the Social Sciences in India'.
54 Ibid., p. 22.
55 Guru, 'Dalit Women Talk Differently'; Rege, 'A Dalit Feminist Standpoint'.
56 See Mohanty 1984 and 2003 for arguments against mainstream Western feminism. Paik's is perhaps one of the few attempts to connect the critique of white Western feminism with Brahmanical feminism in India ('*Amchya Jalmachi Chittarkartha*'; 'The Rise of *New* Dalit Women in Indian Historiography').
57 Scott, 'Experience'.
58 S. Kruks, *Retrieving Experience: Subjectivity and Recognition in Feminist Politics*, Ithaca and London: Cornell University Press, 2001, p. 139.
59 Bhimrao Ramji Ambedkar led people from the erstwhile "untouchable" caste towards claiming their rights and resisting the caste system. He problematised gender in the context of caste and argued for the equality of women. He is also the architect of the Indian Constitution. See S. Rege, 'Introduction: Towards a Feminist Reclamation of Dr. Bhimrao Ramji Ambedkar', in Sharmila Rege (ed.), *Against the Madness of Manu: B.R. Ambedkar's Writings on Brahminical Patriarchy*, New Delhi: Navayana, 2013, for his contribution to gender awareness in India. John Dewey was one of Ambedkar's teachers in Columbia University, where he studied.
60 See his discussion in John Dewey, *Democracy and Education*, Pennsylvania State University Electronic Classic Series, New York: MacMillan, 2001, pp. 145–57.
61 Ibid., p. 277.
62 Ibid., p. 275.
63 Ibid., p. 146.
64 Following Kruks there is a turn to the phenomenological account of experience, with an emphasis on de Beauvoir.
65 S. de Beauvoir, 'A Review of The Phenomenology of Perception by Maurice Merleau-Ponty (1945)', in Margaret Simons (ed.), *Philosophical Writings*, Urbana and Chicago: University of Illinois Press, 2004.
66 de Beauvoir, *The Second Sex*.
67 S. de Beauvoir, 'Literature and Metaphysics', in Margaret Simons (ed.), *Philosophical Writings*, Urbana and Chicago: University of Illinois Press, 2004, p. 270.
68 S. de Beauvoir, 'A Review of The Phenomenology of Perception by Maurice Merleau-Ponty (1945)', p. 161.
69 The collection of testimonies and interviews in Moon and Pawar, 2014, reveal how the participant of experience changes the researcher. Moreover, the researcher has to also labour to reach out to the participant.
70 de Beauvoir, 'Literature and Metaphysics'.
71 D. Bergoffen, 'Simone de Beauvoir', in *Stanford Encyclopedia of Philosophy*, 2004. Retrieved from https://plato.stanford.edu/entries/beauvoir/. Although Bergoffen writes with reference to de Beauvoir, one could extend it to Dewey and the context of Dalit women's lived experience in India.

INDEX

Aayomukhi 117, 119–20
activists 26, 30, 33, 182–3; Dalit 71, 79; Dalit male 164; Dalit women 150–2; feminist 164; health 106; non-Dalit women 61; urbanised women 151; women 150
Adi-maya 167
Advani, L.K. 49
Agastya 119; punishment on Tataka 118
Agnes, Flavia 192–3
Agnishikha Maanch 164
Ain't I a Woman? 144, 189–90
Ain't We Women? 145
Akshara Deepam programme 55
all India association for the preservation of sati 109
All India Dalit Mahilaa Congress 76
All-India Dalit Mahila Parishad 91
All India Dalit Women's Forum 165
All India Scheduled Castes Federation (AISCF) 77
All India Untouchable Women's Council 77
All India Untouchable Women's Federation 93
All the Women Are White 139, 189
'All Women are Niggers' 156
Alochana 165
Alyosius, S.J. 158
Ambedkar, B.R. 4, 8, 11, 24, 63–7, 69, 71, 75–85, 89, 91–3, 95–8, 121, 152, 160–2, 215–16
Ambedkar, Savitabai 98
Ambedkarism 131

Ambedkar movement 80–1, 83, 91, 95, 155, 159–60; women in 90–3
Anand, S. 131
annihilation of caste 96, 104, 195
anti-arrack movement 40, 51–6, 106, 111; Mastan-bi on 56
anti-caste struggles 132
anti-communism 213
anti-discrimination law 139, 142–3
anti-essentialism 212–13
anti-feminist denunciations 28
anti-Mandal agitation 2, 40, 43–8, 52, 55–6, 163
anti-parity positions 28
anti-racist politics 139–40, 144, 147
anuloma (hypergamous) 74
appropriation 16, 64, 72, 154, 175–6, 180, 211, 214, 219
Aydaan 95
Ayodhya *kar seva* 48

Babri Masjid demolition 48–9, 164
Babytai 80–1
Bahishkrut Bharat Bhagini Parishad 82
Bahishkrut Bharat Conference 76
Bahishkrut Hitakarini Sabha 77
Bahujan Mahila Aghadi, Maharashtra 153
Bahujan Mahila Mahasangh (BMM) 167
Bahujan Mahila Parishad 165
Bahujan Mahila Sangh 165
Balagopal, K. 53–4
Balutedari system 216

Bama, F.S. 183
bar dancers 29, 196
Bauddhajan Panchayat Samiti 79
Baudh, Sumit 30
Baxi 107
being Black 5, 190
being women 5, 31, 190
Bhakti movement 114
Bharat, Bahishkrut 131
Bharati, Uma 48, 52
Bharati, Vizia 48, 52
Bharatiya Janata Party (BJP) 29, 52; UCC and 29; and women for election 40, 50; women leaders of 48; women as 'matru shakti' 52
Bharatiya Stree Mukti Diwas or Indian Women's Liberation Day 89, 165, 167
Bhartiya Republican Party 165
Bhikabai 80
bhutyas 74
binary opposition 7, 196
Black feminist, intersectionality and 171; politics 157
Black women 10, 12, 15, 27, 137, 139–47, 156, 188–91, 195; experiences 27, 142, 144, 147, 190; studies on 139, 189
bodies 35; and women's rights 47
Brahmanical: class-caste-based patriarchy 173 (*see also* patriarchy); Hindutva, conceptualisation of 164; principles of patriarchy 179–80
brahmanic-gendered feminist intelligentsia 214
brahmanisation 163, 165–7
brahminism 8, 11, 14–15, 63, 68–9, 71, 104, 114, 155, 159–60, 162–3, 165
brahmin women 68–71, 74, 92, 96, 160
Buddhism 82, 91–2, 96, 114, 213, 215–17; mass conversion to 91
Burton, A. 108
Butler, Josephine 108, 220, 223, 228
Butler, Judith 10, 190, 220

capitalism 23, 34–5, 38, 156–7, 163, 189–90, 194; consumer 51
capitalist globalisation 37
caste: inequalities 42, 104, 134; oppression 8–9, 69, 132–3; Rege on gender matrix and 9
caste-based: division of labour 114, 164, 216; prostitution, 'muralis' against 160; schisms 217
caste-class-gender axis 171, 180
caste/community identity politics 31

casteism 45, 74, 95, 228
caste politics 6–7, 28–9, 34, 69, 189, 196; militancy of 28
caste system 8, 11, 14, 111–13, 132, 160, 175, 178, 180, 215; Ambedkar on 11; characteristics of 112–13
Castro-Gomez, Santiago 217, 219
Chakravarti, Uma 8, 14, 23, 61–2, 67, 94
Chalam 184
Chambhars 77, 90, 215
Chandragutti temple *bettaleseve* (nude worship) 182
chastity 13, 74–6, 114, 146–7
Chatterjee, Partha 155, 159
Chaudhari, Jaibai 76
child marriage 8–9, 11, 35, 71, 84, 107, 160
Child Marriage Restraint Act in 1927 192
Christi Mahila Sangharsh Sanghatana 165, 167
Chunduru sexual harassment 41, 43, 46–7, 55, 163
citizenship 28–9, 46, 50, 80, 93
class 4–5, 8–10, 23–6, 28–30, 36–7, 41–51, 53–4, 83–4, 88–91, 94–7, 104–9, 138–44, 156–9, 162–8, 171, 173–5, 180, 190–1, 217, 223–4
coalitions 105, 110, 112, 115
cohabitation 177, 180
Collins, Patricia Hill 10, 37
colonialism 35, 50, 66, 74, 160, 190–1, 214
communalism 158, 191
conjugal rights, restitution of 41
constitutionalism 49
contraceptive choice, politics of 56
corporate globalisation 33, 194
Crenshaw, Kimberlé 26–7, 31, 35, 189–90
cultural legitimacy 110
Cultural Rights of Community 29
culture: of Bahujans 167; brahmanical 167; (sanskruti) 71, 75, 90, 108, 156, 159, 173, 183, 204, 206–8, 215, 220, 227, 229, 231; (sanskruti), materiality of 167
customary sanctions 112

Dalit: egalitarianism 14; feminist knowledge 215, 220; feminist pedagogies 133; life narratives 131–2; movements 13, 56, 82–3, 88, 112, 132, 134, 155, 161, 184, 187, 193; politics 34, 75, 155, 161, 182, 211–13; radicals 65–7, 71–5, 77, 79–85; *samaaj* 80; streepurush 72, 74; testimonios 132, 134
Dalit difference 9–12, 28, 102, 137, 139, 154, 156; historicising 158–61

Dalit Feminist Theory, against brahmanical feminism 15–17
Dalit Mahila Sanghatans 166–7
Dalit Panthers 79, 162
Dalit Sangharsh Samithi (DSS) 182
Dalit women 7–13, 60–2, 64–6, 68–9, 73–85, 88–93, 101–2, 111–12, 132–5, 150–3, 160–8, 173–80, 182–5, 214–17, 227–32; bodies and sexuality 175, 180; experience 14, 60, 62, 173, 228; in Hindu writings 101; participation of 85, 112; physical contact with 177; prostitution and 4; radical activism 76–83; reality 101; religious representation of 101; representation by non-Dalit women 16; sexual abuse of 47 (*see also* rape; violence); Shiv Sena women attacking 152; subordinate positions of 2; testimonios 132–4; writings 133
Dalit Women Federation 62
Dalit Women's Society (DWS) 185
Dalit Women Talk Differently 165
Dani, Shantabai 77, 80
Dasgupta, Swapan 49
daughters 48, 73, 91, 105, 113, 120, 215
Deanian, Jody 219
de Beauvoir, Simone 10, 16–17, 223–4, 231–3
DeGraffenreid v General Motors 140, 142
dehumanisation 4
de Lauretis, Theresa 224
democratic revolution 29
democratisation 66, 76, 84, 132
democratising movements 158–9
Depressed Class Mission 97
Deshbhratar, Anjanibai 76
Devadasi 11, 91, 104, 121–6, 128, 185
development programmes, 'gender component' to 33
Devi, Bhanwari 9, 34, 164, 184
Dewey, John 231, 233
Dhamma 167
differentiation 43, 85; *see also* Dalit difference
'different voice' 155, 157, 161
discrimination 4, 8–12, 113, 118, 137, 139–44, 148, 152, 174–80, 190–1, 194, 197; caste-based 8; gender-based 8, 174
diversality 38
division of labour 165, 215–16; Rege on 4
domestic violence 40, 81, 186–7, 190, 217; and women's access 41; *see also* violence
dominance/dominant: castes 171, 173–80; intelligentsia 10, 213–14, 220; politics of 42; and sexual exploitation 180; women's experience of 178
Dongre, Sulochanabai 76–7
dowry deaths 41, 106, 162
Draupadi 26, 119
Dumont 215

egalitarian 14, 44, 51, 66, 96, 151, 173, 183, 227, 231, 233
empowerment 11, 34, 40, 80, 152; of women to act as agent 33
endogamy 8, 11, 84, 95, 113, 160, 163, 165, 174–5, 177
Engels, Friedrich 217
engendering development 33–4
equality 2, 44, 66, 71, 77, 92–3, 96, 105–6, 121, 159, 161, 173, 186, 212, 215
eve-teasing 41, 47; campaign against 41

family violence 41
fanaticism 43
female/females: foeticide 105; declining of sex ratio of 105; headed households 105, 111, 140
female labour 105; landless agricultural labour as 105; unionisation and 106, 110
female-gaze 120
femininity 26, 157, 224; controlled 85; masculinities and 85; and masculinity 72, 78; upper-caste 85
feminism 1–2, 5–6, 25, 38, 42, 201; alliance of 157; Ambedkarite 11, 64; brahmanical 15–17; British 67, 108; conceptual homogenising of 211; cultural 157; Dalit 1, 3, 5, 13, 15, 24, 63–4, 89, 134, 171, 211, 217, 220, 231; First World 10–11, 15; of Hindu Right 56; humanist 42; Indian 1–2, 10, 12–13, 15–16, 23–4, 26, 34, 56, 61, 101, 137, 191, 228, 231; mainstream 4, 11, 137, 228; middle-class 156; postcolonial 196; *savarna* 24; theorising 2, 23, 137, 199; UN-driven privileged 34; upper-caste 187; Western 108, 154, 226, 230; white 137
feminist-as-explorer model 133
feminist-as-tourist model 133
feminists: African American 184; Black 12, 88, 137, 139, 145, 154, 157–8; caste-privileged 1, 24, 101; collective 2; Dalit-Bahujan 2–3, 15, 23–4, 29, 88, 168, 184, 215, 219; denial and 95–6; 'difference' 10; emancipation 17, 233; First World 10, 137; historiography 158; imperial 75, 79, 103, 108; Indian 1–2, 5, 7, 9–10,

13, 15–16, 23–4, 64, 102–3, 171–2, 199–200, 227; Latino and African 184; liberal 76; literature 146–7; mainstream 2, 6, 10–11, 15–16, 23, 64, 137, 184, 199; Marxist 3, 23; movements 16, 112, 155, 183–4, 225; Non-Dalit 96, 168; politics 6–7, 12, 25–9, 31, 34–6, 38, 42, 144, 150, 155, 157, 163–4, 167, 195–6, 208; radical 156; Socialist 156; theorization 154, 156–8; Third World 10, 157; upper-caste 89; urban 29, 53; white 11, 145, 154
food allocation 105
Fraser, Nancy 34–5, 212–13
freedom of movement 111, 174
freedom of speech 111, 173
fundamental rights 27, 29, 78, 111
funding 26, 34, 166; international 26, 188

Gaekwad, Sayajirao 90
Gaikwad, Dadasaheb 76
Galanter, Marc 32
Gandhi, Mahatma 27, 212–14
gang rapes 9, 106, 111; *see also* rape; violence
Geetabai 76
Geetha, V. 14, 23, 61–2, 90, 94, 228
gender 8, 33, 47, 115, 152, 196; analysis 42, 56; based oppression 134; as category 41; control 171, 177; as cultural issues 164; governmentalising 33–4; identities 28, 36, 134, 197; mainstreaming 34, 188, 194; reproduction and caste inequalities 104; sensitivity 33
gender-caste axis 175–7
gender-coded bodies 28
gender relations 41, 54; democratizing of 158
Gilroy, Paul 220, 226
girls: Dalit 73, 76, 83, 90–1; of Jadavpur University 45
globalisation 37, 153, 214
global linear thinking 218
goddess 74, 110, 128–9; depiction of 128
Gopal, Meena 5–7, 171, 195
Gopalakrishnaiah, Vavilala 52
governance 33
governmentality 7, 34, 66, 188–9, 193–4
Gowri, Jajula 183
Grabham, Emily 33
grihalaxmi 110
Gudavarthy, Ajay 212–13
guest appearances, of non-Dalit women 152
Guru, Gopal 12–13, 15–16, 23, 90, 112, 132, 137, 161, 166, 219, 223, 229–30
Gyanendra, Pandey 66, 81

Harding, S. 103–4, 224–5
Harishchandra 118
Harriss, John 33
Hartsock, N. 224
health activists 106
hegemony 1, 6, 50, 68–9, 71–4, 111, 114, 193, 195, 199, 208, 219
Hennessy, R. 224, 226, 228
heterogeneity 6–7, 34, 195–6, 228
hijras 31–2; high court judgements on 31; as third gender 32
Hindu: fundamentalists 104; society 49; tolerance 43; woman 48, 71, 107; women as social reformers 107
Hindu Code Bill 78, 89, 93, 95
Hindu laws 78, 93; of marriage 108; of property and marriage 103
Hindu Right 43, 56, 164, 192
Hindutva 41, 48–50, 166
Hintikka, M. 224
homogeneity 6, 31, 196, 227
honour killing 8
humanism 42–5, 50–1, 53
Humanist Marxism 42
'humans' 42, 71, 180
hypergamy 113

idealisations 121
identity 6–7, 26–32, 35–8, 77, 88–9, 109, 152, 165–6, 174, 177–9, 189–90, 192–3, 197, 202, 211–13; marginalised 35; political representation of 32; politics 31, 36, 88–9, 166, 168, 190, 211–13; religious community 28; of 'woman' 28; woman as unstable 7
Ilaiah, K. 52, 90
imagined body 130
imperialism 25–6, 108, 158, 188, 190, 194, 204, 209; *see also* feminists
impurity 24, 114, 161, 165, 177, 180
Independent Labour Party 160
India 5–6, 8, 14–16, 25–34, 44–6, 88–93, 102–13, 158–9, 171–2, 188–9, 191–7, 213–15, 219–20, 229–30
'Indian' 2, 24, 44–5, 63, 107, 109
Indian feminism, women in 26–7
Indian Feminist: community 16; ideology 2
Indian National Congress 161
Indian Nationalism 158
Indian tradition 103, 106–7, 109
Indian womanhood 107–8, 201, 203
individualism 36, 42, 48, 50, 85, 95, 206–7; liberal 36, 42

inequalities 1, 7, 41, 43–4, 77, 101, 106, 114–15, 134, 157, 194, 214
inter-caste alliances, collective violence against 163
inter-caste marriages 91, 177
intermarriage 11, 160
International Planned Parenthood Federation (IPPF) 106
international sisterhood 16, 199, 204, 208
intersectionality 5–8, 10, 13, 23, 25–7, 29, 31–8, 137, 140–1, 144, 146–7, 171–2, 188–97, 224, 227

Jadhav, Shivubai Lakshman 73
Jadhav, Sushila 79
Jahnavi, B.T. 184
Jain, Girilal 49
Janabai 203, 205, 207
Janu, C.K. 183
Janwadi Mahila Sanghatana 166
Jardine, Alice 208
job stigmatising 216–17; *see also* division of labour
jogtinis 11, 73, 91
John, Mary E. 5–7, 9, 33, 171
Joshi, Anandibai 71

Kaasare, Bhagatai 79
Kafila 2
Kakar, Sudhir 121
Kalaram temple-entry satyagraha 76
Kamathipura 76, 127
Kamble, Anusayabai 74
Kamble, Baby 80
Kamble, Devikabai Damodar 82
Kamble, Radhabai 76–7
Kamble, Saroj 90
Kamble, Shivram Janaba 73, 160
Kannabiran, Kalpana 164, 183
Kannabiran, Vasanth 164, 183
Karve, D.K. 90
Ketkar 160
Kelkar, Lakshimibai 48
Khairlanji massacre 10
knowledge, denial of 70
Kondamma 54–5
Kothari, Rajni 151
Kruks 231

labour control 171, 175
Lacan, Jacques 120
Ladke, Nalini 78
land distribution 106
landless agricultural labour 105

law 31
liberalisation 41, 45, 104
literacy campaigns 40
literacy rate 90, 105
literature 37, 41, 107, 117, 131, 145, 187, 201, 224; Black feminist 157; Dalit 131, 183; Dalit women and modern 101; feminist 108, 146–7
lived experience 102, 212, 227, 229–33
Lokhande, Pradnya 134
Loomba, Ania 214
lower caste, men 105, 112–14, 165; violence against 105, 46–7, 55, 68, 72, 89, 104, 109, 111–14, 118, 160–1
lower-caste women 69, 74, 103, 105, 107, 110–11, 114, 119, 160, 165; in Andhra Pradesh 111 (*see also* anti-arrack movement); customary rights of 103; gang rapes of 106
Lucy 203
Lukes, Steven 103–4

Madhalebai 76
Mahaad/Mahad satyagraha 91, 97, 160
Mahaars/Mahars 77, 80–1, 90, 160, 211, 214–17, 219
Mahabharata 117, 119
Mahadevan, Kanchana 15–17, 199
Maharaj, Shahu 97
Maharaj, Shaju 90
Maharashtra Dalit Mahila Sanghatana 165
Maharashtra Dalit Women's Conference 152
Mahar-Mang girls, as Muralis 73
Mainabai 76
male-gaze 120
Malkani, K.R. 45
Manavi 182
Mandal Commission 43, 46–7, 54, 82, 94, 161, 163
Mandal-Chunduru 43, 46, 51
Mandir-Mandal politics 88
Mandodari 117, 120
Mang women 211, 214, 216–17, 219
Mang-Mahars, Muktabai on 69
Mani, Lata 109, 190
Manorama, Ruth 90
Manu 95, 118
Manusmriti 89, 113
Manuvadi Sanskriti 167
marginalisation 11, 111, 140; of Dalit woman 9
marital alliances 174, 177
Marx, Karl 199, 211, 217

242 Index

masculinisation of Dalithood 161–5
Matanga Kanyas 117–18
Mathura rape case 162
matrabhumi 48
McClintock, Anne 190
media 17, 44–6, 51, 96, 106, 112, 114, 121, 123–4, 152, 164, 184, 225, 227, 233
Menon, Nivedita 3, 5, 23, 188
Meshram, Hirabai 78
Meshram, Parbatabai 77
#MeToo 2
Mhatre, S. 203, 207
middle class 44–5, 95, 106, 108–9, 156, 162
Mignolo, Walter 38, 199, 211, 217–19
militancy 28, 206
minoritism 50
misogyny 8, 119
missionaries 90, 103, 107, 109
modernisation 79, 103, 106–7, 109; state-sponsored 104
modernity 37, 48, 55, 66, 71, 75–6, 83–5, 95–6, 134, 186, 212–13
Mody, S. 203, 207
Moffat 215
Moghe, Kiran 166
Mohanty, Talpade 133
molestation 13, 47, 164; *see also* rape
Money, John 190
Moon, Meenakshi 9, 24, 90–1, 96, 160
moral policing 3; *see also* honour killing
mother-in-law, as enforcing agent 110
movement, contemporary women's 104, 155
multiple identities 5, 11, 26, 31, 34, 37, 190
Muralis 11, 73–4, 91, 160
Muslim OBC Sanghatana 163
Muslim Women's Right to Maintenance Act 1986 193

nagnapuja 128; *see also randpurnima*
Naik, Lakshmibai 76, 78
Namaantar movement 78, 161, 163
'name and shame' movement 2; *see also* #Me too
Nandakumar, J. 128–30
Nash, Jennifer C. 26–7
National Campaign on Dalit Human Rights (NCDHR) 4
National Conference of Autonomous Women's Groups in Kolkata 29, 196
National Federation of Dalit Women (NFDW) 4, 150, 152–3, 165
National Integrity 29
nationalism 45, 50, 54, 108, 158–9, 191, 214; First World 50

Nationalist Resolution of the Women's Question' 155, 159
National Women's Conference 229
Nehru, Jawaharlal 44, 93
Nesfield 160
neutrality 27, 49–50
new economic policy 153, 166; *see also* liberalisation
new social movements 155, 161
Niranjana, Tejaswini 13, 23
Nishani (Thumbprint) 183
Nkrumah, Kwame 27
nominalism 157
non-brahmins 68–70, 72–4, 84; democratic movements 159
non-Dalit women 16, 134, 150, 152, 166, 183, 227
non-governmental organisation (NGOs) 26–7
non-Western women 199, 201–2
Nora, Pierre 134
Nyerere, Julius 26
Nzegwu, Nkiru 213

Omvedt, Gail 67, 89, 151, 158
oppression 5, 8–9, 32, 35, 61–2, 68–70, 111, 117, 132–4, 156–8, 189–91, 207–9, 211–13, 216–17, 228–30, 232
Ortelius, Abraham 218
othering 24, 41, 43, 50, 220
Owle, Sudharak 127
Oyewumi, Oyeronke 36–7, 199, 211, 213

Pagare, Sindhutai 79
Paik, Shailaja M. 11, 24, 63, 227–8
Patel, Razia 163
Patil, Indirabai 77
Patil, Sharad 90, 158
Patil, Smita M. 10, 90, 199
pativrata 113–14
patriarchal caste system 181; assimilation of 173–5
patriarchal oppression 8, 62, 224
patriarchy 8–9, 13–15, 37–8, 61–2, 66, 69, 112–14, 120–1, 144–7, 156–60, 162, 165, 177–8, 187, 189–90; Ambedkar on 8, 11; Black 15; brahmanical 8–9, 13–15, 69, 71, 94, 96, 134, 159–60, 164, 173, 178, 195–6; caste-class 178–81; Dalit 12–15, 23, 61–2, 65, 94; forms of 8; as social organisation 37
Pawar, Geetabai 76
Pawar, Urmila 9, 90–1, 95–6, 121
Paxton 108

peaceful co-existence 94
Periyar *see* Ramaswami, E.V. (Periyar)
philosophy 220, 224; Dalit feminist 220; feminist 4, 10, 220; gendering of 224; hegemonic 220; Indian feminist 10; Western (Euro–American) social 26
Phule, Jyotiba 11, 24, 63, 65, 67–71, 81, 84, 90–1, 95, 159; Trutiya Ratna by 68–70
Phule, Savitribai, letters of 160
Phule-Ambedkarite politics 66–7, 84, 101, 131, 152, 162
Pise, Arunadevi 78
pluralism 94
political consciousness 68, 84
Pollock, Griselda 120
pollution, idea of 11, 114, 160, 216
Ponty, Merleau 232
Population Council 106
pratiloma (hypogamous) 74
pre-puberty marriages 114; *see also* child marriage
presuppositions 121–2, 130, 196
pro-sati lobby 109
prostitution 3–4, 29, 64, 91, 111, 193
pseudo-secularism 49–50
Puranik, Ratibai 76
purity 34, 47, 52, 70, 74, 76, 98, 101, 114, 161, 174, 177, 179; women and 52

queer politics 30–1, 197

race 10, 12, 15, 25–7, 31, 36–8, 117, 137–45, 147, 156–8, 168, 190–1, 223, 226, 228
racism 10, 12, 25–7, 31, 36–8, 74, 117, 137–48, 154, 156–8, 190–1, 193, 223, 226, 228
Rajan, N. 212–13
Rajani, suicide of 185
rakshasa women, Rama insulting 117; *see also* Surpanakha
Rama 117, 119–21
Ramabai, Pandita (Ramaai) 24, 63–4, 67, 71, 76, 79, 96–8
Ramabai-Phule-Ambedkarite feminist approaches 63
Rama Rao, N.T. 52–3
Ramaswami, E.V. (Periyar) 80, 84, 91–2
Ramayana 117–20
Ramdas, Anu 186
Rameeza Bee 47
Ramesh, Abihinaya 94
Ramjanmabhoomi movement 40
Ramteke, Chandrikabai 76, 79

Ranade 92, 195; *see also* Ramabai, Pandita (Ramaai)
randpurnima 128
Rani, Swaroopa 13–14, 61
Rao, Anupama 90
Rao, Ramoji 53
rape 9, 12, 47, 89, 103, 105–6, 108, 111–12, 117, 140, 146–7, 151, 162, 164; of Birati 47; custodial 41, 111; of Dalit women 111; NFIW and 162; police 41; of Rameeza Bee 47
Rape and Dowry Prohibition Act 108
Rashtrasevika Samiti 47–9
'real feminism' 9, 137
Reddy, Janardhana 47
Reddy, Vijayabhaskara 52
Reddys vs Dalits 46
reformers, upper-caste brahmanical male 159
reform movement 108
Rege, Sharmila 4, 9–12, 24, 64, 67, 90, 137, 215
Rekharaj 183–5
religious: communities 27, 30, 92, 195; oppression 126
representation 29, 32, 37, 46, 56, 96, 101, 120, 122, 124, 127, 201, 217, 224, 229
Republican Party 79, 166
reservation: politics of 34; for women 28, 44, 192
resistance 3, 34–5, 38, 73–4, 79, 81, 101, 132–3, 137, 172, 206, 228–9
right to property 108, 114
Risley 160
Rithambara, Sadhvi 48
ritual-based caste structure 178
Rudrayamaltantra 128
rural women 40, 54

sacrificing wives 134
Sadalakshmi, Velayudhan 185
Salve, Muktabai 69, 160
Samataa Mahilaa Sainik Dal (Army of Women Soldiers for Equality, the women's wing of the SSD) 78
Samataa Sainik Dal (Army of Soldiers for Equality, SSD) 77
Sangari, Kumkum 46, 114, 158, 165
sanskritisation 62, 75, 92
Saraswathi, Du 183–4
Sarkar, Tanika 47
Sarvagod, Mukta 76
Sarvajanik Satyadharma Pustak 70
sati 8, 84, 104, 109–10, 160; temples by upper caste for 109

sati pratha 11
Sati Prohibition Act of 1829 110
Satya Harishchandra 117
Satyashodak Mahila Sabha 166
Satyashodhak 155, 160
Satyashodhak Communist Party 161
Satyashodhak Mahila Aghadi in Maharashtra 151
Savarkar 48
savarna women 102
savarnisation of womanhood 161–5
Savitribai Phule 68, 98
Sawarkar, Savi 121–2, 124, 127
Scheduled Caste Federation 76, 160
Schmittian, Carl 218
Scott, Joan 190, 223, 228, 230–1
seclusion 105, 107
secularism 30, 41–2, 44, 49
Seetabai 76
self-representation 89–90
Self-Respecters 84
sensationalistic empiricism 231
sex discrimination 139, 141–3; *see also* female/females, foeticide
sexism 139–40, 144–5, 147–8, 190
sexual: exploitation 90, 92, 119, 186; identifications 30, 197; labour 4, 74–5, 114, 165 (*see also* sex-workers); minorities 220; politics 10–11, 163–4; psychotic perversions 128; relationships 177, 180; slavery 124 (*see also* violence, sexual)
sexuality 4, 28, 30–1, 46–7, 67–8, 73–5, 83–4, 110–12, 114, 147, 162–4, 174–80, 184–5, 187, 197; controlling women's 11, 75; control on 68, 73, 114, 165, 171; Dalit women and 111, 171, 179; female 46, 68, 82, 114, 146–7; human 179–80; male 180; normative 146; politics of 34; unbounded female 73; white women's 147
sex-work 3–4, 29, 193; Rege on women and 4
sex-workers 3–4, 216, 232; pan-India survey of 3
Shah Bano case 41, 192
shastras, of Brahmins 113
Shetmajur Shetkari Shramik Aghadi, Maharashtra 153
Shetkari Sanghatana 151
Shevanti 203, 205, 207
Shinde, Tarabai 160
Shinde, V.R. 76, 91
Shivraj, Meenambal 93
Shourie, Arun 44

Shramik Mukti Dal 161
Shramik Mukti Sanghatana 161
Shudra-Ati-Shudras 69–70
Shurpanakha 117, 119
Shyamala, Gogu 183, 185
Singh, V.P. 43
Sinha, Mrinalini 38
sisterarchy 213; brahmanic 211–12
Sita 119–21
Sivakami 183
social: activist groups 104; reform 45, 66–7, 84; reformers 91, 103, 107
solidarity 2, 6–7, 16, 35, 152–3, 195, 216–17, 219–20; feminist 38, 223
Sonalkar, Wandana 67
South Asian Feminisms 214, 219
Srinivas, M.N. 92
standpoint 1, 4, 10–12, 60, 64, 74, 133, 155, 158, 166–8, 199, 211, 224–5; colonial 74; Dalit feminist 10–12, 64, 133, 155, 167–8; of Dalit women 168; feminist 155, 167–8; of Gopal Guru 23; on intersectionality 7; mainstream feminist 7; Marxist feminist 4; non-Dalit feminists 168
Stephen, Lovely 185
Stephens, Julie 16, 199
Strasser, Ulrike 214
sub-caste identity assertions 174
Subhadra, Joopaka 183–4
subjectivity: of Dalit women 66, 81, 85; marginalised 36
Sukirtharani 183–4
Surpanakha 120
Swaroopa Rani, Challapalli 183

talaq 12, 163; *see also* Shah Bano case
talking differently, Kothari and 151–2
Tamasaguna 118
tantric movement 114
Tataka 117–19
temple entry of Dalit women 11
Tersamma 112
Thakur, Rekha 90
Tharu, Susie 13, 23, 90, 171
Third World feminism 2, 154, 199
Thorat, Sukhdeo 90
thought: Black feminist 158; Black Feminist 137, 158; Dalit feminist 2, 9–10, 16, 199, 218, 220; feminist 1, 17, 154, 209, 223–4, 227; Indian feminist 1, 5, 10, 23
Tinsman, Heidi 214
Truth, Sojourner 144, 189

Ujamaa 26
UN Declaration against Racism in Durban 193
Uniform Civil Code (UCC) 5, 29–30, 41, 108, 164, 189, 192
universal citizenship 28
universalisation 26, 162
universalisms 28, 41, 156
universality 36, 189, 193–5, 218
unmarked feminism 133
untouchability 68–9, 73, 84, 92, 113, 171, 176–7
untouchables 68, 70–1, 78, 80, 89–93, 113, 118, 123; education and 90
untouchable women 77–8, 122, 124
Untouchable Women's Reform Association 76
Untouchable Women's Society 76
upper-caste femininity 85
upper-caste men 34, 41, 47, 61, 67, 74–5, 84–5, 112, 163, 185; access to Dalit women 111; sexual rights and 113
upper-caste women 46–7, 61–2, 66, 68–9, 73–4, 84–5, 88, 92, 104–5, 108, 112–14, 133–4, 161–4, 182, 184; employers 110

Vaid, S. 114, 158
Vajpayee, A.B. 49
Varale, Balwant 97
Varale, Radhabai 97
varnasrama 118, 159
victims 66, 105, 109, 119, 127, 134, 141–2, 162, 193
Vikas Vanchit Dalit Mahila Parishad 165
Vinodini 183–4
violence 9, 12, 14, 49, 53, 101, 103–9, 112, 115, 119–20, 162–4, 171, 175–80, 184, 186; against Dalit women 10; against lower-caste men 105; against upper-caste women 105; against women 12, 103–4, 106–9, 112, 115, 162, 179; caste 163, 185; caste-class-gender intersectional 178; communal 49, 109; forms of 107; lower caste women and 8; physical 12, 112, 162, 186; sexual 9, 12, 34, 107, 147, 151, 162–4, 177, 179, 192
Vishwamitra 118–19
Volga 183

widow, burning 105, 107, 109–10, 112, 114; control over sexuality of 109; *see also sati*
widowhood: enforced 8, 11, 71, 107, 159–60; sexuality and 109
Widow Remarriage Act of 1856 109
Wollstonecraft, Mary 10
women 9, 25, 27, 31–3, 36–7, 40, 43, 45–6, 51–2, 69, 161, 192; average consumption of 105; body of 68, 160, 174–5, 177, 180 (*see also* sexuality); Buddhist 215; Dalit-Bahujan 5, 69, 90; death by malnutrition 106; and elections 28; emancipation of 178, 184; experiences of 140, 145, 156, 205, 208, 227; exploitation of 61; groups 41, 89, 106; identities of Black 5, 190; instability of 28–9; labour 105, 110, 175, 228; liberation 67, 89, 104, 165–8; in movements 40; in non-brahmin movement 158–61; as not gendered beings 46; Phule on 70; problems of 107; re-emergence of 46; Third World 10, 103, 154, 157, 201–4, 206–8; of upper caste and right to work 110; visibility of 40
women's movement 6, 27–30, 40, 66, 88, 106, 109, 112, 115, 134, 155, 162–4, 191–2, 196, 214; in global South 27; in India 6, 104, 106, 111, 150, 189, 193; Mandal-Masjid phase of 155
Women's Reservation Bill 5, 189, 192
Women's Rights Conference in Akron 144
Women's Voice, Bangalore 153
World Conference against Racism (WCAR) 26, 35

Yuvak Kranti Dal 161
Yuval-Davis, Nira 26, 34, 37, 193

Zamindari system 107
Zelliot, Eleanor 89